THE UNEMPLOYMENT CRISIS IN AUSTRALIA
Which Way Out?

Since the 1970s the average level of unemployment in Australia has risen each decade. This has imposed huge economic, social and human costs, making unemployment one of the most pressing problems confronting Australia. Governments, however, seem powerless in the face of this problem. Drawing on the expertise of some of Australia's leading economists, this book argues that the currently fashionable approaches of wage cuts and further steps towards labour-market flexibility will not solve the unemployment problem. In reality, unemployment and rising inequality are symptoms of the growing failure of contemporary labour markets to distribute jobs and incomes effectively. The contributors argue that the main solution to this problem is not wage cuts but direct measures to create jobs growth. This important book points to a way beyond the current policy malaise and offers detailed solutions to unemployment.

Stephen Bell has taught at Griffith University, the University of New England and the University of Tasmania and is currently a senior lecturer in the Department of Government at the University of Queensland. He has published widely in leading Australian and international journals and is the author or editor of five books including *Australian Manufacturing and the State* (Cambridge University Press 1993) and *Ungoverning the Economy* (1997).

THE UNEMPLOYMENT CRISIS IN AUSTRALIA

Which Way Out?

EDITED BY

STEPHEN BELL
University of Queensland

PUBLISHED BY THE PRESS SYNDICATE OF THE UNIVERSITY OF CAMBRIDGE
The Pitt Building, Trumpington Street, Cambridge, United Kingdom

CAMBRIDGE UNIVERSITY PRESS
The Edinburgh Building, Cambridge CB2 2RU, UK   http://www.cup.cam.ac.uk
40 West 20th Street, New York, NY 10011–4211, USA   http://www.cup.org
10 Stamford Road, Oakleigh, Melbourne 3166, Australia http://www.cup.edu.au
Ruiz de Alarcón 13, 28014, Madrid, Spain

First published 2000

Printed in China by Everbest Printing Co. Ltd

Typeface New Baskerville (Adobe) 10/12pt. *System* QuarkXPress® [PH]

A catalogue record for this book is available from the British Library

National Library of Australia Cataloguing in Publication data
The unemployment crisis in Australia: which way out?
Bibliography.
Includes index.
ISBN 0 521 64350 3 hardback
ISBN 0 521 64394 5 paperback
1. Unemployment – Australia. 2. Full employment policies –
Australia. 3. Australia – Economic policy – 1990– I.
Bell, Stephen, 1954–
331.137994

ISBN 0 521 64350 3 hardback
ISBN 0 521 64394 5 paperback

Contents

CONTENTS

Figures

Tables

Contributors

STEPHEN BELL has taught at Griffith University and was the co-ordinator of the Graduate Public Policy Program at the University of New England. Before joining the University of Queensland's Department of Government in 1999, he was associate professor and head of the School of Government at the University of Tasmania. His research interests focus on business politics, political economy and the politics of economic policy. He has published widely in leading Australian and international journals and is the author or editor of five books. His most recent sole authored book was *Ungoverning the Economy: The Political Economy of Australian Economic Policy* (1997).

JOHN BURGESS is a senior lecturer in the Department of Economics, University of Newcastle. He has postgraduate degrees from the universities of Sydney, Exeter and Newcastle and has held previous appointments at the University of Sydney and Charles Sturt University. His research interests include employment restructuring, work and gender, employment policy and public-sector economics. He is a joint author of *Introductory Macroeconomics* (1998) and *Introductory Microeconomics* (1999).

ANIS CHOWDHURY is associate professor of Economics, University of Western Sydney, Macarthur. He obtained his PhD in 1983 from the University of Manitoba, Canada. He has taught at the University of Manitoba, the National University of Singapore and the University of New England before moving to UWSM in 1992. Professor Chowdhury has published books, articles and book chapters on a range of subjects. He is the founding editor of the *Journal of the Asia Pacific Economy*. Research interests include political economy, macroeconomic policies, financial sector reform and Asia-Pacific economies.

ROY GREEN has been appointed professor and head of department at the National University of Ireland, Galway. Previously he was director of the Employment Studies Centre at the University of Newcastle. He took his undergraduate degrees at the University of Adelaide and has a PhD in economics from the University of Cambridge where he was also a research fellow. Before coming to Newcastle, he was an adviser to both the British Labour Party and the former Australian Labor government. He has written widely on industry and labour-market issues. His most recent book (with Rodin Genoff) is *Manufacturing Prosperity: Ideas for Industry, Technology and Employment* (1998).

BOB GREGORY is professor of Economics in the Research School of Social Sciences at the Australian National University, Canberra. He has long been closely involved in Australian economic policy development. In 1988, he was a member of the committee that recommended the introduction of student income contingent loans, collected by the Tax Office. He was a member of the board of the Reserve Bank of Australia from 1985–95. From 1986 until 1991 he was a member of the Australian Sciences and Technology Council. Professor Gregory is an elected fellow of the Academy of the Social Sciences (1979). In 1996 he was awarded the Order of Australia Medal. He was president of the Economic Society of Australia, 1996–99.

P.N. (RAJA) JUNANKAR is a professor of Economics and Finance at the University of Western Sydney, Macarthur. He obtained a BSc (Econ) and MSc (Econ) from the London School of Economics, and a PhD from the University of Essex. His current research interests are in the field of labour economics (especially unemployment and long-term unemployment), immigration, and macroeconomics. He has published several books and monographs, including *Investment, Marx's Economics, From School to Unemployment: The Labour Market for Young People, Costs of Unemployment, Immigration, Wages and Price Stability*, and *Immigration and Australia's External Account Balances*. He has published extensively in leading national and international journals.

WILLIAM F. MITCHELL is professor of Economics and director of the Centre of Full Employment and Equity research at the University of Newcastle. He has published extensively on wages policy, unemployment and full employment in the academic and popular literature. His most recent work advocates a buffer stock employment approach to restoring full unemployment, whereby the government provides work for all workers not engaged in the private sector. He has been a long-time critic of deregulation and monetarism.

JOHN NEVILE is emeritus professor at the University of New South Wales. In 1972 he was elected a fellow of the Academy of Social Sciences in Australia. In 1973 he was president of the Economics Section of the Australian and New Zealand Association for the Advancement of Science, and he was president of the Economic Society of Australia from 1980 to 1984. He has served on a number of Australian government advisory bodies and statutory authorities, and has published over 100 articles, the majority on macroeconomic policy, unemployment and inflation.

JOHN QUIGGIN is an Australian Research Council Senior Research Fellow in Economics, based at James Cook University. He has worked in fields including risk analysis, production economics, the theory of economic growth and environmental economics. He was awarded the annual medal of the Academy of the Social Sciences in Australia in 1993 and was elected a fellow of the academy in 1996. Professor Quiggin is also prominent as a commentator on policy topics including unemployment policy, microeconomic reform, privatisation, competitive tendering and the economics of education.

MARTIN WATTS is senior lecturer in the Department of Economics at the University of Newcastle and a member of the Centre for Full Employment and Equity. He completed his PhD at the University of British Columbia and was previously employed at Monash University. His research interests lie in the areas of unemployment theory and policy, the evolution of the wage distribution, and the measurement and evolution of occupational gender and race segregation.

ELIZABETH WEBSTER is a senior research fellow at the Melbourne Institute of Applied Economic and Social Research, University of Melbourne. Her research interests include the economics of intangible investment, labour-market programs and Kaleckian economics.

Preface

These days, the labour-market is not distributing jobs and incomes effectively enough. Unemployment and rising inequality are the results of this kind of labour-market failure. Unfortunately, the dominant argument coming from many economists, policy-makers and the media is that wage cuts and more labour-market flexibility will provide solutions to unemployment. This kind of 'blame the victim' thinking needs to be challenged.

As this book argues, the wage-cuts route is an uncertain one indeed and at best is only likely to produce limited employment growth. Moreover, without a strategy involving some kind of direct redistribution of resources and income, a wage-cutting strategy will drive up inequality, a trend Australia can ill afford to see continue.

This book argues that a direct program of jobs growth is a much better and more direct way to deal with the dual problems of unemployment and inequality. Two strategies are proposed: first, a more expansionary macroeconomic policy; second, direct tax-funded job creation. Together, these solutions will work.

But they will need to be funded, through slightly higher taxes on the already employed. The key aim of this book is to put this kind of *redistributive* agenda on the table in order to open out the unemployment debate. Overall, the social gains from such a policy will outweigh the costs. However, to implement such a program the essentially moral and redistributive elements of the unemployment issue need to be clearly recognised. In the end, no country can keep promising tax cuts and expect decent social and economic outcomes.

Unlike many edited books, this book has been carefully designed to build a cumulative argument. It first challenges the prevailing orthodoxy and then builds an alternative policy position. I would like to formally thank the contributors to this volume for their effort and commitment to the project. Thanks also to the School of Government at the University of Tasmania for support and especially Kate Walepole, for her more than able research assistance. I would also like to acknowledge the wonderful efforts of Carla Taines, the book's copy-editor, as well as the support of Phillipa McGuinness at CUP.

CHAPTER 1

The Unemployment Crisis and Economic Policy

Stephen Bell

Everyone agrees that Australia's unemployment crisis is a national disgrace and that something should be done about it. High unemployment represents the largest single economic policy failure of the last quarter century. Over the last three decades the average unemployment rate has risen each decade. In the 1960s unemployment averaged only 1.7 per cent. In the 1970s average unemployment rose to 3.7 per cent and this rose again to average 7.6 per cent in the 1980s. Thus far in the 1990s, unemployment has risen again to average around 9 per cent. Except for the Depression of the 1930s, we have never had such high unemployment levels for as long, nor have we experienced current levels of long-term unemployment, nor seen net full-time job creation stagnate as it has in the 1990s. Further evidence of a long-term decline in labour-market performance can be found if we compare the significantly weaker employment growth response to post-recession economic recovery in the 1990s compared to the 1980s. As Debelle and Swann (1998, p. 28) report, the rate of employment growth in the first six years of recovery in the 1990s was about half the rate achieved over the same period in the 1980s recovery. In the recovery period between 1994 and 1998, the average rate of unemployment was 8.7 per cent. In early 1999, fully six years after unemployment reached its recessionary peak in 1993, unemployment was still running at 7.4 per cent.

Most commentators agree that the unemployment problem is far bigger than picked up in the official statistics. Governments clearly have an incentive to introduce or modify statistical categories which lower official unemployment. In the UK, for example, the Thatcher government changed the official method of counting the unemployed 19 times in the 1980s alone (Standing 1990, p. 445). In Australia, as Martin Watts shows in chapter 2, the official definition of an unemployed person is very restrictive. As Watts indicates, if we take into account hidden unemployment, under-employment and marginal attachment to the labour-market, the unemployment figure could easily be doubled. In 1997, for example, instead of around 750 000 Australians being afflicted by unemployment and under-employment, the Australian Bureau of Statistics estimated that because of under-counting the real figure was probably closer to 1.9 million Australians (ACOSS 1997, p. 2). Watts estimates that the economic costs of unemployment – in terms of lost output, idle resources and direct burdens on government expenditure – could be as much as $40 billion per annum. There are also incalculable personal and community costs.

The unemployment crisis stretches well beyond Australia. Globally, millions of disaffected workers are being left behind in the wake of changing labour-markets. Across the advanced OECD economies alone, the official number of unemployed is approaching 40 million. Even in the United States, the official figures indicating relatively low unemployment hide an army of under-employed, working poor, the incarcerated, or those that have simply dropped out of the system. Everywhere, governments seem unable or unwilling to tackle this vast human tragedy.

At the centre of the problem are failing labour-markets. Labour-markets are one of the most important mechanisms of a capitalist market system. Yet they are increasingly failing to distribute jobs and incomes effectively. Far too many people are missing the boat and are pushed to the social and economic margins. Under capitalism, this is not an unusual state of affairs. In the midst of the Great Depression the famous British economist, John Maynard Keynes, summed up the situation thus: 'The outstanding faults of the economic society in which we live are its failure to provide full employment and its arbitrary and inequitable distribution of wealth and income' (Keynes 1964 [1936], p. 372). Extraordinarily, between the mid-1940s and the mid-1970s, the postwar 'golden age' was a period of full employment and greater equity, in part because of substantial policy intervention by governments. That era has passed and we are now heading back to the situation described by Keynes.

But why? After all, Australian per capita incomes have doubled since the 1960s. We are much better off. Why then are we throwing hundreds of thousands of Australians on to the economic scrap heap through high unemployment and rising market inequality?

This book tries to answer this question. If the central problem of rising unemployment and inequality is seen as stemming from a failing labour-market, two main causes drive this problem. One has been economic policy. This book argues that since the 1970s, across most of the advanced economies, and certainly in Australia, there has been a major re-orientation of policy away from the postwar commitment to full employment (Bell 1997a; Argy 1998). Under what has variously been described as the new economic rationalist or neoliberal order, the main macroeconomic policy priority has been a two-decade-long fight against inflation waged with policies that have made unemployment worse, especially through policies of slow growth and policy-induced recessions. More recently, at the microeconomic level, neoliberal policies have aimed at labour-market 'flexibility'. Essentially, this means wage cuts and other 'flexibility' concessions to employers, but such policies have had only a limited impact on unemployment and have worsened wage inequality.

The other main source of labour-market failure has been structural change in the economy and in labour-market dynamics themselves. This theme is pursued in chapter 6, by Burgess and Green and by Bell in chapter 12. Briefly, the argument is that structural change in the economy in the last two or three decades has eroded the earlier centrality of the manufacturing sector as a jobs engine providing relatively secure, full-time employment. This erosion has been very pronounced in Australia where the manufacturing sector's share of total employment has declined precipitously. In the wake of these changes, new employment growth has come mainly in the services sector. The upside of this development is that the services sector is relatively jobs intensive. However, and particularly in Australia, employment in the services sector tends to be part-time, casual, low wage and insecure. As Bell, Green and Burgess argue in chapter 8, and as Bell argues in chapter 12, in Australia this trend in employment growth partly reflects a 'low road' developmental path, and aggravates market wage inequality.

One of the themes of this book is that the problems of unemployment and inequality are two sides of the same distributional coin and need to be tackled together. This book argues that *jobs growth* is the best way to deal with both these problems. The book points to a way beyond the current policy framework and offers detailed solutions to unemployment and rising market inequality. Primarily, these solutions involve policies of sustainable economic expansion, and public-sector job creation. There is no other policy alternative if we wish to avoid the vagaries of currently popular wage-cutting strategies and other measures which offer (at best) only limited employment gains and further threaten the fairness of Australian society. As argued in chapter 8, to support such an expansionary and redistributive program, medium-term policies need to be developed to help restructure the economy in order to promote stronger wealth creation in higher value-added industries and a stronger and more competitive export profile. Other redistributive measures such as guaranteed minimum incomes (primarily designed to break the nexus between work and income), wage subsidies and work-sharing are briefly discussed in chapter 12. While the latter two of these policies have merit in some respects, the main approach advocated in this book is the provision of real jobs at reasonable wages for those who need them.

The approach advocated here will have to be paid for, however, by diverting some resources from current private consumption towards public-sector provision. In short, and putting it bluntly, labour-market 'insiders' (the employed) will have to pay for expansionary policy, job-creation and other programs for the under-employed and unemployed 'outsiders'. This 'cost' (at least for those currently employed) must be weighed against the current costs of high unemployment, inequality and social dislocation. Clearly, choices need to be made and the unemployment problem, if diagnosed correctly, poses some stark moral choices. This book hopes to help inform those choices.

It was not always like this

During the postwar 'golden age', trends in the economy and the broad thrust of government policy were able to secure high growth, full employment, reduced inequality, and, for a time, low inflation. Between the mid-1940s and the mid-1970s in Australia, unemployment averaged only about 2 per cent. The Menzies government almost lost the 1961 federal election when unemployment briefly approached 3 per cent!

The underlying economic dynamics of the postwar years were certainly conducive to good employment growth. As argued in chapter 12, employment growth was strongly assisted by a 'virtuous circle' of rapid output, productivity and employment growth in the manufacturing sector, a key jobs engine of this period. Partly supporting and partly driving all this, at both the national and international levels, was a macroeconomic strategy aimed squarely at rapid expansion and full employment. The theoretical inspiration for such a policy approach came from the work of John Maynard Keynes, who had diagnosed the ills of the Depression as one of insufficient aggregate demand. According to this view, the main solution to unemployment was to drive the economy harder to soak up the unemployed through demand expansion, economic growth and the creation of new jobs. As John Nevile argues in chapter 7, Keynes' insight was that governments, especially through the taxing and spending powers of fiscal policy, could help stimulate the economy in the desired direction.

Looking back, what was extraordinary about the golden age was the strong political consensus that underpinned full employment. This was partly born of the experiences of the Depression and World War II. There emerged a view, more or less along traditional social democratic lines, that labour should not simply be treated as a raw commodity subject to the vicissitudes of the market. Instead, the view of the dominant postwar political coalition was that, where needed, the state should intervene in the market economy to ensure full employment. In the postwar era, at least until the 1970s, this new thinking shaped both national macroeconomic policy and international economic govern-ance. Led by the US, new international governance arrangements recog-nised the need to control financial markets and international capital flows in order to support the kind of national economic sovereignty required to pursue full-employment policies. It was well recognised that full-employment capitalism did not necessarily suit conservative finan-cial interests, or indeed certain interests within the business community. The problem, of course, is that full employment inevitably strengthens labour's market power, potentially leading to inflationary wage pressures and challenges to management authority in the workplace. This prob-lem was presciently analysed in the early 1940s by the Polish economist, Michel Kalecki (1943). For Kalecki (1943, p. 326), 'unemployment is an integral part of the normal capitalist system':

> The maintenance of full employment would cause social and political changes which would give new impetus to the opposition of business leaders. Under a regime of permanent full employment, the 'sack' would cease to play its role as a disciplinary measure. The social position of the boss would be undermined and the self assurance and class confidence of the working class would grow. Strikes for wage increases and improvements in conditions would create political tension.

Kalecki's prediction came true. The postwar full-employment order started to unravel in the 1970s, in part because of inflationary pressures generated in the United States and also because full employment for over two decades had helped produce wage pressures that were fuelling high inflation. Structurally speaking, this was the Achilles heel of the postwar order (Armstrong et al. 1991; Glyn 1995; Marglin and Schor 1990). We can learn a great deal from this experience. We now know that strong employment growth and full employment cannot be sus-tained in the long run without a mechanism to control wage pressures and inflation. In varying ways, all sides in the unemployment debate now agree on this. For the neoliberal right, wage moderation or wage reduc-tions are necessary to create employment. For the social democratic and Keynesian left, wage moderation is needed to make a full-employment regime *sustainable*.

Neoliberalism

Since the 1970s, macroeconomic policy under neoliberalism has, in the main, adopted a 'fight inflation first' strategy. In recent years the battle appears to have been won. The cost, however, has been high. Based on a largely correct diagnosis that a major driver of inflation was wage pressures, neoliberal policy has effectively jettisoned the postwar full-employment priority. Instead, macroeconomic policy, through policies of slow growth and the occasional policy-induced recession, has attempted for much of this period to discipline labour through high unemployment. On the fiscal policy front, governments have pursued stringency, aimed at balanced or surplus budgets and low taxes, and this has added a disinflationary and public-sector slimming bias to policy. Monetary policy, through the setting of short-term interest rates, has been used aggressively on several occasions, most spectacularly in the high interest rate squeeze and subsequent deep recession of the early 1990s. Complementing all this, microeconomic and industrial relations policy has focused on increasing labour-market competitiveness and removing market protections and award conditions. Despite sound evidence that Australia already has levels of labour-market flexibility paralleling the much-vaunted levels found in the US (Coelli et al. 1994; Gregory, Klug and Martin 1999), Prime Minister Howard has spoken of the need for an 'infinitely more flexible' labour-market. The main aim is to discipline labour and return it to the status of a commodity subject to the price signal. The combined results of this policy framework thus far have been high unemployment, as well as increasing wage dispersion and rising market inequality, poverty and inadequate provision of government relief in terms of labour-market programs and job creation. Little wonder that by the mid-1990s, over one-third of the unemployed had become long-term unemployed and almost one-third of the Australian population was in receipt of some form of social security benefit (Latham 1998, p. 201).

There have been some policy bright spots. In the 1980s, under the Prices and Incomes Accord, federal Labor governments did attempt to move beyond austerity policies and adopt a Keynesian-style strategy that aimed at expansionary, job-creating economic policy. The idea was to run the economy harder to create jobs while keeping the lid on inflation through a negotiated wage-moderation strategy with the unions – the Accord. The policy worked well for a period but came to grief as the expanding economy ran into a 'banana republic' current account crisis and later suffered from a heavy-handed policy response in the face of an economic boom. Essentially, the economy was running too hard and, because of underlying structural economic weakness, was pulling in too many exports and building up what many considered to be worrying levels of foreign debt. By the late 1980s, as we know, a major boom was under way, soon to be brought down by highly restrictionist policy – later interpreted by leaders such as Paul Keating as the 'recession we had to have'. In the wake of the recession, under the banner of the *Working Nation* program, Labor tried to mount remedial labour-market programs aimed particularly at the growing queues of long-term unemployed. Labor also tried, largely successfully, to compensate for rising market inequality and wage moderation through the welfare system. The problem was that Labor's strategy of compensation was becoming fiscally unsustainable (at least on the existing tax and revenue base) (Dwyer and Larkin 1996). In 1996, the incoming conservative coalition government slashed expenditure on these programs and has since concentrated mainly on privatising and marketising job-broking and employment services. The coalition has tightened fiscal policy further, and wage and labour-market 'flexibility' has become the leitmotif of employment policy.

The unemployment policy debate

To understand the unemployment debate we need to be aware of the various forms of unemployment. There are three of them. So-called 'frictional' unemployment occurs as workers move between jobs and are temporarily out of the labour-market. More important are 'cyclical' and 'structural' unemployment. The former stems from economic slumps or patterns of slow economic growth that destroys jobs and weakens job creation. Here the focus is mainly on the demand or growth side of the economy. Structural unemployment, on the other hand, is usually seen as a labour supply-side problem stemming from skills inadequacies, the debilitating effects of long-term unemployment, wage rigidities, work disincentives and various other forms of labour-market impediments and mismatches.

There is not much consensus among economists about what is driving unemployment. More specifically, opinion is divided across two camps which in turn reflect broader divisions within economic thought. The two camps are the neoclassical and the Keynesian and both are reviewed below.

The orthodox neoclassical school

In Australia and in most OECD economies, neoliberals and orthodox neoclassical economists are the most influential school in policy terms. This school focuses largely on the supply side of the labour market and emphasises the structural problems in labour-markets just noted. For this school, labour supply problems and labour-market 'rigidities' are the main problems driving unemployment. Workers may be under-skilled or ask for excessive wages. They might be inflexible in other ways. Collective organisations such as unions or welfare policies that boost the bargaining strength of labour or that weaken work incentives are also generally seen as problems. The ideal for this school is highly competitive and flexible labour-markets that clear based on price bargaining. To put the case baldly, as Treasury secretary Ted Evans has, people are unemployed largely because they choose to be: they ask for higher wages than employers will pay. Therefore, wage cuts or wage freezes and other concessions to employers are what is required to boost employment.

Neoliberals emphasise that the kinds of structural blockages they identify in labour-markets also place speed limits on the economy, beyond which bottlenecks and accelerating inflation lie. These limits have been variously formalised in concepts such as the natural rate of unemployment (NRU) and the non-accelerating inflation rate of unemployment (NAIRU). The argument is that if the economy is pushed to a point where unemployment falls below the NAIRU, structural problems and bottlenecks will be encountered and accelerating inflation, which will stymie growth, will be the main result.[1] In this sense, a certain level of unemployment is *functional* for an economy with structural labour-market problems. Estimates of the NAIRU for Australia typically vary between 6 and 8 per cent (RBA 1993, p. 7). Hence, levels of unemployment at these magnitudes are essentially redefined as 'full employment'. Neoliberals argue that in the medium to longer term, structural labour-market problems can be eased by various types of labour-market programs, labour-market reform and the vigorous pursuit of wage flexibility. Yet neoliberals also worry about too much growth because, within the NRU or NAIRU framework, growth sufficient to reduce unemployment below, say, 6 per cent, is likely to be inflationary. This concern helps explain the cautious and restrictionist approach Australian authorities have adopted in relation to economic growth (Argy 1998; Bell 1997a, ch. 7), and is also behind rhetorical statements such as the 'recession we had to have'.

Influential officials, such as the governor of the Reserve Bank, Ian Macfarlane, have been prominent advocates of the neoliberal approach to unemployment. In a speech delivered in May 1997, for example, Macfarlane asserted the bank was not solely focused on achieving low inflation and that the bank took the unemployment issue seriously. He argued that in terms of cyclical unemployment, attaining low inflation was the best way to achieve sustainable GDP growth and thus employment growth. He did note, however, that, comparatively, there was not a strong link between GDP growth and unemployment rates. Some countries with good GDP growth had high unemployment, others with moderate GDP growth had low unemployment. The reason, of course, is that factors such as labour-force participation rates and labour productivity growth affect the extent to which GDP growth is linked to unemployment levels. After raising these caveats about growth, Macfarlane gave most attention to structural unemployment, citing the situation in the larger continental European economies as a case in point. There, labour-markets have an institutional framework which promotes 'jobs security, imposes relatively strict minimum wages and conditions, provides easily accessible sickness benefits and unemployment benefits, and increases trade union involvement'. These, Macfarlane argues, 'work against the interests of job creation' (Macfarlane 1997a, p. 6). The solution Macfarlane advocates is to move towards US, UK and New Zealand style labour-market deregulation. This, Macfarlane concedes, will reduce wages and conditions for workers and lead to growing wage dispersion and inequality, but it is a price we must pay, he argues. On the question of fairness, he states that 'while income inequality may not seem very fair, unemployment is not very fair either' (Macfarlane 1997a: p. 6). Essentially we are being offered a grim choice between unemployment and inequality.

A variation on this theme was offered in a set of policies outlined in an open letter to the prime minister in late 1998 by five prominent neoclassical economists (*Australian* 26 October 1998). This drew on earlier work by Dawkins and Freebairn (1997) and has the merit of attempting to deal with the inequality issues that arise from the neo-liberal approach. The core proposal, as usual, is to boost employment by reducing average wage levels. This is to be achieved through one of the few remaining labour-market institutions, the Industrial Relations Commission. The idea is to impose a freeze on safety-net wage increases to low-wage earners. It is argued that a four-year freeze would reduce average wages by 10 to 12 per cent over the period. Some dispute these calculations.[2] In any case, based on Reserve Bank estimates of the wage–employment relationship, the economists claim that the net effect of the package would reduce unemployment to around 5 per cent. The economists admit that freezing wages will increase inequality. Peter Dawkins, one of the five economists, refers to this as the 'diabolical trade-off'. To deal with this dilemma, the economists propose a system of earned tax credits to help supplement falling market incomes. Significantly, this is a proposal for direct redistribution of resources as part of a package to fight unemployment.

The Keynesian school

This last idea points to a linkage to the second major school in the unemployment debate, which follows broadly in the footsteps of Keynes. This approach, in its various forms, is sceptical of the ideal of fully flexible labour-markets and rejects the notion that labour-markets can or should be analysed in terms of simple price signals and raw competition (Quiggin 1997). Structural unemployment and supply-side problems are certainly recognised, but greater emphasis in explaining the growth of and solutions to unemployment is placed on the *demand* side of the economy. As William Mitchell argues in chapter 3, the main factors that have driven unemployment in the last two decades are weak aggregate demand and slow growth, particularly the fall-out from major recessions. These have had the effect of pushing unemployment up to new plateaus and building in increasing blocks of structural unemployment. As Burgess and Green point out in chapter 6, cyclical unemployment increasingly becomes structural unemployment, a problem, it seems, that bears down overwhelmingly on the low skilled (Nickell and Bell 1997; Gregg and Manning 1997, pp. 401–2). In this sense, cyclical and structural unemployment are linked on a continuum. Neoliberals argue that wage flexibility will break this dynamic. An army of unemployed, and particularly those at the low end of the labour-market, will become employed through necessary adjustments on the supply side, especially to wage levels. Keynesians, on the other hand, doubt the magnitude of the claimed links between wage levels and employment growth.

This, then, is a key question in the debate: how much will reducing labour costs (and achieving other flexibilities) influence employment growth and the decision by employers to hire labour? Estimates of the linkage or 'elasticity' between wage rates and employment growth tend to vary in the literature, but overall, as Raja Junankar argues in chapter 4, the link appears not to be a strong one. Factors other than wage rates appear to be stronger influences on the decision to hire labour, and, as Mitchell and Junankar argue in chapters 3 and 4 respectively, it is demand conditions that most strongly influence employment growth. The empirical evidence, then, is not particularly supportive of the neoliberal case. Indeed, labour-markets have become more flexible in the last two decades yet unemployment has continued to rise (Standing 1997). Bob Gregory, in chapter 5, also presents evidence relevant to assessing the neoliberal case. He examines GDP and employment growth as well as the wages and productivity growth over the last 30 years or so in four countries, Australia, the UK, New Zealand and the Unites States. A striking finding is that the two countries that have most aggressively introduced neoliberal reforms over this period have performed relatively poorly in terms of employment growth.

A further major concern about the neoliberal approach can be summed up in the rhetorical question: 'what do you do for an encore?' The problem is that neoliberalism confronts a major medium- to long-term dilemma in its handling of unemployment and inflation. Under NAIRU reasoning, neoliberals agree that unemployment is functional in achieving low inflation. A slight variation on this is the US model where (official) unemployment is somewhat lower than the OECD average, but where inequality, poverty and job insecurity provide a mechanism for labour discipline and the restraint of inflation. Either way, the inflation control mechanism is a blunt and damaging one, especially for low-wage workers. Suppose for the moment that labour flexibility policies work and something like full employment is restored. Unless the US model is adopted (i.e. weakening labour through high levels of inequality and job insecurity), it is hard to see how a repeat of the postwar full-employment scenario could be avoided once full employment rekindled labour's bargaining power and once more set off inflation. The historical cycle that started in the late 1960s would be repeated ending with renewed neoliberal attempts to (re)discipline labour. No wonder Kalecki argued that without major institutional reform, capitalism and full employment are incompatible.

There must be a better way

It is the Keynesian approach to unemployment that is advocated in this book. Broadly, this approach argues that the best way to reduce unemployment and inequality is through a direct emphasis on economic expansion and job creation. There are two versions of this approach. In what might loosely be called 'traditional' Keynesianism, the emphasis is on aggregate expansion of the economy, especially through the activist use of fiscal policy and an accommodating monetary policy. An alternative approach is more overtly redistributive, based on direct, publicly funded job creation. To the extent that the traditional approach runs into constraints on the current account or inflation fronts, the alternative approach should be favoured. The two approaches are clearly complementary, but in practice judgements would need to be made about the appropriate mix.

John Nevile, in chapter 7, argues that in the golden age, fiscal policy was an important expansionary instrument and that expansionary fiscal policy should again be used to achieve lower unemployment. This raises the question of how hard we need to run the economy to bring down unemployment. This issue is covered by Burgess and Green in chapter 6.

The key variables and estimates include the GDP growth rate, the labour-force participation rate and labour productivity growth. Burgess and Green conclude that on current estimates and projections, GDP growth of around 4.3 per cent per annum would bring down unemployment by roughly 1 per cent per annum. If this rate of GDP growth could be sustained for four or so years, unemployment would be reduced to the reasonably respectable low of between 4 and 5 per cent.

So far in the 1990s, GDP growth rates have been short of the mark. If we include the recessionary period in the early 1990s, real GDP growth has averaged only about 2.9 per cent so far in the 1990s. If we look only at the expansionary period since 1994, real GDP growth has been substantially better, running at around 3.9 per cent per annum. On the back of a strong growth figure in 1998, some have begun to argue that we should simply sit back and hope that the recent growth of the economy will continue, thus reducing unemployment to respectable levels through the effects of the economic cycle. Some commentators, for example, have been optimistic enough to suggest that strong growth could continue, so much so that unemployment could fall as low as 5 to 6 per cent in the medium term.

We should be very wary of this kind of 'cyclical solution'. First, the optimistic expansionary scenario might not happen. Other forecasters have pointed out that a major component of recent growth has been based on high levels of private consumption and debt, and are far from sanguine about medium-term growth and unemployment outcomes (see, for example, Brain 1999, pp. 221–3). The point, then, is that a well-founded employment policy should be based on more than 'cyclical hope'. Second, the cyclical path works too slowly. Based on the expansionary cycle of the 1990s, even if we accept some of the more optimistic forecasts, it will have taken over a decade to have shifted unemployment down. This is not good enough, especially given the damage done along the way, particularly to the long-term unemployed who, as noted above, now make up about one-third of the unemployment pool. Third, and inevitably, the next recession will again drive up unemployment and if experience is any guide, the base level of unemployment in the next recovery will be higher than in the last. Arguably, then, the economic growth machine needs a shot in the arm and some form of compensating expansionary policy is required.

This is true for another important reason as well. The labour-market's central role in society is to distribute jobs and incomes: ideally, good jobs and incomes. Yet high unemployment means it is not distributing enough jobs. Nor is it distributing incomes fairly enough, as indicated by rising levels of market inequality and welfare dependency. As mentioned above, and as later chapters will also show, the jobs being produced in

Australia are generally part-time, insecure and low paying. What we need then is not only more jobs, but better jobs. A key argument of this book is that this will not happen without deliberate government intervention.

But what type of intervention? The traditional Keynesianism of aggregate demand expansion driven by the public sector spending is one option. John Nevile discusses this option in detail in chapter 7. Along the way he demonstrates that orthodox objections to fiscal expansionism based on theories such as 'twin deficits' and 'crowding out' do not stand up to serious scrutiny. Nevile agrees that more serious concerns arise from potential growth limits on the Australian economy, based particularly on inflation and the current account constraint.

Chapter 9 by Anis Chowdhury considers the inflation constraint in some detail. As indicated above, the need to control inflation in a full-employment economy is a key lesson of the postwar golden age experience. As that experience shows, wage-push inflation and subsequent wage–price spirals reflect underlying distributive conflict between labour and capital over income shares (Heilbroner 1979; Gilbert 1981). Chowdhury argues that the neoliberal response to the high inflation of the 1970s and 1980s has been to use standard deflationary policies of slow growth and high unemployment as a form of labour-market discipline. Although the strategy has worked on the inflation front, it has been a very costly strategy in terms of lost output and persistent unemployment. Chowdhury argues that the neoliberal disinflationary policy should be replaced by a more civilised alternative. There are two important points to be made at this juncture.

First, in relation to the estimates by Burgess and Green, a sustained rate of GDP growth at around 4.3 per cent per annum would make a big impact on unemployment levels in the medium term. Interestingly, work by Dungey and Pitchford (1998) estimates a so-called steady inflation rate of growth or SIRG for the Australian economy. Their SIRG estimate is 4.37 per cent. That is, they estimate that a GDP growth rate as high as 4.37 per cent is compatible with steady inflation. If this figure is correct, it implies that the prevailing NAIRU estimates are too high and it also gives the green light to a more expansionary approach to macro-economic policy (see also Argy 1998, pp. 124–7).

Second, we need to rethink our approach to inflation in the 1990s and perhaps adopt a less fixated, less stringent position on the problem (Bell 1999; McDonald 1999). There is reason to think that the 'fight inflation first' strategy may have been overdone by attempting to achieve rates of inflation that are perhaps too low. As Bell (1999) and others have argued, there is little evidence that achieving zero to very low inflation is actually good for the economy and plenty of evidence that the achievement of such low rates has been extremely costly. The point is that, on present evidence, there is room for debate about whether the current practice of targeting very low inflation (currently in the 2 to 3 per cent range) should not be relaxed somewhat, allowing a more expansionary policy. Moreover, to the extent that inflation does become a problem in the future, we should avoid standard deflationary strategies and adopt better control mechanisms.

The only alternative to orthodox deflation is a bargained approach where consensus replaces or at least substantially moderates distributional conflict over income shares. Typically, such approaches involve some kind of incomes policy based on negotiations and settlements between labour, government and perhaps business as well. The comparative evidence indicates that such methods generally produce better and certainly lower cost macroeconomic outcomes than any alternative (Schott 1984; Dore et al. 1994). As is well known, however, developing and sustaining an incomes policy is not easy. Ideally, a successful incomes policy should be underpinned by a rough consensus on the distribution of income. This can be buttressed by suitable trade-offs and inducements that support wage moderation. Australia's experience with the Accord between 1983 and 1996 indicates that such policies can be partially successful, at least for a period. However, for various reasons the Accord did not last and the labour movement is not eager to rebuild such a centralised system. Given these difficulties, the only way forward would seem to be a more decentralised form of incomes bargaining. Chowdhury looks at the German model of industry-level bargaining and more sectorally based alternatives to large-scale incomes policies. He also argues that a public-sector-led jobs expansion program would need to develop discrete bargaining forums that linked job provision to wage moderation.

An approach to unemployment based on aggregate expansion of the economy must also deal with potential problems on the current account front. Some argue that we should not be overly concerned about the current account. Their argument is that because most of Australia's current account deficit (CAD) represents the accumulation of *private* offshore debt, this should be of no concern to policy-makers and should not be seen as a limit to economic growth. Others have pointed out that Australia's ability to fund the CAD has improved in the 1990s and urge a more relaxed stance on the CAD. In some ways this might be a good idea, particularly in the wake of earlier overzealous policy reactions.

Nevertheless, the CAD does reflect some worrying medium to longer term structural trends in the economy, particularly the long-term decline in commodity prices and Australia's terms of trade position (the ratio of export to import prices), as well as a rapidly increasing trade deficit in manufactures and other high-end goods. As chapter 8 argues,

Australia is generally following a 'low road' developmental path in an increasingly high-tech world – the main export industries in the commodities sector feature a pattern of 'jobless growth' and low innovation. 'Jobless growth' is also a feature of the manufacturing sector; and there is a predominant pattern of low-wage development in the main jobs arena, the services sector (Marceau et al. 1997). Given that the main labour-market outcome associated with this economic structure is the produc-tion of too many poor quality jobs, a short-term fixation on the CAD number is the wrong focus. Instead we need to focus on the broader structural issues and associated labour-market outcomes. Australia needs policies to better position it in stronger sectors of the world economy, to improve the sustainability of GDP growth and to provide higher skilled and better paying jobs. As chapter 8 argues, co-ordinated industry, regional and industrial relations policies need to be developed.

To the extent, then, that inflation and perhaps even the CAD do not pose a major short-term constraint on an expansionary macroeconomic policy, such a policy should be pursued.[3] To the extent that a higher growth pattern aggravates inflation or CAD problems, these should be dealt with in the ways mentioned above in order to improve the *sustainability* of growth. As Fred Argy (1998, p. 124) has put it, 'it is time to shake off . . . earlier policy timidity and strive boldly for growth of between 4 to 4.5 per cent per annum for at least the next few years. This may require aggressive demand management'.

There is, however, a case for a complementary variation to aggregate expansionism. This is the direct provision of jobs on a more targeted basis, particularly in labour-intensive employment areas, such as public-sector expansion and community services employment. These issues and proposals are covered in more detail in chapters 10 and 12 by Quiggin and Bell respectively. There are two main concerns behind a more targeted approach. First, the long-term unemployed might not be effectively caught up by a broader economic expansion. Second, as Bell argues in chapter 12, only four or five sectors of the economy have displayed significant jobs growth in the last decade or more. Excepting the construction sector, all of these job-rich areas are in the services sector. This reflects a substantial shift away from the postwar developmental model that was based on strong employment growth in the manufacturing sector, which now displays 'jobless growth', not only in Australia but in many other OECD countries. On these grounds, both Quiggin and Bell argue that public-sector services provision and job creation in sectors such as community services offer a path to further employment which should be pursued. This approach would also provide much-needed community spin-offs involving the rebuilding of run-down community services and infrastructure in areas such as health, education, and environmental protection. Complementing such a demand-side focus, labour supply-side policies dealing with education, training, and assisting the unemployed to re-enter the labour-market are also advocated and are covered by Elizabeth Webster in chapter 11.

But how can a more expansionary policy be funded? At present, government macroeconomic policy is fixated on fiscal stringency. Any expansionary alternative must challenge this and find extra resources for the government sector. Essentially, the mechanism advocated here is demand-switching, from the private to public sector in the name of a concerted approach to expansion – something which is not happening at present given the current public–private mix. John Nevile's solution, as advocated in chapter 7, is the standard Keynesian package, with one important variation: instead of deficit spending, the new global realities of potential negative reactions from financial markets to increased government debt require that the spending underpinning stimulation should be mainly tax financed. Bell and Quiggin agree with this financing strategy. Quiggin provides detailed estimates of the jobs and fiscal implications of his proposed jobs program in chapter 10. He estimates that a program with a net cost of around $15 billion per annum would provide for 300 000 places in labour-market programs and 300 000 new public-sector jobs. Such a program would reduce unemployment to between 4 and 5 per cent, which given contemporary labour-market dynamics is a reasonable outcome. As Quiggin emphasises, the extra tax burden would not lift Australia out of its comparative position as a low-tax economy.

The trilemma and quadlemma

Broadly speaking, then, the employment debate is shaped by two policy alternatives. There is the neoliberal or US model in which low-end (mainly services) employment is created by wage reductions and market mechanisms. This approach is questioned in this book on the grounds that it is not likely to be a strong instrument of job creation and that it produces low-wage jobs and thus worsens market inequality. The only alternative approach, the one advocated in this book, is essentially a redistributive route through directly providing jobs at reasonable wages through tax-funded aggregate expansion and public-sector jobs expansion. The downside of this approach is that it compromises government efforts at budgetary stringency.

The two solution paths and their problems constitute what Iversen and Wren (1998) term the 'trilemma of the service economy'. Nowhere, it seems, have governments managed to combine employment growth, greater wage equality and budgetary restraint. 'While it is possible to achieve two of these goals simultaneously, it has so far proved impossible to achieve all three.' As argued above and in later chapters, the growth of private services employment in a deregulated market is typically associated with low-wage employment and rising inequality. On the other hand, the growth of public services employment sacrifices budgetary stringency, which, in recent decades under neoliberalism, has become something of a business and electoral fixation.

The utility of the trilemma framework is that it clearly reveals the stark moral and policy choices that are at stake as we enter the new millennium. Unlike the postwar situation, we are returning to an order where the market economy is breeding inequality and is increasingly divisive. This situation can only be overcome by explicitly confronting distributional issues, something that even in the postwar order was only done in a relatively indirect way, mainly through the trickle-down effects of strong economic growth and full (male) employment.

If we add inflation to this picture, we get the quadlemma: essentially, the task of achieving employment growth, greater equality, low or moderate inflation and fiscal restraint. The neoliberal route can, as we have seen – but at a high cost – achieve two of these: low inflation and fiscal stringency. If one accepts the conventional neoliberal argument about wage flexibility, employment growth is also achievable, but at the cost of rising inequality. That's three out of four. If one questions the neoliberal employment growth argument, as this book does, then employment growth under neoliberalism is nothing special and certainly no better on a proportional basis than that achieved in, say, Australia in the last decade or so. It seems, then, that neoliberalism provides a way to achieve low inflation and fiscal stringency. That's two out of four. In contrast, the strategy advocated in this book will certainly achieve employment growth and reduce inequality. That's two out of four. If, for the reasons outlined above and in more detail in subsequent chapters, inflation could also be kept in check, that's three out of four. The certain casualty, however, is fiscal stringency. Whether this is a great loss, in an era of debilitating cuts to the public sector, is debatable. Even if we try a more humane approach to neoliberalism, as advocated by the five economists, and build in a compensatory welfare component to help offset rising inequality, then this will compromise fiscal stringency anyway, although perhaps not as much as the approach advocated here. Hence, in the worst case scenario (and adding in compensatory welfare measures), neoliberalism is a surefire way to achieve only one of the quadlemma goals – low inflation. This is not much of an achievement.

The aim of this book, then, is to generate a broader debate about unemployment, which has so far not occurred. The costs and benefits of alternative strategies have not been fully canvassed or assessed, and the debate has been too one-sided. Neoliberal 'solutions' have been favoured by powerful interests in government and business. There has also been a worrying degree of community fatalism about the unemployment problem.

As this book argues, solving the problem of unemployment is quite straightforward. With a strong community consensus, low unemployment could be achieved, quite quickly. This book estimates, especially in chapters 7 and 10, the fiscal cost of proposals that would get unemployment down to between 4 and 5 per cent. Essentially, unemployment raises critical issues about distribution and fair shares of work and income. At present the increasingly deregulated labour-market is failing to distribute jobs and incomes effectively. It is also failing to produce enough quality jobs. Only public-sector intervention will fix these problems. In the end it boils down to a moral choice about whether we are willing to share jobs and income more fairly. The neoliberal response to unemployment, seen in distributional terms, is to ask those at the bottom of the heap to take a wage cut: in effect to 'fund' work for themselves through reduced market incomes. The distributional mechanism advocated in this book is to share the burden more widely and to ask those already employed for a contribution. In considering this option, the current massive economic and social costs of unemployment need to be considered. It also needs to be remembered that Australia currently has one of the lowest tax regimes in the OECD. Also, as John Nevile points out in chapter 7, the growth dividend from an expansionary policy would largely offset initial tax increases within several years.

Clearly, politics will determine what happens. Voters put unemployment high on their list of key concerns. They resent being unemployed or becoming so. They also worry about their children's prospects. Governments wring their hands about the issue. The vast majority of voters, however, have jobs and the unemployed are a weak minority. Tax reform not unemployment featured as the major issue in the last two federal elections, and governments retain office despite persistent unemployment. In this context, the *Economist* (1997, p. 19) sums up the European situation thus:

> Voters are almost certainly worried about unemployment. But it is their own jobs they worry about – not the unemployment that is tucked away in poor neighbourhoods, that they rarely if ever visit. Are workers really prepared to sacrifice benefits and make their jobs less secure in order to help the poor? So far, the answer has remained no, even as the dole queues have climbed.

If this is true, there is little hope for the unemployed.

Structure of the book

The broader approach and arguments of this book have been outlined above, but it is useful here to offer a further more explicit guide to the chapters which follow.

One of the aims of this book is to describe the scale and dimensions of the unemployment problem confronting Australia. This is taken up in chapter 2 by Martin Watts who presents data on a range of measures and dimensions of the unemployment problem, including the way in which unemployment is distributed according to age, gender and region. Watts presents estimates of the economic costs of unemployment and examines the links between unemployment and inequality.

A further aim of this book is to critically evaluate two competing theories of the causes of unemployment. The dominant theory in policy terms is the neoliberal supply-side case that excessive or inflexible wages largely drive unemployment. This book rejects this argument, as explained in chapters 3, 4 and 5. In chapter 3, William Mitchell critiques the neoliberal case and presents a demand-side analysis of the unemployment problem. He also assesses the extent to which unemployment is driven by labour-displacing technology, by 'deindustrialisation', and by compositional shifts in the labour-market. In chapter 4, Raja Junankar presents both theoretical and empirical arguments against the neoliberal case. On the empirical front, he shows that the linkage fundamental to the neoliberal case, that between wages and employment levels, is not particularly strong. He also discusses evidence that demonstrates that various forms of labour-market deregulation have not been strongly linked to employment growth. This issue is taken up in more detail by Bob Gregory in chapter 5 who compares the labour-market performances of Australia, the UK, New Zealand and the US over the last 30 years or so. Again, the neoliberal case is not supported. Compared to Australia, radical labour-market deregulation in New Zealand and the UK has not produced superior employment growth. Moreover, compared to the US, the more regulated Australian labour-market has done just as well at producing jobs at the bottom end of the labour-market.

In rejecting the neoliberal approach to unemployment, this book focuses instead on demand-side solutions to unemployment. A key question here is how much economic growth is needed to provide enough jobs to soak up the unemployed. This question is addressed in chapter 6 by John Burgess and Roy Green who estimate that to get unemployment down to what might be considered to be the respectable level of between 4 and 5 per cent, GDP growth would need to run at around 4.3 per cent for three to four years. This of course assumes no recessions, no current account or inflation problems and no interest rate increases, etc. Although the economy has been growing rapidly in the last two years, there are reasons to doubt that this will continue indefinitely. More broadly there is a strong case to be made that GDP growth and employment growth need to be directly stimulated through policy.

John Nevile takes up this issue in chapter 7 and argues that orthodox Keynesian policies still have an important role to play in stimulating economic growth and in avoiding major recessions. Running the economy harder, however, means a greater risk of encountering current account and inflation problems. In chapter 8 by Stephen Bell, Roy Green and John Burgess and in chapter 9 by Anis Chowdhury, it is argued that these problems need to be dealt with as part of a full-employment strategy, and, in contrast to neoliberal strategies, they need to be dealt with in ways that do not involve higher unemployment. Bell, Green and Burgess argue that economic restructuring towards a higher value-added economy is required to reduce the risk of current account problems, to provide the economic wherewithal for stronger employment growth and to help provide higher quality jobs. Chowdhury argues that the only way to deal with the inflation danger in a way that does not rely on the crude instrument of unemployment as a labour discipline is through some form of consensus-based wage restraint.

This book argues that not one but two expansionary strategies should be pursued on a complementary basis. To the extent that aggregate expansion of the whole economy does run into either current account or inflation limits in the short to medium term, and because only some sectors of the economy are jobs rich, attention also needs to be devoted to more targeted, sectorally based jobs programs. These issues are taken up in chapters 10 and 12 respectively. In chapter 10, for example, John Quiggin follows up on the analysis of the sectoral composition of jobs growth conducted by Burgess and Green in chapter 6. He argues that the quickest way to low unemployment is through the provision of publicly funded employment in highly jobs-intensive areas such as the community services sector.

In complementing any expansionary jobs program, there is also a role for specialised labour-market programs. As Elizabeth Webster argues in chapter 11, various forms of training and skill enhancement programs are not a panacea for unemployment but they do offer bridging assistance, especially in terms of assisting the long-term unemployed back into employment.

CHAPTER 2

The Dimensions and Costs of Unemployment in Australia

Martin Watts

Since the early 1970s, Australia, along with most OECD countries, has experienced rates of unemployment that have been persistently higher than during the postwar period from the 1950s to the early 1970s. It is also true that over the last 15 years the Australian unemployment rate has been higher than the corresponding rates of the USA and Japan, as well as the OECD average. The large unemployment rate differential of about 4 percentage points compared to the United States has its origins in the severe recession of the early 1990s. In this chapter a number of issues relating to the incidence and costs of unemployment will be explored. First, labour-market aggregates and the relationships between them will be defined, with a particular focus on the definition of the unemployment rate. The real dimensions of the unemployment problem will be estimated by looking at the notion of marginal attachment to the labour-market. Second, trends in the Australian unemployment rate will be documented and analysed. Third, the incidence of unemployment will be investigated, by reference to the rate and duration of unemployment and its incidence by gender, age, education, sector and region. Fourth, it is shown that sustained high levels of unemployment impose substantial economic and social costs on the Australian community. Fifth, the links between unemployment and the distribution of earnings will be examined. Concluding comments are then presented.

We find that, by taking account of hidden unemployment, the rate of unemployment is in the order of 15 per cent, rather than the current official figure of around 7.5 per cent or so. In the last three decades the official unemployment rate has ratchetted upwards. In addition, the extent of under-employment has increased, which reflects the growing incidence of non-standard forms of employment. Beyond the large rise in aggregate unemployment, several other features stand out. First,

much of the increase in aggregate unemployment is accounted for by a
rise in unemployment rates of male full-time workers. Second, the long-
term unemployed make up an increasing proportion of the unemployed
pool, currently about a third of the total. Third, employment growth is
now heavily biased towards part-time jobs. Fourth, the unskilled are
doing badly in the labour-market: unemployment rates for unskilled
workers are more than double those for skilled workers.

This chapter estimates that the economic costs of unemployment
could be as high as $40 billion per annum, a figure which far exceeds
the most inflated estimates of the costs of microeconomic inefficiency.
Though less easy to measure, when the social costs of unemployment are
taken into consideration, it is evident that a major economic and social
disaster confronts Australia, unless economic policies are designed to
reduce unemployment. Successive governments have abrogated their
responsibility for reducing unemployment, by all too often treating it as
an individual rather than a collective problem. The burden of unemployment by incidence and duration is not spread equally across age,
skill and industry groups. Further, low employment rates and poor
income levels have become concentrated in particular regional and
urban areas which have tended to promote a vicious cycle of poverty and
deprivation. The persistently high rate of unemployment in the last two
decades, along with the increase in earnings inequality, is the most
important economic issue confronting Australia today and requires a
radical change in policy.

The measurement of unemployment

In the official statistics, the population of working age (15–69 years) is
classified as being employed, unemployed or not in the labour force.

$$P = E + U + NIF = LF + NIF$$

where:
P denotes the population of working age,
E is employment,
U is unemployment,
NIF is not in the labour force, and
LF is the labour force.
The employed plus the unemployed constitute the labour force. In turn,
the share of the working-age population that constitutes the labour force
– that is, those who are working or seeking work – defines the labour-
force participation rate, LFP, so that:
LFP = LF/P
The published statistics on the labour-force status of the working-age
population are based on a monthly survey of 35 000 private homes,

which is undertaken by the Australian Bureau of Statistics. Members of the defence forces, diplomatic personnel and overseas visitors are not included in the survey. The ABS classifies an individual as employed if s/he undertook at least one hour of paid work in the survey week or at least one hour of unpaid work on a family farm or in a family business.[1] Hence, according to official statistical methods, even tiny amounts of work render one 'employed'.

An individual is defined to be unemployed if s/he was not employed at all during the survey week, but demonstrated that s/he was seeking a job and was available to take up employment. That is, s/he:

- actively looked for a full-time or part-time job at any time over the previous month; or
- was available for work in the survey week or would have been available except for temporary illness; or
- was waiting to start a new job within a month from the survey week and would have started if there had been an available job; or
- was waiting to be called back to a job from which they had been stood down without pay for less than four weeks (Clark 1997, pp. 146–8).

The term 'actively' means that the individual was taking steps to find a job that includes making direct contact with an employer about work, checking factory noticeboards, being registered with employment placement agencies,[2] advertising or tendering for work and contacting friends or relatives (ABS 1997a, p. 37).

Thus the definition of an employed worker is fairly open-ended, and can underpin significant under-employment,[3] whereas the definition of an unemployed worker is somewhat narrow and restrictive. In short, it is easier to be counted as employed and harder to be counted as unemployed in Australia.

The official unemployment rate clearly understates the true number of workers who wish to work. Those in the working-age population who are classified as not in the labour force are in turn divided into two groups, namely those with and those without a marginal attachment to the labour force.

The first group are subdivided into those who wanted to work and were actively looking for work in the four weeks up to the end of the reference week, but did not meet the criteria for being defined as unemployed; and those who were not actively seeking work (and hence were not in the labour force) but were available to start work within four weeks, with the provision of childcare, if necessary. The second subgroup is divided in turn into discouraged workers and others. Discouraged workers are those people who want to work but believe they are either too old or too

Table 2.1 Employment, unemployment and not in the labour force: Definitions and figures ('000), September 1997

Working age population (15–69 years) 12 919.6 (6456.8, 6462.7)

Labour force		Not in the labour force			
9225.4 (5217.6, 4007.8)[a]		3,694.2 (1,239.2, 2,454.9)			
Employed	Unemployed	Marginally attached		Not marginally attached[b]	
8432.8 (4748.2, 3684.5)	792.6 (469.4, 323.3)	890.5 (259.5, 630.9)		2803.7 (979.7, 1824.0)	
		Wanted to work and actively looking	Wanted to work but not actively looking, but available within 4 weeks	Wanted to work but neither looking nor available	Did not want to work
		53.3 (24.4, 28.9)	837.2 (235.1, 602.0)	298.7 (101.1, 197.6)	2415.4 (819.7, 1595.6)

Within "Wanted to work but not actively looking, but available within 4 weeks" (837.2):

Discouraged	Other
118.4	718.7
(39.7, 78.7)	(195.4, 523.4)

a Bracketed figures denote male and female magnitudes
b Includes persons who were permanently unable to work
Source: ABS (1997a)

young, lack necessary schooling, training, skills or experience, or have difficulties on account of language or ethnic background, or there are no jobs in their locality or line of work (ABS 1997a, p. 35).

The level of discouraged unemployment tends to be anti-cyclical, so that the labour-force participation rate is pro-cyclical. More workers tend to leave the labour force when the economy is in recession, believing that they will be unable to secure a job. In addition to the cyclical influence, male participation rates have exhibited a long-term decline, whereas female rates have exhibited an increase (based mainly on the growth of employment in services).

The group without marginal attachment includes workers who are not looking for work for reasons including: wanting to complete an educational course; looking after children or other family members; and ill-health or physical disability. Langmore and Quiggin (1994, p. 23) note the substantial increase in the number of people with mild disabilities who receive a disability support pension, particularly among older men. This pension is being used as a long-term substitute for the unemployment benefit by many men.

The not marginally attached group is subdivided into those who wanted work but were neither looking nor available, and those who did not want to work. The ABS concedes that the criteria attached to marginal attachment to the labour force, in particular the concepts of wanting work and reasons for not actively seeking work, are more subjective (ABS, 1997a, p. 36). Mitchell and Watts (1997, p. 439, table 1.5) estimate that in February 1997, when the official unemployment rate was 9.8 per cent, there was an underlying unemployment rate of 14.4 per cent, including hidden unemployment (see table 2.2). This is a compiled figure, based on estimating the cyclical responses of labour-force participation rates by age and gender and then calculating potential labour forces for each age–gender group. From table 2.1, inclusion of the marginally attached raises the unemployment rate to 16.6 per cent in September 1997, with a further 300 000 persons who wanted to work but were not marginally attached. Hence the official statistics drastically underestimate the true level of unemployment, something which is acknowledged by the ABS.

In addition to the issue of unemployment, there is also the problem of under-employment. Visible under-employment is defined as individuals working less than their desired number of hours. The presence of under-employment also reduces the accuracy of the official unemployment figures as a measure of the total volume of unemployed labour resources. Under the award system, the number of hours to be worked by full-time employees and their timing were largely prescribed, but now, under a less regulated industrial relations system, employers have significant discretion over the number of hours worked and their timing (see,

Table 2.2 Actual unemployment rates and adjusted unemployment rates (%)

February	Males		Females		Persons	
	Official U rate	Adjusted U rate	Official U rate	Adjusted U rate	Official U rate	Adjusted U rate
1978	6.2	8.5	9.7	18.7	7.5	12.3
1983	9.8	12.2	11.8	21.1	10.6	15.7
1988	7.5	10.1	9.1	17.0	8.2	13.0
1993	12.7	15.8	11.4	20.8	12.2	18.0
1997	9.8	12.2	9.8	17.2	9.8	14.4

Note: Adjusted unemployment rate = Actual + hidden unemployment divided by potential labour force
Source: Mitchell and Watts (1997, p. 439)

for example, Watts and Rich 1991, pp. 173–4). This has coincided with the disproportionate growth of non-standard employment, which is defined as not permanent full-time (see next section). Full-time workers are defined as usually working more than 35 hours a week, whereas part-time workers are usually employed for less than 35 hours per week. EPAC (1996, p. 40) quotes the OECD (1995b) which showed that Australia had the third highest incidence of unemployment and under-employment (19 per cent), as measured by official unemployment, plus discouraged unemployment and involuntary part-time employment, as measured by official data.

Finally, invisible under-employment is defined as workers who are undertaking jobs that are not commensurate with their skills and experience. This form of under-employment is qualitatively different from the visible measures and estimates are not available from the ABS. The figures cited in this section show that the official unemployment figures significantly understate the extent of the underutilisation of labour resources. This means that the task of achieving full employment is even more demanding.

Trends in the unemployment rate and related statistics

Figure 2.1 depicts the long-run trend in the rate of unemployment in Australia since 1951. For nearly thirty years after World War II, the unemployment rate was exceedingly low, with rates of less than 1 per cent being common. After the recession and credit squeeze of 1974, the unemployment rate stayed between 5 per cent and 6 per cent until the severe recession of 1981. There is strong evidence of a ratchetting up of the unemployment rate over the subsequent business cycles.[4] This

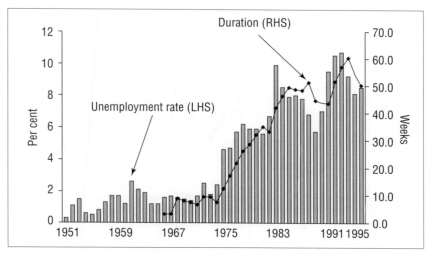

Figure 2.1 Annual unemployment rates and average duration of unemployment in Australia

Source: Foster (1996)

suggests, following the 'hysteresis' concept, that the unemployment rate is strongly path dependent, so that past rates of unemployment influence its future path. The Australian economy grew more rapidly than international competitors over the period 1983–89. The Labor government's overreliance on restrictive monetary policy to slow down the domestic economy initially proved ineffective, so that the unemployment rate fell to 5.4 per cent in November 1989. This was a similar rate to that prevailing prior to the 1981–83 recession. In the early 1990s economic growth slowed dramatically and unemployment grew rapidly, reaching an official maximum of 11.5 per cent in February 1994. In February 1996, prior to the election of the coalition government, the official unemployment rate had declined to 9.4 per cent and in August 1998 the rate was 7.9 per cent.

Figure 2.2 reveals that the Australian unemployment experience has been poor by international standards. Australia has been consistently under-performing relative to Japan and has deteriorated relative to the USA and the UK during the 1990s. Ironically, this is the period over which labour-market supply-side reform has been pursued most energetically. In the recovery since the early 1990s, Australia has experienced lower unemployment than the average of the European OECD countries.

The part-time share of total employment has increased significantly in the last decade, reaching 26 per cent in September 1998. The three-

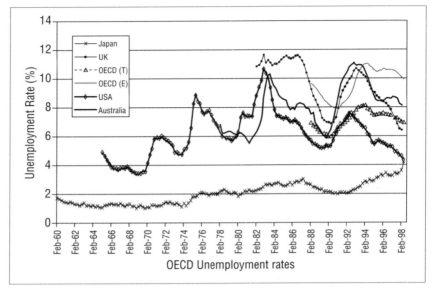

Figure 2.2 OECD standardised unemployment rates, 1960–98

Note: OECD (T) denotes all OECD countries and OECD (E) denotes
European OECD countries. The unemployment rates are centred three-month
moving averages.
Source: OECD Standardised Monthly Unemployment Rates

month moving average figures for part-time employment exhibit some
seasonal variation, but this is dominated by the upward trend (see figure
2.3). On the other hand, the corresponding full-time employment
figures exhibit cyclical sensitivity and slow long-term growth. Shift-share
analysis reveals that increased part-time shares of employment across
occupations are largely responsible for the growth of part-time employment, rather than structural shifts in employment between occupations
(Burgess, Strachan and Watts 1998). The share of male employment
that is part-time has increased from 7 per cent in August 1988 to 12.1 per
cent in August 1998. Many male workers have been placed on short-
time. Sheehan and Gregory (1998) note that if the 1973 ratio of full-time
employment to population of working age had been maintained
through to 1996, 2.8 million more full-time jobs would have been
created.

Langmore and Quiggin (1994, p. 23) document trends in unemployment and under-employment, where the latter is defined as part-time
workers desiring more hours and full-time workers who worked less than
35 hours in the survey week due to economic reasons. In February 1998,
25 per cent of all employees worked part-time and of these, 10.3 per cent

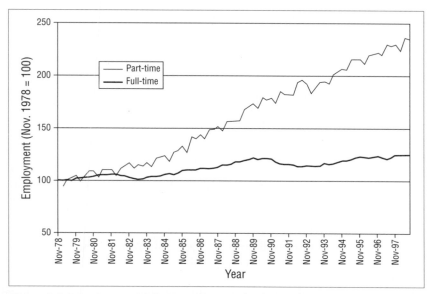

Figure 2.3 Part-time and full-time employment, November 1978 – August 1998
Source: ABS, AUSSTATS *The Labour Force* (Cat. no. 6203.0)

had sought full-time work in the four weeks up to the end of the reference week. A total of 26 per cent of all part-time workers wished to work longer hours, which is double the rate of 20 years ago. No indication is given of the number of extra hours desired by those who had not been seeking full-time employment (see table 2.3). No figures are published, however, on the percentage of workers who seek lower hours. Thus the constraint on the demand for output, along with structural changes towards casualisation, appear to have been forced upon the workforce (Campbell and Burgess 1997). Since mid-1978 the under-employment rate, expressed as a fraction of the labour force, has increased from about 2 per cent to nearly 6.5 per cent in February 1998.[5] The movement through time of the unemployment–vacancy ratio also confirms that there has been a persistent demand constraint imposed on the labour-market. This is reinforced by the steady, but cyclically sensitive, percentage of unemployed workers who desire full-time work.

Mitchell (1996) and Mitchell and Watts (1997) and Mitchell (chapter 3) show that the rise in unemployment is largely due to the failure of governments to maintain growth in GDP sufficient to match the growth in the labour force and in labour productivity. The policy priority of successive governments has been low inflation rather than low unemployment. This is discussed more fully in chapters of this book.

Table 2.3 Summary labour-market statistics

Labour-market measures as at February	1978	1983	1988	1993	1998
Unemployment–vacancy ratio	13.4	44.4	10.4	35.0	11.2
Part-time employment ratio (%)	14.8	17.0	19.0	22.6	25.0
Part-timers who want to work more hours (%)	13.5	19.9	19.9	30.3	26.0
Unemployed who want full-time work (%)	83.1	87.3	80.1	84.1	78.1

Source: ABS *The Labour Force* (Cat. no. 6203.0)

The average duration of unemployment has steadily increased from three weeks in 1966 (the first available data) to 50.5 weeks in February 1998 (see also figure 2.1). The changes in the average duration tend to trail movements in the actual unemployment rate. Increasing unemployment initially manifests itself both in a rise in short-term unemployment with young inexperienced workers unable to secure employment, as well as some of the short-term unemployed moving into longer term unemployment, so that the average duration of unemployment does not necessarily increase immediately. In principle, the burden of, say, a 10 per cent rate of unemployment could be shared equally by all members of the labour force, with each worker unemployed for about five weeks a year. In practice, unemployment is not distributed equally by duration. This is illustrated in figure 2.4 in which the level of unemployment by duration is expressed as a fraction of total unemployment for three years 1978, 1988 and 1998. In 1978 the distribution was bell shaped. Over the last two decades, unemployment of less than six months duration has formed a declining share of total unemployment which signifies a secular deterioration of the labour-market. The rise in the mean duration of unemployment has been accompanied by a more unequal distribution of duration, as measured by the standard deviation. Long-term unemployment (one year or longer) is now entrenched, with its share of total unemployment having increased from 12.3 per cent to 36.2 per cent over the 20-year period.

The probability of exit from unemployment declines with the duration of unemployment. Two possible factors are involved: under the heterogeneity hypothesis, the least qualified do not readily find jobs, due to the process of sorting, whereby the job applicants with stronger labour-market credentials are selected first; and under the state dependence hypothesis, a long duration of unemployment reduces a person's capacity to secure employment, which can result either from unemployed people's loss of confidence after repeated lack of success or from employers believing that the long-term unemployed must have some-

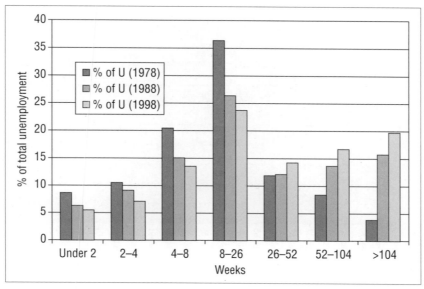

Figure 2.4 Unemployment duration as share of total unemployment, February 1978, 1988, 1998

Source: ABS, AUSSTATS *The Labour Force* (Cat. no. 6203.0)

thing wrong with them. Hence, a long spell of unemployment can have serious repercussions for employment prospects and earnings of individuals in future years.

The incidence of unemployment
Gender and marital status

In figure 2.5 quarterly male and female unemployment rates by marital status and in total are shown for the two decades to August 1998. The broad trends are similar for each cohort by gender. Unmarried males and females have systematically higher unemployment rates than their married counterparts, which is likely to reflect both the younger age of the unmarried group, their lower level of financial commitments and greater job instability.

In the early 1990s the male unemployment rate exceeded the female rate in total and by marital status, after being below it for over two decades. The shift in the distribution of employment from manufacturing to services has contributed to this change in relative rates of unemployment and to the substantial weakening of male full-time employment. Indeed, as Debelle and Swann (1998) point out, the rise in the aggregate unemployment rate over the last three decades is largely

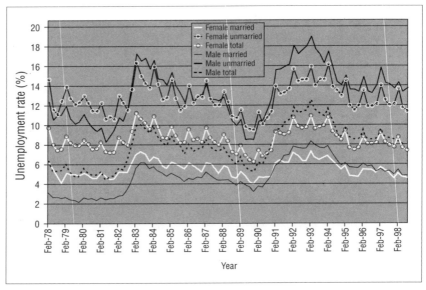

Figure 2.5 Unemployment rates by gender and marital status, February 1978 –
August 1998

Source: ABS, AUSSTATS *The Labour Force* (Cat. no. 6203.0)

accounted for by the rise in the unemployment rate for male full-time
workers, which in turn reflects slower employment growth in male-
dominated industries. Between 1966 and 1997 the aggregate unemployment rate increased from 1.8 per cent to 8.6 per cent. As Debelle and
Swann (1998, p. 5) indicate, fully 5 per cent of this increase can be
accounted for by the increase in male full-time unemployment. On the
other hand, the impact on male unemployment has also been significantly dampened by the long-term fall in male participation rates,
particularly for young and older men. In both post-recession recovery
periods in the 1980s and 1990s, male participation rates declined. The
male participation rate is less sensitive to the state of the business cycle,
however, which is revealed by the greater fluctuations in the male unemployment rates over the cycle. On the other hand, women predominate
in the cohorts of marginally attached and not marginally attached, but
wanting to work. Reflecting the sectoral composition of employment
growth in recent decades, female participation rates have increased in
both the 1980s and 1990s, reflecting better employment prospects for
women. However, as Borland (1997) points out, growth in the female
participation rate for the 1990s recovery was weaker than in the 1980s
recovery. If the growth of female participation in the 1990s had been as

strong as in the 1980s, aggregate unemployment would now be as much as 3 per cent higher.

Age

Unemployment rates by age group can only be understood by reference to their respective patterns of labour-market behaviour. Table 2.4 shows labour-force participation rates, the employment rate and the incidence of unemployment by age group for February 1998. The labour-market behaviour of teenagers (15–19-year-olds) is markedly different to that of the rest of the labour force and this is reflected in their pattern of employment and incidence of unemployment. Also, the youth labour-market is heterogeneous because it includes young people seeking full-time employment and others who try to combine full-time study and part-time employment (Wooden 1996; Flatau and Simpson, 1996).

About three-quarters of this cohort are in full-time education, of whom nearly 50 per cent are also in the labour-market. Nearly 95 per cent of these employed students worked part-time. This group had an unemployment rate of approximately 17 per cent, but unemployment is likely to be a temporary problem, given the relationship between educational attainment and labour-force status (see below).

Those teenagers not in full-time education had an unemployment rate of about 20 per cent with the majority seeking full-time employ-ment, despite having little or no post-school education and in some cases not having completed year 12 schooling. Unemployment is recurring and there is a greater likelihood of being trapped in involuntary part-time and/or casual employment, with little training, limited career prospects and low pay (NBEET 1992; Flatau and Simpson 1996).

Youth unemployment rates have never recovered from the large cuts in public-sector apprenticeship schemes in the mid-1970s. Freeland (1997, pp. 29–31) argues, however, that despite exhibiting some cyclical fluctuations over the 1980s and early 1990s, apprenticeships have pro-vided a stable component of youth full-time employment opportunities, which have declined significantly in aggregate over this period.

The overall problem of teenage unemployment has been somewhat attenuated, however, by the large increases in school retention rates, the changing demographic distribution of the labour force, and the decline in teenage labour-force participation (Biddle and Burgess 1998). Young job-seekers tend to be the victims of recession, because vacancies decline and many of these workers have either not yet secured employment or have had short job tenure and typically lack skills and credentials, in addition to experience. When the economy recovers, job vacancies

Table 2.4 Participation, employment and unemployment rates by age,
February 1998

| Age | LFP (%) | Unemployment Rates (%) | | | | | E/P (%) | Part-time employment share (%) |
		FT	PT	Total	Born in Australia	Born outside Australia		
15–19	59.1	28.7	16.6	21.8	21.1	28.9	46.2	60.5
20–24	83.4	14.9	11.1	14.1	13.5	17.5	71.6	23.2
25–34	80.7	8.0	5.9	7.6	7.3	9.0	74.6	18.5
35–44	81.4	7.5	6.2	7.2	6.8	8.3	75.5	22.6
45–54	77.4	6.6	3.7	6.0	5.2	7.4	72.8	22.0
55–59	57.3	8.9	5.7	8.1	5.8*	8.5*	52.7	23.9
60–64	31.7	7.4	5.2	6.6			29.6	34.0
Total	*63.3*	*9.5*	*8.0*	*8.9*			*57.7*	*25.2*

Note: Employment/Population is computed by multiplying Labour Force
Participation by (1 – UR)
*Unemployment rates for those over the age of 55
Source: ABS, AUSSTATS *The Labour Force* (Cat. no. 6203.0)

increase, but so does the labour-force participation rate of youth (Clark
and Summers 1982). The unemployment rate is a declining function of
age up until the age of 54 for full-time and total employment. The rates
of participation and employment of workers between 20 and 54 exceed
70 per cent, with this part of the lifecycle typically corresponding to the
period of the heaviest financial commitment. Above the age of 55, there is
the combination of reduced participation, or at the least resort to part-
time employment, and an increasing rate of full-time unemployment. The
latter is associated with the inability of some less skilled workers
in this age group to secure new employment, due to structural changes in
the economy. Langmore and Quiggin (1994, p. 18) note that in 1979,
unemployment was disproportionately concentrated among single young
people, with a third of the unemployed aged between 15 and 19, whereas
unemployment is now more evenly distributed across age groups.

Freeland (1997, p. 25) argues that the employment base, measured
by the ratio of total employment to total population, has not exhibited
any long-term decline since 1966. This result is not an artefact of the
rising share of part-time employment, because average weekly hours of
employment per head of population have not exhibited any long-term
decline over this period. Bell (see chapter 12) confirms that the employment intensity of growth increased over the period 1980–94, as
compared to 1960–73, in a number of countries, including Australia, the

USA, Japan and Germany. This reflects the shift in the distribution of employment away from manufacturing to labour-intensive services and shorter average weekly hours of work in these growing industries. Freeland (1997, p. 26) notes the significant declines in male employment to population ratios by age, in particular prime age males (25–54), that are largely driven by the decline in their full-time employment to population ratios. Gregory (1991a) argues that there is the prospect of long-term shortages of male full-time employment opportunities, given the structural shifts in the economy and the nature of male and female participation behaviour.[6] Despite the decline in participation rates of young males and males over the age of 54, the unemployment rate for males is likely to remain high, because prime age males will tend to exhibit high participation rates, reflecting their breadwinner status, even if there are limited job opportunities. On the other hand, women's employment to population ratios have increased for all age groups except 15–19-year-olds, with the full-time ratios rising in the prime age range and the part-time ratios increasing across all age groups (Freeland 1997, p. 27). The overall female participation rate has risen from 43.4 per cent in November 1978 to 54 per cent in August 1998. Thus, despite the increased job intensity of growth, the rising participation rates of women and the failure of male participation rates to decline in line with job opportunities have contributed to sustained high rates of unemployment. The employment base, measured as average weekly hours of work per head of population, has remained unchanged. Workers born overseas have higher rates of unemployment than their Australian-born counterparts, particularly those of non-English-speaking backgrounds. Wooden (1994) identifies four contributory factors to the differences in unemployment rates, namely proficiency in English; period of residence (with those who have resided longer in Australia more closely resembling the Australian born); refugee status (with refugees performing poorly on average); and whether qualifications were obtained in Australia or overseas, with the latter tending to be less useful.

Educational attainment

Table 2.5 below shows the relationship between educational attainment and unemployment and participation rates. Individuals who have invested in post-school education have higher rates of participation than those without post-school qualifications. In addition, there is an inverse relationship between educational attainment and the unemployment rate, and a positive relationship between educational attainment and occupational status. Also full-time shares of total employment tend to be higher for workers with post-school qualifications. As table 2.5 indicates,

Table 2.5 Labour-force status and educational attainment, May 1997

	Participation rate (%)	Full-time share (%)	Unemployment rate (%)
With post-school qualifications	85.3	80.8	5.4
Higher degree	93.0	87.8	3.1
Postgraduate diploma	88.4	80.1	3.8
Bachelor degree	87.9	80.3	3.6
Undergraduate diploma	80.2	71.2	4.6
Associate diploma	87.0	81.5	5.0
Skilled vocational qualification	88.4	90.9	6.1
Basic vocational	78.6	71.4	8.6
Without post-school qualifications	69.5	71.6	11.2
Completed highest level of school	75.3	68.9	8.9
Did not complete highest level of school	66.5	73.2	12.5
Still at school	36.5	73.1	19.6
Total	*74.1*	*74.4*	*8.7*

Source: ABS *Transition from Education to Work* (Cat. no. 6227.0), May 1997

the unemployment rate for poorly trained (low-skilled) workers is almost twice as high as for workers with higher educational attainments. Low rates of unemployment for highly educated workers do not imply that increases in educational attainment across the labour force will reduce the rate of unemployment (see Albo 1994), any more than the solution to the unemployment problem is for the whole working-age population to get married (see figure 2.5). The acquisition of credentials provides a signal to prospective employers. Hence, educational attainment should be seen as a means of relocating individuals within the labour queue, rather than necessarily reducing the length of the queue. Junankar and Kapuscinski (1992, p. 56) explore the relationship between unemployment and the skill composition of migration to Australia. They show that high levels of unemployment have an adverse impact on the immigration of highly skilled labour.

Industry and occupation

In table 2.6, unemployment rates by industry and occupation and gender are shown. Some workers cannot be identified with a particular industry or occupation, because of not having worked full-time within the last two years. In particular, many teenage workers have not had full-time employment during their short working lives. With the exception of transport and storage, property and business services, cultural and recreational services, and personal and other services, males have a

Table 2.6 Unemployment rates by gender and industry and occupation

	Unemployment rate		
	Males	Females	Persons
Industry division			
Agriculture, forestry and fishing	6.1	3.4	5.3
Mining	6.4	7.3	6.5
Manufacturing	6.5	6.1	6.4
Electricity, gas and water supply	6.4	2.7	5.8
Construction	6.6	1.3	5.9
Wholesale trade	4.2	4.2	4.2
Retail trade	5.4	4.7	5.0
Accommodation, cafés and restaurants	6.2	5.2	5.7
Transport and storage	4.6	4.8	4.6
Communication	3.6	2.0	3.1
Finance and insurance	2.7	2.4	2.5
Property and business services	3.6	3.8	3.7
Government administration and defence	5.3	3.6	4.5
Education	3.4	2.3	2.6
Health and community services	2.5	2.2	2.3
Cultural and recreational services	4.0	4.1	4.0
Personal and other services	2.7	3.7	3.2
Occupation group			
Managers and administrators	1.5	0.6	1.3
Professionals	2.3	1.9	2.1
Associate professionals	3.1	2.6	3.0
Tradespersons and related workers	5.1	3.4	5.0
Advanced clerical and service workers	1.5	2.1	2.0
Intermediate clerical sales and service workers	5.5	3.9	4.3
Intermediate production and transport workers	7.1	9.4	7.4
Elementary clerical, sales and service workers	4.4	4.7	4.6
Labourers and related workers	11.1	7.5	9.8

Source: ABS *The Labour Force* (Cat. no. 6203.0)

higher rate of full-time unemployment than females. This reflects the greater commitment of males to full-time employment, which is revealed by their higher rate of participation.

The male-dominated, declining industries such as mining, manufacturing, construction, and electricity, gas and water typically exhibit the highest unemployment rates. The problem of structural change cannot be understood solely by reference to industry unemployment rates, however, because the capacity of individuals to shift between industries will reflect the occupations which they are engaged in. To the extent that the declining industries have disproportionate numbers of relatively low-skill workers, their re-employment will be difficult.

The second half of the table confirms that the more highly skilled occupations exhibit lower unemployment rates. This reflects both the rising shares of total employment in these occupations and the greater employability of skilled workers.

Region

DEETYA produces quarterly figures for employment, unemployment and participation rates across 29 regions (DEETYA 1998). The overall unemployment rate was 7.9 per cent, with the rate ranging from 4.3 per cent in North Sydney and the Central Coast to 15.1 per cent in Wide Bay–Burnett (Qld). Unemployment rates tend to exhibit significant variation within states, with less than 10 per cent of their total variance being explained by between-state variations in unemployment in June 1996 (Borland 1997, p. 396).

Using census data, Gregory and Hunter (1995) examine the significant increase in income inequality across smaller geographical areas (collectors' districts) within urban centres over the period 1976–91. Gregory (1994) shows that in 1976 employment/population ratios lay between 0.65 and 0.69 across areas of different socioeconomic status. The collapse of employment opportunities over this period in neighbourhoods of low socioeconomic status, along with declining incomes, has been accompanied by increasing employment to population ratios and rising incomes in the high socioeconomic status neighbourhoods. Now the relationship between socioeconomic status and employment/population ratio is strongly positive with the latter lying between just under 0.50 and 0.70. These outcomes are giving rise to a higher incidence of poverty in the low SES neighbourhoods and more inequality, due to bad neighbourhood pathologies (see also Sheehan and Gregory 1998). Gregory (1994, p. 111) concludes that:

> In 1976, if you walked across Australia crossing from high socio-economic status areas to low socio-economic status you would notice that access to employment did not change very much. The income differences produced across areas were derived from different wages not from different levels of employment. If you walked across Australia along the same path in 1991 you would notice that the income differences among some areas have become exaggerated. The principal reason is the change in employment opportunities. The income of the poor areas is falling because of lack of jobs.

Latham (1998, p. 109) notes the close link between low socioeconomic status, educational disadvantage and unemployment. He points to the critical role of education and skills development in breaking entrenched cycles of disadvantage, but acknowledges the need for 'demand side interventions targeted at the creation of new forms of employment, in balance with the supply of labour force skills at a neighbourhood level'. The apparent correlation between educational disadvantage and the incidence of unemployment does not imply that an investment in the development of education and skills will reduce unemployment. It may merely reorder the queue of unemployed workers. Furthermore, the priority placed on education and skill development ignores the incentive for firms to train their workforces in the appropriate skills in a tight labour-market. In short, Latham should be placing a greater priority on demand expansion, albeit regionally focused, rather than potentially inefficient skill development which is not attached to new job opportunities.

Costs of unemployment

Some economists view unemployment as the outcome of voluntary choice made in response to generous unemployment benefits, excessive wage expectations, idleness or lack of motivation of the unemployed (e.g. Moore 1997). In this case the costs of unemployment would be rather small, unless externalities, such as crime and family breakdown, were significant. Despite the difficulty in measuring vacancies, the persistently high ratio of unemployment to vacancies would suggest that a significant proportion of unemployed workers are involuntarily unemployed (see table 2.3). Further, the tightening of the activity test by the Howard coalition government has not led to a dramatic reduction in the official rate of unemployment. The majority of commentators would agree that sustained unemployment imposes significant economic, personal and social costs that include (see Sen 1997; Junankar and Kapuscinski 1992):

- the loss of current output;
- an increase in the government fiscal burden;
- social exclusion and the loss of freedom;
- skill loss;
- psychological harm;
- ill-health and reduced life expectancy;
- the loss of motivation;
- the undermining of human relations and family life;
- racial and gender inequality; and
- the loss of social values and responsibility.

In this section of the chapter these costs will be documented in more detail and, where possible, quantified.

Output loss

Economists usually focus on the forgone output resulting from unemployment and under-employment. A number of conceptual and empirical issues arise. First, the choice of the target rate of unemployment is
important (see Junankar and Kapuscinski 1992, p. 23). The chosen rate
of unemployment must reflect estimates of frictional and any obdurate
structural unemployment. Second, there are two methods of calculation
which reflect the two sides of the national accounts, income and output.
In the income method, it is assumed that the wage reflects the additional
output produced by a newly employed worker. In the absence of knowledge about the distribution of output (and hence employment) across
sectors arising from the implied increase in employment, a somewhat
arbitrary wage has to be adopted. To obtain a measure of the value of
output forgone, this wage is multiplied by the number of additional
employees consistent with the target rate of unemployment being
achieved. The productivity of newly employed workers is likely to decline
at high rates of employment, so that the use of a constant wage is
inappropriate. The rate of decline of the wage will reflect the extent of
unused plant and machinery, as well as the skills and experience of the
unemployed workers.[7] On the other hand, the use of the wage to
measure the additional output produced by newly employed workers
ignores the additional output of co-operating factors of production
(Junankar and Kapuscinski 1992, p. 25).[8]

In the output approach, the forgone output due to unemployment is
proxied by a direct measure of output per worker, that is in turn multiplied by the number of additional employees. Again the assumption of a
constant loss of output per worker ignores skill differences across the
newly employed. Ignoring hidden unemployment, Mitchell and Watts
(1997, p. 438, table 3) calculate the daily loss of output associated with
the failure to achieve the target rate of 2 per cent unemployment for the
years 1972–96, based on economy-wide productivity per worker per
annum. Wooden (1997, p. 446) is critical of these computations, arguing
that they are based on the assumption that the unemployed are as productive on average as the employed, even in the public sector. A number
of comments can be made by way of rebuttal. First, with unemployed
workers and underutilised capacity, there will be some unemployed
workers whose productivity is in excess of the average productivity.
Second, using ABS calculations for those people who were marginally
attached to the labour force in September 1996, namely 880 000, the
adjusted rate of unemployment was 16.6 per cent. If it is assumed that
75 per cent of the hidden unemployed have returned to the labour force
when the (official) unemployment rate drops to 2 per cent, then an

extra 1.26 million jobs would be required. Approximately 78.6 per cent of unemployed workers were seeking full-time employment in September 1996, so using this figure, the number of full-time equivalent jobs required to reduce the unemployment rate to 2 per cent is given by 0.898 × 1.26m = 1.13m.[9] Nominal gross national product for the year ending June 1996 was $475 411m and average full-time equivalent employment over the year ending June 1996 was 7.28 million. Then annual productivity per full-time equivalent employee was about $65 000. Taking into account the claim that some of the unemployed are less productive, the modest figure of $30 000 per newly employed full-time equivalent employee is used to represent the additional output. Then the total loss of output, associated with the official unemployment rate being above 2 per cent, is $33.9 billion or 7.1 per cent of nominal GDP. Kenyon (1998) estimates a loss of output in the order of 4 per cent of GDP in 1996, based on a target rate of unemployment of 4.7 per cent and the assumption that the unemployed are as productive on average as the employed. He does not take account of hidden unemployment. More broadly, Kenyon (1998) estimates that Australia lost between 1.5 and 3 per cent of GDP per year for the past 20 years because it has not implemented policies which would have resulted in full employment. Junankar and Kapuscinski (1992) estimate the output loss due to unemployment during the recession of 1991–92 to be at least 5 per cent of GDP.

In its *1991–92 Annual Report*, the Industry Commission initially estimated that the annual cost associated with microeconomic inefficiency was $22b, but they now appear to be less committed to this figure (Mitchell and Watts 1997, pp. 437–8). In any case, the static cost of income (output) losses dwarfs the estimates of losses associated with microeconomic inefficiency, even if the estimated costs of microeconomic inefficiency are increased by 20 per cent, say, to account for the passage of time since the annual report. Langmore and Quiggin (1994, p. 28) estimate that, taking into account the hidden unemployed, the static costs of income loss lie in the range of $30–40b per year. Thus there is persuasive evidence that the macroeconomic costs of unemployment overwhelm the costs of microeconomic inefficiency. Finally, taking account of the cumulative costs of sustained recession, Langmore and Quiggin (1994, p. 28) note that if the more rapid growth of GDP per head over the period 1960–73 had been sustained, national income would have been nearly 50 per cent higher in the early 1990s. These calculations reflect the dynamic costs of unemployment, because they pick up the loss of future output arising from the reduced human and physical capital stock due to skill atrophy and the lower investment in physical capital stock (Junankar and Kapuscinski 1992, p. 24).

Costs to government

Junankar and Kapuscinski (1992, p. 47) argue that government should be treated as an economic agent in the quantification of costs of unemployment. They distinguish between the provision of services to the unemployed, which represent the expenditure of real economic resources, from outlays on transfer payments, such as unemployment benefits or reduced taxation receipts. They note, however, that the secondary effects arising from transfers will have an effect on the allocation of real economic resources, through the operation of multiplier effects.

On the revenue side, using the September 1996 employment figures, a fall in unemployment to 2 per cent requires an extra 1.13 million full-time equivalent jobs. If all these workers were receiving unemployment benefit of $160 per week and were placed in jobs paying, say, $400 per week, then the increase in tax revenue, assuming a tax rate of 25 per cent, would be $60 per employee per week or $3120 per annum. Then a conservative estimate of the total increase in taxes would be approximately $3.5b. Expenditure on labour-market programs, in the form of assistance to job-seekers and industry, over the year 1995/96, the final year of the Labor government, was $2.1b.

Outlays on unemployment benefits were $6.6b over the year 1995/96. Langmore and Quiggin (1994, p. 29) argue that much of the increase in sickness benefits and disability support pensions can be attributed to unemployment. Over the year 1995/96 outlays on sickness benefits were $354 m and invalid and permanent disablement benefits were $5b (ABS 1997c). Langmore and Quiggin (1994) estimate that about half of these recipients are people who could undertake employment if jobs were available. Taken together, this means that the total unemployment-related transfers were $9.2b in 1995/96. Finally, it should be noted that the social costs of unemployment are felt in most areas of government, including police, community welfare, health and education services. Hence, on these figures, achieving full employment, defined as 2 per cent unemployment, would net the government $14.8b, through significant savings in employment assistance and unemployment and related benefits, and through increased tax revenue. This figure is a similar order of magnitude to the estimates of Langmore and Quiggin (1994, p. 29) of savings on direct outlays of about $12b in 1992/93. Since the election of the coalition government in 1996, there has been a radical restructuring of the system of employment assistance. The Jobs Network took over many of the functions of the Commonwealth Employment Service in May 1998. Most labour-market programs have been scrapped. Projected outlays on labour-market programs and employment services have declined, but the Jobs Network was severely underfunded and the coalition government has already taken some remedial action.

Individual and social costs

The replacement ratio measures the extent to which the system of unemployment benefits compensates for the loss of work income. It is computed as the ratio of the level of net benefits to net income from work. Benefits are computed net of tax and any costs associated with job search, whereas income from work is adjusted for the costs of commuting, work uniform and taxation. Junankar and Kapuscinski (1992, p. 51) note that the main problem with the replacement ratio is that it is non-unique, because benefits depend on factors including marital status and number of dependants. An assumption must be made about the level of work income and the associated level of taxation. Junankar and Kapuscinski (1992, p. 55) find that in the June quarter 1992 for single adults, the replacement ratio for females lay between 27.1 per cent, based on full-time female average adult earnings, and 35.5 per cent for average total adult female earnings. The corresponding figures for males were lower, 22.6 per cent and 23.6 per cent, respectively, which reflect their higher average wages. The ratio can exceed 50 per cent for families with low earnings and, say, four children. A single period computation of the replacement ratio, while conveying the extent of the immediate loss of income from unemployment, often fails to indicate the long-term potential loss of income from a sustained spell of unemployment. For example, an individual's long-term capacity to secure employment (Junankar and Kapuscinski 1991) and income (Bradbury, Ross and Doyle 1990) is often reduced by a period of unemployment and/or if benefits are only available for a limited period. Finally, the authors note that any move to reduce unemployment benefits will have the greatest impact on those unemployed persons least able to bear the costs, namely the long-term unemployed.

The non-pecuniary costs to individuals of unemployment include the loss of social and professional contacts in the workplace that can undermine self-esteem, along with psychological problems, including stress and loss of self-worth, and medical problems which can be linked to lifestyles, involving poor diet and/or excessive consumption of alcohol (Junankar and Kapuscinski 1992). Burgess and Mitchell (1998) note that the human rights of the unemployed are undermined by their loss of freedom. Without access to labour income, they are forced to rely on social and/or family transfers, non-labour income or savings. Many unemployed people do not have access to these sources of support, and thus their ability to participate in the market economy is limited. Choices over lifestyles, personal development and access to 'basic' goods and services are restricted.

Unemployment has been linked to truancy and non-completion of schooling, family break-up, substance abuse, alienation, discrimination, illness and premature death, and poverty (Siegel 1994, p. 8). Junankar and Kapuscinski (1992, p. 57) show that higher unemployment tends to reduce the incidence of marriage and raise the rate of divorce. Burgess and Mitchell (1998) note that social and economic exclusion encourages anti-social behaviour and fosters the growth in illegal activity as a means of generating income. Borland and Kennedy (1998) also find evidence suggesting a positive link between crime rates and unemployment. Unemployment adversely affects the health and levels of life satisfaction of unemployed persons. Dixon (1992) finds a four-fold increase in unemployed offenders as compared with the total number of offenders in South Australia during the 1970s. Withers' (1984) study also shows a strong association of unemployment with poverty, and crime. Thus, prolonged high unemployment poses a serious threat to the social and economic fabric of our society.

As mentioned above, unemployment is unevenly distributed across regions and within cities, with the unemployed tending to congregate in areas of cheap housing. Further, the incidence of youth unemployment appears to be related to the labour-market status of their parents. Finally, increasing fiscal conservatism by governments combined with a prevailing attitude that unemployment benefits are a privilege rather than a right has led to the financial pressures on the unemployed intensifying and to gaps in the welfare system opening up (Siegel 1994, p. 8). In Australia, there has been the tightening of eligibility conditions for benefits, the abolition of the youth unemployment benefit and the introduction of work for the dole programs (Biddle and Burgess 1998; Burgess, Mitchell, O'Brien and Watts 1998). Quoting from the OECD (1997a), Lombard (1998, p. 69) notes that the income replacement ratio, defined as the unemployment benefit for a single earner household as a fraction of average production worker's earnings, was 34 per cent in Australia in 1994, compared to the OECD average of 55 per cent and 74 per cent in the Netherlands. The measurable pecuniary costs of unemployment are massive and, as calculated above, a conservative estimate of government outlays on assistance and transfers to the unemployed plus forgone output, would be in excess of $40b per annum. In addition, there are significant costs of law enforcement, community services, health and education, along with costs to individuals arising from their marginalisation due to their inability to secure employment and a living wage. These costs are not confined to the unemployed individual, but also impact on her/his family and other relationships within the local community and society as a whole. It is ironic that successive governments have been quick to provide assistance in the event of significant natural disasters, such as floods and bushfires, but appear to consider that an economic and social disaster of a much greater magnitude merely requires further deregulation of the market system and increased training for the unemployed.

Unemployment and inequality

The direct link between unemployment and wage inequality lies in the absence of wage income for the unemployed, but official statistics only record the earnings of those who are employed. Watts (1997) notes that there are two opposing theories of the relationship between unemployment and wage inequality of employees. Under Okun's upgrading hypothesis (1973), employment expansion over the upturn gives rise to a compression of the wage distribution, via increases in earnings for the less well paid, whereas skilled employees can be attracted into the better paid jobs without a higher wage, possibly via a relaxation of hiring standards (see also Cornwall 1983, p. 83). Thus wage rates vary in their sensitivity to changes in excess demand across segments of the labour-market.[10] A high-pressure economy is viewed as efficient with growing wages promoting productivity enhancing investment. In a cross-country study, Galbraith (1996) finds that for most countries, including Australia for the period 1971–92, the time series relationship between unemployment and wage inequality is usually positive and often strongly so.

On the other hand, the OECD *Jobs Study* (1994a) points to the alleged benefits of the greater wage flexibility which characterises the American model, in the form of increased employment opportunities for low-skilled workers, so that the efficient allocation of labour is not being inhibited by rigidities in relative wages. Labour-market liberalisation is alleged to lead to stronger growth and higher average levels of employment which imply larger income gains for the economy, thereby offsetting the social implications of wider wage differentials and hence the growth of low-wage jobs. Australian studies have shown that the distribution of earnings has become more polarised since the mid-1970s (King, Rimmer and Rimmer 1992; Gregory 1993). Mitchell and Watts (1997) find that over the two phases of the business cycle (1986–96) the trend towards more polarised full-time wage distributions for adults has continued, despite the cyclical forces outlined by Okun. This dispersion has taken the form of the disappearing middle, which is defined as an increase in the incidence of low- and high-wage employment (Morris, Bernhardt and Handcock 1994, p. 207). Further, the main factor driving the increase in polarisation appears to be differential rates of wages growth across occupations (Watts 1997), in contrast to Okun's arguments about the narrowing of skill differentials in the upturn. Despite the failure of private-sector management to achieve significant productivity growth, upper income earners, who operated outside the Accord, earned substantial increases in the late 1980s and early 1990s (Langmore and Quiggin 1994, p. 34). The high rate of unemployment has contributed to downward pressure on wage rates of the less skilled, whereas the skilled are generally protected through internal labour-markets and are less easy to replace (McGuire 1994, pp. 43–4). Borland and Kennedy (1998) find that unemployed persons are disproportionately concentrated in the bottom two deciles of the income distribution. This has the effect of increasing the level of poverty.

Recent changes in the underlying institutional arrangements have also played a role in widening inequality. An additional contributory factor to this polarisation could be the widening distribution of hours of paid work, through a dramatic increase in the number of persons working over 60 hours per week from about 3 per cent in the 1970s to 7 per cent in 1995, including 10 per cent of male employment (Dawkins 1996). There has not been a corresponding increase in paid overtime and the increase in multiple job-holding only explains a small fraction of this increase (Wooden, Sloan, Kennedy, Dawkins, and Simpson 1994).[11] The growth in part-time employment contributes to the rise in dispersion of all wages. The recent strong growth of employment in the USA and low official unemployment rate appear to support the claim that the prerequisite for sustained employment growth and falling unemployment is a deregulated system of wage determination with a relatively low level of minimum wages. Yet Australia was relatively more successful in generating low-wage full-time jobs for both males and females and in aggregate than the USA over the decade since wage indexation was abandoned (1986–96), in the context of the net increase in full-time employment for each country and their corresponding 1986 wage distributions (Mitchell and Watts 1997; see Gregory 1996 for similar computations for the period 1976–91, also McGuire 1994).

Thus, while the Australian full-time wage distribution is more compressed than the corresponding US distribution, it has exhibited more relative flexibility with respect to low-paid employment over the last decade. Gregory (1996) concludes that the US population has not become better off relative to the Australian, despite faster employment growth. Mishell and Schmitt (1995) argue that a relative wage reduction of low-skill workers in the USA implies a high explicit cost per job associated with the increased employment. For purposes of welfare, the relevant unit is not the individual but the income unit, which consists of a group of related people who form a single income-earning and spend-ing unit (Dawkins 1996, p. 279). A number of income units may inhabit a single household. An important influence on living standards is the distribution of jobs across families. In February 1998 about 25.1 per cent of families had no family member employed, an increase from 22.7 per cent in February 1988. Over the decade, the percentage of these families with one or more dependants rose from 30.7 to 32.8. Of the families with one or more dependants, the percentage with no parent working rose from 13.1 to 16.2. On the other hand over the decade, the percentage of this group with both parents employed rose from 42.1 per cent to 44 per cent. Thus there is evidence of a polarisation in the distribution of employment opportunities across families, with an increased percentage of families with dependants having either no parent or two parents working (see also Dawkins 1996, p. 280). The decline in the employment to population ratios by age for males has contributed to this polarisation, since the spouses of unemployed men are unlikely to secure employ-ment (Freeland 1997, p. 27). There is now alarming evidence emerging that unemployment is being inherited across generations, with youth unemployment being much higher in households where no person is employed (OECD 1996).

Concluding comments

Australia's unemployment record over the last two decades or so has been poor by OECD standards (see figure 2.2). The increase in jobless-ness has been accompanied by the collapse of full-time employment growth and a rise in the extent of poverty. Urban ghettos that used to be identified with cities in the United States are becoming entrenched in Australia. Since the election of the Labor government in 1983, economic policy has been largely oriented towards the achievement of deregulated markets, notwithstanding the Accord and the Labor government's brief experiments under the *Working Nation* policy. This shift towards free-market policies accelerated under the coalition government with further labour-market, product market and industrial relations deregulation. Policy-makers appear to believe that the high rate of unemployment is structural in origin, so that the unemployed can be blamed for their inadequate skills and lack of employment experience. In this chapter the measurable pecuniary costs of unemployment in the form of government outlays on assistance and transfers to the unemployed, plus forgone output, have been estimated to be in excess of $40b per annum. These calculations exclude the significant costs of law enforcement, community services, health and education, along with the personal costs to individuals and their families arising from their marginalisation due to limited access to income. Governments in many countries have attempted to shift the responsibility for the massive economic and social problem of unemployment to the victims. A more realistic interpretation of the Australian data is that the high level of unemployment is the outcome of demand-deficiency. These theoretical and policy issues will be addressed in later chapters of the book.

CHAPTER 3

The Causes of Unemployment

William F. Mitchell

The crucial issue of macroeconomic theory today is the
same as it was 60 years ago when John Maynard Keynes
revolted against what he called the 'classical' orthodoxy of
his day.

James Tobin (1996)

With persistently high unemployment rates in the OECD economies
since the 1970s, there are still economists who cling on to the 'Treasury'
view of the 1930s and blame supply-side issues such as excessive real wage
levels. Derivatives of this view source the persistently high unemploment
in institutional arrangements in the labour-market (wage-setting mechanisms and trade unions) and government welfare policies (encouraging people to engage in inefficient search) (see for example, Layard,
Nickell and Jackman 1991). There is, however, an alternative Keynesian
view that focuses on the demand side of the economy, explaining
unemployment as stemming mainly from sluggish growth, inadequate
aggregate demand and too few jobs. There are also economists who
point to the pace and nature of structural change, technological change
or demographic change as the cause of the unemployment malaise.
These competing explanations are considered in this chapter.

In the quote above, Tobin is referring to the dispute between orthodox economists and those who follow the lead given by Marx and Keynes
in linking effective demand to the causes of mass unemployment. In this
chapter, it is argued that the principal reason that OECD countries have
experienced more than two decades of high unemployment lies in an
unwillingness of policy-makers to use fiscal and monetary policy in an
appropriate expansionary manner. The rapid inflation of the mid-1970s
left an indelible impression on policy-makers who became captive of the
emergent 'new labour economics' and its macroeconomic counterpart,
monetarism. The goal of low inflation replaced other policy targets,
including low unemployment. The result has been that GDP growth in
OECD countries has generally been below that required to absorb the
labour-force growth and the growth in labour productivity.

For the unemployment rate to remain constant, real GDP growth must be equal to the sum of labour-force and labour productivity growth, other things equal. In the midst of ongoing debates about labour-market deregulation, minimum wages and taxation reform, the most salient, empirically robust fact that has pervaded the last two decades is that the actual GDP growth rate has rarely been above this required rate (see chapter 6 this volume; Mitchell 1996; Mitchell and Watts 1997). The two decades of slow growth and high unemployment with rising numbers of long-term unemployed is a pattern common across OECD economies. The real task is to explain this deficiency in output growth.

The chapter is organised as follows. We begin with a critique of orthodox supply-side explanations of unemployment. The critical role of growth and aggregate demand as the main drivers of unemployment is then explored. This is followed by a discussion of technological change as allegedly driving 'jobless growth'. The impact of 'deindustrialisation' is then examined, and, in Australia's case, is found, in tandem with weak aggregate demand, to be a significant contributor to the rise in unemployment. Compositional shifts in economic output and the growing importance of services employment are also examined and this is followed by a look at the impact of age and gender compositional shifts on unemployment.

Problems with orthodox neoclassical explanations

Orthodox economists have concentrated mainly on the supply side of the labour-market in explaining unemployment, hypothesising that 'full employment' now occurs at much higher unemployment rates than in the past, mainly due to structural problems in labour-markets. This is expressed in technical language as a rise in the non-accelerating inflation rate of unemployment (NAIRU).

The NAIRU is related to the concept of the natural rate of unemployment (NRU). Originally, Milton Friedman (1969) coined the term NRU in an attempt to explain the links between wage or price inflation and the rate of unemployment. The fundamental idea in the NRU and NAIRU framework is that supply-side rigidities and various structural problems in labour-markets produce the level of unemployment that is consistent with stable inflation. Attempts to reduce unemployment below the NAIRU level result in accelerating inflation. Hence, the level of unemployment at which inflation is constant is the equilibrium rate of unemployment, or NAIRU. In this view, unemployment is a crucial factor, which acts to control inflation. Also, unemployment is redefined as essentially a voluntary affair: workers choose to be unemployed because they refuse to accept low enough wages or because they refuse

to move to seek jobs elsewhere, etc. Neoclassical economists agree that
the level of the NAIRU has risen in recent decades (essentially tracking
the unemployment rate).[1]

Several reasons have been suggested in the literature for the rise in the
NAIRU. The most important are:

- Excessive unemployment and other social security benefits distort the
  choice between labour and leisure – this might be called the search
  argument.
- Excessive minimum wage rates and hiring and firing cost promoted by
  trade unions and government.
- Mismatch between the skills of the unemployed workers and the jobs
  on offer.
- Excessive real wage levels.

The basis of all these explanations is a view that the labour-market is
essentially a price-auction market like any microeconomic market and
that an understanding of unemployment must focus on market rigidities
or optimising individual behaviour. Thurow (1983, p. 185) says:

> Usually some market imperfection is hypothesised and as we shall see, each is
> posited ad hoc and after the fact. At some point it becomes necessary to
> examine the weight of the evidence to see the extent to which the labour
> market is or is not working in accordance with the theories of the equilibrium
> price-auction model.

Whenever market imperfections exist, there is a profit opportunity (for
example, a price above equilibrium allows someone to profitably under-
cut). The pursuit of these margins eliminates the imperfection. A striking contrast exists between this notion, which would suggest short-term
market imperfections at most, and the persistence of mass unemployment. The argument is that the only way an imperfection can continue
despite market forces is if it is backed by the weight of government or a
trade union. The problem is that attempts to control inflation by tight
fiscal and monetary policies have pushed unemployment to persistently
high levels. The idea that eventually the economy would stabilise at a
NAIRU, which has driven orthodox policy, has been very damaging in
terms of idle resources. There are a number of unanswered questions in
the NAIRU theory. For example, what is the natural rate of unemployment? Why does it require very high and persistent unemployment for
inflation to be brought down? We will see that the labour-market is
'certainly not the simple full-employment world predicted by a simple
interpretation of the price-auction model' (Thurow 1983, p. 186).

Some orthodox economists attempt to define the problem away by arguing that 'what appears to be persistent and lengthy periods of unemployment is really nothing of the kind' (Thurow 1983, p. 190). Accordingly, an unemployed person considers the attainable real wage to be below their reservation wage (the wage that reflects the margin of indifference between work and non-work). They either prefer to take leisure (which increases the reservation wage) or they have a poorly estimated reservation wage relative to their own abilities. Welfare benefits and minimum wage laws can also inflate the reservation wage. We will examine these arguments in turn and explore their problems.

The unemployment rate in Australia (and elsewhere) rose sharply in the early to mid-1970s. In Australia, it rose from 2 per cent in September 1971 to 5.3 per cent by December 1975. Why did the reservation wage rise over that short time? Even if it had risen in this period, why didn't unemployed workers quickly review their reservation rates relative to market information? The fact that they remained unemployed might therefore be explained by a taste change towards leisure. What motivated that change? What motivated more than 30 per cent of the labour force to make radical changes in their preferences towards leisure in the 1930s? It is difficult to believe that these factors explain the rise and persistence of unemployment.

We also observe low-paid workers cycling in and out of the unemployed pool. When they do work, they re-enter the labour-market on more or less the same conditions as they had when they left. Why would they do this? Why does their reservation wage rise and fall over these spells of unemployment and work?

Several sources of rigidity or imperfection are hypothesised by economists, which inflate the individual's reservation wages. Layard, Nickell and Jackman (1991), who represent the view that the cause of unemployment can be traced to institutional rigidities in the labour-market, hint that the USA economy has been spared the worst of the rise in unemployment because they have experienced a fall in welfare benefits. The argument is simply that the provision of welfare benefits subsidises unemployment and increases the job-search duration.

The OECD *Employment Outlook* (July 1996, p. 29, chart 2.2) shows movements in replacement ratios in OECD countries from 1961 to 1995. The replacement ratio is mainly a measure of the difference between the average wage and unemployment benefits and is taken as a guide to the level of generosity of the welfare system and the implied work 'disincentives' built into the system. Interestingly, there has been no systematic relationship between the direction of the benefits and rise or fall in the employment/population ratio (the most stable measure of labour-market activity). For example, Australia has seen a rise in both, whereas

Belgium has seen a fall in both. It is also possible that the causation is exactly the opposite of that proposed by the new labour economics. With low economic growth and activity moderating money wages growth, the replacement ratio will rise if in the face of persistently high unemployment rates, the governments bow to the pressure for increased benefit rates. Most striking is the fact that in the Scandinavian countries where unemployment has not been as bad as in Australia, the replacement ratios are more than twice that found in Australia. The OECD (1997a) shows the replacement ratio for Sweden is 80 per cent (the ratio of unemployment benefits to average earnings), for Denmark 86 per cent, Netherlands 70 per cent, OECD average 55 per cent and Australia 34 per cent. The same countries also have much more regulation when it comes to employment protection, employer social service contributions, compulsory superannuation, and hiring and firing rules than in Australia. Importantly, one has to ask why have their unemployment rates generally been low relative to Australia.

Layard, Nickell and Jackman (1991, p. 4) also argue that the level of unemployment has risen sharply relative to the level of vacancies and suggest this is due to a failure of the unemployed to seek work as effectively as before compounded by the search distortion introduced by the welfare system. Mitchell (1996) concluded that for most OECD countries the unemployment–vacancy ratios have risen since 1973 with interspersed cycles. But if search behaviour was to explain these increases, we might expect an upward trend in unfilled vacancies, which is absent in the data. In September 1997 there were 12 unemployed for every vacancy. Had the unemployed taken all the unfilled jobs there would still have been 730 000 people without work. It is more plausible that the problem has been demand-side oriented and the rising ratios of unemployed to unfilled vacancies signal this.

Search theory explanations are generally difficult to sustain as a comprehensive explanation of unemployment. Unemployment is seen in this theory as a time allocation used by persons to seek better paying employment. Searching becomes an iterative process of sampling the labour-market against the reservation wage and ultimately accepting employment with improved circumstances or revising the reservation wage to match the reality found. This representation, however, is at odds with the facts. Thurow (1983, p. 194) argues persuasively that if 'unemployment is a matter of workers testing the labour market, why should 25 per cent of them be doing it in 1933, while only 3 per cent in 1953, and 1 per cent in 1943?' As noted above, many unskilled persons have repetitive spells of unemployment and work without any career development. Further, in career labour-markets job changes usually are not accompanied by an intervening spell of unemployment. In other words, search is done on the job in the employer's time (Burdett 1978; Black 1980; Mattila 1969). The most damaging empirical fact for search explanations is the fact that quit behaviour is strongly counter-cyclical – falling when unemployment is rising.

Tobin (1972) was an early critic of the search–voluntary unemployment story. Tobin (1972, p. 6) noted that 'a considerable amount of search activity by unemployed workers appears to be an unproductive consequence of dissatisfaction and frustration rather than a rational quest for improvement'. Tobin indicates that evidence from Reynolds (1951), Hall (1970), and Doeringer and Piore (1971) conflicts with the price-auction explanation. He confines the usefulness of search theory to explaining frictional unemployment, a very small percentage of total unemployment.

Overall, there has been very little evidence presented to substantiate these structural labour-market effects in any economy in the world. They are largely predictions, emerging from the orthodox competitive model, which lack empirical substance. As Davidson (1998, p. 818) argues:

> By adopting the same axiomatic foundation as the old classical system, natural unemployment rate analysis suffers the same shortcoming, namely that the 'characteristics' of these models happen 'not to be those of the economic society in which we actually live, with the result that . . . [such a theory] is misleading and disastrous if we attempt to apply it to the facts of experience' (Keynes 1936a: 3).

Piore (1979, p. 10), also an antagonist to the orthodox position, argues that:

> Presumably, there is an irreducible residual level of unemployment composed of people who don't want to work, who are moving between jobs, or who are unqualified. If there is in fact some such residual level of unemployment, it is not one we have encountered in the United States. *Never in the post war period has the government been unsuccessful when it has made a sustained effort to reduce unemployment.* (emphasis in original)

Summers (1988, p. 19) also argues that:

> In Britain today, about 60 per cent of all unemployment is due to persons in the midst of spells lasting two years or more. Can anyone seriously maintain that this outcome is the result of intertemporal substitution, misperceptions, or inefficient search? For that matter, what factor or factors could have doubled the NAIRU over the last seven years?

The excessive real wage level argument has long been used to explain unemployment and is derived directly from a price-auction labour-market with a production sector subject to diminishing marginal productivity. In the absence of legal constraints or powerful trade unions, the theory suggests that any individual 'can get a job by knocking on the door of some employer and offering to work for less than those already employed' (Thurow 1983, p. 187). In the real economy, however, no employer would accept this sort of offer for several reasons.

Nominal wage rigidity has actually been associated with an efficient labour-market where skills are heterogeneous and are acquired on the job. Okun (1981) presented the 'invisible handshake' hypothesis, which formed the basis of implicit contract theory. The point is simple – employers and employees agree not to cut wages when there is an overall excess supply of labour in return for productivity gains. Both parties gain from the contract and dynamic efficiency is enhanced as skills are passed on down the workforce.[2] This body of literature has expanded into a comprehensive model of the labour-market, which is at odds with the major conclusions of the price-auction approach (Okun 1981).

The orthodox arguments usually invoke two sources of rigidity which lead to excessive real wages. First, legally enforced minimum wages, and, second, trade union power. A striking fact is that in economies like the United States there were no minimum wages in 1930 yet unemployment skyrocketed. There is also considerable evidence that employers willingly pay over the legal minimum wage rates to increase quality of labour input (Junankar et al. 1998). In Australia, this means that it is typical for an employer to pay over-award wages. To then claim that it is the regulated award system that is a culprit is problematic. Junankar et al. (1998) show that the over-award phenomenon is salient in youth employment and conclude that the claim that youth wages should be cut to improve their employment prospects is erroneous.

Trade unions may be able to enforce higher wages than would otherwise occur by reducing the supply competition. However, in all the major countries in the last 25 years trade union coverage has fallen considerably. In Australia, trade union coverage is now around one-half of what it was in 1970. In that time, unemployment has risen and shown a persistence to remain at high levels.[3]

There are some major differences between the way the actual labour-market operates and the competitive market on which the neoclassical explanation is based. Thurow (1983, p. 212) provides a good summary.

1. Labor supplies are endogenously acquired and the labour-market is not an auction market based on price, but one that is structured to maximise the transfer of knowledge (training) over time. Static efficiency is relatively less important than dynamic efficiency.

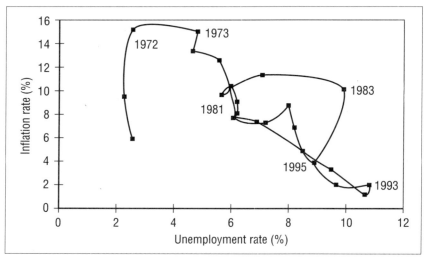

Figure 3.1 Unemployment rate and inflation, Australia, 1970–95
Source: ABS, AUSSTATS

2. The productivity of each individual worker is unknown and variable.
   Motivation is important, since individual workers control their own
   productivity and can offer a wide range of productivities.
3. Happiness (utility) is heavily conditioned by interdependent preferences. If violated, these preferences can lead to reductions in productivity – team and individual.
4. Total output is heavily determined by team as opposed to individual
   productivities. But with team productivity an indeterminacy is created
   in individual wages, since there is a team bonus to be allocated.

An empirical examination of the wages issues also poses problems for
the neoclassical approach. Consider figure 3.1, which shows the Phillips
Curve (the relationship between price inflation and unemployment) for
Australia from 1970–95. It helps to shed light on the argument that
excessive wages have increased unemployment.

An examination of similar charts for the OECD economies reveals
four notable things (Mitchell 1996). First, the instability in the trade-off
in the mid-1970s after the first OPEC shock is apparent in every country
except perhaps the Scandinavian economies of Finland, Norway and
Sweden. At first inflation rose sharply between 1972 and 1974 and then
unemployment followed after 1974. Second, there is a second wave of
instability in the early to mid-1980s in almost every country except
Finland, Italy, Germany, Japan, Norway, and Sweden. Third, in recent

years, the Scandinavian countries seem to have had very sharp declines in their inflation rates at significant cost in terms of unemployment. Fourth, the annual changes in inflation when unemployment is rising are significantly larger than changes when unemployment is falling.

Mitchell (1996) compared figure 3.1 with another chart substituting wage inflation for price inflation. The feature, which emerges from the comparison, is that the instability in the mid-1970s implicated both wage and price inflation. However, although there were some large wage rises in the early 1980s, the recession of 1983, combined with the re-introduction of wage-setting guidelines, killed the wage inflation quickly, while price inflation persisted for two more years.

Are there any differences between the two periods of instability? Tables 3.1 and 3.2 provide some additional but incomplete information. Table 3.1 shows the growth in real unit labour costs (RULC) in selected countries for various periods.[4] The instability of the Phillips Curve in the 1970s was associated with rising RULC in every country (not shown), which reflected sharp rises in money wages relative to inflation, then sharp decreases in economic activity and labour productivity. There was a large redistribution of real national income towards wages in this period.

It is interesting to note that in this period, Australia experienced rising RULC and rising unemployment, whereas countries like Sweden and Norway shared the redistribution to the wage share but did not experience any substantial rise in unemployment. For the countries shown, except Sweden, RULC fell during the period of instability in the 1980s. There was a large redistribution of real national income over this period towards profits. Over the entire post-oil shock period, RULC have on average been falling in most countries.

Table 3.2 shows the growth in real hourly earnings for various periods. Every country experienced rapid rises in real hourly earnings in the period after the first OPEC shock. However, the experience in the early 1980s is mixed. Some countries had strong real earnings growth but different unemployment and inflation experiences (for example, Japan and the United Kingdom), while many countries had steady real earnings. Australia and Belgium (in addition to the OECD bloc as a whole) saw real earnings growth decline but still unemployment rose and price inflation persisted.

It seems, then, that in the 1970s, some case could be made for a wages-driven inflation, which led to rises in unemployment as governments finally stopped accommodating the wage–price spiral. However, in the 1980s, no such argument is possible. The crucial point is that high unemployment and persistent inflation do not appear to be wages-driven.

In summary, the orthodox account of unemployment has major conceptual and empirical difficulties. At best, it can help to explain

Table 3.1 Average annual growth rates (%) in real unit labour costs for selected OECD economies

	Canada	USA	Australia	Japan	Germany	Norway	Sweden	UK
1970–95	−1.56	−2.69	−0.20	−0.76	−0.55	−0.50	1.82	−1.08
1970–78	−1.21	−1.72	0.47	−0.58	0.35	3.07	4.70	−0.74
1978–95	−1.73	−3.14	−0.51	−0.85	−1.00	−2.24	0.50	−1.24
1984–95	−1.86	−2.98	−0.36	0.00	−0.73	−2.08	0.97	−1.43

Source: OECD *Main Economic Indicators*, various issues

frictional unemployment. It has a major problem accounting for the business cycle. Even the relatively recent real business cycle theories (not examined here) strain credibility by explaining the business cycle in terms of random supply shocks or temporary misinformation.

The debate over unemployment depends in part on whether we can conceive of an aggregate labour-market in the same way we might out-line a small market for bananas where demand and supply combine to determine the prevailing price and the quantities that are traded. Keynes (1936) negated the conception of an aggregate labour-market on the basis that an aggregate labour supply curve specified in real wage terms was untenable. Galbraith concludes (1997, p. 95) that:

> If there is no aggregative labour market in any sense meaningful to economics, then theories based on shifts in wages clearing labour markets will fail to hold. From a proper Keynesian perspective, the correct response to the neo-Walrasian formulation of the natural rate hypothesis is simply, 'Sorry, but the "labour market" is a misconception; it doesn't exist'. Aggregate demand for output, and not supply and demand for labour, determine employment. By these lights, the aggregative labour market, lacking a defensible supply curve as well as any internal clearing mechanism, is simply a failed metaphor, unsuitable for use as the foundation of a theory.

Output gaps and the required GDP growth rates

In this section we provide empirical support to the notion that the major reason that unemployment has persisted at high levels for the last 20 years is because output growth has been deficient. We can estimate the deficiency in GDP growth, which has led to the rise in unemployment rates, by relating the major output and labour-force aggregates. These relations allow us to calculate changes in the aggregate unemployment rate that would occur under different output growth rates. The so-called Okun's Law arithmetic helps us to understand why unemployment rates have risen. Take the following output accounting statement:

Table 3.2 Average annual growth (%) in real hourly earnings in selected OECD economies, 1970–97

	1970–97	1970–79	1975–79	1980–84	1985–89	1990–97
Canada	0.8	2.5	1.5	0	−7.6	0.4
United States	−0.2	0.7	0.7	0	−17.4	−0.1
Australia	−0.7			1.4	−31.5	−0.6
Japan	2.26	4.14	2.17	1.7	46.4	1.1
New Zealand	−0.2	1.9	0.4	−2.7	−14.3	−0.29
Belgium	0.2			−0.5	8.6	0.56
Denmark	1.8		1.1	−1.1	34.5	
France	2	4.4	3.3	1.9	13.1	0.7
Germany	2	3.4	2.2	−0.3	61	0.9
Italy	2.31	6.2	4.2	1.4	4.1	0
Netherlands	1.01	2.8	0.51	−1.1	22.8	0.14
Spain	3.8	7.7	7.1	2.9	28.8	1.37
Sweden	1		0.3	−0.5	51.8	1.8
United Kingdom	2.1	1.7	0.7	2.8	59.4	2
OECD	−2.1			−2.6	−38.1	−1.3

Source: OECD *Main Economic Indicators*, various issues

$$Y = GH (1 - UR) L \tag{1}$$

where:

Y is real gross domestic product

G is labour productivity,

H is the average number of hours worked per period,

UR is the aggregate unemployment rate, and

L is the labour force.

Equation 1 says that total output produced in a period is equal to total labour input times the amount of output each unit of labour input produces.

We can convert this into an equation expressing percentage growth rates, which, in turn, provides a simple benchmark to estimate, for given labour-force and labour productivity growth rates, the increase in output required to achieve a desired unemployment rate. The rule of thumb that emerges (with the lower case letters indicating percentage rates of change per period) is:

$$ur = lf + g - y \tag{2}$$

Labour-force growth, lf, and productivity growth, g, increase the jobs that are required to maintain a given unemployment rate. For the change in unemployment to be zero, output growth, y, must generate enough jobs to match the increased requirements.

Thus, equation 2 shows that if the unemployment rate is to remain constant, the rate of real output growth must equal the rate of growth in

Table 3.3 Required real output growth and output gaps (per annum)

Country	Unemployment rate 1987	Unemployment rate 1997	Labour-force growth (1)	Prod'y growth[a] (2)	Required real GDP growth (3)	Real GDP growth (4)	GDP growth gap (5)
					Average % per annum, 1987–97		
Canada	8.9	9.2	1.3	0.8	2.1	2.0	0.11
USA	6.2	5.0	1.3	1.1	2.4	2.6	−0.20
Japan	2.9	3.4	1.1	1.8	2.9	2.8	0.04
Australia	8.1	8.6	1.7	1.3	3.0	3.0	0.02
Belgium	10.0	9.2	0.5	1.1	1.6	1.1	−0.18
Denmark	6.1	5.2	0.02	1.9	1.9	2.1	−0.20
Finland	5.1	13.1	−0.1	2.8	2.7	1.7	1.00
France	10.3	12.4	0.5	1.7	2.2	2.1	0.17
Germany	8.9	10.1	0.4	2.2	2.6	1.5	1.10
Italy	9.9	12.1	−0.1	2.0	1.9	1.7	0.30
Netherlands	8.1	5.2	2.5	−0.4	2.1	2.8	−0.70
Spain	20.5	20.8	0.9	1.4	2.3	2.6	−0.30
Sweden	2.3	9.9	−0.4	2.0	1.6	1.1	0.50
Switzerland	0.8	5.2	1.2	1.9	3.1	1.1	2.00
UK	10.6	7.0	0.3	1.4	1.7	1.9	−0.28
OECD	6.7	7.3	1.1	1.7	2.8	2.5	0.30

[a] Productivity growth (output per person hour)
Source: OECD *Main Economics Indicators,* OECD *Labour Force Statistics,*
OECD *Economic Outlook,* July 1998

the labour force plus the growth rate in labour productivity. Cyclical movements in labour productivity and the labour force can modify the relationships in the short run.[5]

The calculations are shown in table 3.3. Columns 1 and 2 show the actual labour-force and productivity growth (output per person hour employed) from 1987 to 1997. Column 3 is the sum of 1 and 2 and shows the rate of real GDP growth, which would be required to maintain a steady (unchanging) unemployment rate. Column 4 is the actual real GDP growth over the period 1987 to 1997. Column 5 then calculates the extent to which the real GDP growth rate has been sufficient to reduce the unemployment rate (some rounding approximations are made). A positive sign in 5 indicates a growth gap (real GDP growth below the required rate), while a negative sign in 5 indicates that real GDP growth is contributing to reductions in the unemployment rate over the period shown.

A positive sign will thus be linked to a rising unemployment rate over the period due to the rate of GDP growth being deficient. The size of each effect is measured by the magnitude of the growth gap (positive or negative).

The calculations, while somewhat approximate given the difficulty in using this type of data, are supportive of the contention that the changes in unemployment over the period are largely explained by the fact that real GDP growth was insufficient given labour-force and productivity growth rates. For Australia, the cumulative GDP gap provides a reasonable estimate of the actual rises experienced. Hence, as table 3.3 indicates, for the OECD as a whole, real GDP growth over the period 1987–97 was below the level required to reduce unemployment. Table 3.3 also indicates that for Australia in this period, real GDP growth, averaged over the period, only achieved a level which would roughly stabilise but not reduce unemployment (see also chapter 6).

Deflationary policy and its impacts

The data and analysis of table 3.3 raise the question of why GDP growth has been insufficient to prevent unemployment from rising over the last 20 years. The short answer, as mentioned above, has been the decision by the authorities, strongly supported by financial markets and other business interests, to 'fight inflation first' using deflationary, slow growth policies (Eatwell 1995). The major reason why policy-makers have allowed the level of unemployment to rise over the last 20 years is that they have been increasingly loath to use discretionary fiscal and monetary policy to stimulate the economy. The battle against unemployment has been largely abandoned in order to keep inflation at low levels. In recent years, this crude deflationary strategy has been augmented by deregulation policies at the microeconomic level that have exacerbated the hardship of the unemployed. There has been a surprising lack of interest among economists in measuring the relative costs of these policies (see Mitchell and Watts 1997). This helps explain why GDP growth since the 1970s has averaged about half the level experienced during the postwar 'golden age' era. Hence, as Mitchell (1996) has argued, excessive reliance on tight monetary policy via high real interest rates by governments intent on fighting inflation led to private-sector demand conditions which caused the unemployment rates to rise throughout the OECD. Arguably, an important conduit was through failing private-sector investment. First, the restrictive policy held real interest rates at high levels for extended periods. The high real interest rates resulted, after lags, in lower than otherwise private capital

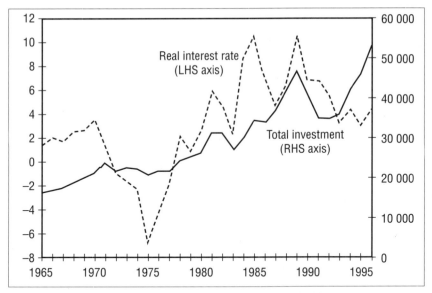

Figure 3.2 The relationship between real interest rates and total investment in Australia, 1964–96

Source: ABS, AUSSTATS

expenditure which reduced the potential medium-term growth path of the economy and worsened the relationship between output capacity growth and labour-force growth.

Figure 3.2 seems consistent with the view that high real interest rates were a determining factor shaping total private capital formation. The lags in the response to investment to real interest rates are clear. The graph is supported by a calculation of investment growth rates for various periods before and after the abandonment of Bretton Woods in the early 1970s. Davidson (1998, p. 820) argues that the annual rate of growth in investment in plant and equipment in the OECD was 6 per cent prior to 1973 and has fallen to less than 3 per cent since 1973. He argues the evidence is irrefutable.

There is no doubt that growth in investment fell after 1973. Table 3.4 calculates growth rates in total investment and its components for Australia for selected periods. The cyclical nature of investment is clearly demonstrated. That is the only irrefutable fact. The lagged relationship between investment flows and the leading real interest rate levels is also evidenced in the data.

The contribution of investment to GDP has also fallen in Australia. The investment ratio fell from 10.5 per cent (average rate from 1960 to 1972) to around 9.2 per cent from 1974–79, 9.8 per cent 1982–84,

Table 3.4 Growth rates (% p.a.) in total investment and components and the average level of real interest rates in Australia for selected periods

Period	Total investment	Plant and equipment	Buildings	Average real interest rate
1960–73	5.28	5.29	5.27	1.35
1974–96	4.03	4.42	3.21	3.65
1974–83	2.18	2.93	0.66	0.29
1984–89	9.44	6.84	15.16	7.85
1984–96	4.92	4.74	5.36	6.23
1990–93	−4.25	0.08	−12.38	5.56
1990–96	4.34	6.54	0.11	4.85

Note: The real interest rate is the 3-monthly money market interest rates after adjusting for the annualised percentage change in the consumer price index
Source: ABS, AUSSTATS

9.7 per cent 1974–84, was 11.2 per cent 1984–90, 9.6 per cent 1990–94 and 10.3 per cent from 1959–1997.

Figure 3.3 shows the inverted unemployment rate and the total capital expenditure/GDP ratio for the OECD. There appears to be a strong association between the two. One might be tempted to assert that the major determining factor accounting for the changes in the level of unemployment in the OECD has been movements in the investment ratio. Figure 3.4 shows a similar relationship for Australia. The pattern is in fact common across the major OECD economies.

Of course, it has long been recognised that private investment variations are responsible for the swings in activity in capitalist economies. The difference in the last 20 years has been that the governments have been unwilling to use active fiscal policy to resolve the demand-deficiency. The graphs are consistent with this hypothesis. Economists who wish to argue that the unemployment has been generated by supply-side rigidities have to first explain the relationships implied by figures 3.3 and 3.4.

The OECD (1997) published a comparison between Australian real interest rates and selected economies (see table 3.5). It can be seen that Australia's short-term real interest rates were higher during the growth period than those of the three largest world economies and the differential between our rates and the others has widened. Over the last two decades, our unemployment problem has been commensurately worse.

Capital expenditure was also retarded directly by public spending cuts (including widespread privatisation strategies). Governments, seeking quick and visible improvement in budget deficits, found it easier to cut capital expenditure before cutting into recurrent, 'vote-attracting'

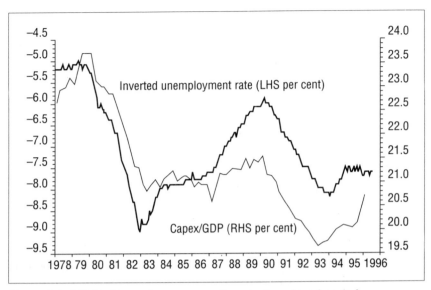

Figure 3.3 OECD: Unemployment rate (inverted) and total capital expenditure/GDP, 1978–96

Source: OECD *Main Economic Indicators,* various issues

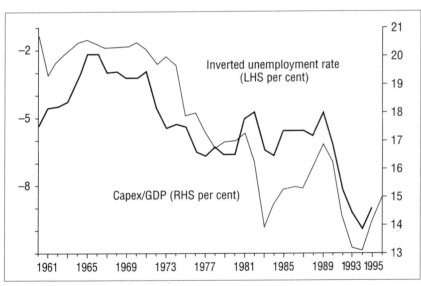

Figure 3.4 Australia: Unemployment rate (inverted) and total capital expenditure/GDP, 1960–96

Source: ABS, AUSSTATS

Table 3.5 Real interest rate comparisons (annual average percentage rates)

Period	Australia	USA	Japan	Germany
1983–89	6.9	3.8	4.0	3.7
1990–96	4.9	1.4	2.3	3.7

Source: OECD *Main Economic Indicators*, various issues

programs and services. As these cuts impacted on the unemployment rate, the resulting high cyclical budget deficits led governments to further cut public capital spending. Inflation mania was joined with balanced budget mania over the decade from 1975. Both have persisted with damaging consequences. European countries have been locked into the restrictive requirements of the Maastricht Treaty, while other countries, like Australia, used spurious current account/national savings arguments to pursue budget surpluses.

It is here that macroeconomic policy in Australia became very muddled. The high interest rates were designed in part to stifle demand to reduce imports and directly attack the current account deficit. However, the Reserve Bank argued that the high rates were designed to stabilise inflation by maintaining a higher than otherwise exchange rate. At the same time the government was pursuing economic restructuring (tariff cuts) aimed at stimulating exports. For a small trading nation like Australia, the high real interest rates pushed the exchange rate up which squeezed the export sector and allowed an advantage to imports. The very policies that were designed to counter the so-called current account constraint have pushed the economy further up against it. This in turn has led to further fiscal constraint, which has reduced the ability of the economy to significantly reduce unemployment (see Anderson 1995; Pitchford 1989, 1990).

The impact of technological change: Jobless growth?

If it is true that slow growth and inadequate aggregate demand have been the main factors driving unemployment, it is also true that other subsidiary factors may be playing a role. The question we turn to in this section is: what role has technological unemployment or 'jobless growth' played in driving unemployment?

An argument emerged in the 1990s that the relationship between economic growth and employment growth had been displaced by technological change such that the former no longer guaranteed the latter. The concept of jobless growth was touted as further evidence of the poverty of Keynesian remedies, which relied on the government stimulating aggregate demand to generate growth and hence jobs. If the growth no longer delivered the same numbers of jobs as it had previously then the strategy was in need of major overhaul. Some adherents to the jobless growth hypothesis pointed to the fact that information technology is intrinsically more labour saving than previous technologies (see Padalino and Vivarelli 1997).

The issue is essentially an empirical one. Three questions are relevant in addressing whether there is evidence to support this view of technological unemployment. First, has the link between employment growth and GDP growth – the employment/growth elasticity – decreased? Second, can we detect a break in the employment/growth relationship at any point in time? Third, can any evidence of jobless growth be found at the sectoral level, specifically in the manufacturing industry? It is possible that while the economy overall is still producing jobs in accordance with previous growth elasticities, the manufacturing sector, traditionally the engine-room of jobs growth, has now seen the technological displacement or jobless growth referred to above.

The jobless growth hypothesis runs counter to the usual view that technological change brings with it new opportunities and stronger employment growth after the so-called *compensation mechanisms* start working. Padalino and Vivarelli (1997) outline the pro and con arguments for technology. The positive effects of technology on employment are in italics with the counter-argument, emphasising the weakness of the compensation mechanisms, following.

1. *New jobs arise in the capital goods sector to make the new machines.* But labour-saving technology spreads into the capital goods sector where new investment results in obsolete machines being scrapped.
2. *Lower prices and competition increase demand.* There is a loss of demand as sacked workers lose income. For this compensation mechanism to work, a strong version of Says Law must operate in a perfectly competitive economy. In oligopolistic markets, which are the norm, prices may not fall.
3. *Profits from lower costs (before prices are lowered) are invested elsewhere.* If investments are not forthcoming or if they are labour saving, then the compensation is limited.
4. *Wage cuts can compensate.* This contradicts the entire Keynesian theory of effective demand and relies on the flawed neoclassical view of wage-cutting. The argument is subject to the fallacy of composition that says that if one firm cuts its wages it will be better off then the same effect will endure if all firms follow suit. Of course, the lower wages lead to cuts in demand and sales fall if all workers receive the cuts.

5. *Unions may participate in redistribution of wealth generated by lower costs.* Higher incomes lead to higher demand but the labour-market no longer allows the unions to redistribute higher incomes via productivity growth. Wages are more competitive now.

6. *New products are created.* New branches are created which lead to 'welfare effects' (positive employment creation) which have to be compared with 'substitution effects' (displacement of mature products and jobs); this remains the best way of counterbalancing the labour-saving effects of new technology.

Padalino and Vivarelli (1997, pp. 210–11) label the period since the 1970s as the 'post-Fordist' era and conduct a series of econometric tests, concluding that:

> Clearly, the conclusion of this analysis is that the short-run linkage between growth and employment did not weaken in the post-Fordist period in the whole economy or in the manufacturing sector alone, either in terms of number of employees or in terms of working time. Thus, the transition to post-Fordism brought about an obvious slow-down in economic growth but not a break in the short-run relationship between growth and employment.
>
> This evidence suggests that fostering growth and investments specifically in manufacturing may have very limited direct employment effects, but fostering aggregate economic growth should contribute to employment, especially in the short run.

So much for 'jobless growth', at least at the economy-wide or aggregate level. Using Australian data, the claim that employment elasticities have changed over time, a necessary condition for the jobless growth hypothesis, can be tested.[6] The jobless growth hypothesis would be consistent with declining and negative elasticities,[7] but no evidence was found to support a hypothesis that there has been a regime shift in the relationship between employment growth and output growth.

The results are presented in table 3.6. They show that more recent elasticities have been significantly higher than in the period from 1974 to 1990, especially in terms of employment by hours (see also chapter 11). These results are not at all consistent with the jobless growth hypothesis. They are consistent with the changes in the industrial composition of employment and output with the labour-intensive service sector growing faster than the goods-producing sector. The significance of the rise of services employment is discussed more fully in later chapters, especially chapters 6, 10 and 12.

To substantiate the technological change hypothesis, it would be expected that the period of rising unemployment should be associated with rising labour productivity growth. Eatwell (1995) fails to find evidence of this in the G-7 countries. His conclusion (p. 273) is that:

Table 3.6 Regression tests of the jobless growth
hypothesis in Australia

Sample	Long-run elasticity	
	Total persons	Total hours
1960(2) to 1997(3)	0.62	–
1967(2) to 1997(3)	–	0.37
1960(2) to 1974(2)	0.95	–
1974(3) to 1997(3)	0.45	0.37
1974(3) to 1982(4)	0.35	0.24
1983(1) to 1989(4)	0.24	0.28
1983(1) to 1997(3)	0.41	0.49
1990(1) to 1997(3)	0.59	0.66

Note: Missing numbers reflect gaps in data.

there has been a sharp slow-down in productivity growth. Indeed the
slowdown in productivity growth has been greater than the slow-down in
overall growth of demand, which means that low productivity growth has
contributed to the creation (or at least preservation) of jobs, rather than their
destruction.

For Australia, a similar pattern has been observed. Table 3.7 shows a
decline in productivity growth over the period 1960 to 1997. Part of this
decline has been due to the structural shift in the economy away from
manufacturing towards the more labour-intensive service industries,
which we examine in the next section (see also chapters 6 and 12).

In summary, there appears to be no evidence for jobless growth at the
aggregate or economy-wide level (see chapters 6 and 12 for a discussion of
the sectoral dimensions of jobless growth). The jobless growth hypothesis
suggests that productivity growth is faster than output growth which
means that employment growth is negative. Technological change, which
induces productivity growth in innovating sectors, is usually considered
to create job opportunities elsewhere as costs rise throughout the
economy. Using regression techniques there appears no evidence that the
relationship between employment growth and output growth has shifted
and supports the jobless growth hypothesis. Yet if the jobless growth
hypothesis does not hold for the Australian economy as a whole, evidence
presented in chapter 6 shows that it does hold for various sectors of the
economy, such as manufacturing. This is a major departure from postwar
experience as the manufacturing sector had been a major jobs engine in
the economy. The data presented in chapter 6 also indicate significant
changes in the industrial composition of employment towards the
low-productivity services sector. In the section below we look more closely
at the jobs fall-out from deindustrialisation in Australia.

Table 3.7 Overall productivity growth in
Australia: GDP per person employed

Period	% per annum
September 1960–69	2.33
September 1970–79	1.89
September 1980–89	0.91
September 1988–97	1.38

Source: ABS, AUSSTATS

Deindustrialisation?

Some have claimed that the decline of manufacturing or deindustrialisation has led to a substantial rise in unemployment. This section supports that argument. But first, what is deindustrialisation? The literature is unclear on the use of the term. Some use it to refer to a decline in employment in manufacturing or a decline in manufacturing output. On the other hand, does not a mature economy, à la Rostow, go through phases of growth where agriculture declines relative to industrial production, which in turn gives way to services? Why focus on the manufacturing sector? With freer trade and financial flows since the 1970s, it is possible that the proportionate decline in manufacturing is just a response to changing international demand and supply conditions (see Singh 1977).

The causes of the relative decline in the manufacturing sector can also be questioned. Krugman (1994b) focuses on the liberalisation of trade in the 1980s. He argues that the increase in unemployment is partly due to the relative contraction of the manufacturing sector as a share of the economy due to trade liberalisation. He estimates the impact of the US manufacturing trade deficit on US employment by calculating the trade deficit as a proportion of manufacturing value added. He shows that the manufacturing trade deficit in the US only amounts to around 2 per cent of manufacturing value-added and is therefore only responsible for a reduction in the manufacturing sector, and manufacturing employment, of around 2 per cent.

The manufacturing sector has long been seen as the major source of growth and rising living standards in industrial economies. Bacon and Eltis (1976) first developed the Cambridge theory that the decline in manufacturing was a reflection of an endogenous process of deindustrialisation. They make a distinction between marketable and non-marketable output and define deindustrialisation as the decline of the former relative to the latter. The marketable sector is defined as goods and services whose prices are determined in the market place by demand and supply factors. Bacon and Eltis claim that the underlying real standards of living in an economy are determined by the productivity of the marketable sector firms. Real wealth is sourced in these industries. The manufacturing sector is the hub of the marketable goods sector.

Bacon and Eltis trace the decline in the prosperity of the British economy to the shrinking manufacturing sector. This contraction was exacerbated by the growth of the non-marketable sector (services). The services sector raised the demand for labour and forced the marketable sector to pay higher wages. The rising costs and subsequent price rises eroded the competitiveness of the manufacturing firms in the face of a rise in competitive production in the Southeast Asian economies.

Bacon and Eltis argue that the rise of welfare provision by governments also contributed to the pressure on the manufacturing sector. The welfare services were provided from tax deductions out of profits and wages. They claim that business investment declined because the marginal profits were now reduced. In addition, trade unions militantly defended the real wages of their members, with the subsequent squeeze on profit margins further constraining investment. To see the growth of the services sector as a 'crowding out' effect, however, cannot be substantiated. The labour-force growth of married women has largely fed the demand for labour in the services sector while the manufacturing sector has been shedding prime age, blue-collar males (see Moore and Rhodes 1976, for an early insight). The compositional shift in industry employment may in fact be viewed as being fortuitous in a time when manufacturing was in decline and labour-force participation rates were beginning their spectacular rise.

Singh (1977) suggests that nations will lose their manufacturing employment share if they fail to maintain an adequate excess of exports over imports of manufactured goods due to declining competitiveness. Krugman's trade argument above is a variant on this general notion. A question that arises is why exchange rate movements do not overcome the declining competitiveness. But the process of declining competitiveness would require continual exchange rate falls. The initial loss of competitiveness squeezes profits, which leads to declining investment and a vicious circle emerges. In other words, the supply side of the economy contracts as an adjustment to the initial demand shock. As Shone (1989, p. 391) argues:

> What some economists are worried about is whether, over the last two decades or so, the manufacturing base of the economy has not only declined,

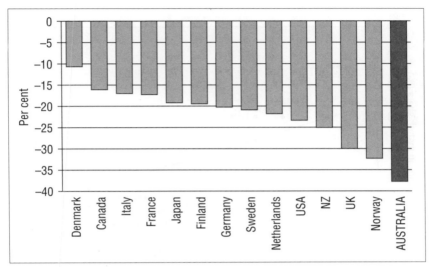

Figure 3.5 Change in manufacturing share of GDP for selected OECD countries, 1970–90

Source: OECD (1994b)

but declined to such an extent that here is a serious problem for the future. The point about this argument, if true, is that no 'tinkering' with the macroeconomy will solve this underlying structural problem.

The claim that some problems are exclusively microeconomic and are invariant to aggregate demand management is the basis of the natural rate hypothesis. However, what appears to be a structural imbalance is often a manifestation of demand failure (see Mitchell 1987a).

Figure 3.5 shows the relative declines in the share of manufacturing output in GDP for a range of OECD countries. It is clear that Australia's relative decline has been the most severe. Figure 3.6 suggests that there is an association between increases in unemployment rates and declines in manufacturing shares of GDP across a number of OECD economies.

Using Krugman's (1994b) approach to estimate the impact on unemployment of the relative contraction of the manufacturing sector as a share of the economy, we see that the outcomes for Australia are considerably larger than Krugman found for the USA. In fact, the combined impact of deflationary policy on investment in Australian manufacturing, plus the poor trade competitiveness of manufacturing under a regime of vanishing tariffs in the last two decades, would appear

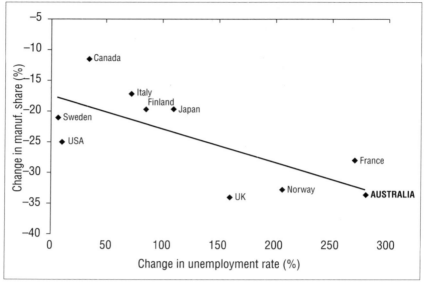

Figure 3.6 The change in the unemployment rate and the change in manufacturing share of GDP, 10 OECD countries, 1970–90
Source: OECD (1994b)

to be a major component of Australia's unemployment problem. The relevant calculations are shown in table 3.8.

Krugman's approach was anticipated by Singh (1989) who concluded after studying the performance of the UK economy during the 1970s, that it lost manufacturing jobs to Japan and Germany due to its inefficient manufacturing sector. This is a new dimension to the deindustrialisation argument. There are two components: the relative shifts between sectors (service and goods-producing) within a country and the relative competitiveness of comparable sectors across countries. The trade effect allegedly works through the latter dimension.

Appelbaum and Schettkat (1995b, pp. 616–17), however, reject the view that deindustrialisation has occurred through trade liberalisation between industrialised countries. They examine the relationship between employment and productivity growth. They find a negative relationship between employment growth and productivity growth by industry applying to the whole OECD bloc. They conclude that:

> although it may have had a disproportionate effect on countries with an 'inefficient' manufacturing sector [cf. Australia], trade between the industrialised economies is not the fundamental explanation for the negative inter-industry relationship between employment and productivity growth rates.

Table 3.8 Contribution of manufacturing trade deficit to manufacturing unemployment

Manufacturing sector trade deficit 1993	$33 billion
Reduced by services component of manufactured exports (40%)	−$13.2 billion
Net effect of manufacturing deficit	$19.8 billion
Total manufacturing value-added	$66.2 billion
Percentage reduction in manufacturing sector (19.8/66.2)	29.9%
Manufacturing workforce 1992–93	1.05 million
Therefore potential employment cost of deficit (29.9% × 1.05m)	314 000
Total Australian unemployed 1992–93	916 000
Potential contribution of manufacturing trade deficit to total unemployment:	*34%*

Source: ABS, AUSTATS

What about trade with less developed economies? There has been a massive increase in the proportion of exports from the newly industrialised economies (NIC). Singh (1994) shows that the majority of these exports go to the mature industrialised economies. Appelbaum and Schettkat (1995b, p. 618) convincingly put to rest the myth that manufacturing jobs in mature economies have been lost to the NICs. They conclude, 'this conventional view of trade with the Third World cannot, therefore, explain the inverse relationship between employment and productivity growth rates in the industrialised countries'.

The interaction between aggregate demand, employment growth and productivity growth

Richard Freeman (1988) raised the issue of a trade-off between productivity and employment growth. The experience of Europe and the USA appeared to provide casual support for his hypothesis. Europe had slow employment growth but relatively strong productivity growth compared to the USA, which experienced the opposite trends in both.

Appelbaum and Schettkat (1995b, p. 611) argue 'that the shift from full employment to unemployment in industrialised countries is caused not by exogenous factors, rigid labour markets or policy mistakes, though these may exacerbate the problem, but rather by the endogenous development process itself'. Clearly, the impact of mistaken policy positions has been crucial. The debate is really about whether the deflationary policies worsened an underlying structural trend or was itself a primary cause of the declining job opportunities. The analysis earlier suggests that the policy change towards fighting inflation at the expense of unemployment was a primary cause. Certainly, the structural changes were ongoing throughout. But the large-scale withdrawal of the public sector as an employer, especially of youth, meant that Australia no longer had an employer of the last resort. Appelbaum and Schettkat appear to take a slightly different view.

To understand their position, a brief review of the endogenous growth theory is necessary. The first to really articulate the notion was W.E.G. Salter (1960) who studied the relationships between the growth of labour productivity, earnings, prices, real output and employment. The relevant conclusion here was that industries with the strongest employment growth also exhibited strong productivity growth. Salter also noted that the employment effects of productivity growth depended on the balance between labour saving and the increased demand that was possible via lower costs (lower prices). The positive relationship between productivity growth and employment growth found by Salter rested on the fact that relative prices fell in industries experiencing the productivity growth, and product market demand for the resulting goods was responsive and price elastic (see Appelbaum and Schettkat 1995a).

The general process of development then was driven by the relative price movements that accompanied productivity growth, which shifted the patterns of output, employment and demand towards the higher productivity industries. At least in the postwar period, manufacturing was the main sector driving the productivity and employment growth. Appelbaum and Schettkat (1995b, p. 609) refer to this pattern as the endogenous growth process.

The feature of this period of expansion following World War II was that household durable industries grew rapidly as household incomes grew. Stability in income growth was ensured by the practice of Keynesian fine-tune and pump-priming policies. As incomes rose, the demand for goods from the relatively high-productivity sector grew and the resulting relative price movements enhanced the overall process. The process was also strengthened by the use of mass production, which further lowered prices in the higher productivity sectors.

Appelbaum and Schettkat (1995b, p. 609) argue that: 'In these circumstances, institutional differences among the industrialised economies were largely, though not entirely, irrelevant to labour market outcomes'. The real explanation lies in the balance between output demand growth and productivity growth. By the 1980s, however, it was becoming apparent that the industries with the most rapid employment growth were those in the service sectors with low productivity growth.

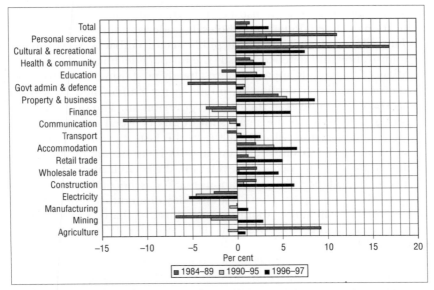

Figure 3.7 Changes (%) in industry employment in Australia for selected periods

Source: ABS, AUSSTATS

The previously strong employment industries failed to achieve demand conditions that allowed employment growth to outstrip productivity growth. Hence, Appelbaum and Schettkat (1995b, p. 611) argue that 'Countries which have not been successful in shifting employment from manufacturing activities to service activities have generally experienced little employment growth'.

Figure 3.7 shows the changes in industry employment in Australia over three periods: 1984–89 a period of rapid aggregate employment growth in Australia; 1990–95 a period of recession and early recovery; and 1996–97 a period of government cutbacks and slower growth.

There has been a fundamental shift in the composition of industry employment in the last decade which, prompted by the severe public-sector budgetary cutbacks in 1996 and 1997, has accelerated. The production industries (mining, manufacturing, electricity, gas and water, agriculture, forestry and fishing, and construction) have been flat or in decline over the recent period. Manufacturing is the largest production industry and since March 1996 it has not only declined absolutely but its share in total employment has also declined from 15 per cent to 13 per cent.

The service industries showed dichotomous behaviour. Personal services, cultural and recreational services, health and community, property and business demonstrated growth, while communications and education declined. Retail and wholesale trade were stifled. The decline in education reflected the harsh public-sector cutbacks. Government administration and defence (mostly the former) declined substantially.

Many of the trends apparent were already established prior to 1996. However, the sharp decline in public-sector employment has been exacerbated by policies of the current government. The other notable aspect of this period is the sharp shift in mix between full-time (down 31 900) and part-time (up 216 300). In the fastest growing industries (like property and business), part-time work is fast becoming the norm. This sharp change in mix is also evident in the retail industry.

There is evidence that the labour-market is becoming more segmented than in the past. There is a vast body of literature that describes the manner in which the labour-market adjusts to changes in economic activity (see Reder 1955; Wallich 1956; Wachter 1970; Okun 1973; Thurow 1975; Vroman 1978). The literature also ties in with some versions of segmented labour-market theory and provides the basis of a theory of cyclical upgrading, whereby disadvantaged groups in the economy achieve upward mobility as a result of higher economic activity. Okun's (1973) paper firmly entrenched the idea that employment growth and productivity growth are complementary – and hence there are upgrading effects.[8]

In the light of widespread evidence that many economies experienced a productivity slowdown during the 1970s, Okun's results have been questioned (see Mitchell et al. 1995). Thurow (1983) argues that the productivity slowdown has been mainly due to changes in the occupational structure of the economy, characterised by a switch away from jobs which actually make things towards those which are essentially administrative and do not directly produce anything. He cites the fact that between 1978 and 1985, the number of blue-collar employees in the US fell by 1.9 million (6 per cent), while real business GDP rose by 16 per cent. Productivity for blue-collar workers seemed to be rising. An alternative explanation is that the slowdown may have been due to a slump in productivity in the goods-producing industries and therefore a shift in composition of output away from the goods-producing sector is thus not necessarily the source of the problem.

Table 3.9 shows that for Australia, the share of employment of the goods-producing aggregate (manufacturing, construction and transport) has fallen since 1985 (from 34 per cent of the total in 1985 to 25.3 per cent in 1997). In contrast, the services aggregate (wholesale and retail trade, accommodation, cafés and restaurants, communications, finance and insurance, property and business services, health and community services, cultural and recreation, personal and other services)

Table 3.9 Composition of employment in Australian industries, 1985–97

	Goods sector	Service sector	Selected service industries							
	% of total	% of total	WRT % of total	Accom % of total	Com % of total	F&I % of total	P&BS % of total	H&CS % of total	C&R % of total	Pers % of total
1985	29.1	49.4	19.8	3.2	2.4	4.2	6.6	8.1	1.8	3.2
1986	28.9	50.1	20.0	3.5	2.3	4.4	6.6	8.3	1.8	3.3
1987	28.1	51.3	19.8	3.6	2.1	4.7	7.1	8.5	1.8	3.6
1988	28.4	52.0	20.3	3.8	2.0	4.5	7.3	8.6	1.9	3.6
1989	28.7	52.3	20.7	3.8	1.9	4.5	7.7	8.3	2.1	3.4
1990	27.6	52.9	20.5	4.0	2.0	4.8	7.7	8.6	1.9	3.5
1991	25.9	54.4	20.6	4.4	1.8	4.5	8.1	9.2	2.1	3.6
1992	25.7	54.7	20.7	4.4	1.6	4.4	8.3	9.2	2.1	4.0
1993	25.9	53.8	20.7	4.4	1.6	4.0	8.1	9.2	2.1	3.7
1994	26.1	55.1	20.8	4.6	1.7	4.0	9.1	8.9	2.3	3.7
1995	25.4	55.7	20.6	4.7	1.8	3.9	9.7	9.2	2.3	3.6
1996	25.4	56.0	20.8	4.5	2.0	3.8	9.8	9.2	2.3	3.7
1997	25.3	56.8	20.1	4.7	1.8	3.7	10.7	9.4	2.4	4.0

WRT = Wholesale and retail trade
Accom = Accommodation, cafés and restaurants
Com = Communications
F&I = Finance and insurance
P&BS = Property and business services
H&CS = Health and community services
C&R = Cultural and recreation services
Pers = Personal and other services

Source: ABS, AUSSTATS

rose from 49 per cent of total to 57 per cent of total over the same period. The major part of the rise came from property and business services (6.6 per cent to 10.7 per cent), and accommodation, cafés and restaurants (3.2 per cent to 4.7 per cent). Given this marked shift in the composition of employment away from 'goods-producing' industries, towards 'administrative, service and overhead' industries, what patterns of productivity growth have the industries shown over the same period?

Table 3.10 compares the employment growth and the productivity growth for the goods-producing sector and the service sector industries. As a benchmark, the annual average growth in GDP divided by employment for all industries for the period 1986 to 1997 was a meagre 1.3 per cent. For the market sector, over the same period, the average annual growth rate was slightly higher at 1.8, and for the non-farm

Table 3.10 Employment and productivity growth (% p.a.) in goods and services sectors, Australia, 1986–97

	Goods sector		Service sector	
	Productivity growth (% pa)	Employment growth (% pa)	Productivity growth (% pa)	Employment growth (% pa)
1986	1.4	3.1	−2.7	5.3
1987	−2.5	−0.3	−4.6	4.8
1988	5.0	4.6	0.1	5.1
1989	2.8	6.2	2.0	5.7
1990	1.8	−2.8	−2.0	2.3
1991	1.1	−8.2	−2.5	0.5
1992	4.8	−0.7	0.9	0.4
1993	3.9	0.6	4.0	−1.6
1994	4.4	4.4	1.7	5.9
1995	1.1	1.5	1.0	5.5
1996	1.1	1.2	2.9	1.7
1997	1.4	−0.6	−2.3	1.3
Average annual compound growth	2.3	0.7	−0.2	3.0

Source: ABS, AUSSTATS

sector, it was 1.7 per cent per annum. The annual average employment growth for all industries was 1.5 per cent per annum over the same period.

The goods-producing aggregate (manufacturing, construction and transport) exhibited a comparatively healthy 2.3 per cent average annual growth in productivity over the period 1986 to 1997. Manufacturing's average annual growth rate over the period 1986 to 1997 was a relatively strong 3.04 per cent, while transport was 2.86 per cent per annum and construction was 0.5 per cent per annum. While the goods-producing sector has shown above-average productivity performance since the early 1980s, its annual average compound employment growth has been more than half the all industry average.

The service industries shown in table 3.11 reveal that within the sector there have been disparate outcomes over the 1986–97 period. The trend is consistent with the goods-producing sector where the higher productivity industries have the lowest employment growth. Taken together though, the service industries have shown very poor productivity growth, yet strong to very strong employment growth. A large redistribution in employment to these industries, given that they account for nearly half the total employment, has been a major part of the declining economy-wide productivity performance. The results also help us understand the

Table 3.11 Productivity and employment growth (% p.a.) in selected services, Australia, 1986–97

	Productivity growth	Employment growth
Wholesale	1.8	0.8
Retail	−0.3	1.9
Communications	8.1	−0.3
Finance and insurance	3.8	0.1
Cultural and recreational	−0.9	3.7
Services sector	−0.2	3.0
All industries	1.3	1.5
Market sector	1.8	
Non-farm market sector	1.7	

Source: ABS, AUSSTATS

reduced sensitivity of productivity growth to the closing of the employment gap (see Mitchell et al. 1995).

These results suggest that Okun's upgrading hypothesis may have to be modified to take account of the changing composition of industry employment. The low-productivity service sector is responsible for most of the growth in employment since the late 1970s. If two further related facts are added to the discussion, namely, that these industries have higher part-time employment shares, and greater female and teenage participation, then a less glamorous picture of upgrading emerges. We should expect to see more jobs created in the service sector as the employment gap is closed. We should also expect teenagers and females to receive a significant number of these jobs. But whether we would want to construe this as a ladder-climbing shift is questionable. The new jobs are likely to be biased towards low-pay, fractional positions. Further, the effect on aggregate productivity, as the composition of output and employment shifts further to these service industries, is likely to be less than desirable.

Overall, the results are consistent with the argument of Appelbaum and Schettkat (1995b). The endogenous development process that they believe established the strong relationship between employment growth and productivity growth in the postwar era has been interrupted by these compositional shifts. They argue that (p. 611):

This shift from a positive (or zero) correlation between productivity growth and employment growth to a negative correlation has contributed to the end of the virtuous circle of economic development in industrialised countries. It marks a change that is often, though imprecisely, described as the shift from an industrial society to a service economy. This change in the inter-industry pattern of employment growth and productivity growth has weakened the feedback link from income growth to productivity growth, a link which operated through the economies of scale achieved by mass production industries as markets for output of high productivity growth industries expanded.

The question that is important in this analysis is what factors are important in explaining the compositional shifts. Appelbaum and Schettkat (1995b, table 2.2) show the correlation between growth rates in productivity and a number of indicators including employment, wages and prices growth. They conclude (p. 612) that there is 'no systematic inter-industry relationship between the growth rates of wages and those of productivity in industrialised countries'.

There is a distinction between the changing composition of employment and output. Rowthorn and Wells (1987) argued that the share of output between services and manufacturing used to be relatively constant. The changing employment composition in favour of larger shares in the services sector is due to the productivity growth disparities, of the type shown in the analysis above. Rowthorn and Wells (1987, pp. 15–16) argue that, 'With a given pattern of output, differential productivity growth will always cause the pattern of employment to shift away from the most dynamic sectors towards those in which productivity is rising more slowly'.

The constancy of output shares, however, is now doubted. Appelbaum and Schettkat (1995b, p. 619) find that in several countries the share of services in real output rose. For Australia, the share of total manufacturing in GDP was around 28 per cent in the late 1960s and dropped to 19 per cent by the end of the 1980s. So the loss of employment is not just due to productivity growth. The failure to maintain the same output growth rate as the services sector has also led to the declining contribution to total employment.

Whatever the compositional changes that have led to employment shifts across industries, none of the discussion in this section negates the view that ultimately mass unemployment is due to demand-deficiency exacerbated by the failure of governments to employ appropriate expansionary policies.

Changes in the age–gender composition of the labour force

Are age and gender compositional shifts in the labour force also contributing to unemployment? Perry (1970) seeking a 'non-natural' explanation for the ostensible shift in the Phillips Curve during the late 1960s popularised the idea that the full-employment/unemployment rate had increased because the share of groups with higher than average unemployment rates in the labour force had increased (for example, women). On the other hand, Mitchell (1984, p. 137) argues that 'if demographic factors are to blame for the upward shift in Australia's unemployment rate, then the groups experiencing high unemployment rates must have grown drastically as a proportion of the work force. This has not been the case in Australia where conflicting tendencies have been at work'.

Table 3.12 shows the labour-force weights and unemployment rates by age and gender from 1968 to the present. The 15–24 age groups for both males and females have the highest unemployment rates. This segment of the labour force has declined substantially since 1968. The evidence is contrary to the compositional argument.

Table 3.13 uses this information to calculate different measures of the unemployment rate in July 1998 using different weights. The unemployment rate shown in column 2 is the specific unemployment rate for the group in question as at July 1998 and the aggregate unemployment rate (total) is the weighted-average of these specific rates using the July 1998 labour-force weights. Columns 3 to 6 calculate the weighted-average of the specific unemployment rates for July 1998 using the weights of the various periods shown. For example, the male unemployment rate for July 1998 in total was 8.16 (using the actual July 1998 weight). If we had weighted the actual July 1998 unemployment rates (by age) with the 1978 labour-force weights, the unemployment rate for males would have been 8.78. Both the male and female unemployment rates, and the aggregate rate, would have been higher if the labour-force composition had remained as it was in August 1978.

Columns 7 to 10 convert the weighted unemployment rates for each age–gender group into a measure of the percentage contribution of each group to the July 1998 unemployment rate. It is clear that groups with the high relative unemployment rates have *reduced* their impact on the overall unemployment rate. The offsetting nature of the compositional changes is also shown. For example, the 15–19 and 20–24 and 25–34-year-old age groups now contribute less to the aggregate unemployment rate, but the two older groups (35–44 and 45–54) now contribute relatively more.

This empirical analysis shows that the demographic groups with high relative unemployment rates have actually reduced their impact on the overall unemployment rate, thus refuting the argument that the rising unemployment rates are due to compositional changes in the labour force, especially as a result of women becoming a rising percentage of the total labour force. In fact, the overall unemployment rate would have been higher in 1998 had the labour-force demographic composition remained as it was in August 1978.

Table 3.12 Labour-force weights and unemployment rates by age and gender

	1968	August 1978		August 1984		August 1989		August 1997		July 1998	
	Weight	Weight	UR	Weight	UR	Weight	UR	Weight	UR	Weight	UR
Males											
15–19	9.00	9.85	16.30	8.75	22.08	8.83	12.87	6.75	20.23	6.99	19.698
20–24	13.00	13.13	8.83	13.55	14.24	12.29	7.98	11.27	15.32	11.28	13.033
25–34	22.00	26.86	3.85	27.17	7.64	27.11	5.09	25.51	8.21	25.15	7.927
35–44	22.00	19.75	3.27	23.12	5.03	24.43	3.51	25.03	5.73	24.75	5.803
45–54	19.00	17.65	3.27	16.06	5.68	16.43	2.97	20.31	5.78	20.50	5.442
55–59	9.00	6.98	3.70	6.68	5.41	5.76	4.58	6.10	9.69	6.21	7.370
60–64*	5.00	4.14	3.09	3.33	8.13	3.77	7.22	3.11	6.83	3.22	8.372
65+		1.65	2.53	1.35	1.68	1.39	1.20	1.92	2.72	1.89	1.795
Total	100.00	100.00	5.46	100.00	8.67	100.00	5.39	100.00	8.65	100.00	8.155
Females											
15–19	19.00	15.72	17.22	13.13	19.70	11.67	14.60	8.62	18.39	8.81	17.320
20–24	19.00	17.17	9.57	17.80	10.28	15.12	7.88	13.04	12.06	12.78	10.625
25–34	17.00	24.78	6.35	25.90	7.07	26.74	5.84	25.02	7.17	24.54	6.266
35–44	20.00	19.70	4.20	22.84	5.62	25.86	3.86	25.99	6.73	25.09	6.011
45–54	17.00	15.30	4.04	14.05	4.61	14.98	4.07	20.35	5.60	21.16	5.100
55–59*	8.00	4.58	3.37	3.87	3.68	3.43	2.60	4.39	5.14	4.75	5.910
60–64		1.81	0.95	1.55	1.21	1.49	2.58	1.77	1.89	1.88	2.760
65+		0.94	1.37	0.86	0.44	0.70	1.27	0.83	1.86	1.00	0.247
Total	100.00	100.00	7.56	100.00	8.34	100.00	6.20	100.00	8.12	100.00	7.343

Persons											
15–19	13.00	11.99	16.79	10.40	20.95	10.00	13.69	7.55	19.34	7.78	18.119
20–24	15.00	14.60	9.14	15.16	12.48	13.45	7.92	12.03	13.80	11.93	11.915
25–34	21.00	26.10	4.71	26.69	7.43	26.96	5.40	25.30	7.77	24.89	7.217
35–44	21.00	19.73	3.60	23.01	5.25	25.02	3.66	25.44	6.17	24.89	5.898
45–54	19.00	16.79	3.51	15.30	5.31	15.83	3.39	20.32	5.70	20.79	5.296
55–59	7.00	6.10	3.61	5.62	4.94	4.80	4.00	5.36	8.09	5.58	6.811
60–64	4.00	3.29	2.66	2.65	6.61	2.83	6.21	2.53	5.30	2.64	6.642
65+		1.39	2.25	1.17	1.33	1.11	1.22	1.45	2.43	1.50	1.349
Total	*100.00*	*100.00*	*6.22*	*100.00*	*8.54*	*100.00*	*5.72*	*100.00*	*8.42*	*100.00*	*7.772*

* for 1968, the 60–64 age group for males includes 64+, and the 55–59 age group for females includes 60+
Source: ABS, AUSSTATS

Table 3.13 Weighted unemployment rates and percentage contribution to July 1998, unemployment by age and gender

	July 1998	Weighted unemployment rate				Percentage contribution to July 1998 unemployment rate			
	UR (2)	1978 Weight (3)	1984 Weight (4)	1989 Weight (5)	1998 Weight (6)	1978 Weight (7)	1984 Weight (8)	1989 Weight (9)	1998 Weight (10)
Males									
15–19	19.69	1.94	1.72	1.74	1.38	22.1	19.9	20.3	16.9
20–24	13.03	1.71	1.77	1.60	1.47	18.0	20.4	18.7	18.0
25–34	7.93	2.13	2.15	2.15	1.99	24.5	24.9	25.1	24.5
35–44	5.80	1.15	1.34	1.42	1.44	17.6	15.5	16.6	17.6
45–54	5.44	0.96	0.87	0.89	1.12	13.7	10.1	10.4	13.7
55–59	7.37	0.51	0.49	0.42	0.46	5.6	5.7	5.0	5.6
60–64	8.37	0.35	0.28	0.32	0.27	3.3	3.2	3.7	3.3
65+	1.79	0.03	0.02	0.02	0.03	0.4	0.3	0.3	0.4
Total	8.16	8.78	8.65	8.57	8.16	100.0	100.0	100.0	100.0
Females									
15–19	17.32	2.72	2.27	2.02	1.53	32.5	27.9	25.7	20.8
20–24	10.63	1.82	1.89	1.61	1.36	21.7	23.2	20.4	18.5
25–34	6.27	1.55	1.62	1.68	1.54	18.5	19.9	21.3	20.9
35–44	6.01	1.18	1.37	1.55	1.51	14.1	16.8	19.8	20.5
45–54	5.10	0.78	0.72	0.76	1.08	9.3	8.8	9.7	14.7
55–59	5.91	0.27	0.23	0.20	0.28	3.2	2.8	2.6	3.8
60–64	2.76	0.05	0.04	0.04	0.05	0.6	0.5	0.5	0.7
65+	0.25	0.002	0.002	0.002	0.002	0.0	0.0	0.0	0.0
Total	7.34	8.39	8.15	7.87	7.34	100.0	100.0	100.0	100.0

Persons									
15–19	18.12	2.17	1.89	1.81	1.41	25.5	22.6	22.1	18.1
20–24	11.92	1.74	1.81	1.60	1.42	20.5	21.6	19.5	18.3
25–34	7.22	1.88	1.92	1.95	1.79	22.2	23.0	23.7	23.1
35–44	5.89	1.16	1.36	1.48	1.47	13.7	16.2	18.0	18.9
45–54	5.29	0.88	0.81	0.84	1.10	10.5	9.7	10.2	14.2
55–59	6.81	0.42	0.38	0.33	0.38	4.9	4.6	4.0	4.9
60–64	6.64	0.22	0.18	0.19	0.18	2.6	2.1	2.3	2.3
65+	1.35	0.02	0.02	0.02	0.02	0.2	0.2	0.2	0.3
Total	7.77	8.50	8.36	8.20	7.77	100.0	100.0	100.0	100.0

Source: ABS, AUSSTATS

Conclusion – The way ahead

This chapter has examined various hypotheses about the causes of unemployment. It initially considered the neoclassical orthodoxy, which sources its explanation in supply-side factors. The orthodox theory assumes that unemployment is ultimately a voluntary phenomenon representing maximising individual choices. In that sense, it poses no particular problem that policy needs to address. In fact, the role that policy plays in distorting individual choice is highlighted. So we see that welfare benefits distort the choice between labour and leisure by subsidising search activity.

The labour-market is also seen by orthodoxy to be subject to 'artificial' rigidities like excessive minimum wage rates and excessive hiring and firing cost promoted by trade unions and government. These rigidities are said to distort the workings of the market and lead to maximising choices, which involve unemployment. Trade unions pursuing excessive real wage increases are implicated in this approach. The orthodox theory was shown not only to have serious conceptual difficulties but also to be at odds with the empirical evidence. It does not stand as a credible explanation of unemployment.

The chapter examined the much simpler argument that demand-side deficiencies have been the major factor driving unemployment and found it to be well supported by an array of empirical indicators. The pursuit of deflationary policies following the rapid escalation of inflation in the 1970s as a result of the oil price hikes was accompanied by the sustained high unemployment that still afflicts the economy today. The manifestation of this policy change appears in the fact that output growth has been consistently below that required to fully employ a growing labour force once labour productivity growth is taken into account.

The depressed state of demand has also worsened the impacts of structural and technological changes, which in a buoyant economy would normally not have negative consequences on unemployment. The jobless growth hypothesis was rejected at the economy-wide level but there is evidence that it is valid for the manufacturing sector. The deindustrialisation hypothesis was also examined. The argument is that compositional shifts in output, specifically in terms of the declining contribution of the manufacturing sector, contribute to rising unemployment. The sources of the decline are often related to increased trade liberalisation whereby higher costs economies lose employment to third world economies. There is some evidence that the decline in manufacturing has been associated with the rising unemployment. But this decline is related, in part, to the conduct of macroeconomic policy, with high real interest rates discouraging investment. The argument that the high unemployment in mature economies is due to jobs being exported to third world economies is rejected by the work of Appelbaum and Schettkat (1995a, 1995b).

The chapter then considered the argument by Appelbaum and Schettkat (1995a, 1995b) who focus on the balance between output demand growth and productivity growth. Appelbaum and Schettkat (1995a, 1995b) argued that if a country could not shift employment from manufacturing activities to service activities, then it would see little employment growth. By the 1980s, it was becoming apparent that the industries in Australia with the most rapid employment growth were those in the service sectors with low productivity growth. The previously strong employment industries failed to achieve demand conditions that allowed employment growth to outstrip productivity growth. The share of total manufacturing in GDP was around 28 per cent in the late 1960s and dropped to 19 per cent by the end of the 1980s. So the loss of employment is not just due to productivity growth. The failure to maintain the same output growth rate as the services sector has also led to the declining contribution to total employment. This is an aggregate demand problem.

Whatever the compositional changes that have led to employment shifts across industries, none of the discussion in this section negates the view that ultimately mass unemployment is due to demand-deficiency exacerbated by the failure of governments to employ appropriate expansionary policies.

A final orthodox argument relates to the argument that the rising unemployment rates are due to compositional changes in the labour force, especially as a result of women becoming a rising percentage of the total labour force. The empirical analysis refutes this notion and shows that the demographic groups with high relative unemployment rates have actually reduced their impact on the overall unemployment rate. In fact, the overall unemployment rate would have been higher in 1998 had the labour-force demographic composition remained as it was in August 1978.

As later chapters argue, the main solution to unemployment is to use government to help stimulate the economy and to act as an employer. The capitalist system has cast aside the long-term unemployed and rendered them 'valueless' in terms of their contribution to production. The social costs of this are enormous and threatening. The role of the government has to lie in getting the unemployed back to work. This will require considerable re-orientation of the way we think about employment and government. Unfortunately, we are some way from that change.

CHAPTER 4

Are Wage Cuts the Answer?
Theory and Evidence

P.N. Junankar

> When the rich argue that tax cuts for the rich and wage or
> social benefit cuts for workers are the only way to cure
> unemployment about which the rich care deeply, every
> economist's eyebrows should rise.
>
> *Freeman 1998, p. 15*

A comparison over time and across different countries leads to an inevitable conclusion: deregulated labour-markets do not necessarily lead to full employment and regulated markets do not always lead to high unemployment. In the 1960s unemployment rates in the USA (which has a deregulated labour-market) were higher than in Japan (a regulated labour-market). In the 1960s and 1970s West Germany (a regulated labour-market) had very low unemployment rates, but it has very high unemployment in the 1990s! The USA in the 1990s has relatively low (official) unemployment rates but had high unemployment rates in the 1960s and 1970s. The UK deregulated its labour-market under Margaret Thatcher from 1979 onwards but its unemployment rate rose sharply and remained very high, declining slightly in the last couple of years. There are many economists, politicians and policy-makers who believe that a simple remedy of wage cuts exists to cure unemployment. This is certainly the consensus in Canberra. This chapter argues that this argument is specious and false.

The chapter proceeds as follows. The next two sections discuss orthodox accounts of unemployment. This is followed by three sections which probe and critique orthodox accounts, particularly in terms of unemployment in models of imperfect competition, efficiency wage models and so-called insider/outsider models. The question of whether governments have the capacity to impose wage cuts is then addressed. This is followed by an examination of the evidence on labour-market flexibility and unemployment. A final section concludes the chapter.

Unemployment in a neoclassical model of a competitive economy

The orthodox (or neoclassical) view of the labour-market is based on an idealised market: there are a large number of buyers and sellers of labour services who act independently of each other (i.e. there are no unions and there are no monopolies). The market behaves like an auction market: if there is excess demand the price is bid up, if there is excess supply the price is bid down and trade only takes place at an equilibrium price (wage rate).

In this abstract world, the demand for labour is determined by profit-maximising firms facing a given production function (technology) and given prices of output and inputs (including labour). Firms can hire as many workers (or as many hours of work) as they please at a given wage rate. Since it is assumed that firms are maximising profits, they would hire workers until the extra revenue they get by selling the extra output produced by an additional worker just equals the additional cost of hiring the worker, i.e. the wage rate.[1] Workers are assumed to be driven by maximising utility (doing as best as they can given the conditions they face) where they can work as many hours as they wish at the given wage rate. Labour supply and labour demand determine equilibrium employment and unemployment, independently of the goods market or the money market.

Unemployment in this model is voluntary: the unemployed are those people who are unwilling to work at the current market wage but would be willing to work only if they were paid higher wages. In this model monetary or fiscal policies that affect aggregate demand have no impact on unemployment as these policies (by assumption) do not affect the marginal productivity of labour. Only supply-side policies that affect the production function (and hence the marginal product of labour) or changes in labour supply due to changes in tastes or due to tax or social security policies would influence unemployment.

In this model, involuntary unemployment is possible if for some reason wages are fixed above equilibrium, either by governments imposing minimum wages or by non-competitive forces like unions. With wages artificially fixed above market clearing rates unemployment would result. In this case a reduction in real wages would lead to an increase in employment and a reduction in unemployment. Hence, the orthodox case for cutting wages relies on a labour-market that operates like an auction market for (say) fresh fish or tomatoes (Quiggin 1997): if there is an excess supply for the commodity, its price falls; if there is an excess demand, the price rises to clear the market. The only reason for the market to not clear is due to 'interference' by the government or by unions.

Orthodox economists would argue that if we abandoned minimum wages we would solve the problem of unemployment. Their argument is essentially based on a simple competitive labour-market as discussed above. In the discussion below of alternative models, we show how this conclusion is invalid in a model where employers have monopsony power (i.e. an employer has to pay higher wages if they wish to hire more people) or where productivity of workers is linked to the wages paid (see under efficiency wages below).

The orthodox version of the labour-market was criticised by Keynes (1936) when he argued that the labour-market was different from an auction market. Keynes maintained that if nominal wages were cut for one group of workers, it would affect the *relative* wages of that group, who would oppose the wage cuts. He also argued that a cut in everyone's wages would lead to a fall in aggregate demand (as wages were incomes for workers) which would then lead to a fall in consumption expenditures and hence a *rise* in unemployment.

Another set of the criticisms of a classical/neoclassical model came from Keynesian theorists, e.g. Barro and Grossman (1971). Essentially these criticisms were based on the view that there was a co-ordination failure: because the output market did not clear (prices were not perfectly flexible), demand for labour was constrained to less than what was required to produce full employment. For example, during a recession automobiles pile up in yards until eventually the firms cut back production and decrease overtime, stop replacing staff who leave, start laying off workers, and eventually make workers redundant. In other words, they do not cut prices to clear the inventories that are piling up in the yards. Hence, the problem of unemployment was not due to rigidity of wages (either due to governments or unions) but due to a failure of the price system to operate in the real world without any problems.

If for some reason the output price did not adjust in the face of excess supply, then firms would be quantity constrained (minimum of the demand and supply curves) and hence would only demand labour to produce the non-equilibrium output level which was less than the equilibrium level. This would lead to unemployment: cutting wages in this case would not be a solution as the problem was in the output market, not in the labour-market.

The importance of this literature was to shift the focus: blame for unemployment lay not with the workers but with the output market. This led to much debate about the problems of co-ordination failure of the price system: the Walrasian auctioneer[2] was a fiction invented to solve an important theoretical problem by allowing trade to take place only at equilibrium prices.

Some further neoclassical models of unemployment

Another set of models that argue that unemployment is essentially a voluntary phenomenon is based on views of imperfect information in the labour-market. An early version of this is due to Lucas and Rapping[3] (1969) who argued that unemployment is a result of individuals 'intertemporally substituting leisure'. The distinctive feature of this model is that unemployment (leisure) in the current period is substituted for unemployment (leisure) in the future period. Unemployment is voluntary: it is the difference between normal or long-run labour supply and short-run or current labour supply. The reason there is unemployment is because the unemployed are 'enjoying' leisure now while the wage they are being offered is low, and they would work in the future when they expect to have a higher wage offered. It is assumed that they can borrow from their friendly banker to cover their expenditures now based on their expected future earnings.[4] To put it graphically, the unemployed are choosing to be unemployed because they expect to work in the future at a million dollars a week.

The model assumes that we are always in short-run equilibrium, and fluctuations in unemployment are due to fluctuations in the current wage relative to expected future wages. This intertemporal substitution of leisure argument would suggest that workers would quit their jobs in a recession voluntarily: unfortunately (for the authors), the data show clearly that quitting rates are acyclical. Quit rates are low in a recession period and high in a boom. This model was tested on time series data and results did not support the theory of intertemporal substitution of leisure.

A more sophisticated version of this model is based on search theories of unemployment (Phelps 1970; Mortensen 1970). According to these theories, unemployment is a voluntary choice on the part of workers who believe that they would get a higher wage offer than they have received to date. They are simply maximising their utility (satisfaction) by waiting for a higher wage offer. It is assumed that everyone receives wage offers (there is a normal distribution of wage offers). Unemployed workers decide on a 'reservation wage' based on their estimation of the wage distribution, their discount rate and any income they may receive in the absence of accepting a wage offer (e.g. income from assets, unemployment or other social security benefits). The higher the unemployment benefits the higher their reservation wage and hence the longer their duration of unemployment (they can afford to wait longer for this ideal wage offer which exceeds their reservation wage).

A critical assumption made in these models is that job search is either not possible when the worker is employed or that search is more efficient when the person is unemployed. However, for most people job search is in fact more efficient when employed, when stationery, phones and, most importantly, a network of contacts are accessible. To be unemployed provides a negative signal to the prospective employer.

It is, however, strange that most of the unemployed people happen to come from poor families, with low levels of education and training, etc. The highly educated and the well off somehow seem to spend less time searching for a highly paid job! To quote Phelps (1970):

> It would be as senselessly puritanical to wipe out unemployment as it would be to raise taxes in a deep depression. Today's unemployment is an investment in a better allocation of any given quantity of employed persons tomorrow; its opportunity cost, like that of any other investment, is present consumption. (p. 17)

It is difficult to believe that 700 000–800 000 unemployed people are busily investing like crazy when firms are cutting back on investment in real capital goods.

In this model wage cuts would simply lead to searchers spending longer looking for work since they would have formed expectations about their reservation wage on the basis of the previous wage distribution. In other words, a cut in wages would not lead to a fall in unemployment until the labour-market participants changed their reservation wages in response to the wage cuts. Unless there was an accompanying cut in unemployment benefits, this theory would suggest that wage cuts would *increase* unemployment.

Unemployment in models of imperfect competition

Models of imperfect competition are based (essentially) on a paper by Bob Rowthorn (1977) (a Marxist scholar from Cambridge University), although developed independently by Layard, Nickell and Jackman (1991). In these models, unemployment is the mechanism by which the distributional claims of the workers and capitalists (employers) are made compatible, given the available national output. If the demands of the workers and employers exceed the national output, a wage–price spiral ensues until a higher level of unemployment eliminates it. If unemployment is too low, wage-setters would try to raise their relative wages, only higher unemployment would stop this leap-frogging. In equilibrium, what people expect is just realised.

The model consists of firms that use a markup system of pricing where the markup is an increasing function of the level of activity in the economy, proxied by the employment rate (or negatively related to the unemployment rate). Firms set prices by putting a markup on *expected* wages. Wage-setting is done by unions who set wages on a markup on expected prices, with the markup as an increasing function of the employment rate and negative function of the unemployment rate. In other words, firms are not maximising profits but simply use given rules to fix prices.

In this model, the equilibrium point of unemployment is reached when the interaction of the demands of workers, who are more aggressive in times of low unemployment, and the profit margins of employers, which are higher when unemployment is low, balance.

Note that in this model real wages and unemployment are determined simultaneously, so we cannot argue that the cause of unemployment is the high level of wages. Instead the interpretation is that workers expect wages that are too high for the level of unemployment. Alternatively, employers expect too high a profit margin given the workers' demands. Since wages are determined by this interaction of the workers' demands and the employers' bargaining, we cannot prescribe wage cuts as a solution to the problem of unemployment (see below for a further discussion of this issue).

Efficiency wage models

If we find that there is unemployment, why do real wages not fall to clear the labour-market? An interesting explanation is provided by the efficiency wage model (see Akerlof and Yellen 1986). There are several variants of the efficiency wage hypothesis. One version of the theory can be traced back to Marx's *Capital*, while another one can be traced to Leibenstein's theory for less developed economies. The crucial assumption of this theory is that the productivity of a worker is some function of the wage paid to the worker. The different versions of this theory are:

Shirking model: This model is best known from a paper by Shapiro and Stiglitz (1984) where they argued that employers would pay a higher wage (higher than market clearing) and if the workers did not perform adequately they would be fired. Given that unemployment exists, this would provide an incentive for workers not to shirk. This is similar to Marx's argument that unemployment is necessary in a capitalist system to force workers to work hard so that they are not thrown on the scrap heap and do not demand higher wages which would erode the capitalists' profits.[5]

Costs of turnover model: Firms pay higher than market wages in order to lower the costs of turnover of employees. This would be especially important where the workers had job-specific skills and the loss of an employee would entail the firm spending on recruitment and training costs. Again firms choose to pay higher wages in order to get higher profits, which implies an unwillingness to cut wages.

Adverse selection model: The higher the wages paid, the better the quality of workers who apply for the job, and hence productivity and profits are higher. In other words, firms choose to pay higher wages in order to get higher productivity and would not want to cut wages.[6] This is related to the adage, 'if you pay peanuts you get monkeys!'

Sociological models: Higher wages may improve worker morale and hence lead to higher productivity. This may be an important motivation where teamwork is necessary in the workplace. One version of this kind of model comes from Akerlof (1982) which he calls a 'partial gift exchange relationship'. Employers pay more than they have to (i.e. higher wages than the market clearing wage) as a gift and employees return this in part by being more productive than they have to be. This is based on studies by sociologists, psychologists and anthropologists who emphasise the cultural context of decision-making and the importance of treating people well to get the maximum productivity from them.

The assumption behind these theories is that we can calculate the wage which would maximise profits. Obviously, an employer will not be willing to pay an infinitely high wage. There is a trade-off: the higher the wage, the greater the effort provided by workers and thus, the higher the productivity; however, the higher the wage the greater the costs of production and hence the lower the profits. While productivity increases with wages, the increases become smaller and smaller until a profit-maximising wage (called the 'efficiency wage') is reached. Beyond this point, further increases to wages would lead to a greater increase in costs than in revenues.[7]

One important result from efficiency wages models is that wages do not clear the labour-market, that is, wages do not adjust to eliminate unemployment. Employers *deliberately* choose a wage above the market clearing rate in order to get increased effort from the workers (and increased productivity) and hence higher profits. As a result, wages do not respond to changes in supply and demand: there is wage rigidity which is not due to union or government 'interference' in the labour-market but due to the conscious maximising behaviour of the employers. Therefore, unemployment is a necessary feature of a capitalist economy with profit-maximising behaviour. An important implication of this set of theories is that firms *choose* to pay higher wages to extract increased effort and higher productivity from workers. They would not wish to cut the wages of their employees! Wage cuts are not even a rational response to the problem of unemployment.

Insider/outsider theory

In a series of articles and books, Lindbeck (1993) has argued that unemployment is due to bargaining between employers and unions where the unions are concerned about the plight of their employed members (the insiders) and tend to ignore the plight of the unemployed (the outsiders). Wage bargaining then sets wages which are 'too high' to clear the labour-market and unemployment persists. If for example productivity increases because of improved production methods, the workers would demand higher wages for the 'insiders' and ignore the 'outsiders'. Gregory (1998) argues that the different time paths of US and Australian unemployment rates are partly explained by the insiders in Australia capturing the productivity gains (especially after the introduction of enterprise bargaining), whereas in the US, they did not.

Can government policy impose wage cuts?

The theoretical material above suggests reasons to question orthodox accounts of wage cuts as a solution to unemployment. However, assuming a government was committed to a wage-cuts policy, could such a policy be implemented? To answer this question, it is first necessary to distinguish between money wages and real wages. At the level of the employment relationship, an employer may be able to cut the money wages of employees but whether it leads to a cut in real wages depends on whether the price level remains constant. If all employers cut money wages, then everyone would probably be worse off and workers would cut their expenditure on consumption goods (see Malinvaud 1982). Consumer goods prices would then fall, and the fall in money wages might be alleviated or real wages might even rise. Hence, the money wage cut may or may not lead to a real wage cut. What is necessary according to orthodox economists to increase employment (or decrease unemployment) is a cut in *real* wages. Malinvaud (1982) also argues that low wages may hinder capital accumulation and lead to lower productivity in the long run. Although wage cuts may be advantageous from the point of view of one firm/employer, wage cuts by all firms simultaneously could have negative consequences on the economy as a whole. It should also be noted that what is important for firms is not the level of wages, but the unit labour costs of production which also depends on productivity. Therefore, wage cuts are not a solution if they lead to a fall in productivity – and a rise in unit labour costs.

The simple solution of cutting wages to lower unemployment, as proposed by some politicians and some economists, is not feasible. According to models that assume perfect competition in the labour-market, wage rates are determined by the demand and supply of labour. The only way to affect wage rates is to influence the demand or supply of labour. As we saw above, in more realistic models that assume imperfect competition, wage rates are determined by the joint behaviour of firms who use a markup pricing system and workers who are bargaining for higher wages. Again, government policy has to lead to a change in the behaviour of employers or workers: it is not obvious which policies would lead employers or employees to change their behaviour such that they increase employment but at lower wage rates. In efficiency wage models wage rates provide an incentive to workers to raise productivity. In this situation, government policy to encourage firms to cut wages would be counterproductive.

Finally, wage cuts are feasible when minimum wages are legislated. In Australia the complex system of minimum wages is slowly being eroded (first by Keating's enterprise bargaining, and now by the coalition government's Australian Workplace Agreements). The government could certainly introduce legislation to cut minimum wages for low-paid workers (especially for youths). However, it would be difficult for the government to change the award wage system for the low-paid workers without changing the industrial relations system even further, or by abolishing the Australian Industrial Relations Commission. Such drastic changes would require some form of agreement with the unions or an election victory following an announced platform to remove award wages completely. The Hawke–Keating Accord on wages was a significant agreement forged at a time of consensus politics and is unlikely to be repeated. The impact of the Accord on wages and employment is considered later when the evidence is discussed for the impact of wage cuts on employment and unemployment.

However, as noted above, and as argued more fully below, the simple theory that a cut in minimum wages would lead to an increase in employment and a decrease in unemployment is based on a competitive labour-market model which appears to be at variance to real world experience. If we use the efficiency wage arguments a cut in minimum wages may increase the turnover of low-paid staff, lower the average productivity of labour, and lower the profits of the employer.

Evidence on labour-market flexibility and unemployment

For some time now, orthodox institutions like the OECD have been arguing that labour-market flexibility is likely to lead to higher rates of employment and lower rates of unemployment. What does 'labour-market flexibility' mean? Generally, it is taken to mean an absence of minimum wages, no restrictions on employers firing workers, an absence of unions, and limited social security benefits (low unemployment benefits relative to wage levels and restricted for short periods of time) (see OECD *Jobs Study* 1994a and Gregg and Manning 1997). In other words, labour-market flexibility is usually taken to mean shifting the power balance in bargaining towards the employer and away from workers, with attendant downward pressure on wage levels.

Yet if we compare Australia over the period of the Accord with the UK after the labour-market deregulation of the Thatcher era, it is clear that labour-market flexibility does not necessarily provide ideal outcomes (Gregg and Manning 1997, pp. 409–10). Australia followed a quasi-corporatist strategy with a tight incomes policy (the Accord) and maintained its award wage system, while the UK deregulated the labour-market. By any of the usual criteria used to judge economic performance, Australia outperforms Britain. Looking at GDP, industrial production, employment, unemployment, long-term unemployment, inflation, net trade, Australia did significantly better (see Junankar 1997; Gregory this volume). The reason for the relative success of the Accord was not simply that real wages were kept under control, but also that industrial peace had been declared, which gave investment a boost which helped a rapid growth of employment (see Chapman, Dowrick and Junankar 1991).

Minimum wages

There is now a significant literature that shows that, in contrast to what orthodox theory maintains, minimum wage regulations have either a zero or positive effect on employment outcomes. This has been demonstrated in microeconomic studies in the US by Katz and Krueger (1992) and Card and Krueger (1995), and in the UK by Machin and Manning (1994). Card and Krueger's 1995 work, for example, shows that if we relax the assumption of perfect competition, a cut in minimum wages may actually lead to a decrease in employment. They show that if we allow for a monopsonist employer, then the solution of wage cuts breaks down.

In a more recent study of the impact of minimum wages on employment, the OECD *Employment Outlook 1998* estimated cross-country (pooled over time) regressions for a sample of OECD countries which had minimum wage legislation (curiously excluding Australia). It found that:

- the results suggest that a rise in the minimum wage has a negative effect on teenage employment;
- negative employment effects for young adults are generally close to or insignificantly different from zero;

- for prime age adults, the most plausible specifications suggest that minimum wages have no impact on their employment outcomes (pp. 47–8).

However, the investigators are cautious in their conclusion and emphasise the 'fragility of the results in Table 2.5' (OECD 1998a, p. 47). They add, however: 'At the same time, it is important to note that these estimated effects are relatively insignificant in terms of explaining the large decline that has occurred in the teenage employment-population ratio in some countries' (OECD 1998a, p. 48). The employment elasticities are statistically significant for the 15–19-year-old groups but are relatively small, of the order of about −0.4. These are particularly small for a group of young people whose education level has increased significantly. In other words, they have not allowed for young people choosing to stay on in education, but have assumed that the differences in employment over time and country are due to employers' cost-minimising demand functions. The OECD (1998a, p. 70) indicates that differences and changes in school retention rates are likely to affect the estimates and this is a matter for further research.

Most estimates of the responsiveness of employment to wage cuts suggest that it is relatively small (Freeman 1998; Boltho and Glyn 1995, p. 464). However, in a study of the youth labour-market for the Productivity Commission, Daly et al. (1998, pp. xii, xiii) assert:

> even among teenagers, who are often most affected by minimum wages, the proportion being paid the minimum wage is relatively small. Minimum wage studies do not say anything about what would happen if the wages of the remaining teenagers were changed relative to employees in other demographic groups. Studies that can examine this question look at substitution between particular types of labour. The estimated responsiveness of youth employment to youth wages in these studies is considerably higher than the estimates from the minimum wage studies. The weight of evidence suggests a relatively large (much more than proportionate) decline in youth employment in response to an increase in the youth wage.

However, Junankar, Waite and Belchamber (1998) criticise the paper on several counts, but especially because, rather than using minimum wages, Daly et al. use average wages, which are chosen by the firm to get increased efficiency. Many of the workplaces in the Daly et al. study pay youths more than the minimum wage, presumably because they believe, along efficiency wage lines, that they would get higher productivity, and higher profits, as a result. In their research Junankar, Waite and Belchamber (1998) use minimum wages and detailed data for employment of youths for every separate year of age, but they are unable (in general) to find significant wage elasticities. That is, the link between wage levels and employment is relatively weak.

Debelle and Vickery (1998) estimate that it would require a 10 per cent cut in the *real* wage to increase employment by a mere 4 per cent. Argy (1998, p. 97) concurs, arguing experience shows that changes in the relative wages of women and youth do not have a strong effect on employment and that 'the wages of low-skilled workers already in employment are likely to adjust downwards in response to competition from the low-skilled unemployed leaving the job prospects of the latter largely unchanged' (1998, p. 97). In a similar vein, Freeman (1988) reports that mechanisms that reduce the price of labour, such as publicly funded wage subsidies, do not generally produce strong employment growth.

In an important recent paper, Hancock (1999) presents data from a sample of 19 OECD countries that indicate there is no relationship across countries between labour-market flexibility (as measured by wage dispersion) and employment levels. He also tests the orthodox idea that lower wages will increase employment. Using Australian data from the last two decades, he finds little or no relation between employment and the wage share of national income. Testing this idea across a sample of 10 OECD countries, Hancock comes to the surprising finding that: 'superior employment performances are associated with *higher* wage shares' (1999, p. 15) (original emphasis). He concludes that the evidence 'calls into question the *realism* of seeking to compress wages further . . . Arguments about excessive real wages do not, on this evidence go to the heart of the unemployment problem' (original emphasis).

As many critics have pointed out, employment and unemployment dynamics involve critical market segmentation and spatial dimensions that mean that labour-markets do not operate as the textbook model predicts (Quiggin 1997). In a highly differentiated skill-driven economy, these effects have become even more pronounced in recent decades (Latham 1998, p. 95). Only at the less differentiated bottom end of the market are price-driven effects (i.e. lower wages) likely to impact on employment levels but, as pointed out above, the effects are small. This suggests that the magnitude of wage reductions required to make serious inroads into unemployment presents an unattractive trade-off. As Gregory (1994) explains:

> The argument is that in a deregulated labour market the wage of the long term unemployed will fall and as a result jobs will be created for them. The issue is what is the empirical magnitude of the elasticity of demand for labour? The greater the elasticity the less the wage need fall and the greater the number of jobs created. There is an older econometric literature which suggests that the elasticity might be 0.3. That is, to increase employment by

ten per cent wages need to fall by 33 per cent. To estimate the proportionate increase in the number of jobs needed is not easy but suppose the 300,000 long term unemployed effectively compete with a group of workers that number about one million. If this was a reasonable estimate then to create 300,000 jobs would require a 30 per cent increase in employment and therefore a 90 per cent wage reduction (if the elasticity were 0.3). This is a very large wage reduction indeed. Perhaps the long term unemployed compete with two million workers, if so the wage would need to fall by 45 per cent. These are very large wage falls. (p. 104)

Gregory (1996, p. 100) argues that in Australia, 'if the earnings distribution was to widen further the major effect would be to create greater levels of inequality rather than sufficient jobs at low levels to deliver full employment'. As US experience in the last two decades shows, the neoliberal model offers unacceptable increases in inequality and mass poverty.[8]

Centralisation

There has been a debate in the literature on whether deregulated labour-markets provide better outcomes than regulated markets. Calmfors and Driffill (1988), for example, using cross-section data from studies of OECD economies, showed that there appeared to be a hump-shaped relationship between centralisation and unemployment. Very low and very high levels of centralisation were good for reducing unemployment, but intermediate levels were poor. Freeman (1988) found some supporting evidence although he emphasises the considerable diversity of performance and argues that there is no 'particular set of labour-market institutions as the simple key to success' (p. 79). In a more recent paper Freeman (1998) is circumspect about the hump-shaped relationship and discusses the problem that institutions themselves are influenced by economic history.

Similar results were obtained by Rowthorn (1992) – he showed that countries with high levels of wage dispersion (i.e. with unregulated labour-markets) had worse labour-market outcomes than those with low levels of wage dispersion. Moreover, the OECD (1997, ch. 3) casts strong doubt on the original Calmfors and Driffill findings, arguing that there is no statistically significant hump-shaped relationship between unemployment and centralisation. In fact it found that centralised/co-ordinated economies had a *lower* wage inequality and *lower* unemployment rates. As Chowdhury (1994) and Soskice (1990) point out, the Calmfors and Driffill study suffers from a major problem: countries and associated industrial relations systems are empirically misspecified and their results are strongly influenced by the existence of outliers such as Switzerland and Japan, and the treatment of the Japanese and German systems as laissez-faire.

Nickell (1997) argues that the popular view that the flexibility of the labour-market in North America has led to low unemployment, while the inflexibility of the labour-market in Europe has led to high unemployment is wrong. In the 1950s and 1960s unemployment rates in the USA were generally higher than in most European countries, while in the 1980s and 1990s the situation has reversed even though labour-market institutions have remained more or less unchanged over the period (except for, especially, the UK). Moreover, in a study comparing Australia, the UK and New Zealand, Sloan and Wooden (1998) found that labour-market outcomes did not vary much between these countries, despite the fact that the UK and New Zealand had much more deregulated labour-markets than Australia. Australia in fact, over the last decade or more, has enjoyed faster employment growth than both New Zealand and the UK.

Rowthorn (1992), using cross-section data for the OECD, finds a positive relationship between wage dispersion and decentralisation: where wage bargaining is decentralised, overall wage dispersion is higher. He also finds little empirical support for the view that wage flexibility (as proxied by wage dispersion) has a positive impact on employment.

In an interesting paper Gregory and Sheehan (1998) argue that employment growth in Australia has been more rapid than in the US in the bottom two deciles of the earnings distribution although wage inequalities have increased more in the US. In other words it is not necessary to reduce wages to increase employment. 'There is no evidence for the view that legislation to make the wage system more flexible will have any significant impact on unemployment' (Gregory and Sheehan 1998, p. 348).

Finally, research by the Reserve Bank also cautions against a narrow policy focus on 'labour market flexibility' (Coelli et al. 1994). In a study which examined 14 OECD countries, the researchers probed relationships between wage flexibility (measured by wage dispersion), macroeconomic performance and labour-market institutions. The key findings were as follows:

- on a comparative basis, there appears to be little connection between wage flexibility and labour-market institutions;
- Australia in the 1980s scored well on wage flexibility despite having relatively centralised labour-market institutions;
- wage flexibility in the 1970s and 1980s in Australia was similar to that found in the US, a country which is widely considered to have one of the most decentralised wage bargaining systems among the advanced economies;
- and from the above, any further moves towards wages decentralisation in Australia may not increase wage flexibility;

- finally, and most importantly, wage flexibility does not appear strongly related to macroeconomic performance.

As the report (Coelli et al. 1994, p. 29) concludes, 'A country's macro-economic performance is not obviously related to its wage setting institutions'. Similar findings are reported in a study by Gregg and Manning (1997). They examined links between various forms of labour-market regulation and labour-market performance across 16 OECD countries. They summarised their conclusions as follows:

> If the conventional analysis of labour market regulation is correct, we should expect to find labour market performance to be negatively correlated with benefit duration, replacement ratios, trade union density and coverage, the minimum wage, job tenure . . . Yet when one looks at the results . . . the most striking thing is that it is very rare to find any significant relationships at all . . . There is simply no strong evidence for the conventional view that regulation is associated with poor unemployment performance. (p. 406)

Surveys of employers

In some fascinating research conducted over several years, Bewley (1998) has surveyed a large number of firms with in-depth questioning about the role of wages and employment. He finds that in most cases firms laid off workers due to a decline in product demand or financial setbacks, but not due to demands for wage increases. Firms were unwilling to cut wages in response to a fall in demand as reduced wages would affect productivity through lower morale, as noted by Akerlof (1982; see also Akerlof et al. 1996). Workers would resent pay cuts and their attitude would affect the reputation of the firm which would harm its chances of hiring good workers in good times. Lay-offs affected only a minority of workers, whereas pay cuts would affect the whole workforce and the laid-off workers are no longer on the premises to affect the productivity of the remaining workforce. In separate research, Freeman (1998) also rejects the view that workers have unrealistic expectations about wages leading to their unemployment: 'There were few indications that unemployed people had excessive wage expectations. On the contrary, many unemployed people were too flexible and found themselves rejected by firms as over qualified' (Freeman 1998, p. 459).

Summary

To summarise: money wage cuts may not lead to real wage cuts. Money wage cuts may lead to increased unit costs due to a fall in productivity. Even if money wage cuts led to a fall in unit labour costs, the impact on employment and unemployment is likely to be very small. Finally, wage cuts are not a sensible policy because firms do not want to cut wages as it affects workplace morale and hence productivity. If firms do not want to cut wages then the government cannot impose wage cuts. The policy is neither economically rational nor is it feasible.

Wage cuts do not solve the unemployment problem. Cuts in welfare benefits do not solve the unemployment problem. Unless the government is willing to expand demand by direct government expenditures and by providing incentives to the private sector to expand investment and production, high unemployment will continue. Labour-market programs in conjunction with appropriate macroeconomic policies would help the unemployed to find satisfying work. We cannot afford to continue to run an economy with high levels of unemployment. Besides the obvious waste of resources which could be producing large amounts of consumer goods, we are dampening future levels of GDP as investment is lower and human capital is being destroyed due to unemployment. What is needed is a concerted program by the OECD countries to expand aggregate demand in the economy. The old monetarist remedies which have been pushed by the IMF and many neoclassical economists have clearly not worked. It now seems that a change in thinking is taking place: even the IMF is telling Japan it should expand government expenditure and cut taxes. That is a good Keynesian remedy. We should try it in Australia as well!

CHAPTER 5

The Impact of Labour-Market and Economic Reforms in the UK, NZ, Australia and the US

R.G. Gregory

Free-market reforms of various kinds have dominated economic policy in the advanced economies since the 1970s. Some countries, notably Britain and New Zealand, have made sweeping changes in the direction of small government, privatisation and labour-market deregulation. But how much influence do such shifts in economic reform policy have on the macroeconomies of the advanced economies? Do increases in the pace of reform deliver a noticeable increase in the rate of economic or employment growth in countries such as New Zealand, Australia and the UK?

Once the task of assessing the impact of economic reforms is begun, a number of important lessons are learnt very quickly. Perhaps the most important is that assessment is not a straightforward exercise.

One problem is that the potential gains from reform are exaggerated during the process of gathering support for the changes. This process often leads to a loss of objectivity, after the reforms, as assessors of the outcomes tend to produce evidence that is consistent with their initial position as supporters or opponents of the reforms. All economies experience good and bad changes through time and by the appropriate selection of facts it is always possible to tell good or bad stories. Putting together what would be widely regarded as a balanced assessment is very difficult.

Another problem relates to the timing of the assessments. It is often suggested that the costs of reform occur quite quickly – job displacement and business failures for example – and that the gains take longer. New businesses do not grow up and thrive overnight and new jobs take time to be created. But there is no clear view as to how long it will take before reforms pay off. Hence, when faced with disappointing evidence, reform advocates claim that the evaluation is too soon. In the longer term, when reforms are likely to have their greatest permanent impact, there may be a new political agenda and the careful linking of current outcomes to reforms in the distant past is not a high priority. Longer run balanced assessments of reforms are often quite scarce.

Finally, in many countries, and in so many instances, post-reform macroeconomic outcomes seem surprising and disappointing, which suggests either that reforms do not deliver promised results or that their impact is easily swamped by other influences on the economy. The impact of non-reform factors on the economy, and their potential to mask post-reform outcomes, raises the difficult problem of the counter-factual, that is, what would have happened to the economy if the reforms had not taken place. Perhaps the lack of good outcomes from reforms is the result of negative non-reform factors swamping good reform outcomes.

The isolation of reform impacts is a difficult problem that is often handled by construction of a computer model of the pre-reform economy that is then subject to the reform change and the reform results simulated. The obvious inadequacy with this approach is that the model is usually designed to deliver good results from the reforms. The arguments for the reforms and the design of the model are based on the same theoretical view of the economy. The counterfactual problem therefore will always remain.

These difficulties suggest that it would be unwise to be too dogmatic when evaluating reforms, that inevitably there is no escape from exercising considerable judgement and that the assessment of outcomes may change over time as new evidence is accumulated. The difficulty of the task explains, in part, why opinions vary so much as to whether particular reforms are a success or a failure.

In this chapter we focus on labour-market and economic reforms and their impact on economic growth, employment and wage outcomes in the longer term. To make the task more manageable, we describe the economic growth experiences of four English-speaking countries. We look at the impact of the Thatcher reforms in the UK, the Douglas reforms in New Zealand, and the Hawke Accord period and subsequent labour-market reform in Australia. The US is taken as a comparison country that has not been subject to substantial shifts in government-introduced labour-market and economic reforms except, perhaps, in the area of immigration and very recently in the area of welfare reforms. The welfare reforms are substantial but it is too early for their impact to influence our comparisons significantly.

We adopt a very aggregative approach. The focus is on four data series taken from the OECD Economic Outlook database: the analysis is based on measures of:

- output produced for the residents of each country (GDP per capita);
- the proportion of the population employed (the employment–population ratio);
- the changing living standards of the employed population (the rate of growth of real compensation per employee); and
- the changing distribution of full-time weekly earnings.

It is important to present the macro data because it helps set the framework for other chapters in this volume.

The major advantage of this aggregative analysis is that it provides a macro framework that acts as a constraint on exaggerating the losses and gains that may be identified from a more piecemeal assessment. The disadvantage, of course, is that the diversity of experience within the aggregates is lost.

A brief guide to the reforms

For the past 40 years at least, governments seem to have been promising that a new bout of economic reform will quickly lead to faster economic growth, higher incomes and more jobs. This strong belief in the suddenness of the large 'pay-off' from government-induced economic reform became clearly apparent in the UK during the 1960s. Harold Wilson, the Labour leader, promised that, if elected, he and the Labour Party would reform the British economy and the electorate would experience the white heat of a technological and economic revolution. All would gain. Reform was to be achieved by more government involvement in the economy especially in the planning of economic growth and the development of new technologies.

A decade and a half later, in 1979, Prime Minister Thatcher was also to promise radical reform and gains to all in the UK but the meaning of economic reform had changed in a very fundamental way. Reform now meant that the economy should become less subject to government involvement and all should be less dependent on government. The labour-market was to be subject to special attention. Where possible, centralised wage-fixing authorities were to be weakened and more of the responsibility for wage outcomes and employment conditions was to be negotiated between individual firms and their workers. The power of unions was to be reduced.

This shift in the nature of reform has occurred in most OECD countries. Economic reform is now primarily thought of as a change from more to less government intervention and as a process that frees up product and labour-markets. This change in emphasis has also occurred in Australia, although the change was not quite as stark as in the UK and the timing was different. The Whitlam Labor government during the early 1970s initially promised more government intervention in the economy and faster economic growth that would benefit us all. But, once in office, the government tended to pursue less regulation and intervention by implementing policies, such as tariff reductions and less restrictive immigration, which led to more involvement in the world economy. After the defeat of the Whitlam government there was, for a while, a move back to greater government intervention in the economy. Industry policy became more interventionist and wage outcomes became more centralised. But from 1983 onwards, the new Hawke Labor government slowly began the process of free-market economic reform and policy was increasingly directed towards integrating Australia more with Asia and increasing the degree of competition in product markets. Tariffs were reduced and exchange rate targeting abandoned. It was hoped that Australia would be dragged upwards by the faster economic growth of the Asian region. The emphasis on government involvement with the labour-market was to continue in the context of an Accord with the unions and, unlike the UK reforms, not a great deal was done to deregulate the labour-market.

More recently, the Howard Liberal and National government has accelerated the process of economic reform and, like the Thatcher government, has been advocating the benefits of labour-market reform and less government involvement in the economy. Industrial relations legislation has been changed and public utilities privatised. Wherever possible, more competition has been introduced to the government and private sector. Our political leaders believe that we should all become less dependent on government for education, health and industry assistance.

Across the Tasman, the New Zealand experience has been similar. During the late 1970s government intervention into the economy and 'think big' strategies were to save New Zealand. Then, following upon the lack of success, the New Zealand government became the most radical of free-market reformists in an attempt to move the economy away from government dependency towards more competition and more expansion into world markets. The reforms, which began in 1984 with the election of a Labour government, have been quite exceptional in their extent, consistency, and speed, and for the level of intervention from which they began. Among OECD countries the New Zealand reforms represent an extraordinary experiment. The reforms were also unusual in that they were based on a 'new' theoretical structure of economics which stressed contestability in markets, transaction costs and public accountability (see the *Reserve Bank Act 1989* and the *Financial Responsibility Act 1994*).

The initial New Zealand reforms of 1984–86 began in the capital and financial sectors and in international trade and monetary policy. During those years wage, price and interest rate controls were removed and the exchange rate initially devalued by 20 per cent and set free to float. These changes were followed by reforms to taxation, corporatisation and public expenditure. The labour-market reforms were introduced during 1990/91. The introduction of the 1991 *Employment Contracts Act* decentralised the New Zealand labour-market and replaced multi-employer collective contracts with individual and single employer agreements. The legislation abolished centralised wage-setting and made compulsory unions illegal. More recently, radical welfare reforms have been introduced.[1]

Finally, the US has also been subject to similar advocacy for reform but the ability of government to intervene or withdraw from the economy is more limited and it is more difficult to marshal political coalitions for reform. Although the US has embarked on extensive and radical welfare reforms that have influenced the labour-market, these changes have only recently occurred and do not affect our analysis. The US economy therefore provides a counterfactual or a backdrop against which the evolution of the other economies can be judged.

Evaluating the reforms

Many of the reforms could and should be evaluated on a micro basis. Thus, where a public utility is privatised, the evaluation should focus on such things as changes in price and quality of customer service, and changes in the cost of production and workplace practices. There are some studies that adopt this approach (see various chapters in Silverstone et al. 1996) but in the rhetoric associated with reforms there is clearly a macro focus and a belief that the reforms will speed up the process of economic growth. The Productivity Commission in Australia, for example, always argues that Australian living standards in aggregate will noticeably drop behind those of other countries unless the process of free-market reform is continued and perhaps increased. In this chapter therefore we adopt a macro focus and search for interrelationships between periods of reform and changes in the macroeconomic growth rate.

The history of GDP per capita
The long sweep 1960–96

The purpose of most economic reform is to increase the amount of goods and services available for the citizens of the country. Therefore, as a first approximation, the reforms might be assessed by their impact on the growth of GDP per capita, that is, the amount of goods and services produced per man, woman and child. Of course, this is not an ideal measure of economic progress. GDP, as conventionally measured, does not take into account many of the economic costs of reform such as loss of well-being and perhaps ill-health associated with job displacement, changes to the environment, movements towards a less desirable income distribution, and so on. Furthermore, GDP per capita does not take into account the cost of producing the output. The same GDP per capita with more voluntary leisure is obviously better than the same GDP per capita produced by more workers, longer hours of work and less voluntary leisure. Nevertheless, GDP per capita is probably the best place to begin.[2]

We take real GDP per capita in 1960 for each of the four countries, create an index number and set it equal to unity. We then trace out the change in the index over the thirty-six years to 1996 (figure 5.1). By setting the index at unity for each country we put aside differences in the level of GDP per capita across countries and direct our attention to changes in GDP over time.

There are two very noticeable features of figure 5.1. First, for Australia, UK and the United States, there is very little difference in the rate of growth of GDP over the three and a half decades. In terms of changes in output per capita, the three economies seem hardly distinguishable. This is an important and somewhat surprising result. The average growth rate of GDP per capita from 1960 to 1996 is 1.8, 1.9 and 1.7 for Australia, the UK and the US respectively. The difference in growth rates is less than .02 per cent.

The following observations seem to follow from the fact that three countries have experienced similar growth rate outcomes.

- Per capita income growth seems to be largely independent of population growth. Over this period the population of Australia doubled, that of the US increased 60 per cent and that of the UK increased 11 per cent. And yet, the growth of GDP per capita is approximately the same in each country.
- The reformist periods may not have had far-reaching effects on these economies. In terms of GDP per capita growth rates, the Australian and UK histories do not seem very different from that of the US. Of course, if the reforms had not occurred, the time path followed by GDP per capita may have been different across countries but that is doubtful.
- Because the GDP growth rates are similar across the three countries, there has been no obvious and consistent income catch-up to the US. Australian and UK income levels are still approximately 20–30 per

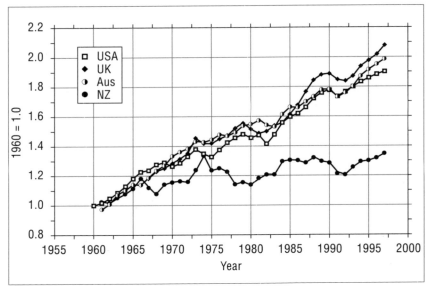

Figure 5.1 GDP/population indices: Australia, UK, USA, NZ
Source: OECD Economic Outlook Database

cent lower than the US. It is possible that with increases in the rate of
international capital flows and technology across countries that the
income gaps between the US, UK and Australia might have narrowed
in a way that was noticeable. The hope that, as Australia becomes
more linked into the world economy, our growth rate would increase
and income levels would approach those of the US has not been
fulfilled.

- There seems to be some advantage from looking at a long period of
  time because there are sub-periods when one country does better
  than the others, only to fall back again during a later period.
- The data for Australia, UK and the US trace out a relationship with
  time that seems to be linear. Consequently, in growth rate terms, there
  is evidence of a slowing down in the GDP per capita growth rate,
  although this reduction is not very substantial. The average rate of
  growth of GDP per capita of the three economies averaged 2.5 per
  cent between 1960 and 1975 but only 1.0 per cent between 1975
  and 1996.

The second noticeable feature of figure 5.1 is that the New Zealand
growth performance is clearly quite different from that of the other three
countries. Among OECD countries, and especially over the last two and a

half decades, New Zealand has been the worst performer by a very large margin. This deterioration stemmed largely from the separation of the New Zealand economy from UK primary product markets during the 1970s. The deterioration in growth rates created a sense of crisis in New Zealand and established the preconditions for radical reform over a decade later.[3] Quite clearly something was wrong – government felt that something must be done in an attempt to increase the growth rate. Initially, during the 1970s, New Zealand tried the interventionist policies of Prime Minister Muldoon but as these policies failed, the pressure to do something else was growing with each passing year.[4] This is an important point. The better performance in Australia during the 1970s and 1980s helps to explain, in part, why reform was not as radical here and was introduced more slowly. There seemed to be less need for change in Australia.

The shorter period

Although it appears that any reform influence is slight when measured against the long sweep of history, and in terms of per capita GDP growth rates, reform effects may be more apparent if the period of analysis is shortened. To examine the effects of the Thatcher reforms, we rebase the GDP per capita indices at unity in 1979, the first year of the Thatcher government. We then subtract the UK GDP per capita index from that of Australia and express the difference as a proportion of the UK GDP per capita index. This indicates the change in the GDP/per capita between the two countries relative to 1979. Then the gains and losses of UK output, relative to Australia, are accumulated by applying a running sum to the gaps (figure 5.2).

For the first six years after 1979, the increase in the GDP per capita index was greater in Australia, then the UK gradually narrows the gap. If the difference in the path of GDP per capita between the countries was only a product of the reforms, then at the beginning of the period we would expect to see the usual costs of reforms, in terms of lost GDP, but the eventual improvement in GDP some years later. This is the pattern we observe.

It was eleven years after the reforms began before the UK made up for lost output, relative to Australia, and then the UK continued to gain an additional increment in output each year. By 1997, after almost 20 years, the UK has accumulated approximately two months, the equivalent of a little less than an additional three days work for each of the 20 years. A similar calculation shows a falling behind of the UK relative to the US in the early period and a catch-up later. But over the period as a whole the accumulated gains and losses of output per capita offset each.

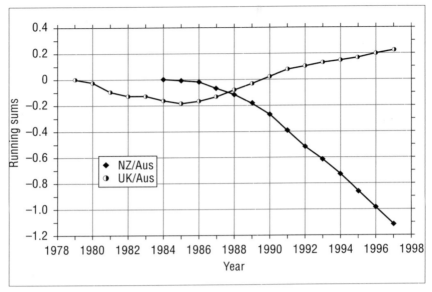

Figure 5.2 Running sums NZ–Australia and UK–Australia GDP/population
indices

Source: OECD Economic Outlook Database

These are obviously crude calculations – they attribute all the differences between Australia and the UK and between the UK and the US to
the greater pace of reforms in the UK. Despite their crudity they do
suggest that the differences in GDP per capita growth rates between the
countries are very small and that promises of large changes in growth
rates in response to reform seem astray. The calculations suggest that
relative to Australia there was a very small gain from the Thatcher
reforms but the gains took at least six years to become evident. Relative
to the US there was no gain.

To focus on the New Zealand reforms, we perform the same calculations but rebase the indices at 1984, when the NZ reforms began (figure
5.2). The story is very different from that generated by the UK reforms.
The relative deterioration of New Zealand growth of GDP per capita is
very marked since 1984 and there is no evidence of a recovery relative to
any of the other three countries. New Zealand has increased its output
per person ratio by 4 per cent over the 13 years while the UK and
Australia have increased their output per person ratios by 34 and 23 per
cent respectively. Thirteen years after the reform process began, New
Zealand has lost one and a quarter years of GDP per person relative to
Australia and the loss continues to grow. A similar story is evident from
a comparison of NZ with the US.

These crude calculations present us with the first set of puzzles. Why were the gains from reforms in the UK so small, relative to Australia, and non-existent, relative to the US? Why is New Zealand so different and why has New Zealand lost so much relative to the other countries? It is not clear how these questions can be easily answered but given the high hopes for the New Zealand reforms, their consistency, their wide-ranging nature and their development against a consistent theoretical model, the results must be extremely disappointing to New Zealanders and to those who advocated the reforms. Indeed, it is perhaps difficult to believe that the outcomes could have been worse if there had been no reforms at all.

Employment outcomes

GDP per capita is only one macro measure of the potential impact of reforms.[5] We now turn our attention to other measures that focus on labour-market impacts. We begin with employment outcomes and then turn our attention to changes in the average wage and its distribution.

The long sweep 1960–96

Since the mid-1970s the average unemployment rate among OECD countries has increased. Among our four countries, all except the US have experienced large increases in unemployment and for Australia and New Zealand the increases, relative to the very low unemployment rates of the 1950s and 1960s, have been very large. For all except the US, unemployment seems to have moved to a new range approximately between 6 per cent and 10 per cent.

Much of the advocacy for labour-market and other economic reforms has been based on the belief that economic reform will increase employment and reduce unemployment. The commonly heard phrases are 'reforms will lead to faster economic growth' and 'faster economic growth will create more jobs'. The relationship between employment and economic growth, which we measure as the growth of GDP per capita, can be summarised by the following identity,

$$Q/P = E/P \times Q/E \tag{1}$$
where:
Q/P is GDP divided by the population,
E/P is the employment–population ratio and
Q/E the level of labour productivity.
This identity can be rewritten in growth rate terms as
$$q = l + p \tag{2}$$

that is, the rate of growth of GDP per capita, q, is identically equal to the sum of the rate of growth of the employment–population ratio, l, and labour productivity, p.

It is clear from equation 2 that an increase in economic growth, q, need not be associated with a faster rate of job creation. The identity is consistent with a wide range of possible relationships between the variables. Faster economic growth, for example, may be associated with a faster rate of productivity growth and if the increase in the productivity growth rate exceeds the increase in the economic growth rate, then employment will fall, relative to the population.

In the economic literature, there is little theory applied specifically to the impact of economic reform on the division of the growth of GDP per capita between the two right-hand components of equation 2. There are different theories for different sets of circumstances. Here are some examples to illustrate the point. When considering economic development in Asia, it is usual to think of the two terms on the right-hand side as independent and to assume that reforms to free up labour and product markets will increase labour productivity and GDP per capita but not reduce the employment–population ratio. This relationship seems to prevail not only in Asia but wherever low-income countries begin to experience fast economic growth.

But what might be expected from labour-market and economic reform in the high-income English-speaking countries? Here there seem to be many different possibilities. One story that is told is the same that is applied to economic development in Asia. It is argued that labour-market reform will increase labour productivity and leave the employment–population ratio unaffected. Under these circumstances, increases in labour productivity are unambiguously a good thing.

Another story, often told by treasurers and prime ministers who are advocating more reform, is that labour productivity increases will add to both employment and GDP per capita. The positive impacts of labour-market and other economic reforms proceed along two channels to increase GDP per capita. Once again reform is unambiguously a good thing.

Finally, it might be argued that reforms that lead to productivity increases, generated by job-shedding, may give rise to lower employment levels and not affect the rate of growth of output. The impact of reform, under these circumstances, is on the two right-hand-side variables of equation 2. The effects are equal and offsetting. This is a version of the Luddite view of technical progress. The Luddites – a group of textile workers based around Nottingham in the early 1800s – believed that new textile technology reduced employment. In response, they set about destroying machines. For nineteenth-century Britain and for the macroeconomy as a whole, we know that the Luddites were wrong. Productivity growth added to income per capita and did not detract from employment

In the short to medium run, it is still possible that lower employment levels may accompany productivity increases. If so, it is important to know whether the reduction is involuntary and adds to unemployment, or whether the extra leisure is valued and taken as shorter working hours or additional holidays. Where the additional leisure is not valued, and reform reduces employment and increases unemployment, productivity improvements may not be a positive force for increased well-being.

The reason why so many different views can be held as to the relationship between economic reforms, productivity and employment is that equation 2 is an identity and not a theory. As an identity equation 2 describes how variables must be related together. To understand the links among the variables, a theory is needed along with additional equations to embody that theory. We will not go down this path but instead focus on actual outcomes.[6]

Figure 5.3 plots the four-country history of the first term of the right-hand side of the identity, the employment–population ratio. The employment–population ratio at 1960 is set equal to unity for each country. So, once again, the focus is on changes through time rather than on the level of the employment–population ratio in each country. Five features are noticeable from figure 5.3.

First, during the 1960s and into the mid-1970s, each country maintained approximate constancy in its employment–population ratio. Economic cycles and variations in economic growth exerted little influence on the employment–population ratio. The large swings in the employment–population ratio date from the mid-1970s and this instability has continued in all countries.

Second, the New Zealand employment experience has been very poor and noticeably different from the other three countries. Over the six years following 1984, when the New Zealand reforms began, the employment–population ratio fell 10 percentage points. New Zealand did not share in the rapid employment growth that was widespread throughout the OECD during this period. There was a strong employment recovery in New Zealand from the 1991 recession but this recovery is not enough to return the employment–population ratio to previous levels.

Third, the Australian and UK experiences are very similar until 1980. Then, during and after the Thatcher reforms, the UK employment performance *deteriorates* relative to Australia. The deterioration appears concentrated in the two periods 1980–83 and post-1990, when UK employment does not significantly recover from the recession.

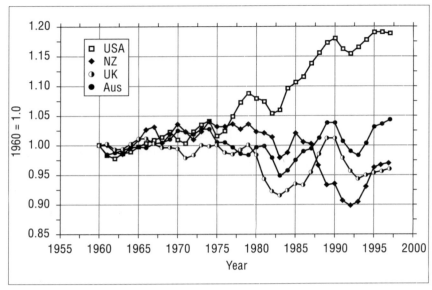

Figure 5.3 Employment/population indices, 1960–97
Source: OECD Economic Outlook Database

Fourth, it is noticeable that the UK and New Zealand employment performances were very poor during the five to seven years after the reforms began. The UK experienced the worst employment outcomes from 1979–84, and New Zealand experienced the worst employment outcomes from 1985–92.

Fifth, the US is very different from the other countries in our sample. Since 1975 the US employment–population ratio has increased 20 per cent while the Australian and UK ratios are not very different from early 1970 levels. The last two decades have seen unprecedented job growth in the US. It is not true therefore that the introduction of computers, or the development of new technologies, has led to job shortages in all developed countries. The US, which has led or shared the adoption of new technologies, has a very different job-growth experience from other OECD countries. For the US the relevant question is: how has the economy achieved such an envious job growth? For Europe, the UK and Australia the relevant question is just the opposite: why has their employment record been so poor relative to the increased demand for employment?

It was shown earlier that the UK, Australia and the US experienced similar growth paths in GDP per capita. That is, there appears to be a fixed relationship across these countries in the right-hand variable of equation 2. But the growth paths of the employment–population ratio are very different. If these differences can be attributed to economic and labour-market reforms, then it appears that reforms exert their most significant impact on employment rather than output.

Given that the growth rates of GDP per capita are similar but the growth rates of the employment–population ratios are different, it follows, from equation 2, that the labour productivity performance must be different across these countries. For these three countries, the dominant experience has been that changes in the two terms on the right-hand side of equation 2 have been offsetting to maintain the identity. Where the employment–population ratio has increased most, the labour productivity index has increased least. Since the mid-1970s therefore the relationship between the employment–population ratio and productivity across these countries seems consistent with a Luddite view of macro outcomes.

This is a very disturbing and surprising result. It follows that the US has achieved a much better employment outcome not by faster economic growth but by lower labour productivity growth. To produce the same rate of output growth as the UK and Australia, the US needed to employ more workers. For the UK the marginally worse employment–population growth rate, relative to Australia, has been offset by a marginally better labour productivity performance. These results suggest that the major differences among these countries relate to employment issues and not different growth rates of GDP per capita.

Does this suggest that we should attempt to prevent technical change and productivity improvements to preserve employment? That would not seem to be a desirable response because the resources being freed by productivity improvements represent opportunities for additional output or additional and desirable leisure if the economy can find ways of utilising these resources. The traditional way of doing this was to increase government involvement in the economy either by training of workers to increase their employability or by adding to demand by producing labour-intensive community outputs. Unfortunately, the present political climate seems to discourage government activity in this area, and, as this book argues, this situation will need to change if unemployment is to be successfully addressed.

Wage changes

In most economies increases in labour productivity are usually associated with increases in average wages. This relationship is very noticeable among our four countries as seen in figure 5.4 which plots the real compensation per employee. The New Zealand data are available only

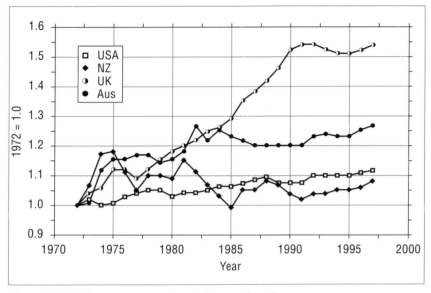

Figure 5.4 Real wage compression indices, 1972–97
Source: OECD Economic Outlook Database

from 1972 and therefore 1972–97 is adopted as the period of analysis. Figure 5.4 tells the following story.

From the mid-1970s, before the Thatcher reforms, the real wage series in the UK grows strongly and this growth continues until 1990 and then the growth is arrested. In terms of real wage increases, the UK has performed much better than the other three economies. It alone has managed to maintain substantial real wage increases through the 1980s. The growth is quite spectacular and, although the growth seems to have begun before the reforms, this experience does lend support to the argument that the UK reforms have increased labour productivity and increased substantially the real wages of the employed workforce.

Australian and UK real wages increase at much the same rate until the early 1980s and then, from the beginning of the Accord period, the path of wages in Australia deviates from that of the UK and there is approximate real wage constancy. The Australian government adopted the policy that real wage moderation was necessary to foster employment growth and while Australian employment grew faster than that of the UK, the additional employment growth was not as great as the additional wage growth in the UK.

New Zealand outcomes are again very poor. Real wages in 1997 are lower than in 1974 and 1975 and there is no clear evidence of the labour-market and economic reforms being associated with average real wage increases.

Finally, it is surprising how sluggish real wage growth has been in the US. By 1996 US real wages are only 11 per cent higher than in 1972. The US real wage series also appears to have much less variation over time, suggesting a very different type of labour-market. What may be said about the distribution of wages among the employed? There is a marked tendency for the distribution of wages to widen in each of these labour-markets. There are no adequate data from NZ, so the focus is placed on the US, UK and Australia.

The tendency for the wage distribution to widen is documented from the full-time weekly earnings for males and females. Weekly earnings are ranked from the lowest to the highest in each country and the ratio calculated for the 90th to the 10th percentile. Table 5.1 presents this ratio for a number of years. The wage distribution is widest in the US, narrowest in Australia. The UK wage distribution lies somewhere in between.

The greatest increase in wage inequality occurred in the UK. The gap between the male wage at the 10th and 90th percentile increased 36 per cent between 1983 and 1996. The increase in inequality is a little less in the US and a little less again in Australia. It appears that in Australia, the Accord process may have slowed the tendency for the wage distribution to widen, but since the early 1990s the rate of growth of inequality has accelerated.

Although the real wage distribution has widened, it is only in Australia and the US that wages have fallen in real terms among the low paid. In the UK wages among the low paid have fallen relative to the median but the increase in the median wage has been sufficient for wages of the low paid to have continued to increase in real terms.

Concluding remarks

It is important, when evaluating reforms, that we keep our eye on the big picture to clearly establish the macro outcomes. In any economy – those that produce good macro outcomes and those that produce bad macro outcomes – there are always some success stories of individual firms, plants and products. The big picture, however, cannot present all the outcomes and must inevitably involve some simplifications. Nevertheless, a very powerful picture emerges with very clear and bold brush strokes.

The major result is that over a period of three and a half decades the UK, Australia and the US have experienced very similar growth rates of GDP per capita which seem largely independent of labour-market and economic reforms. It is as though these countries are all linked together

Table 5.1 Full-time weekly earnings: Ratio of 90th to 10th percentile, wage and salary earners, 20–64 years

	1983	1991	1996	Change 1983–96
Males				
Australia	2.43	2.47	2.76	13
UK	2.75	3.15	3.75	36
USA	4.00	4.31	4.64	16
Females				
Australia	2.32	2.29	2.60	12
UK	2.70	3.02	3.36	24
USA	3.28	3.69	4.09	24

Sources: US   March, *Current Population Survey*
         UK   *General Household Survey*, Office of Population and Census
                    Surveys
         Australia ABS *Weekly Earnings of Employees (Distribution)*,
                    Cat. no. 6310.0

in output terms. Those countries which have introduced the most wide-ranging reforms have not grown any faster. This does not mean that labour-market and economic reforms do not affect output, or are not worthwhile in output terms, it is just that the macro effects are not great enough to be easily observed. The promise of a noticeable change in GDP growth per capita following reforms has not been delivered. We should be very sceptical therefore of claims that particular institutional changes, which may be worthwhile in their own right, will noticeably affect the growth rate of GDP per capita.

Unlike GDP per capita growth rates, there are significant differences in labour-market outcomes. The employment history is very similar across these three countries until the mid-1970s and then employment paths diverge. It appears as though labour-market institutions and reforms are capable of affecting employment–population ratios without substantially affecting GDP per capita. Since the mid-1980s, UK labour productivity has increased relative to Australia and, given that the rate of growth of output seems unresponsive to the reforms, UK employment has fallen, relative to Australia. Something similar has occurred in Australia relative to the US. Australian labour productivity performance has been superior to that of the US and, given that output growth rates do not differ significantly across these countries, the effect of a better labour productivity performance is a worse employment performance.

The real wage history also differs substantially across the countries. The UK has managed to achieve substantial real wage increases throughout the 1980s. By 1990 real wages in the UK were 50 per cent higher than in 1972. This is by far the best performance among these countries and suggests that the reform process may have substantially advantaged those with jobs. The New Zealand experience, however, does not support this conjecture. Average real wages in 1997 are lower than in the early 1970s. There does not seem to be a simple relationship between the extent of economic reforms and real wage growth.

The three countries for which data are available share a growing inequality of wages. The change is greatest in the UK. Despite the Accord process and centralised wage-fixing, Australia has also experienced increased inequality, especially post-1990.

New Zealand presents us with the largest puzzle. The country with the greatest rate of reform has experienced the worst economic outcomes and has lost considerable ground to Australia, the UK and the US in terms of the growth rate of GDP per capita. The reforms have not delivered any noticeable improvement. Employment losses relative to the other three countries far exceed anything that has been seen in any other period over the last fifty years. It now appears, in growth rate terms, that the falling employment–population ratio relative to Australia, the UK and the US may have ceased but there is no obvious evidence of any clawing back of the accumulated losses to date. Real wages have failed to increase in NZ.

The issue for New Zealand commentators therefore is to begin with the knowledge that the reforms have not been successful in terms of the macro aggregates presented here and to try to establish why. What could have been done better? The need to understand what happened in New Zealand is fundamental. After all, the reforms there were consistent with the advice emanating from the World Bank, the IMF, the OECD and most economists. It might be argued that the rate of GDP per capita decline in New Zealand, relative to Australia and the UK, has substantially slowed and that this is the positive outcome from the reforms. But there is no closing of the GDP per capita gap that existed between New Zealand and our sample of countries.

For the UK the reform story is more complicated. In GDP terms, the UK seems to have gained marginally since 1979. In terms of employment though, the losses have been significant but the evidence suggests that the rate at which employment losses are accumulating may have stabilised. Both NZ and the UK share this common experience of early employment losses but no subsequent clawing back of employment losses. The UK, however, has at least gained very large real wage increases.

In terms of output per capita and employment growth, what went wrong in these two countries? Why was the promise of a faster rate of GDP per capita not fully realised? Why were all outcomes so poor in New

Zealand? These questions are difficult to answer. I offer the following observations.

First, in both NZ and the UK, inflation control was a dominant concern in the early reform period rather than labour-market reform. Perhaps, therefore, a considerable amount of the failure to increase the growth rate is related to the role of monetary policy and the costs of reducing inflation. If this is a large part of the reason for the poor performance, then the evidence suggests that the New Zealand monetary reform was particularly poor. Monetary policy has been too tight throughout the whole period and the costs of establishing credibility of monetary policy far higher than the authorities would have imagined.

Second, perhaps despite all the rhetoric and promises, labour-market and economic reforms exert a very small influence on economic growth in a high-income country where the degree of regulation is not that restrictive and where product and factor markets are well developed. Growth rates respond more to other more basic factors such as technical change and saving rates.·

Third, despite the clear evidence of the macro data presented here, there is by no means a unanimous view on reform outcomes for New Zealand (Bates and Snape 1998). Some authors are more optimistic. They tend to focus on other variables, believe that the reforms will take longer to pay off and emphasise that accepting macro outcomes from Australia, the UK and the US as implicit counterfactuals is misleading. It is argued, with some validity, that the need for reform in New Zealand was so great that any reforms must have a high short-run cost. The disjuncture between the old New Zealand economy and that needed for a modern high-income country was too great for the adjustment to be smooth and relatively costless. The major mistake was to believe that the change in the New Zealand economy could be made without paying a high price.

We conclude with a few remarks on unemployment which is the central theme of this book. The official unemployment rate at mid-1998 was 8.2 per cent in Australia, 6.2 per cent in the UK, 7.7 per cent in NZ and 4.5 per cent in the US. The two reform economies, NZ and the UK, have high unemployment rates that are slightly lower than in Australia. It is only the US that has an unemployment rate similar to 1960s levels.

In the long run, differential unemployment outcomes are largely independent of differential rates of economic growth. Each of these countries has experienced similar growth rates per capita since 1960 but unemployment outcomes have been different. During the 1960s unemployment rates were low in the UK and Australia, and relatively high in the US. In the 1980s and 1990s unemployment rates were high in the UK and Australia, and relatively low in the US.

The relationship between productivity growth and unemployment is also not straightforward. Low productivity growth has accompanied low unemployment in the US and high unemployment in NZ.

These results suggest that it is not possible to be certain as to the effectiveness of predicted 'cures' for unemployment. Understanding the unemployment problem is not as straightforward as is often suggested.

To make the discussion of unemployment a little more complicated, let me tie this chapter back to some of my earlier work. My view is that large average real wage increases in Australia and most OECD countries during the mid-1970s were largely responsible for the rising unemployment rates over the following seven or eight years (Gregory 1993). But this emphasis on large average real wage increases, which fits this period well, does not sit well as the explanation of high unemployment since then. There are four problems.

- During the Australian Accord period, average real wages did not increase but there was no growth in the male full-time employment–population ratio. Male unemployment reduced because the male participation rate fell as males withdrew from the labour force (Gregory 1991a). Employment growth was directed primarily towards part-time jobs and jobs traditionally held by women (Gregory 1991a). These jobs did not reduce the unemployment rate but added to the participation rate of women. This experience suggests that the pattern of job growth and its impact on labour-force participation can be important.
- The UK experience of strong real wage growth during the 1980s impacted adversely on employment growth as predicted, but the impact on unemployment was much less than might have been expected. In the UK, male unemployment has also been reduced by withdrawal of males from the labour force. Again the pattern of job growth and its relationship to labour-force changes mattered.
- Three or four years after the 1990s recession, the reduction in Australian unemployment was slow, despite insignificant average real wage increases. In this instance, relative to previous economic recoveries, there was a switch of new job growth away from females and towards males.
- The real wage distribution is widening within these countries as the relative wages of the unskilled, especially males, are falling. This suggests a strong technological influence on unemployment independent of average real wage outcomes. The widening of the relative wages has been greatest in the UK. A similar and smaller growth of wage inequality has occurred in Australia and the US. The pattern of real wage changes, however, does not map into unemployment outcomes across the three countries (Gregory 1996).

Perhaps we cannot proceed far with simple analysis as it has been applied here except to show that common views and prescriptions do not accord well with the data. This suggests that more complex analysis capable of taking into account many influences at the same time is needed. This is the technique of applying econometric models to the economy. The trick will be to use these models to analyse the causes of unemployment without building into the models the results we are seeking.

CHAPTER 6

Is Growth the Answer?

John Burgess and Roy Green

Growth is the answer to unemployment, but it is only part of the answer. This begs the questions of how much growth is required and how it is to be achieved. Growth rates can increase, yet unemployment rates will persist if labour productivity growth accelerates. Growth rates can decline, yet the unemployment rate can also decline if labour-force growth or labour-force participation rates contract. There is no simple or stable relationship between growth and unemployment since there are a number of intervening links, which are neither cyclically nor secularly stable, including productivity growth and labour-force participation rates. The unemployment rate has demonstrated a secular upward trend over the past 25 years and this corresponds with a secular decline in the economy's growth rate (see table 6.1). At the same time there has been a decline in productivity growth and considerable shifts in the distribution of output and employment. As Mitchell briefly showed in chapter 3, and as explored in more detail in this chapter, unemployment has increased and persisted in Australia because growth rates have not been sufficient to generate enough jobs to accommodate both the unemployed and labour-force growth. Why growth rates have declined is beyond the scope of this chapter; however, the Australian experience in this regard mirrors similar experiences across the OECD (Maddison 1991; Glyn et al. 1991) (see table 6.1).

The purpose of this chapter is to investigate the relationship between growth and unemployment in some detail, to identify the unemployment stabilising growth rate, to suggest what growth rate Australia requires over the coming decade in order to achieve full employment, to discuss the obstacles to achieving a sustainable growth path and to briefly outline policies for achieving these growth targets.

Table 6.1 Australia and OECD: Growth rates and unemployment rates

Time period	Real GDP growth %		Unemployment rate %	
	Australia	OECD av.	Australia	OECD av.
1970–79	3.6	3.7	3.7	4.6
1980–89	3.2	2.7	7.7	7.3
1990–96	2.3	1.7	9.2	7.6

Source: OECD *Economic Outlook* June 1988; June 1997

The chapter is organised as follows. The second section reviews the connection between growth and unemployment; in particular it touches on the cyclical versus structural explanations for unemployment together with developments in the relationship between inflation and unemployment (the Phillips Curve) over the past three decades. The third section traces the longer term relationship between Australia's growth rate and its unemployment rate; in particular it highlights the enduring effects of recessions since the mid-1970s on the unemployment rate. Section four sets out the derivation of the unemployment stabilising growth rate, indicates how this can act as a rule of thumb guide for macroeconomic policy and suggests why it should be regarded only as an approximation. Section five investigates the relationship between structural change in the economy and employment growth, and in turn the implications for structural change on the unemployment stabilising growth rate. At issue is whether Australia has entered into a new 'post-industrial' employment phase characterised by aggregate and sectoral shifts in the relationship between growth and employment, and between growth and productivity (Appelbaum and Schettkat 1995a). The sixth section outlines why the unemployment stabilising rate of GDP growth has declined over the past decades in Australia and what realistic and sustainable economic growth target is required in order to eliminate mass unemployment. Section seven outlines a policy program for realising this growth target and discusses why even this may not, in itself, be sufficient to achieve full employment. Finally, the eighth section summarises the debate about whether higher growth can reduce unemployment rates, what the obstacles to higher growth are and whether a policy program for sustaining economic growth is possible.

Unemployment as a cyclical or a structural problem?

Conceptually, a number of explanatory models account for persistently high rates of unemployment in Australia and throughout much of the

OECD, but only one dominates official policy advice from treasuries and central banks. This is the general equilibrium model of neoclassical economics – a 'perfect competition' model where prices and quantities are simultaneously determined in all commodity markets, including the market for factors of production such as labour. To the extent that 'imperfections' are conceded in the model, they are attributed to structural impediments, primarily trade unions and minimum wage regulation, which prevent the theory from operating as it should. Optimal outcomes, including full employment, are achieved in the model only when markets clear, and, correspondingly, the main source of unemployment is found in unions pursuing 'monopoly rents' in the labour-market and tribunals artificially imposing wages in excess of market clearing levels (Green and Burgess 1997). According to the orthodox neoclassical approach, or 'economic rationalism' as it has come to be known in Australia, these impediments explain the breakdown of the empirically established Phillips Curve trade-off between inflation and unemployment, which was thought to be a reliable guide for macroeconomic policy from post-1945 until the early 1970s. With the stagflation of the 1970s and early 1980s, the Phillips Curve was overhauled by the monetarists to incorporate inflationary expectations and an equilibrium unemployment rate (Friedman 1977; Humphrey 1982). Inflation first strategies and the stabilisation of price expectations became the prime function of macroeconomic policy across many OECD economies, including Australia, during the 1980s (Bell 1997a, ch. 6; ILO 1995; Smith and Mahony 1993).

A related innovation by the monetarists was the concept of the 'natural rate of unemployment', or 'non-accelerating inflation rate of unemployment' (NAIRU), which is defined as the rate of unemployment consistent with stable wage and price inflation, taking into account the existing configuration of structural impediments and rigidities within the labour-market. The clear policy implication of the theory is that some proportion of the unemployment rate is structural and cannot be eliminated through higher growth rates. Indeed, higher growth rates can be counterproductive through raising inflation expectations, pushing up wage claims and eventually generating further structural unemployment. A lower NAIRU can only be achieved through labour-market deregulation, entailing legislative restrictions on the role of wage-setting tribunals and trade unions, the removal of minimum wages, restricted access to unemployment benefits, the removal of unfair dismissal provisions and the facilitation of decentralised and individual bargaining (Kniest, Lee and Burgess 1997, ch. 8). In Australia, this approach has provided a justification for key provisions of the 1996 *Workplace Relations Act* concerning the reduced scope of awards and the shift of emphasis from union-negotiated collective agreements to individual contracts. It is also behind the introduction of the work for the dole program and the introduction of the Jobs Network (Burgess, Mitchell, O'Brien and Watts 1998). However, the evidence suggests that such measures affect only the most vulnerable groups in the external labour-market, while pay negotiations in relatively stable internal labour-markets proceed with less regard to the legislative and policy environment. The result is *not* generalised pay restraint but a reinforcement of the tendency to a two-tier workforce, with increasing disparities between a high-status, well-paid core, and a growing periphery of low-paid, insecure part-time and casual workers consisting mainly of women and young people (Burgess and Campbell 1998).

An additional and remarkably pervasive implication of the neo-classical approach is that demand expansion policies will be ineffectual in reducing unemployment below the NAIRU since demand management policies can only eliminate cyclical unemployment in the short term, but have the potential to increase the NAIRU in the long term through increasing price expectations. In this context, the role of demand management is to give priority to inflation, specifically through stabilising price expectations and the target inflation rate. Unemployment reduction becomes secondary and dependent upon a stable inflation environment. The argument suggests that in such an environment, consumer and business confidence will increase, expenditure will expand and unemployment will decline through both the expansion in output and as a result of reduced wage claims associated with lower price expectations (Kniest, Lee and Burgess 1997, ch. 8).

The above approach is reflected in the inflation targets, micro-economic reform proposals and the 'fiscal consolidation' stance of the past and present governments and their orthodox advisers in Treasury and the Reserve Bank (Bell 1997a, ch. 7; Debelle and Vickery 1998; Macfarlane 1997a). However, the evidence of the 'hysteresis' of the natural rate of unemployment makes the orthodox policy position one of supporting increasing unemployment where inflation is above target rates. Hysteresis arises when the natural unemployment rate follows the actual unemployment rate upwards. Cyclical unemployment becomes translated into structural unemployment as the average duration of unemployment increases and the proportion of the unemployed who are in long-term unemployment increases (Green, Mitchell and Watts 1997). As a result, the orthodox model develops an asymmetry in that demand contraction increases the natural rate of unemployment while the natural rate is invariant to demand expansion. As a consequence, there is a bias towards an increasing and justifiable unemployment rate.

In the hysteresis model, little distinction is made between cyclical and structural unemployment. Demand insufficiency generates cyclical cum structural unemployment. In this context, the lack of effective demand remains an important reason why high unemployment rates are sustained in Australia. The orthodox approach assumes that, once inflationary expectations are stabilised and product and labour-markets are deregulated, the economy will approach full employment. Despite nearly a decade of microeconomic reform policies in product and labour-markets, sporadic attempts at fiscal consolidation and an inflation first strategy, unemployment rates have averaged above 8 per cent during the 1990s. Market deregulation may generate static efficiency gains, it may also increase unemployment and undermine business and consumer confidence, yet despite the plethora of extravagant claims associated with the microeconomic reform agenda (Quiggin 1996a), the reality is that growth rates in the Australian economy are not sufficient to make inroads into the unemployment rate.

Deflationary policy, low growth, recession and unemployment in Australia

Four broad propositions summarise Australia's growth and unemployment experience since the early 1970s:

- There has been a decline in average growth rates and an increase in average unemployment rates (table 6.1).
- Each cycle over this period has been associated with higher average rates of unemployment; that is, Australia has entered the recovery phase of each successive cycle with a higher unemployment rate than the previous cycle. In turn, this points towards the presence of hysteresis of the natural rate of unemployment (Stevens and Robertson, 1993).
- The employment intensity of economic growth has in general increased through time as the full-time/part-time, male/female and industry composition of jobs has shifted (Debelle and Swann 1998).
- Recessions have a very damaging, and difficult to reverse, impact on the unemployment rate (Phipps and Sheehan 1995).

Each of these propositions will be briefly discussed in turn.

First, the decline in growth rates and the accompanying increase in the unemployment rate have been well documented (Burgess and Green 1997; Quiggin 1993b) as has the discussion of the reasons for the growth slowdown (Argy 1998, ch. 3; Drake and Niewenhuysen 1988).

Australia's growth experience is very similar to that of the rest of the OECD (Maddison 1991). On this characteristic, the Australian experience suggests that the impacts of systems and institutional change common across countries (e.g. oil price shocks, the demise of the Bretton Woods system of regulated international finance, the emergence of inflation first macroeconomic policy and the growing internationalisation of markets and production) have played a part in contributing to the slowdown (Bell 1997a, ch. 5; Eatwell 1995). In this new environment, more obstacles were placed on sustaining high growth rates; policies that worked in the post-1945 period were now operating in a different institutional and policy environment that reduced their effectiveness. It is important to recognise not only the growth slowdown, but the context in which the slowdown occurred. Unemployment became a consequence of this new, low-growth economic and policy environment.

Second, through time, rising unemployment rates became a permanent feature for many OECD economies as growth rates moderated. What started out as cyclical unemployment soon became structural unemployment as the average duration of unemployment increased as did the proportion of the unemployed in long-term unemployment. Here we have an asymmetry of significant policy consequence: a growth slowdown generates unemployment, but if that slowdown persists, this implies that an acceleration in rates of economic growth will be less effective in reducing unemployment since a component of the unemployed have been excluded from work for so long that generating job vacancies is not in itself sufficient for them to find employment. Since the early 1970s the growth slowdown has been part of the hysteresis process which increases structural unemployment and contributes to the problem of labour-market mismatch (Indecs 1995, ch. 4). Later discussion will demonstrate that despite the asymmetry problem, higher rates of economic growth are still very powerful in reducing unemployment, especially in the context of the employment intensity of economic growth increasing. The hysteresis issue suggests that governments should do at least three things if they wish to avoid secular increases in unemployment rates. They should: ensure that economic growth rates are sufficient to avoid cyclical unemployment; not use deflation and increasing unemployment as a policy to stabilise the inflation rate; supplement growth policies with active labour-market programs to ensure that the transition from unemployment to employment is quick once economic growth rates increase.

Third, when we examine the business cycle over this period, we see that Australia moved into each subsequent business cycle with a higher unemployment rate than was present at the beginning of the previous business cycle. Lower or even negative growth in an already low growth environment generates more extensive structural labour-market problems. Australia never quite recovers from the previous recession before it enters the next one. The business cycle accentuates the pernicious impact of the secular growth decline on the labour-market. Unlike the post-1945 period, in the post-1973 period Australia does not enter a cyclical downturn with less than 2 per cent unemployment – it enters the downturn with 5 or 6 per cent unemployment at least one-quarter of whom are in long-term unemployment. The characteristic of each cycle in terms of its impact on employment is neither regular nor predictable since the impact of the cycle differs across sectors, the structural composition of output shifts through time and structural shifts occur within industries. Factors such as technological change, international trade, wage dispersion and interest rates impact upon these structural developments. Within-industry and between-industry shifts in productivity growth also change the employment intensity of growth. The post-1945 period, in general, was associated with a positive correlation between economic growth, employment growth and productivity growth, in aggregate and across sectors (Drake and Niewenhuysen 1988). This is no longer the case. As indicated below, some sectors are responding to growth purely in terms of productivity growth without employment growth, with the spectre of jobless growth (Burgess and Green 1997). For other sectors, particularly the services sector, the response is employment growth with little productivity growth. The cycle can accelerate structural shifts, and, as a result, the employment intensity of growth in the recovery and in the slowdown does differ from cycle to cycle. So while the general relationship between economic growth and employment growth can be confirmed, the relationship is neither constant through time, across the cycle, nor across sectors.

Finally, economic downturns are very destructive in their impact on the labour-market in the environment outlined above. As figure 6.1 makes clear, recessions ratchet up the average duration of unemployment (and the proportion of long-term unemployed) and make it difficult for the economy to return to unemployment rates existing prior to the downturn. Deflationary policies have a significant structural impact on the economy's labour-market from which it is difficult to recover (Phipps and Sheehan 1995). The subsequent recovery will occur in a context of higher unemployment rates, a longer average duration of unemployment and a higher proportion of long-term unemployed than the previous recovery.

The story then of Australia's unemployment experience is one in which a secular decline in growth rates was exacerbated by the occasional cyclical decline in growth rates, and cyclical unemployment

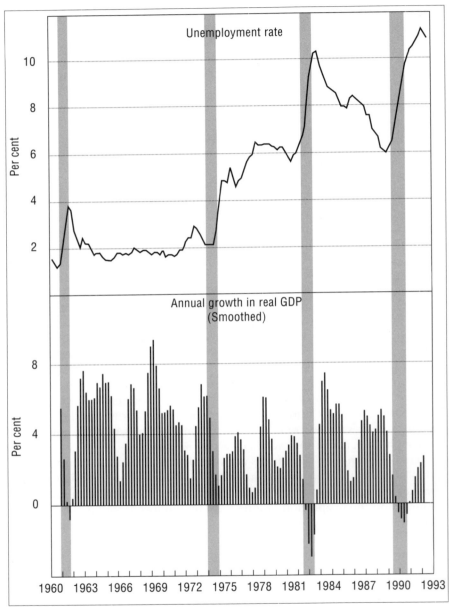

Figure 6.1 GDP growth and the unemployment rate, Australia, 1960–93

Note: Shaded areas represent periods of falling GDP.

Source: RBA (1993)

quickly became much more entrenched structural unemployment. Despite a strong recovery phase and strong employment growth over the 1983–90 Prices and Incomes Accord, Australia entered the 1990s in a recession, double-digit unemployment and over 350 000 persons in long-term unemployment. Deflationary policies, especially the 1989–91 recession, had an important role to play in this process since it has been through the dramatic increases in unemployment that inflation and inflationary expectations have been reduced (see figure 6.1).

This argument demonstrates why insufficient growth rates are the reason for unemployment, but also why higher growth rates are not the complete answer to reducing unemployment. The policy dialectic is that while lower growth rates have undoubtedly contributed to the secular increase in unemployment rates, higher growth rates will not necessarily erase the structural unemployment generated by the lower growth rates as more and more of the unemployed move into long-term unemployment. Finally, there is not a stable relationship between growth and employment, the structure of the economy and the composition of employment changes through time. Structural change occurs hand in hand with cyclical change, the blueprint of each cyclical episode is different from the previous cyclical episode, businesses will react differently due to differences across cycles in product market conditions, regulatory arrangements, technological conditions and external conditions.

The unemployment stabilising growth rate

For a given rate of unemployment, we would expect that, in aggregate, real GDP growth will be translated into employment growth. Increased sales translate into increased production, and increased production generally translates into growing demand for labour input or extra jobs. However, as noted above, the relationship is not exact and depends upon a number of structural and technical conditions. First, there is the extent to which firms are utilising existing capacity, including labour input. Labour hoarding and averaging labour input over the business cycle means that economic growth does not necessarily translate into employment growth since firms may utilise labour input more effectively through work intensification, increasing average hours of employment through overtime hours and through more effectively utilising capital inputs. Second, there is the underlying production function that dictates by how much labour input must be increased in order to increase output. If production were very capital intensive, then GDP growth would not be translated into many additional jobs. Third, there is the average number of hours of employment, which determines how many new jobs are required to meet the increase in real GDP. The gap between GDP growth and employment growth is filled by the growth in labour productivity. With a more productive workforce, fewer workers are required to produce a given level of output. This raises an immediate policy dilemma. Economic growth is more effective in increasing employment the lower the growth rate in labour productivity, but here we run into causality problems. Since labour productivity growth is one necessary ingredient for increasing economic growth, the lower the growth in labour productivity, the lower will be the rate of economic growth for any given increase in labour inputs.

Re-arranging labour-force identities leads to the concept of the unemployment stabilising rate of economic growth which is that growth rate (Y) that is sufficient to maintain the existing unemployment rate (UR) for the given growth in the labour force (LF) and labour productivity growth (LP). If output growth (Y) exceeds the sum of labour productivity and labour-force growth (LF + LP), the unemployment rate (UR) will decline. On the other hand, if Y < (LF + (Y/E)), then the unemployment rate (UR) will increase.

There is a critical threshold rate of growth above which GDP growth is translated into a reduction in the unemployment rate. This threshold is determined largely by the growth in labour productivity and the growth in the labour force; their summation is equal to the unemployment stabilising growth rate. In order to maintain the existing unemployment rate, the rate of GDP growth must at least equal the rate of labour-force growth plus the rate of labour productivity growth. In order to reduce the unemployment rate, the rate of GDP growth should exceed the unemployment stabilising growth rate, hence:

where Y = [LF + LP], U is constant
where Y < [LF + LP], U increases
where Y > [LF + LP], U declines

In this discussion, productivity growth is a residual that enables us to consider the relationship between output and employment. As a residual measure, labour productivity growth is sensitive to fluctuations in either output or employment growth. We are not considering labour productivity as it is more popularly understood – that is, the relationship between output (value added) and the input of labour services, usually labour hours per period. We are concerned about the average relationship between growth and employment on a per person basis; not on a per person hour basis, our interest is in what growth rates are required to sustain employment levels on a per person basis; not on an hours basis, and what growth rates are required to reduce the rate of unemployment. In this analysis, average hours of employment are assumed to be constant.

The relationship between real GDP growth and the unemployment rate has been largely considered in the context of Okun's 'rule of thumb' (Okun 1970). Arthur Okun developed a rule of thumb for the relationship between real GDP growth and the unemployment rate for the USA in the postwar period. The question he posed was by how much is the unemployment rate reduced for every 1 per cent GDP growth above the trend rate in GDP growth. For the USA, the relationship was approximately a 1 per cent reduction in the unemployment rate for every 2.2 per cent increase in GDP above its trend rate (Dornbusch and Fischer 1987, p. 15).

Okun's rule of thumb applies to the relationship between GDP growth above this threshold and the subsequent reduction in the unemployment rate. In terms of this analysis, the Okun coefficient (K) is equal to the difference between actual economic growth (Ya) and the unemployment stabilising growth rate (Yu) divided by the change in the unemployment rate (dU):

$$K = (Ya - Yu) / dU$$

For Australia, the Indecs estimate (Indecs 1995, p. 78) for the unemployment stabilising GDP growth rate is 3.5 per cent and the Okun coefficient is estimated to be 2.15. For example, to reduce the unemployment rate by 1 per cent per year requires a rate of real GDP growth equal to 3.5 per cent (the required unemployment stabilising growth rate) plus 2.15 per cent (the Okun coefficient), or 5.65 per cent per year. Earlier estimates for Australia by Nguyen and Sirwardana (1988) put the GDP growth threshold at 3.2 per cent and the Okun coefficient at 3.0. The economic growth projections contained in the 1993 unemployment Green Paper are in line with the Indecs estimates with the high-growth scenario of 4.75 per cent real GDP growth per year being translated into an annual 0.5 per cent (that is $(4.75 - 3.5)/2.15$) reduction in the unemployment rate (Commonwealth of Australia 1993, p. 52). In the following discussion we suggest that both the unemployment stabilising growth rate and the Okun coefficient are currently smaller than the above estimates. In other words, the impact of economic growth on reducing unemployment is increasing.

Labour-force growth and labour productivity growth are both cyclically sensitive. In particular, labour-force participation rates increase during the growth phase and decline during a slowdown phase. Discouraged workers leave the labour force as unemployment increases and return to the labour force when job vacancies increase (Norris 1996, p. 228). Labour productivity growth increases during an expansion as labour and capital utilisation rates improve, and, during a downturn as utilisation rates decline, labour productivity growth declines (Indecs 1995, ch. 4). In addition, both labour-force and labour productivity growth are subject to structural shifts in the longer term. Labour-force growth will be affected by immigration rates, natural population increases, the demographic distribution of the population, shifts in gender participation rates and participation rates in post-secondary education (Norris 1996, ch. 2). Productivity growth will be affected by the sectoral composition of output, the introduction of new technology, shifts in relative factor costs and government policies towards industry and investment (Indecs 1995, ch. 4). All this suggests is that there is no reason to believe that the unemployment stabilising growth rate should be constant over the cycle or in the longer term.

In table 6.2, the trends since the post-1950 period are presented and can be summarised as:

- falling average rates of real GDP growth;
- falling employment growth;
- falling rates of average labour productivity growth;
- a falling unemployment stabilising rate of GDP growth;
- an increasing average unemployment rate;
- apart from the 1980s, a ratio of employment growth to GDP growth of about 0.4;
- GDP growth has been on average less than the combined growth in the labour force and in labour productivity since the early 1970s; that is, below the unemployment stabilising threshold.

In the 1950s and 1960s, low unemployment rates were maintained since the rate of GDP growth kept pace with the required unemployment stabilising growth rate. In the 1970s, and especially in the 1980s and 1990s, the growth in real GDP was well below the unemployment stabilising growth rate, with the consequence being an increase in the average rate of unemployment. Put simply, decade by decade, economic growth has been insufficient to stabilise unemployment rates, let alone reduce them. In the 1990s, the annual average GDP growth rate has been 0.3 per cent below the unemployment stabilising growth rate. The unemployment situation might have been even more alarming had not the unemployment stabilising growth rate continued to decline.

However, the estimated growth rates for employment and average labour productivity are potentially misleading as a result of the shift towards part-time employment in Australia (Norris and Wooden 1996,

Table 6.2 Trends in real GDP growth, employment growth, labour productivity growth, labour-force growth, the unemployment stabilising rate and the unemployment rate

	(1)	(2)	(3)	(4)	(5)	(6)	(7)	(8)
			Empl. /GDP	Lab. prod.	Lab.	Unempl. stabil. rate		Unempl.
	GDP	Empl.	(2/1)	(1/2)	force	(4+5)	(6–1)	rate
1950–59	4.5	1.8	0.40	2.5	1.9	4.6	0.1	1.5
1960–69	5.1	2.4	0.47	2.1	2.3	5.0	0.1	2.0
1970–79	3.6	1.6	0.44	2.3	2.0	4.0	0.4	3.7
1980–89	3.2	1.9	0.59	1.7	2.5	3.8	0.6	7.8
1990–97	2.7	1.1	0.40	2.5	1.4	3.0	0.3	9.0

All figures (except unemployment rate) as percentage growth rates
Sources: Foster and Stewart (1991); OECD (1995a); *Reserve Bank of Australia Bulletin,* December 1997

p. 7). A growing part-time employment share has a number of effects which influence the trends shown in table 6.2. With a growing part-time employment share:

- a given GDP growth rate, other factors constant, can support more jobs;
- average labour productivity as measured on a per person basis will decline since the average hours of employment will decline;
- the unemployment stabilising rate of GDP growth is reduced because average labour productivity growth on a per person basis is depressed.

Intuitively, without the shift towards part-time employment, the unemployment stabilising growth rate and the average unemployment rate would be much greater than revealed in table 6.2. However, for this to hold, the average weekly hours worked by full-time and part-time workers should remain constant; then the overall average weekly hours would decline. However, in reality, the trend of declining average hours of employment has been reversed over the past decade, with the average worked per week for both full-time and part-time workers increasing (Norris and Wooden 1996, p. 6). As a consequence, an increasing part-time employment share over the past decade has not been translated into a decrease in the average hours of employment.

While the growing part-time employment share over the past decade has assisted in reducing the unemployment stabilising growth rate, this effect has been partially offset by increasing hours of employment for both full-time and part-time workers since 1987 (see table 6.3 and

Table 6.3 Trends in part-time employment and average weekly hours of employment

August	Part-time employment ('000)	Part-time employment share (%)	Average weekly hours of employment
1966	475	9.8	39.1
1974	728	12.4	37.1
1984	1148	17.8	36.2
1987	1421	20.0	35.6
1994	1924	24.4	36.8
1997	2126	25.4	36.3

Sources: Foster and Stewart (1991); ABS *The Labour Force*, Cat. no. 6203.0, August 1994, 1997

Burgess 1998). In 1984, 23.7 per cent of the workforce, or 44 per cent of full-time workers, worked more than 40 hours per week. In 1994, 31.4 per cent of the workforce, or 50 per cent of full-time workers, worked more than 40 hours per week.

What is the Okun coefficient for Australia? In table 6.4 the Okun coefficient is estimated for the recoveries of 1983/84–1989/90 and 1992/93–1996/97. The data in table 6.4 refer to average annual changes. The unemployment stabilising growth rate was identical at 3.6 per cent per year in each recovery phase. However, the composition differs. In the 1980s recovery strong labour-force growth was tempered by high employment growth and moderate productivity growth. In the 1990s recovery, labour-force growth declined, but so did employment growth, the result was an increase in productivity growth. Overall, the annual average gap between the actual and required growth rates was similar, as was the Okun coefficient of 1.4 in the 1980s and 1.2 in the 1990s. Yet, the Okun coefficient is lower than expected from the previous studies. This suggests an increasing employment intensity of growth or a declining growth in labour productivity. These possibilities are discussed in the following section.

Two other aspects of the relationship between growth and employment warrant discussion. First, and following from Padalino and Vivarelli (1997), the Australian evidence (table 6.2) indicates that there remains a strong, albeit changing, relationship between growth and employment. There is no evidence of a break in the relationship between aggregate output and employment growth. As yet, the spectre of jobless growth does not apply to Australia as a whole, though it may apply to some sectors such as the manufacturing sector (discussed below). Second, and following from Appelbaum and Schettkat (1995a),

Table 6.4 The Okun coefficient for Australia over the past two recoveries (annual average percentage growth rate)

	1984–90	1993–97
Real GDP growth	4.4	4.3
Employment growth	3.8	2.5
Labour-force growth	3.0	1.8
Productivity growth	0.6	1.8
Annual reduction in unemployment rate	0.57	0.57
Unemployment stabilising growth rate	3.6	3.6
Difference between actual and required growth	0.8	0.7
Okun coefficient	1.4	1.2

Source: *Reserve Bank of Australia Bulletin*, December 1994, 1997

there is no evidence of a negative secular relationship between output growth and productivity growth. Although average rates of productivity growth (and output growth) have declined since the early 1970s (Maddison 1991), a positive relationship remains between output and productivity growth.

Sectoral trends in employment and productivity

In this section, we turn to the relationship between employment growth and productivity growth on an industry sector basis. As Lowe (1995, p. 100) demonstrates, the aggregate level of labour productivity is the weighted average of productivity in each industry. As a consequence, aggregate labour productivity growth is the consequence of productivity growth within industries and/or the shift in shares of output and employment between industries. That is, there is a within-industry effect and a structural or between-industry effect reflecting changes in the shares of output and employment across industries. What has been the growth record and the employment record for each sector? To what extent has there been a compositional shift in the distribution of GDP and employment? This question is directly related to whether the employment intensity of growth has shifted and whether the positive relationship between output and productivity growth has been reversed.

Essentially, table 6.5 highlights the shift in employment share towards the service sectors of finance/business services, community services and recreation/personal services (Norris and Wooden 1996, p. 6). By 1993, almost one-half of all employment was located in these three sectors. If we add trade (retail and wholesale), then table 6.5 demonstrates that virtually all the growth in employment since 1967 has taken place in these four service sectors.

Table 6.5 The shifting sectoral composition of employment, 1967–93[1]

	Empl. share 1967 (%)	Empl. share 1993 (%)	Change 1967–93	Empl. 1967 ('000)	Empl. 1993 ('000)	Change 1967–93 ('000)	% change 1967–93
Agriculture	8.9	5.4	−3.5	430	416	−14	−3.2
Mining	1.2	1.2	0.0	58	90	42	55.2
Manufacturing	27.4	14.1	−13.3	1233	1081	−152	−12.3
Construction	8.4	7.2	−1.2	406	557	151	37.2
Retail/ wholesale trade	20.6	20.9	0.3	994	1603	609	61.3
Finance and bank	6.1	11.1	5.0	294	850	556	189.1
Community services	10.0	19.0	9.0	486	1455	987	199.4
Recreation and personal services	5.9	8.1	2.3	287	632	345	120.2

Sources: Foster and Stewart (1991); ABS *Australian Economic Indicators,* Cat. no. 1350.0, March 1995

As indicated above, there are major problems in attempting to measure labour productivity on an industry basis with some output and price deflator estimates subject to a range of weaknesses (Lowe 1995). Nevertheless, we can look at broad trends over the 1984/85–1992/93 period to demonstrate some fundamental implications for our analysis.

Table 6.6 is very approximate and not directly comparable to table 6.5 since for a start it contains different industry subdivisions. This difference, however, does not affect the substance of the analysis. The growth rates refer to total change over the period, not average growth rates, so starting and finishing dates can and do affect the results. Once again, we are dealing with productivity on an average employment or per person base, not a labour input base. Labour productivity growth rates may reflect changes in the average hours of employment worked, changes in the intra-industry distribution of output and employment, and statistical difficulties in estimating output and price deflators on an industry basis. Despite the methodological shortcomings of table 6.6, it does demonstrate several points pertinent to this analysis:

• high-productivity growth has in general been achieved in those sectors that have reduced their levels of employment, e.g. mining, utilities, transport and communications;

Table 6.6 Industry output, employment and productivity growth, 1984/85 – 1992/93

Sector	Output growth (%)	Employment growth (%)	Labour productivity growth (%)	Productivity per worker 1992/93 ('000)
Agriculture	12.3	0.0	12.3	39.8
Mining	40.8	−6.5	47.3	201.0
Manufacturing	12.3	−4.1	16.4	51.5
Utilities	28.5	−29.0	58.0	127.0
Construction	−0.4	16.2	−16.0	48.0
Retail/wholesale trade	15.3	22.7	−7.4	39.9
Transport & communication	48.7	−2.9	51.6	60.0
Finance & property	37.3	37.6	−0.3	52.1
Public admin.	34.0	12.7	21.3	41.2
Community services	41.3	26.9	14.4	31.6
Recreation & personal services	21.3	42.3	−21.0	26.8

Source: ABS *Australian Economic Indicators*, Cat. no. 1350.0, August 1991, March 1995

- those sectors with the highest levels of labour productivity are those sectors that have experienced net employment contraction: mining, manufacturing, utilities and transport and communications;
- the service sectors are accounting for virtually all employment growth, but they have relatively low productivity levels and low labour productivity growth rates

Contrary to the traditional models of economic development (Chenery and Syrquin 1975), there has in effect been a transfer of employment from high-productivity sectors (levels and growth) to low-productivity sectors. In turn, as outlined above, this reduces average rates of economic growth and average labour productivity growth, and reduces the growth potential of the economy. This is an important policy paradox. If we are interested in job generation, then it is appropriate that the employment share of the service sector increase; however, if we are interested in increasing economic growth, then it is appropriate that the employment share of the primary, secondary and utilities increase. In the process of employment restructuring in Australia, low-productivity service jobs have replaced high-productivity primary/secondary sector jobs. This is broadly in accordance with Appelbaum and Schettkat's (1995a) view that there has been a shift to a post-industrial employment model where employment growth is almost exclusively located in the service sector. Unlike the industrial model of development which generated employment and productivity growth in the industrial sectors, the current process is delivering employment growth in the service sector and productivity growth in the industrial sectors. A schism or dualism has emerged in Australia's economy between the sectoral location of productivity growth and the sectoral location of employment growth. Overall, the positive aggregate relationship between output growth, employment growth and productivity growth remains; the difference is that this relationship is now very different across sectors.

This observation provides a useful insight on the process of 'microeconomic reform' as it has been preached and practised in Australia over the past decade. Essentially, the largest job losses have occurred in those sectors associated with tariff cuts (manufacturing) and public-sector rationalisation (utilities). Productivity levels and productivity growth have lifted in these sectors but redundant workers have been forced either outside of the labour force or into the much lower productivity service sectors. In general, shifting employees from high-productivity to low-productivity employment will depress productivity growth rates and aggregate growth rates. This depresses the growth potential of the economy, but where it is associated with an expansion in low-productivity service sector employment it means that the unemployment stabilising growth rate declines. It also raises the fundamental question, posed by Appelbaum and Schettkat (1995a), of whether market-based reforms can generate both productivity and employment growth within the same sectors. The best that can be hoped for may be a bifurcated economy where improved productivity and competitiveness in the manufacturing sector addresses the balance of payments constraint on demand expansion, thereby creating scope for low-productivity and labour-intensive sectors such as recreation and community services to expand employment. This is explored further in the chapter on the current account and in chapter 10 by John Quiggin.

Future growth prospects and requirements

We now turn to the likely *aggregate* relationship between real GDP growth, employment growth and the unemployment rate over the coming decade. The following predictions are made on the basis of our analysis:

- the relationship between employment growth and real GDP growth, or the employment intensity of growth, will continue to hold at around 0.4 (see table 6.2);
- average labour productivity growth on a per person basis is likely to

decline given growing part-time and service sector employment shares;

- the unemployment stabilising rate of output growth is also likely to decline to less than 3 per cent per year as a result of the above development together with a predicted decline in the labour-force growth rate;
- despite this, there will still be a need for rates of economic growth that are high relative to Australia's recent experience (above 3.5 per cent p.a.) in order to reduce the unemployment rate; as outlined below, in order to cut the unemployment rate by 1 per cent per year, the growth in GDP should be between 4.0 and 4.5 per cent per year.

What will happen to employment growth and economic growth over the coming decade? Will the unemployment rate decline or increase? To answer this question, we turn to two projections for growth and employment: the 1993 Employment Green Paper (Commonwealth of Australia 1993) and the 1995 Department of Employment, Education and Training *Workforce 2005* projections (DEET 1995).

The Green Paper discusses two scenarios: a base growth scenario and a high growth scenario. The base growth scenario extends average GDP growth for 1970–90 from 1992/93 to 2000/01. The base growth rate is 3.5 per cent per annum; the high growth rate is 4.75 per cent per annum. To achieve the high growth rate requires a policy program to boost productivity growth (Commonwealth of Australia 1993, ch. 2). These different scenarios are outlined in table 6.7.

The labour-force growth rates are not made explicit, but we can imply them by the underlying unemployment stabilising threshold. For the base estimates, the unemployment rate falls by 0.5 per cent per year. With an Okun coefficient of 2.0, this implies an underlying unemployment stabilising growth rate of 2.5 per cent and average labour-force growth of 1.5 per cent. For the high growth scenario, the annual average reduction in the unemployment rate is 0.75 per cent, the unemployment stabilising growth rate is 3.25 per cent and the labour-force growth is once again 1.5 per cent. These projections, as compared to past experience (see table 6.2), reveal some interesting developments, in particular:

- a reduction in labour productivity and labour-force growth rates;
- a reduction in the unemployment stabilising rate of GDP growth;
- an increase in the employment growth to GDP growth ratio.

In 1998, with the benefit of hindsight, we can see that at best the base scenario outcome may be achieved by 2000/01. With over five years of continuous growth, an unemployment rate of 7 per cent appears

Table 6.7 Green Paper growth and unemployment scenarios

	Actual 1992/93	Forecast 2000/01	
		Base growth	High growth
Real GDP growth	3.0	3.5	4.75
Labour productivity growth	3.0	1.0	1.75
Employment growth	0.0	2.5	3.0
Unemployment rate	11.0	7.0	5.0
Employment intensity of growth	0.0	0.7	0.6

Source: Commonwealth of Australia (1993, p. 52)

realisable by 2000/01, the 5 per cent target appears less likely. One problem with the projections is labour-force growth rates. In general, we would expect labour-force growth rates to decline in line with an ageing of the population, increased participation in post-secondary education and earlier retirements. However, labour-force participation rates are pro-cyclical (Quiggin 1993b, p. 94), so the high growth projections would be associated with higher rates of labour-force growth, one suggestion being 2 per cent per year (Quiggin 1993b, p. 95). In this case, the unemployment rate would be closer to 7 per cent, not 5 per cent, by 2000/01 even under the high growth scenario.

One final point concerning the Green Paper projections is that they imply a much higher employment growth to GDP growth ratio (E/Y) than in the past (see table 6.2). We would expect this ratio to increase given the continuation of the trend towards part-time and service sector employment, and the Okun coefficient therefore to decrease.

From the DEET projections in table 6.8, we can see that the highest growth in labour productivity will be achieved in those sectors that are sustaining output growth in combination with employment contraction (mining, utilities). The highest rates of employment growth are anticipated in wholesale trade, accommodation/cafés and in finance. Not surprisingly, those sectors with the highest employment growth to output growth ratio tend to be located in the public sector or in direct personal service sectors such as accommodation.

In the DEET (1995) workforce projections, the labour force is expected to grow by 1.6 per cent per year. This represents a decline from the long-term trend and is a response to the decline in natural population growth, the decline in net immigration and an ageing population. This is in line with the ABS (1991) labour-force projections, which forecast a gradual decline in labour-force growth rates from 2.1 per cent in the early 1990s to 1.1 per cent in 2005, and with the implied labour-force projections contained in the Green Paper.

Table 6.8 The DEET projections: Industry employment growth, 1994–2005 (% p.a.)

Sector	Real GDP	Employment	Employment intensity	Labour productivity
Total	3.5	2.2	0.63	1.3
Agriculture	3.1	2.5	0.80	0.6
Mining	4.9	0.0	0.00	4.9
Manufacturing	3.8	0.1	0.03	3.7
Utilities	3.4	−2.3	−0.68	5.7
Construction	4.0	2.4	0.60	1.6
Wholesale trade	5.3	4.0	0.75	1.3
Retail trade	4.0	3.2	0.80	0.8
Transport	3.0	−0.4	−0.13	3.4
Communication	6.7	3.3	0.49	3.4
Finance	4.9	3.7	0.76	1.2
Property	3.7	1.2	0.32	2.5
Public adm./defence	2.9	2.7	0.93	0.2
Education	2.9	2.6	0.90	0.3
Health	2.8	2.7	0.96	0.1
Recreation	3.3	0.6	0.18	2.7
Personal services	4.2	2.9	0.69	1.3
Accommodation, cafés	5.0	4.0	0.80	1.0

Source: DEET (1995, pp. 10, 13)

The DEET projections also forecast an increase in the female employment share and the continuing growth of the share of employment that is part-time (to over 30 per cent in the next century). The DEET projections imply an unemployment stabilising growth rate of 2.9 per cent (1.3 plus 1.6) and an employment growth to GDP growth ratio of 0.63. Using an Okun coefficient of 1.5 implies an annual reduction in the unemployment rate of around 0.4 per cent (3.5 less 2.9 divided by 1.5) through to 2005. We can highlight a number of points from the DEET forecasts:

- employment will continue to shift towards the low-productivity, low-productivity growth service sectors;
- without the growing part-time employment share, the productivity growth rate would be higher and the unemployment stabilising growth rate would be higher;
- the projected annual employment growth is above that achieved since the 1960s, but this is not inconceivable with a growing service sector employment share and a growing part-time employment share.

What we can predict with confidence is that both service sector and part-time employment share will increase over the next decade. This should increase the employment growth potential and the employment growth to GDP growth ratio (the employment intensity of growth). The Okun coefficient will be around 1.5, reflecting this increase in the employment intensity of growth. The downside will be relatively low-productivity growth, but if the DEET labour-force projections hold, labour-force growth rates will actually decline from the past trend of 2 per cent per year. The unemployment stabilising growth rate will be under 3 per cent – much lower than that required in preceding decades to reduce the unemployment rate. Under this scenario, a rate of economic growth of around 3.5 per cent per year, if sustainable, will reduce the unemployment rate by an average of 0.4 per cent every year. If the unemployment stabilising growth rate were 2.8 per cent and the Okun coefficient 1.5, then a growth rate of around 4.3 per cent would be required in order to reduce the unemployment rate by 1 per cent per annum. This is not spectacular, but it does give recognition to Australia's current account and external debt constraint (see chapter 7). It also assumes no exogenous shocks, no interest rate increase, wage–price stability, stable commodity prices and a stable exchange rate.

The above forecasts highlight the growing duality of the economy. High-productivity sectors are low-employment sectors, and high-employment sectors are low-productivity sectors. However, to the extent that many of the low-productivity sectors (e.g. education, health) provide inputs and generate externalities for other sectors, their contribution to output is understated through market-based output estimates. On the other hand, to the extent that high-productivity sectors address the current account imbalance, their contribution to employment growth in other sectors via demand and multiplier effects is also understated.

Yet the present federal government is moving towards a polarised wage system in which the emerging dualism within the economy will be institutionalised. Employees in high-productivity growth sectors have been able to secure relatively large wage increases, while those in services, including the public sector, have had difficulty in securing wage increases. This duality is further compounded by the general disparity in unionisation rates between the high-productivity and the low-productivity sectors. A centralised wage determination system offered a mechanism for sharing the benefits of productivity growth across the workforce and for moderating aggregate wage outcomes. Unless new fair wage and comparability instruments are devised, the enterprise-based bargaining system will allow a few sectors to appro-priate those gains acquired through technological change, work reorganisation and the redundancies of fellow employees and through the repositioning of parts of the workforce in relatively low-productivity sectors. Moreover, those outside the enterprise bargaining and unionised award sector can expect few, if any, benefits under such a system. In common with other OECD economies, such as the United Kingdom and the USA, Australia has to confront this growing duality within the economy, especially where it translates into growing earnings and income disparities (OECD 1996).

Conclusions and policies for growth

Despite the favourable structural developments noted above, such as an increased employment intensity of growth, economic growth above 3.5 per cent per year remains imperative over coming years if unemployment is not to worsen. Based on the estimates in this chapter, to move beyond this and to reduce unemployment at the rate of 1 per cent per year will require a GDP growth rate of around 4.3 per cent per annum. Even if this is achieved, the Green Paper persuasively demonstrated that special labour-market measures are also required to address long-term unemployment and different forms of labour-market disadvantage (Cwth of Australia 1993, chs 4–6, see also chapter 10). In other words, it is not enough to secure sustainable rates of economic growth of at least 3.5 per cent per year; we need to do better, and on a sustained basis. Policies also need to be developed to address the structural issues of long-term unemployment, regional unemployment disparities and the uneven access to jobs and income across the community.

In the current policy deliberations of the federal government, unemployment is a low priority. In the 1996/97 federal budget, the problem of unemployment was considered in budget statement no. 2 under the heading of structural budget and labour-market reform. The unemployment problem was represented as one of 'structural impediments to an efficient labour market' (Cwth of Australia 1996/97, 2.41). As with microeconomic reform, 'the potential benefits from removing or reducing structural impediments in the labour market are substantial. Reform offers the potential to achieve faster economic growth and lower unemployment' (Cwth of Australia 1996/97, 2.43). The path to achieving these reforms centred on two policy initiatives: industrial relations reform and a privatised employment services market. The efficacy of these proposals is not assessed here, but the point to emphasise is that these initiatives address the supply side of the labour-market and the wage determination process. Nowhere is there a strategy for addressing the longstanding deficiency in the derived demand for labour. Nowhere is there a policy for unemployment reduction through sustained GDP growth above the unemployment stabilising growth rate.

In October 1996, the prime minister announced the formation of a special cabinet committee to co-ordinate a policy program for unemployment. GDP growth was slowing, monetary policy remained tight and employment growth was falling. Yet the requirement for higher rates of growth together with measures to address the problems of the long-term unemployed have since been largely absent from policy discussion. The overriding policy emphasis has been towards industrial relations reforms (the 1996 *Workplace Relations Act*), unemployment benefit reform (Work for the Dole Program, 1998) and job-search and placement reforms (the Jobs Network, 1998). There remains a heavy bias towards the inflation first strategies of the Reserve Bank, despite the dangers that such an approach entails for both growth and employment (Fraser 1996; Argy 1998, Bell 1999). The public spending cutbacks have restricted opportunities for growth in those labour- and skill-intensive sectors with the most potential for cost-effective job creation, and they have also undermined exports, training and R&D in sectors with the most potential for reversing Australia's current account imbalance, and hence overcoming the balance of payments constraint on output and employment growth in the economy as a whole. In addition, real interest rates remain high to counter pressure for a lower $A exchange rate, with the effect of limiting investment in the capacity to create new jobs across industry sectors.

As John Nevile explains in chapter 7, an alternative approach would be to pursue active demand management. This should occur in conjunction with interventionist supply-side measures, such as labour-market programs and industry and regional development policies, which take as their starting point the failure of the market to deliver satisfactory employment outcomes (Argy 1998; Genoff and Green 1998). As this chapter has shown, the approach will have to tackle the issue of growth in a way that recognises the interdependent roles of high-productivity sectors in addressing the current account and of low-productivity, labour-intensive sectors in generating employment. It will also have to be accompanied by industrial relations policies which ensure a fair distribution of the gains from productivity in a decentralised pay-setting system through fair wage and comparability mechanisms. Today, an employment strategy must be about much more than job creation. It must also be an integrated approach to the quality and distribution of jobs, to availability of training and career paths, to equal opportunities for women and disadvantaged groups, to equal pay for work of equal value, and to fair treatment and job security for all categories of employees. However, the strategy must begin with the recognition that balanced, sustainable growth is an essential precondition for the creation of sufficient numbers of net additional jobs to bring down the rate of unemployment and secure a return to full employment.

CHAPTER 7

Can Keynesian Policies Stimulate Growth in Output and Employment?

J.W. Nevile

There is widespread agreement that a faster, sustained rate of growth of the Australian economy is required to achieve a substantial lasting reduction in unemployment. As John Burgess and Roy Green argued in the previous chapter, on current estimates of the relevant variables, including productivity growth and labour-force growth, GDP growth of around 4.3 per cent per annum is required to reduce unemployment by 1 per cent per annum. It is abundantly clear that such a level of GDP growth is much bigger than the trend rate of growth, of about 3 per cent a year, achieved over the last 25 years. It is also higher than the average rate of real GDP growth achieved in the 1990s of about 2.9 per cent. The required increase in the medium-term trend rate of growth is large enough to require a major change in the overall policy mix. This chapter argues that Keynesian policies can increase the growth rate by the required amount, but that it will not be easy and will entail some cost, in the form of higher taxation, to those already employed or receiving a comfortable income from rent, interest or dividends.

The next section very briefly outlines the main types of Keynesian policies. Then follow two sections: the first reviews historical evidence about the effectiveness of Keynesian policies in Australia and the second considers the major theoretical arguments that have been mounted against Keynesian policies. These two sections together provide a convincing case that Keynesian policies can increase the rate of growth of output and employment, by making business cycle recessions shallow and short. While Keynesian policies generally act on the demand side of the economy, short shallow recessions will also help increase supply by reducing the deterioration of the quality of the labour force caused by long-term unemployment and increasing the rate of growth of the capital stock by fostering more optimistic expectations about future output levels which will increase the amount of investment. Successful Keynesian policies will both increase the capital stock so that workers drawn from unemployment to employment can be more productively, and more profitably, employed and also reduce the number of workers suffering from the barriers to re-employment that are caused by long-term unemployment. In addition, when there is substantial unemployment, Keynesian policies can increase the trend rate of growth directly by raising aggregate demand, as long as there are also policies which ensure adequate supply, especially labour-market programs.

However, successful Keynesian policies to reduce unemployment will have undesirable side-effects, if they cause balance of payments crises and increased inflation. These issues are discussed more fully in chapters 8 and 9, but a preliminary treatment here is in order. The trend to globalisation makes these side-effects more likely and more serious if one economy, other than an extremely large one, raises its rate of growth substantially while the rest of the world grows at the same rate as before. This is the biggest problem in using Keynesian policies to reduce unemployment substantially. However, the section devoted to these side-effects concludes that, despite globalisation, it is possible to avoid balance of payments problems and keep any rises in the rate of inflation relatively small. An outline of a policy package which could achieve this is set out in the penultimate section before the threads are drawn together in a brief conclusion.

The nature of Keynesian policies

There are many varieties of Keynesians. The one thing that unites them is a belief that if left to itself, a free-market economy will not automatically tend towards a situation in which there is no involuntary unemployment – a situation in which everyone who wants a job can find one within a reasonable length of time. Keynesians believe that there is an important role for government, or economic policy, in keeping economic activity close to the desirable level so that there is neither substantial involuntary unemployment nor excess demand in the economy as a whole leading to accelerating inflation.

Although Keynes himself thought that both aggregate demand and aggregate supply were important (1973, p. 513), the central Keynesian policy instruments are those that operate on aggregate demand, or the total amount of goods and services demanded in the economy as a whole. In particular, fiscal policy and monetary policy have been the most discussed in the literature and the most used in practice. Fiscal policy is concerned with the effects of government expenditure and revenue on the economy at an aggregate or economy-wide level. It is not concerned with effects on individuals, on individual industries, or on particular classes of people, such as old age pensioners.[1] The key to fiscal policy is that, in both direct and indirect ways, government expenditure increases aggregate demand, at least according to Keynesians, and government receipts reduce aggregate demand. When governments increase spending, this immediately increases the demand for those things the money is spent on, from the construction of roads to the labour of tax collectors. If governments increase spending on pensions or unemployment benefits, it is a reasonable assumption that the recipients spend the increase in their incomes or at least a large part of them. These first round effects are not the end of the increase in aggregate demand. There will be a rise in the incomes of those who produced the goods and services sold because of the first round increase in demand. They in turn will spend more, increasing others' incomes, and so on. Each subsequent round the expenditure will be less because of leakages into savings, taxes and imports, until additional expenditure is insignificant. In a country like Australia, with a high propensity to import, successive rounds will peter out quickly, but nevertheless the total increase in aggregate demand will be greater than the initial increase in government expenditure. Similarly, a cut in tax rates will increase households' income and increase their expenditure, at least to some extent. Again this initial increase in expenditure will be followed by second and higher round effects. In the case of both expenditure and revenue, the effects work in reverse when government expenditure is cut or tax rates increased.

Monetary policy operates on the quantity of money circulating in the economy and on interest rates. One of the revolutionary claims in (1964 [1936]) Keynes' *General Theory* was that these monetary variables affect 'real' variables like output measured in constant prices, whereas neo-classical economists argue that, except in the very short run, monetary variables affect only prices. By its very nature the major effects of monetary policy are economy-wide[2] and they too operate primarily on aggregate demand. Monetary policy has its major initial impact on investment expenditure, both by firms and by households investing in dwellings. As consumer credit becomes more important, there may also be a direct effect on consumption expenditure. In addition, falls in interest rates increase the prices of financial assets and this spills over to a greater or lesser extent to the prices of other assets such as shares and property. Those owning such assets may increase their expenditure as they become wealthier. As in the case of fiscal policy, the various first round effects are followed by second and higher round effects on expenditure.

However, governments must be concerned about inflation as well as unemployment. If inflation increases, monetary and fiscal policies can only reduce inflation by reducing the growth in demand and increasing unemployment. Incomes policies, such as the Accord under the Hawke and Keating governments, were designed to try to overcome this problem by reducing inflationary pressures through consensual wage moderation. Incomes policies operate on the supply side, seeking to influence wages, or the prices of one class of productive inputs. They also often seek to influence profits and rents as well. While necessary, if the cost of controlling inflation is not to fall on the most vulnerable in society, incomes policies come and go. Monetary and fiscal policies are always central in Keynesian economic policy-making. Both have been used extensively in Australia in the last 50 years, and this history is reviewed in the next section to see what lessons can be learnt.

Learning from the past

The first 25 years after World War II were a 'golden age' in which the average rate of growth of the Australian economy was high, unemployment was very low, even in recessions, and inflation was under control though somewhat precariously at times. Similar conditions prevailed in most other OECD economies. Some believe that this was largely due to adoption of Keynesian macroeconomic policy. If so, this suggests strongly that the question posed in the title of this chapter should be answered in the affirmative.

An alternative point of view has been put, among others, by Ian Macfarlane (1997c). Partly because of Macfarlane's position as governor of the Reserve Bank of Australia, the article has proved influential, and his arguments are worth close attention in an assessment of the implications of the golden years experience for current policy.

Macfarlane (1997c, p. 1) throws cold water on two propositions. The first and most important is that activist and expansionary macroeconomic policy was the major, if not the sole, cause of the excellent economic performance in the golden age. The second proposition Macfarlane rejects is that what brought this golden age to an end was an OPEC-induced oil price rise in 1973 and consequent cost-push inflation, reinforced by a second oil price shock in 1979.

An impartial review of the period provides a great deal of evidence to support both of these propositions and, in my view, in rejecting them Macfarlane downplays the role of Keynesian policy far more than is justified.

As Macfarlane mentions, two factors were of considerable importance in explaining the good economic performance in the 25 years following World War II. One was the large gap in fixed capital (both public and private) to be made up after the Depression of the 1930s and the war years. The second was the low level of inflation expected by most people. This was a result of decades of low inflation, apart from a brief interlude of high inflation in some countries caused by the Korean War. Macfarlane also mentions liberalisation of international trade, to which I would add the certainty generated by exchange rate stability.[3] Both these features of policy encouraged high levels of investment.

However, macroeconomic policy also had an important role to play, and not just by not being over-ambitious, as suggested by Macfarlane. A major problem with Macfarlane's analysis is his use of the budget deficit as one of his major indicators of the stance of fiscal policy. Although widely used in the media, the budget deficit is a deeply flawed indicator of fiscal policy. It is true that in part it reflects fiscal policy decisions, but it also reflects the level of economic activity in an economy. Without any change in fiscal policy, a boom will reduce the budget deficit substantially, since tax receipts rise with rising income and payments by the government to those in need decline as under-employment declines. When unemployment is low, other things being equal, the budget deficit will be low. In Australia, and in a number of OECD countries, fiscal policy was far more activist than Macfarlane acknowledges.

In the 20 years 1954/55 to 1973/74, Commonwealth tax rates were changed in all but five years (Nevile 1975, p. 128). In seven years they were reduced and in eight years they were increased. This of course was apart from increases in tax revenues due to fiscal drag, as inflation pushed individuals into higher tax brackets. Similarly, there were frequent and substantial changes in the rate of growth of government expenditure.

Moreover, and more importantly, macroeconomic policy reacted relatively quickly with Keynesian expansionary measures whenever there was a significant recession and also sometimes when there was just a faltering in the rate of growth of the economy. There were only two significant recessions in the golden years,[4] one in 1952/53 and one in 1961/62. The 1952/53 recession was countered by a notable easing of monetary policy, a substantial cut in Commonwealth tax rates and a large rise in government expenditure. The last mentioned included money given to the states by the Commonwealth to supplement funds raised in the loan market to finance public works. The value of this supplementary finance was greater than 1.5 per cent of the value of total output or gross domestic product!

Again in the 1961/62 recession the federal government pursued very active macroeconomic policies. It instituted the biggest tax cut since the 1952/53 recession and the largest percentage increase in government expenditure over the same period (Nevile 1975, p. 129). Monetary policy was also eased. With expansionary macro policy, both recessions were short lived. The Australian economy grew by 6.3 per cent in 1953/54 and 6.8 per cent in 1962/63.

This success of macroeconomic policy in overcoming the two significant recessions of the period was important because it sustained the belief that the government was in control and, not only was it committed to full employment, but it also had the power to ensure that recessions were very brief. To some extent this was a self-fulfilling belief. If recessions are always brief, it makes very good sense to increase spending on capital equipment during a recession while prices are stable or discounted and there are no bottlenecks. Also, the belief that the government could and would keep recessions short and small reduced uncertainty. In my judgement, this confidence that recessions would be short lived and growth would soon be back to around 5 per cent, or more in the short run, was very important in keeping entrepreneurs optimistic and thus sustaining private investment and the growth process.

Macroeconomic policy was not, of course, always expansionary. Restrictive policy was used when there were fears of rising inflation, notably in 1956, and when there were substantial concerns about the balance of payments as in 1960 (Nevile 1975, pp. 128–9).

It is instructive to look at the response of policy to the significant recessions that have occurred in Australia since the golden age. There have been two such recessions: the first occurring in the year 1982/83 and the second in the two years 1990/91 and 1991/92. In both cases monetary policy was eased. However, the fiscal policy response to the 1982/83 recession was far more expansionary than it was eight years later. The Labor government, elected in March 1983, followed an aggressive policy of expanding government expenditure, both on its own account and in state jurisdictions. After allowing for inflation, government expenditure on goods and services increased by 3.7 per cent in 1983/84,[5] the largest increase for eight years. Transfer payments to households (or pensions and cash benefits) increased by 9 per cent but some of this would have been due to the higher level of unemployment over the year 1983/84 as a whole than in 1982/83.[6] There was a small fall in tax rates. With this expansionary fiscal policy, output increased by 6.1 per cent in 1983/84.

Over the final years of the 1980s, macroeconomic policy became more and more restrictive. Then in the recession that started in 1990/91 monetary policy was the principal policy instrument used to try to stimulate the economy again. The official cash rate had fallen by 2 percentage points in the first half of 1990, but was still 15 per cent at the beginning of the 1990/91 financial year, an extraordinarily high figure for an economy no longer in a boom. There was a further fall of

4 percentage points in 1990/91 followed by another fall of 4 percentage points in 1991/92. Little more than a quarter of these falls merely matched the fall in the inflation rate.

However, interest rates were so high at the beginning of the recession that, even with a fall of 4 percentage points, monetary policy in 1990/91 could be judged as still tight. Fred Argy (1998) has commented:

> The evidence suggests that . . . both the RBA [Reserve Bank of Australia] and the Treasury (with the tacit acceptance of the Treasurer and his personal advisers) decided it was worth taking a risk with unemployment in order to entrench low inflation in the medium term. (p. 41)

Argy goes on to quote Ian Macfarlane as saying that, in order to reduce the inflation rate greatly, 'we had to run monetary policy somewhat tighter than in earlier recessions and take the risk that the fall in output would be greater than forecast'.

In addition to this caution in easing of monetary policy, fiscal policy was much less expansionary than it had been in response to the early 1980s recession. In 1990/91, after allowing for inflation, government expenditure on goods and services rose by only 0.6 per cent. In 1991/92 it rose by a further 1.9 per cent. The total rise over the two years was much less than the rise in the single year 1983/84. Pensions and cash benefits increased substantially each year, but part of this could be accounted for by increased unemployment benefits. Tax rates were cut in 1990/91 but not by a large amount.

Not surprisingly the recession dragged on. In 1991/92 output increased by only 0.25 of a percentage point. In 1992/93 it grew by 3.3 per cent, or virtually the same as the average rate of growth since the slump year 1982/83. Relatively rapid growth, though still only 4.9 per cent, was finally restored in 1993/94.

The length of the 1990–92 recession and the slow recovery may reflect not only the cautious and tardy approach to expansionary policy but also in part the old adage that using monetary policy to cure a recession is like pushing on a piece of string. Expansionary monetary policy makes it easier and cheaper for firms to increase expenditure on equipment and construction but, if there is little incentive to invest, this does not increase spending. For reasons already discussed, this was not important in the golden years when rapid growth was expected to be the norm. However, all that changed after the mid-1970s. In the decade starting in 1973/74 growth was anything but rapid, unemployment rose greatly and uncertainty about the future was much greater.

In any case, no matter what may have happened had monetary policy been eased more rapidly, what did happen is clear. The macroeconomic policy response to the 1982/83 recession was very expansionary and along traditional Keynesian lines with an emphasis on fiscal policy to cure the recession and an incomes policy, in the form of the Accord, used to control inflation. Output grew by 15.6 per cent in the three years following 1982/83. The response to the recession which bottomed in 1990/91 was much less expansionary. Output grew by 8.6 per cent in the three years following 1990/91. Not only the experience of policy reactions to recessions in the golden years, but also experience in the period since then suggests that Keynesian macroeconomic policies are potent in boosting output and employment in an economy undergoing a recession.

Macfarlane discounts the importance of fiscal policy in the golden years by pointing out that government expenditure was larger, as a proportion of output, after 1973/74 than in the years before. However, as argued above, fiscal policy helped keep recessions short, and this in itself was important in maintaining the high rate of growth. Moreover, in the context of growth, a focus on the level of government expenditure is misdirected. The rate of growth of government expenditure is more important. Government expenditure grew strongly in the 20 years to 1973/74. It is true that government receipts also grew rapidly, but an extra dollar spent by the government normally gives more boost to the economy than is offset by an extra dollar of tax revenue. When tax revenue goes up, the effect is split between reducing aggregate demand and reducing savings in the private sector. All of an increase in government expenditure is an addition to aggregate demand.[7] As the Americans say, with expenditure you get a bigger bang for your buck (see Nevile 1997, pp. 96–9).

The steady rise in government expenditure in the golden years was a major source of economic growth, even though it was largely matched by rises in tax receipts. Nevile (1975, p. 129) shows that fiscal policy was responsible for over half of the growth in output in Australia over the 20 years starting in 1953/54. Thus it was more important than all the other sources of growth combined, i.e. it was more important than growth in exports, autonomous investment resulting from technological change and the effects of population growth on private-sector expenditure.

Of course this impetus to long-run growth operated largely on the demand side, not the supply side, and would have led to rising inflation (as it did in the first half of the 1970s) if aggregate supply had not matched the growth in aggregate demand. However, growth in demand as well as in supply is important, and fiscal policy also contributed on the supply side through increasing public and private investment in fixed capital.

After 1973/74, government expenditure grew noticeably less rapidly in Australia. This was despite a slight rise in the rate of growth of social security payments due to the rise in unemployment and unemployment benefits. The rate of growth of government expenditure on goods and services (after corrections for inflation) fell from 4.8 per cent a year over the 20 years to 1973/74, to only 2.7 per cent a year over the next 20 years. Expenditure on goods and services has, dollar for dollar, a bigger effect in stimulating economic activity than do social security payments (Nevile 1975, p. 114). The fall in the rate of growth of government expenditure on goods and services was one of the important factors reducing the rate of growth of the Australian economy after 1973/74.

Macfarlane's second major point, that it was not the first oil shock that caused the end of the golden age, is well taken. The very large inflationary pressures, which originated in the United States and were rapidly transmitted to other OECD countries under the Bretton Woods system, combined with mounting domestic wage pressures in a range of countries, were what brought the golden age to an end. The US inflationary pressures that were transmitted overseas had their genesis in President Johnson's determination to finance his Great Society programs, as well as fight an expanding war in Vietnam, despite the delay by Congress in allowing a substantial increase in tax rates (Okun 1970, ch. 3).[8] The inflationary pressures were well entrenched *before* the first oil shock.

The general picture that emerges from this review of economic policy and growth over the last 50 years in Australia is that Keynesian policies can be remarkably successful in reducing the size of fluctuations in economic activity. In the context of concern about unemployment, in the three recessions in which vigorous Keynesian policy was used to stimulate the economy the recessions were brief. In the one recession, in which policy was much more hesitant, the recession dragged on. Moreover the rapid rise in government expenditure on goods and services was a major source of growth in the golden years.

While the review of historical experience in this section has concentrated on Australia, its conclusion is confirmed by overseas experience. The most obvious example in overseas evidence is the varying experience of countries after the 1982 recession. In general, the countries in which unemployment fell substantially were those with expansionary Keynesian policies. In those with much less expansionary policies, unemployment fell very slowly. Perhaps the two most extreme cases were the United States and Germany. In the United States, President Reagan's policies provided, perhaps inadvertently, a massive Keynesian stimulus and unemployment fell from 9.6 per cent in 1983 to 5.5 per cent in

1988. In conservative Germany, unemployment was 6.9 per cent in 1983 and still 6.2 per cent in 1988.[9] On a more formal level Boltho (1989) carried out a statistical study showing that the period 1950–79 had much smaller business cycles than the interwar period or the 44 years before World War I. Boltho attributes this to 'the greater influence of government which operated via automatic and discretionary policies and by changing expectations' (p. 1709). Boltho's article contains an extensive list of references on the topic. It is clear that overseas evidence confirms the conclusion that Keynesian macroeconomic policies can reduce the size of the business cycle. As pointed out above, this in itself will increase the longer run growth rate.

Also interesting in this respect is a cross-section regression study of 20 OECD countries by Boltho and Glyn (1995) that is specifically concerned with the medium-term relationship between various macroeconomic policy measures and growth in output. They find that the measure most likely to increase economic growth is growth in government expenditure on goods and services. However, their method assumes, rather than demonstrates, the direction of causation. Consequently they are careful in the way they present their results and it is worth quoting their own summary of their empirical findings on this question. These they say:

> provided some evidence that countries in which government spending (on goods and services) increased faster after 1973 recorded a higher growth rate of GDP. Two points are worth emphasising. First, the effect does not seem to have depended on budget deficits, since the impact of the rapid growth of expenditure was almost as great when the structural deficit was controlled for. These results represent, therefore, the effects of a positive balanced budget multiplier process rather than those of a traditional deficit-financed expansion. Public spending directly generated more output within the government sector and in those private industries supplying it, whilst the additional taxation choked off any increase in consumption.
>
> Second, however, this impact weakened through time. Not only did public spending growth slow down (from some 3 per cent per annum on average in 1973–79 to barely 2 per cent per annum in 1982–93), but the size of the coefficients and their statistical significance diminished. (p. 462)

The weakening of the relationship in more recent years could be due to a number of causes. The most plausible is that when, following financial deregulation, fiscal consolidation (or the reduction of government deficits) became fashionable, governments in countries where output was growing more strongly felt more able to pursue fiscal consolidation so that there was some causation in the opposite direction. At least, in the regressions for the 1980s the coefficients were still positive even if they were statistically significant at about the 15 per cent level.

Arguments against Keynesian expansion: Crowding out and related issues

The previous section gave examples where expansionary Keynesian policy was associated with brief recessions and where lack of expansionary fiscal policy was associated with recessions that dragged on. This is important because we now know from experience that recessions are a major factor in driving unemployment. The cumulative effect of these examples of expansionary policy is very convincing, but does not constitute an incontrovertible proof that Keynesian policies can stimulate growth and reduce unemployment at least in an economy in a recession. The case for this will be further strengthened if an examination of the arguments designed to show that Keynesian policy is ineffective finds that these arguments lack conviction or supporting empirical evidence.

The four major arguments against the effectiveness of Keynesian policies go back at least 20 years. Perhaps the most important argument is that expansionary policy, operating through increased government expenditure, will not work because any increased government expenditure will 'crowd out' private investment expenditure, so that there will be no net increase in aggregate demand and no stimulus to output and employment.[10] An increase in government expenditure can be financed by increasing taxation or increasing the budget deficit. It was argued in the previous section that an increase in both government expenditure and revenue will provide a stimulus to the economy. This proposition is usually ignored by proponents of crowding out, who focus on deficit-financed increases in public expenditure.

Crowding-out theory maintains that an increase in the deficit will cause a rise in interest rates and this rise in interest rates will reduce private investment expenditure. If increased public expenditure increases economic activity, more money will be demanded by the public to carry out this increased economic activity. Purchasers will try to borrow this extra money, forcing up interest rates. As long as economic activity is above the level holding before the increased government expenditure, there will be upward pressure on interest rates.

This argument is of particular importance because, unlike others examined later in this section, it is not just an interesting intellectual proposition argued about by academics. It has been held by many policy advisers and has been put strongly in the media, both influencing public opinion and placing pressure on politicians to take note of it. For example, in his 17 June 1993 column in the *Sydney Morning Herald*, Max Walsh talks of the capacity of the public sector 'to undermine the private sector by confronting it with a high interest rate regime as a consequence of large structural deficits' and concludes that, despite the depressed state of the economy, expansionary fiscal policy will not be effective because 'further expansion of the public sector deficit will simply create higher hurdles for private sector investment'.

An implicit, or often explicit, assumption underlying this crowding-out thesis is that the monetary authorities are successful in maintaining a constant stock of money. This assumption is necessary if interest rates are to rise. It is not clear, however, why the monetary authorities would want to reduce the effects of expansionary fiscal policy in a recession by allowing interest rates to rise. Moreover, the analysis that shows increased government expenditure leading to higher interest rates if the stock of money is held constant also shows that any increase in private expenditure, for example, on investment or even foreign expenditure on Australian exports, will also lead to a rise in interest rates in Australia if the monetary authorities are successful in preventing changes in the stock of money. In this respect, expansionary fiscal policy is no different from any sort of stimulus that might lift the economy out of recession.

In any case, the monetary authorities in Australia, and elsewhere, do not maintain a constant volume of money. Even before widespread financial deregulation, targeting the volume of money was remarkably unsuccessful. Now, after financial deregulation that volume adjusts to whatever size is desired, in total, by all those with an effective demand for money. Monetary authorities operate directly on interest rates and the rate of growth of the money supply is only one of many factors that they take into account when determining interest rates. In the case of Australia this has been documented by Reserve Bank officers, for example in Macfarlane and Stevens (1989, pp. 5–6). In effect, those supporting crowding out in today's world of deregulated financial markets are arguing that, whenever government expenditure increases, the central bank actively tightens monetary policy to the extent necessary to reduce private investment by an amount equal to all, or most of, the increase in public expenditure.

There is one qualification that should be made to this conclusion. It is short-term interest rates that are the monetary policy instrument. Long-term interest rates may be more relevant to investment decisions in the private sector. It is possible that large budget deficits might increase the spread between short-term and long-term interest rates so even if short-term interest rates were held constant, long-term rates could rise, crowding out private investment. However, there is no evidence of this happening in Australia. There is virtually no correlation between the budget deficit for all levels of government in Australia combined, as a percentage of gross domestic product, and the spread (or gap) between long-term and short-term interest rates. Over the period from the floating of the exchange rate to 1996/97, the adjusted squared correlation coefficient is 0.07 which is nowhere near being statistically significant. In theory the spread should be bigger when short-term interest rates are expected to rise in the future (because of increased inflation or because they are unusually low as a result of easy monetary policy, or other factors). If larger deficits lead to expectations of greater inflation in Australia, this change in attitude could lead to a rise in long-term interest rates, but there is no evidence that large deficits have affected expectations in this way.

Hence, if a bigger deficit leads to higher interest rates in Australia, it must cause monetary authorities to increase short-term interest rates since it does not affect the gap between long-term and short-term interest rates. If one examines changes in the size of the deficit and changes in short-term interest rates in Australia, it is hard to find a relationship, but if anything the relationship is inverse (Nevile 1997, pp. 101–3).

Thus, in Australia the crowding-out argument falls down at the first step. There is no evidence that larger deficits cause a rise in interest rates. This is also the case overseas. Heilbroner and Bernstein carried out a cross-sectional analysis of the G-7 countries. Pressman (1995, p. 215) summarised their findings as follows:

> those countries whose public debt increased most during the 1980s did *not* also experience the largest increases on real interest rates. In fact, if anything the actual relationship seemed to be the reverse. Canada, whose public debt increased the most among G7 countries between 1980 and 1986 experienced the smallest increase in real interest rates among the G7 countries over the same time period. Conversely the United Kingdom experienced the smallest increase in government debt and the largest increase in real interest rates. [Emphasis in the original]

So far, discussion has been about the possibility of increased public expenditure crowding out private investment expenditure through a rise in interest rates. Another possibility is that it may discourage private consumption. Barro (1974) revived interest in the so-called Ricardian equivalence theorem, the name given to the assertion that an increase in the budget deficit will be matched by an increase in private-sector savings as households try to increase their wealth in order to cover the increase in tax liabilities that they expect in the future. This proposition, rightly, has had few committed supporters among Australian economists or policy-makers. It is likely that any debt will be repaid, not by those increasing their savings, but by their children or grandchildren. Some will not have children and others may not care overmuch about their children's tax liabilities. Many, perhaps most, may not even think about future tax liabilities in this way.

Moreover the empirical evidence, both in Australia and overseas, is against the Ricardian equivalence theorem. Edey and Britten-Jones (1990), in their study of saving and investment in Australia, comment that Australian experience in the second half of the 1980s is close to a natural experiment for the purpose of testing the Ricardian equivalence theorem. They conclude that the theorem fails the test. Among the points that they note are:

> Between 1985/86 and 1989/90 the public sector deficit was reduced by 5 per cent of GDP and public savings was dramatically increased from 1.1 to 6.6 per cent of GDP . . . private savings fell only 1.2 percentage points over the period . . . private savings ratios were quite stable throughout the 1960s, 1970s and 1980s despite the major swings in public savings after the mid-1970s. (p. 121)

Overall, overseas evidence is also unfavourable to the Ricardian equivalence theorem. In many countries, saving rates fell while deficits rose. In the United States Summers and Carroll (1987) found a clear inverse relationship between private savings rates and budget deficits and Pressman (1995) notes similar relationships in Canada, France, Germany and Japan.

There is one final very important point why the Ricardian equivalence theorem is not an argument against effective fiscal policy. Unlike almost all supporters of the theorem, Edey and Britten-Jones are careful to talk about public-sector savings rather than budget deficits. The budget deficit is not a measure of public dissavings. Savings is the difference between income and consumption, not the difference between revenue and expenditure. Public savings is the difference between public revenue and public current (or non-investment) expenditure. Public investment should produce a return in the future, just as private investment should. This return should be enough to pay off any debt incurred in financing it, as well as interest on that debt. Increases in government expenditure on capital equipment and construction, as well as on human capital such as education, should increase the tax base so that even if households act according to the principles underlying the Ricardian equivalence theorem, they will not have to increase their savings rate.

A third theory, the twin deficits theory, implies what could be called international crowding out. If expansionary policy increases aggregate demand, some of the extra demand will be spent on imports. This leakage into imports is uncontroversial and is not an argument against the effectiveness of Keynesian policies. It occurs because policies are effective and do increase aggregate demand, though it is one of the factors that determine the extent to which aggregate demand is increased (Nevile 1975, ch. 4). The twin deficits theory goes much further and argues that if the budget deficit is increased, either because of an increase in expenditure or because of a cut in revenue, the balance of payments current account deficit will increase by the same or very similar amount so that all or nearly all of the expansionary impact will go overseas. The twin deficits theory is the exact opposite of crowding out and Ricardian equivalence. While these last two see an increase in the budget deficit causing a decline in private expenditure, the twin deficits theory argues that private expenditure and savings are very stable and not affected by what happens in the public sector. Thus, for example, if public expenditure increases and the increase is deficit financed, neither private-sector expenditure nor savings is much affected. The deficit must be financed by selling bonds to foreigners and the current account deficit rises by the same amount as the budget deficit, with the resources to meet the demand coming from the additional expenditure being provided by imports.

Empirical evidence does not support the twin deficits theory. Many studies, cited to support it by those opposed to Keynesian economic policy, show the current account deficit increasing by up to one-third of a change in the budget deficit (e.g. Berheim 1987, and Sachs and Roubini 1988). This is not empirical evidence in favour of the twin deficits theory but merely shows that imports increase when aggregate demand increases because of effective macroeconomic policy. A simple test of the twin deficits theory is the experience in OECD countries in the early 1990s. From 1990 to 1993 in the G-7 countries as a whole, budget deficits more than doubled and the current account deficits fell to zero. This was not an isolated incident. A similar story applies to the years 1980 to 1983. The twin deficits theory fails this test conclusively.

Although the twin deficits theory is contradicted by experience in most G-7 countries (and Australia) in most recessions, the Keynesian point, that when an economy expands imports also usually rise, still stands. This does not matter when the level of economic activity is low, but may cause problems in the context of longer run growth. We will return to this point in the next section.

So far we have considered arguments about the effectiveness of fiscal policy. The next proposition applies equally to monetary and fiscal policy. A school of economics, known as new classical economics, holds that macroeconomic policy is ineffective except for the short period when people are surprised by it and do not take it into account in their decision-making. A completely fair exposition of new classical economics would be more technical than is appropriate in this context, but the following gives the flavour of the arguments.

The key assumption, from which all else flows, is that wages and prices adjust rapidly enough so that labour and product markets clear with virtually no delays. That is, everyone who wants a job at the going wage can find one and every firm can sell as much as it wants at the going price. Given this, and abstracting from economic growth, the amount of output and employment will only change when there are unexpected changes in the general level of prices. At the level of the individual worker or firm, the amount of labour or goods supplied depends, it is asserted, on the perceived real wage or real prices – that is, on the wage or price received relative to the general price level. At the macro level, in the words of a prominent new classical economist:

> Unexpected rises in the price level . . . boost aggregate supply, because suppliers (of which suppliers of labour are one important example) mistakenly interpret surprise increases in the aggregate price level as increases in the relative prices of the labour or goods which they are supplying. (Sargent 1973, p. 435)

The next question, of course, is what determines the expected price level. The assumption of rational expectations begins with the belief that the public cannot form their expectations in a way which would lead to a permanent bias in one direction or another, because if it did, sooner or later people would notice this and correct for it. If people are rational, in the way the new classical school assumes, they will use the best information possible in forming their expectations and assume that everyone else does the same. That is, they will use the best economic theory or econometric model available (which the new classical economists immodestly assume is their own). If the government acts in such a way as to increase the general price level, and people realise that this is happening, then there will be no effect on supply or on unemployment. The level of unemployment is determined by unexpected inflation (and is lower the higher the unexpected inflation). Unexpected inflation can result only from unexpected and unnoticed actions by the government (or unexpected changes in other exogenous variables). Thus the government can affect real output and unemployment only in a time period so short that its actions are unexpected and unnoticed.

For many, the market clearing assumption, on which the whole edifice of new classical economics rests, is so absurd that little further discussion is needed. However, empirical evidence does not support new classical economics either. There are many econometric studies which demonstrate that Keynesian policies have been effective (e.g. Boltho 1989) and a number that do not. These studies have given rise to arguments about technical econometric points. There is an easy way to cut through all these arguments about technicalities and, in a straightforward way, to test new classical economics empirically. A prediction at the core of new classical economics can be shown not to hold. New classical economics holds that economic policy can affect the general price level and the rate of inflation but that, except in the short period when people are taken by surprise by policy changes, variables such as output, employment and unemployment cannot be changed through economic policy actions. If this is so, tight monetary policy, well heralded in advance so that it surprises no one, will stop inflation immediately without affecting output and employment. This has not happened and experienced central bankers believe that it is most unlikely to happen in the future. On his retirement, as governor of the Reserve Bank of Australia, R.A. Johnston said 'To deal with inflation in a permanent way is to accept a fairly great deal of pain' (*Sydney Morning Herald*, 19 June 1998). In more formal language, Max Corden, in summing up the conclusions of a Reserve Bank conference, stated: 'Consensus did exist on three crucial matters . . . [of which the first was] you cannot disinflate without some cost' (1992, p. 341). With this refutation of new classical economics, none of the theories discussed in this section are supported by the empirical evidence.[11]

Inflation, the current account deficit and globalisation

While arguments that Keynesian policies cannot stimulate growth in output and employment have been refuted by empirical evidence, the argument that they have potentially disastrous side-effects must be taken more seriously. Anything that raises the growth of output sufficiently to reduce unemployment substantially will usually increase inflationary pressure. Unless the source of growth is an export boom, it will also usually cause a deterioration in the current account deficit on the balance of payments. Unfortunately, these two side-effects are likely to interact, each making the other worse. Even in the golden years they caused problems from time to time. The response was unusually tight macroeconomic policy, as occurred in 1956/57 and 1960/61.

Inflation is not a problem in Australia at the moment, being at the lowest level for 25 years. This does give room to manoeuvre, but the very low inflation rate was bought at considerable cost in terms of a recession that was both deep and long. This occurred even though the recession came after seven years of a successful incomes policy had reduced the inflation rate while unemployment was also falling. Given that inflation is currently at extremely low levels, the first priority now must be to reduce unemployment and under-employment. Nevertheless, policies should be devised which will do this without throwing away the benefit of low inflation, which was obtained at such a high cost.

In the short to medium term the rate of inflation rises as the unemployment rate falls unless incomes policies such as the Accord are put into place to prevent this from happening. This trade-off between inflation and unemployment has been well documented empirically and is widely accepted by Keynesian and neoclassical economists alike. Not quite so uncontroversial but still widely accepted is that there is a rate of unemployment (or narrow range of unemployment rates) above which the inflation accelerates, or increases even if the rate of unemployment is constant. When unemployment is below this rate, inflation declines. This rate of unemployment is known as the NAIRU or non-accelerating inflation rate of unemployment.

It is important to realise that the NAIRU is not a number set in stone. It can be changed by policies, especially incomes policies and labour-market policies. In many countries it is not independent of the actual rate of unemployment and grows over time when unemployment is high. Hence, overall macroeconomic policy can influence the NAIRU by influencing the level of actual unemployment. Australia's experience in the 1980s shows that it is possible to have lengthy periods of growth without the rate of inflation rising. From 1982/83 to 1989/90 output grew at an annual rate of 4.3 per cent in Australia and unemployment fell from 9.0 per cent to 6.2 per cent. Over the same period inflation fell from 10 per cent to 6 per cent.[12]

A tendency to rising rates of inflation may interact with current account deficit problems. In the past 25 years in Australia, whenever output and employment have grown fast enough to significantly reduce unemployment, and this rate of growth is sustained, the leakage of aggregate demand into imports causes uncomfortably high current account deficits on the balance of payments. If consequent market forces, or even government policy, result in a devaluation of the value of the Australian dollar against foreign currencies, imports will become more expensive adding to inflationary pressure. A rising rate of inflation will put further pressure on the foreign exchange rate and it is easy to slip into an inflation–devaluation vicious circle. This can be prevented, though often at the cost of a fall in real wages,[13] if wages are not allowed to rise to offset the increased cost of living caused by higher import prices.

It is easier to stop an inflation–devaluation vicious circle, even without increasing unemployment, than it is to cure the underlying problem with the current account deficit. Some academic economists have argued that large current account deficits are more of a perceived problem than a real one. The current account deficit is Australia's net borrowing from foreigners over the relevant period. If imports rise, and nothing else changes, we have to borrow more to pay for the extra inputs. Some academic economists argue that since this borrowing from foreigners is largely done by firms in the private sector, who presumably believe that it is profitable to do so, it is not something to be concerned about (see Pitchford 1995). The majority of economists, and virtually all of those responsible for policy advice to government, disagree. The basic reason is that Australia already has a large foreign debt, and the amount we are already borrowing from abroad is a high proportion of our output (or GDP). If we continue to borrow increasing amounts from abroad (i.e. if the current account deficit increases as a proportion of GDP), sooner or later foreigners will wonder if we will be able to service the debt and cease lending to Australia. Moreover, Australia confronts a volatile external environment, especially in terms of potentially large swings in commodities prices. As Sjaastad (quoted in Grattan and Gruen 1993, p. 168) has pointed out,

> the basic reason for concern about the large build-up of private Australian debt is that some unexpected events can lead to a sudden and pronounced change in overseas investor sentiment about their exposure to the excessively high levels of (private) debt of Australian firms.

This can precipitate a massive devaluation of the Australian dollar on foreign exchange markets and hence large falls in real consumption and a rapid, painful adjustment in our economy. Moreover, the devaluation may be precipitated by currency speculators before it would occur if foreign investors were left to make the judgement themselves. If currency speculators have reason to think that signs of weakness will cause investors to stop lending, a speculative attack is likely to be successful. Although the circumstances are different, the East Asian crisis of 1997/98 is an outstanding example of what can happen when financial markets take fright. It is, at the least, only prudent to have policies that address current account deficit problems.

If rapid growth in the Australian economy occurs when there is also rapid growth around the world, any current account deficit problems are not likely to be severe. Not only will the volume of Australian exports increase but their prices are likely to rise, even compared to the prices of Australian imports. It is when Australia tries to go it alone that the current account deficit can raise severe problems.[14] The following analysis assumes that growth in output is greater than growth in exports.

The current account deficit is equal to the difference between imports and exports (the trade gap) plus the net amount that Australians pay to foreigners in dividends, interest and gifts. It is also equal to the difference between investment and savings (the savings gap) plus again the net amount paid to foreigners in dividends, interest and gifts. This follows from the definitions of the various items in the national accounts so that when the statistician measures what has happened in the economy, the savings gap is the same as the trade gap and must be so by definition. But what if the trade gap which would result from the plans of participants in the economy does not equal the savings gap which would result from those plans? Will the trade gap change or will the savings gap adjust? If with a rising rate of economic growth there is a surge in imports, in the short run the savings gap will adjust through an increase in trade credit. The extra imports will not encourage foreigners to lend to Australian institutions, on the contrary. Hence, in the somewhat longer run the inflow of foreign financial capital will decline unless interest rates rise to make lending to Australia more attractive. The decline in foreign lending to Australia will cause the value of the Australian dollar to fall on the foreign exchange market. If, for fear of inflationary consequences or some other reason, the government wishes to avoid this devaluation, the usual response is to raise interest rates enough to sustain the flow of foreign lending. Policy-induced rises in interest rates will encourage foreign lenders not only because of the higher interest returns, but also because it may reassure them that the government is determined to avoid a substantial devaluation which would cause losses on loans denominated in Australian dollars. However, the higher interest rates will discourage investment by private firms. This will reduce the savings gap, but it will also reduce growth of output and any fall in unemployment.

If interest rates do not rise and the Australian dollar's value falls on foreign exchange markets, exports and import-competing industries will be encouraged, but only in the very short run unless, as discussed before, real wages fall. Otherwise an inflation–devaluation vicious circle will be set up. Even if this does not occur, a substantial devaluation may make foreign investors more nervous than is necessary leading to a further devaluation. While a small devaluation can be helpful, it is not likely to be enough by itself and it is hard to make a large one successful. It requires a strong incomes policy and perhaps other policies also which reassure foreigners that the Australian dollar has underlying strength. Rather than devaluing, it is almost always easier to tackle the savings gap, not by reducing investment, but by increasing savings in Australia. To some extent, savings increase automatically as output and income rise, but in the absence of policies to increase savings this is not enough to match the rise in imports. Although increasing savings is only part of the solution, it is probably a necessary condition for Keynesian policies to increase growth in output and employment in the long run, in a country like Australia.

This conclusion is made much stronger when account is taken of the effects of the financial deregulation and globalisation that have occurred over the last two decades. Globalisation is a term coined to describe the greater interdependence, even integration of national economies, which, in part, has been facilitated by the computer revolution in the transmission of information. It is most obvious in financial markets. Vast sums of money cross national boundaries each day. Transactions are made by computer, institutions all around the world are linked by computers and professionals can deal as easily in a country on the other side of the world as in their own city. The consequences of this virtual integration of financial markets around the world are seen every day in our newspapers, e.g. when Australian share prices fall, the day interest rates rise in New York.

The globalisation of financial markets has given these markets considerable influence on government policy. Financial markets now have great power in determining the exchange rate for an economy, and the exchange rate has such a widespread influence on the economy that, in many countries, governments must be constantly looking over their shoulder with concern about the effects of policy actions on financial markets (Nevile 1996, p. 323).

The practical effect of this globalisation is not necessarily that national sovereignty in policy-making has been superseded by tailoring policies to please financial markets. While there have been assertions that this is the case, careful empirical studies suggest that 'governments still have policy choices and fiscal policy may be the most important instrument for choice' (Keohane and Milner 1996, p. 248), to quote from the conclusion of a major book on the extent to which domestic policy-making has been constrained by globalisation. Keohane and Milner certainly do not argue that choices in macroeconomic policy-making have not been reduced. The quotation is largely based on the chapter by Garrett in their book. After a careful cross-country study of 15 countries, Garrett (1996) concludes that monetary policy is constrained by increasing capital mobility, but that the evidence that there are important constraints on fiscal policy is weak. Moreover, Moore (1998) has shown that much of the evidence found to support the loss of national autonomy in policy-making is based on the experience of members of the European Economic Community who have gone much further along the road of integration of their economies than is generally the case.[15] Nevertheless, the problems of inflation and current account deficits, which always were important when Australia tried to grow faster than the rest of the OECD, have become even more important, with less margin for error in policies designed to overcome them.

It is difficult to strike the correct balance between blithely ignoring the financial markets' reactions to macroeconomic policy changes on the one hand, and giving up independent macroeconomic policy for fear of those reactions on the other. The reason for financial markets' concern about the size of current account deficits is obvious. Anything which suggests that a currency may be about to fall in value on foreign exchange markets is likely to lead to actions that precipitate a devaluation. Financial markets also give great weight to keeping inflation low as this is good for their profits. In a speech the former governor of the Reserve Bank of Australia, Bernie Fraser, commented that 'monetary policy was becoming the hostage of influential financial markets with a vested interest in making the Reserve Bank give greater weight to inflation than unemployment' (quoted in the *Sydney Morning Herald*, 16 June 1996). Financial institutions have a vested interest in keeping inflation low because a rise in interest rates reduces the value of the fixed interest securities that they hold. Also, and perhaps of more importance to foreigners investing in financial assets in Australia, a rate of inflation that is consistently above that in most other countries is a reliable sign that sooner or later the currency will be devalued. Financial markets also seem to be worried by large budget deficits which they fear may lead to a rise in interest rates or devaluation. However, there is little or no evidence that the size of the public sector is a matter of concern if expenditure is balanced by revenue.

Financial markets have, no doubt, always been concerned about inflation and the current account deficit. Globalisation gives them much more power to make their wishes prevail in that it makes a disastrous outcome much more likely if they decide that the exchange rate for a country's currency is unsustainable. While governments do not have to make the desires of financial markets their first priority in economic policy-making, at least those in countries with a large foreign debt have to convince financial markets that their actual (or potential) policies will prevent a large devaluation.

Policies for a sustained large fall in unemployment

The previous sections have indicated that, if Keynesian policies to raise the rate of growth of output and employment are to be successful in producing a sustained fall in unemployment, more than expansionary monetary and fiscal policies are required. The following package of policies is put forward:

- an effective incomes policy (see chapter 9);
- substantially expanded and better designed labour-market programs (see chapter 11);
- a substantial increase in government expenditure, especially on economic infrastructure, education, training and labour-market programs and on labour-intensive socially useful community services (see chapters 10 and 12);

- an equally large, or even larger increase in taxation revenue;
- measures to increase savings in the private sector;
- measures to increase net exports (see chapter 8).

Incomes policy and expanded labour-market programs are necessary to reduce inflationary pressures and to help prevent any inflation–devaluation vicious circle developing. The incomes policy will have to be strong enough to withstand the strain put on it by increases in tax rates as well as by falling unemployment. Successful incomes policy and labour-market programs are needed to reduce the NAIRU, not only to reduce inflationary pressures, but also because while the exact level of the NAIRU in Australia at present is not clear, it certainly is above any socially acceptable long-run goal for the unemployment rate. Labour-market programs are an important complement to Keynesian macro policies.

The increase in government expenditure is necessary to stimulate growth in aggregate demand and private investment. Expenditure on economic infrastructure, education, training and labour-market programs should also increase both labour and capital productivity and help offset to some extent the fall in the real value of take-home pay caused by the rise in taxation rates. There is mounting evidence that in many countries, increased public investment in economic infrastructure increases the productivity of private-sector investment. Otto and Voss (1994) document this for Australia. Using Australian data, Kearney, Chowdhury and Fallick (1996) find that public infrastructure investment has positive externality effects and 'crowds in' private investment (see also Dowrick 1994a). Making private investment more productive will normally increase the rate of private investment which will help increase aggregate demand. Education, training and labour-market programs obviously increase labour productivity, but indirectly can also contribute to increasing capital productivity.

Because of the need to avoid large government deficits (if only to avoid negative financial market sentiments), increasing taxation revenue is at the heart of the expansionary policies advocated here. It almost certainly would involve some new taxes and these would have to be introduced with careful consideration of both equity issues and effects on private-sector savings. This is not the place for a detailed discussion of tax reform but a couple of unusual suggestions can be put forward for consideration (see also chapter 10). The first is the imposition of a uniform tariff, say at 5 per cent on all imported goods, and on as many imported services as it is reasonably convenient to catch in the tax net. Revenue tariffs are not meant to be part of a policy of protection and are allowed under World Trade Organization rules when a country faces current account deficit problems. Any effect on the price of imports would be smaller than those of acceptable fluctuations in the exchange rate, partly because the exchange rate will be a little higher than it would be in the absence of a revenue tariff.

The second suggestion relates to the merits of a goods and services tax versus Australia's present wholesale sales tax. It is desirable to tax consumption of services as well as consumption of goods. The equity problems involved in the introduction of a goods and services tax could be overcome by zero rating food, housing and health expenditures and by retaining the wholesale sales tax on some luxury items, for example expensive cars.

Taxation revenue will have to increase sufficiently to increase national savings to such an extent that the current account deficits are not unduly high. Equally important, it will have to ensure that, despite increases in government expenditure, the budget deficit does not become large enough to alarm financial markets. In the short to medium term, it is essential that financial markets do not have undue concern about the Australian dollar. This rules out budget deficits that are large and increasing. There is scope to increase taxes in that Australia has one of the lowest ratios of taxes to income and output in the OECD (see table 10.1).

In the longer term, solving the current account deficit problem will be eased by measures that increase private savings without reducing private-sector investment or public-sector savings. One possibility is to increase the superannuation levy, but thought should be given to other measures.

As argued in chapter 8, increasing net exports will also ease current account problems. There are numerous examples where Australian governments have not proved good at picking winners. Nevertheless, policies that encourage export and import-competing industries across the board can be devised.

Keynesian policies to increase the rate of growth of output and employment can be successful, but they do not provide a free lunch. Even in the short term, they are likely to increase income per head as the unemployed are drawn back into productive activity. However, at least in the short term, the increased taxation required will reduce a little the incomes of those already in steady full-time employment and those with comfortable incomes from rent, interest and dividends or profits. How big is the required rise in tax revenue? It is impossible to be precise. It will depend in part on what is happening in the rest of the world. The faster economies overseas are growing, the faster the volume and value of Australian exports will grow. Thus, fast growth in the rest of the world will both stimulate output and employment growth in

Australia and help prevent the current account deficit growing too rapidly. However, the prospects for rapid growth in the world economy over the next five years are anything but good.

The size of the required increase in taxation will also depend on how rapidly unemployment is to be reduced. Over the eight years to June 1998 the unemployment rate in Australia averaged 9.3 per cent. This period roughly covers one complete business cycle of boom and slump. An ambitious, but not completely unrealistic, target would be to reduce unemployment by half in five years so that after that five-year period the average level of unemployment over boom and slump is 4.7 per cent.

Given this target, and assuming that the world economy will grow slowly over the next five years, a ball-park figure for the increase in the ratio of tax revenue to GDP is 10 per cent. Current government revenue, which includes dividends from government business enterprises and fees and fines as well as taxation, would have to rise from a little over 34 per cent of GDP to around 38 per cent of GDP. This rise will be needed to cover the increase in government expenditure. The low rate of growth of the world economy will make it unlikely that the current account deficit will fall as a proportion of GDP. To reassure financial markets, it will be necessary to finance increases in both current and capital expenditure by increases in current revenue. At least on average over boom and slump, all government expenditure must be balanced by current government revenue.

The rise in government expenditure and current revenue should be sustained, as a percentage of GDP, over the whole five years. Obviously, those who move from unemployment, or under-employment, to full employment will have a rise in real income. On average other Australians will suffer a short-run decline in real income because of the increase in taxation. This will be greatest (3 to 4 per cent) at the beginning of the period, but will become progressively smaller because of the more rapid rate of growth of GDP. By the end of five years, the higher rate of growth will have completely offset the increased tax rates so that the real incomes of those already fully employed will be just as high as they would have been if the policy package had not been implemented.

Conclusion

Both a review of past experience and an examination of the theoretical arguments of those opposed to Keynesian economics suggest that Keynesian policies can stimulate growth in output and reduce unemployment. Even if policy does no more than make recessions shorter and not so deep, the average level of unemployment will be reduced. However, this chapter argues that Keynesian policies can do more than this.

Well-chosen policies can significantly increase the trend rate of growth of output and employment, reducing unemployment substantially. Halving the rate of unemployment in five years time is quite possible.

However, halving unemployment five years hence, or even seven or eight years hence, cannot be done without short-run cost to the majority of Australians. While the package of policies outlined in the previous section will increase the average income of Australians as a whole, it will increase greatly the incomes of those unemployed or substantially under-employed but reduce slightly the average income received by other Australians. This reduction is because of the increase in taxation which is an integral part of the policy package. It will be about 3 or 4 per cent at the beginning of the period and will steadily decline over time.

The question is how much do Australians wish to reduce unemployment substantially and relatively rapidly. How much are we prepared to pay in higher taxation to achieve this? The cost, in the form of a fall in after-tax income, will only be short lived. The more rapid rate of growth of GDP will, despite higher tax rates, restore real income: after about two years to the level that held in the year before the policies were implemented, and after about five years to the level that they would have reached at the slower rate of growth which would have occurred without the policy changes. Is this too big a sacrifice for the majority of Australians to make to halve the unemployment rate?

CHAPTER 8

Speed Limits to Growth and the Quality of Jobs: Economic Structure and the Current Account

Stephen Bell, Roy Green and John Burgess

As outlined in previous chapters, an expansionary economic policy aimed at reducing unemployment runs the risk of exacerbating Australia's current account problem. An expansionary policy could suck in too many imports or create too much foreign debt, potentially bringing about a current account crisis, thus acting as a speed limit to growth. As argued briefly in chapter 1 and more fully in chapter 7, Australia's current account position should remain an important focus for policy. We should, however, also learn from experience and avoid highly restrictionist – 'the recession we had to have' – responses to the current account deficit (CAD) (Leeson 1993; Burgess and Mitchell 1998). This applies especially to monetary policy. Instead, the best approach is a medium-term one and this is the focus of this chapter. At present, as this chapter argues,[1] complacency about the CAD in some circles masks deeper medium-term structural problems in the economy. These relate not only to our deteriorating terms of trade but also to the employment structure.

Australia's current account position is mainly defined by the trade account and our foreign debt position. Although the trade account is not seriously out of balance, this chapter argues that our reliance on low value-added commodities exports in an increasingly high-tech world poses medium to longer term problems. This chapter also argues that the best way to fund and stabilise our foreign debt[2] is through strong export growth. Both these issues highlight the need in the medium term to restructure the Australian economy in order to better position it in world trade and pursue a 'high road' developmental path. Ultimately, we need a better mix of industries and less reliance on low value-added commodities exports.

Such restructuring is important for another reason. Australia's economic structure and developmental path are producing too many low-

175

quality, low-paying jobs. There has been virtually no net full-time job creation in the 1990s with the vast majority of net job generation being part-time and casual centred in low-paying sectors (Brosnan and Campbell 1995; Burgess and Campbell 1998). The only way to improve this situation is through a better economic structure that produces higher paying, better quality jobs. In short, we need a stronger mix of industries that will better reflect the developmental realities of the new millennium. We argue in this chapter that, despite gains in a few areas, the last two decades of economic restructuring have not achieved these goals. In some ways we have gone backwards.

The chapter begins by outlining the type of economy we need to secure good jobs and jobs growth. Then the type of economy we now have is reviewed. The weakness of current policy settings is explained. Finally, a more appropriate policy framework is briefly outlined: the key argument being that without a new package of properly co-ordinated, funded and administered industry, training and labour-market programs, present structural economic trends will only continue.

The economy we should have

As we enter the twenty-first century, it is increasingly clear that economies dominated by high value-added, brain-based manufacturing and high-end services industries (and the boundary between the two is increasingly blurred) are far better off than countries dominated by low value-added commodities or low-wage services sectors (Reich 1991; Thurow 1996). Economic structure matters! One reason is that high-end industries are the main growth sectors in the world economy. Figure 8.1 illustrates this trend clearly in terms of the fate of manufactures vs commodities in global trading markets in recent decades.

A major reason for this trend is that as the world economy develops, there is less reliance on commodities as production inputs and more reliance on knowledge and skill-based inputs (Drucker 1986). This helps to partially explain why there has been a long-term trend decline in the real price of commodities in world markets and a corresponding increase in the real prices of high-end manufactures. It also explains why, in recent decades, countries heavily reliant on basic commodity exports, such as Australia, have experienced such adverse terms of trade (i.e. a fall in the price of exports relative to imports). These basic characteristics underpin a common pattern across the world: namely, that successful economies are sustained by strong trade performance in manufacturing and related higher end industries. As Porter's extensive work on the competitive advantage of nations shows:

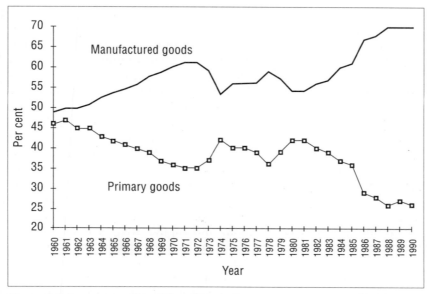

Figure 8.1 Percentage share of world merchandise trade by value, 1960–90
Source: GATT

> One of the very few features that successful economies in the post-war era do have in common is a very strong sense of national mission. That national mission always includes the central concept that they are going to export, and that they are going to export manufactures. There isn't a single experience which contradicts that feature. (quoted in Carter 1992, p. 20)

The Australian Manufacturing Council's *Global Challenge* (Pappas Carter Evans Koop-Telsis 1990, p. 16) report agrees, arguing that 'No large modern economy has managed to stay wealthy without substantial diversity and a strong manufacturing base'. This is partly a matter of linkages within the economy. A strong manufacturing sector typically fosters a range of high value-added sectors in the service economy, particularly in consultancy areas such as law and accounting, marketing, engineering, and trade and currency analysis, etc. (Cohen and Zysman 1983; Daniels 1993). A capable manufacturing sector is also typically linked to a robust indigenous research and development and technology capacity. Manufacturing is also typically associated with strong input linkages from other parts of the economy. For example, in 1992/93, every dollar of manufacturing output in Australia relied on 55.1 cents worth of inputs from the domestic economy. The nearest rival was agriculture with inputs of 43.4 cents per dollar of output (Sicklen 1998, p. 45).

The importance of high-end manufacturing and service sectors to the fate of national economies is also emphasised in recently revised understandings about the causes of economic growth and trade specialisation (see Dowrick 1993; Marceau et al. 1997). The new findings embodied in theories such as new growth theory, strategic trade theory and evolutionary economics question the key assumptions of conventional neo-classical theories of growth and trade, particularly perfect competition, decreasing returns to scale and the assumption that technology is independent or exogenous to the growth process. By substituting imperfect competition, increasing returns to scale and by seeing technology and innovation as embedded within and indeed driving much of the growth process, the new approaches end with a very different view of economic development. These shifts in understanding about growth and trade reflect the need to move beyond conventional nineteenth-century views that crude inputs of land, labour and capital drive growth, to a late twentieth-century view where it is clear that what matters just as much or more in driving growth is information, knowledge, skill, technology and firm size or market power. For example, imperfect competition in industries dominated by a small number of major players can help foster increasing returns to scale as firms grow, particularly through strategies of market capture and barriers to entry, brand loyalty and product differentiation. Imperfect markets and 'externalities', particularly where there are large spillovers of skill, knowledge and innovation capacity beyond the host firm to other firms and sectors, are now recognised to be important in spurring growth and competitiveness. It is also recognised that such spillovers can be fostered by co-operatively organised inter-firm networks and clusters which purposefully share resources and knowledge.

Hence, the process of economic development depicted by the new theories is one where growth is based not on perspiration but inspiration (to paraphrase the economist Paul Krugman). It is a world of strongly linked high-end industry and service sectors, of clustering, of research and development, of 'national systems of innovation', of technological breakthroughs, of human capital development, of 'learning by doing', of spillover effects, scale economies and first mover advantages. Marceau et al. (1997) characterise this type of economy as a 'learning economy' and stress that economic structure, relationships between economic actors and the policy environment are critical determinants of such an economic system.

Developing high-end manufacturing, however, is not likely to create many new manufacturing jobs because this sector is essentially one of productivity-driven 'jobless growth' (see also chapter 6). Even in the case of Australia's relatively low- to medium-tech manufacturing sector, this has been the case in recent decades. As indicated in chapter 6, for example, between 1984/85 and 1992/93 the manufacturing sector increased output by 12.3 per cent and productivity by 16.4 per cent while employment in the sector *fell* by 4.1 per cent. Nevertheless, as indicated above, high-end manufacturing (and high-end services industries) are the major source of growth and dynamism in the world economy and they are important high-wage and high-skill sectors. Manufacturing and other high-end industries are also important sectors of innovation and learning in the economy. The recent trend in the manufacturing sector has been to outsource not only low-wage activities but also a range of high-wage services, such as design, marketing, training and maintenance, which are then counted for statistical purposes as services rather than manufacturing employment. It is in this sense that we live not in a 'post-industrial' society, but one in which the distinction between manufacturing and services is increasingly blurred (Jaikumar 1986; Reich 1991). Indeed, manufacturing has historically given rise to a 'clustering' effect, with the establishment of formal and informal customer–supplier chains which include services as well as other manufacturers. Hence, while the manufacturing sector itself is not a major jobs generator, it is important in spurring jobs growth in other sectors, such as high-end services.

Another mechanism by which manufacturing helps create jobs is less visible but of even greater significance. Here, improvements in productivity and competitiveness enable manufacturers to export to world markets and to replace imports at home. It is this process, based on private and public-sector investment, that allows us to reduce the current account deficit and hence to overcome the balance of payments 'speed limit' on economic growth. It is our argument that the most effective strategy for overcoming the balance of payments constraint on growth and jobs is to tackle the merchandise trade component of the current account deficit. The aim should be to create a surplus that offsets the net income deficit and enables us to reduce external debt as a proportion of GDP to lower levels. While this does not automatically generate faster growth, it provides policy-makers with the opportunity to do so through investment in public infrastructure and community services, which not only creates new jobs directly but also via multiplier effects across the economy. Indeed, as John Quiggin argues in chapter 10, the public sector can and should be the major source of additional employment in the next century, because as manufacturing becomes more productive, government is in a better position to mobilise resources, including people, to tackle unemployment and meet clearly identified social needs (Langmore and Quiggin 1994).

The economy we have

There is a big difference between the economy we should have and the one we've got. Structurally, Australia's economy has three basic problems: its overreliance on commodities, its weak manufacturing sector and the strong growth of low-wage, low-productivity service industries. Australia is on what Marceau et al. (1997) in a major recent report call the 'low road' of economic development – increasingly, a 'Mcjobs' economy.

In terms of the first problem, Australia's commodity-based economy makes it very different from our major trading partners in Europe, North America and even Asia. Australia's heavy reliance on basic commodity exports and weakness in elaborately transformed manufactures (ETM) exports is strikingly clear from table 8.1. As indicated, in 1993, Australia's export profile was closer to that of New Zealand and Papua New Guinea than any other country in the region. It featured an almost 60 per cent reliance on unprocessed or semi-processed commodities with only a 17 per cent share of ETM exports. Most of our APEC trading partners had the opposite pattern, with only about a 20 per cent reliance on commodities exports with an ETM share averaging almost 60 per cent of total exports.

The problem with Australia's economic structure and export profile is that, as argued above, specialising in commodities is increasingly a counterproductive approach in the world economy. Because of this and because commodity prices are weakening in world markets, Australia's terms of trade collapse has been the most severe in the OECD, as figure 8.2 indicates.

Given this situation, Australia has to export almost twice as much by volume as it did in the 1950s in order to fund the same level of imports. Beardow has estimated that if Australia had maintained its terms of trade and real incomes at 1975 levels, unemployment today would be around 4–5 per cent (*AFR* 4 May 1998).

Australia's weak, low- to medium-tech manufacturing sector is also a problem. As Sheehan (1998, p. 247) points out, because of the nature of the industries which dominate Australian manufacturing (and despite gains in recent years), the overall research and development intensity (the ratio of R&D to value-added) of Australian manufacturing is only about half the OECD average. Moreover, in the last decade in particular, manufacturing has limped along at about half the speed of the rest of the economy with output expanding only 14 per cent in the nine years from 1987/88 (*AFR* 8 October 1996). The sector has struggled since the early 1990s recession, only experiencing one short-lived growth spurt in 1994.

Exposing the sector to international competition through successive rounds of tariff cuts in recent decades, combined with the impacts of an unsupportive policy environment, has led to a process of rapid 'deindustrialisation' as the manufacturing sector's share of GDP shrank from 26 per cent in 1963 to 15 per cent by 1993. The majority of manufacturing firms are now reducing their production within Australia and

Table 8.1 Composition of export income, APEC countries, 1993

	Elaborately transformed manufacture (%)	Simply transformed manufacture (%)	Services (%)	Processed food (%)	Other primary and miscellaneous exports (%)
1. Australia	16.6	6.9	20	8.8	47.7
2. New Zealand	15.3	9.1	20.7	29.9	24.6
3. USA	51.7	6.2	26.1	3.3	12.7
4. Canada	51.9	12.6	11.9	3.6	20
5. Mexico	30.1	6.2	33.9	2.8	27
6. Chile	30	4.3	22	10.5	33.2
7. Japan	78.5	6	12.5	0.4	2.6
8. Taiwan	76.2	5.6	12.9	2.7	2.5
9. Korea	71.7	8.2	14.2	1.7	4.2
10. China	65.4	6.9	11.2	4.5	12
11. Hong Kong	75.1	6.0	13.6	2.2	3.1
12. Thailand	49.7	4.7	23.6	10.3	11.7
13. PNG	6.2	0.5	12	10.4	70.9
14. Singapore	54.3	4.2	24.7	3.4	13.3
15. Philippines	29	1.9	29.1	6.2	37
16. Malaysia	53.9	3.6	12.5	7.9	22.3
17. Indonesia	43.5	4.8	9.9	5.6	36.2
18. Brunei	na	na	na	na	na
19. Total APEC	57.8	6.5	19.3	3.3	13.1

Source: AMWU (1998, 3.3)

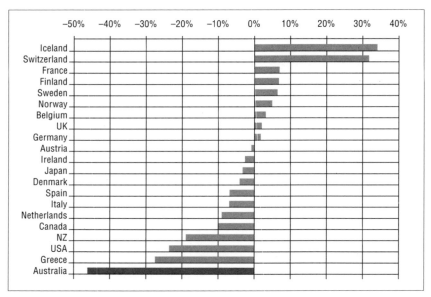

Figure 8.2 Changes in terms of trade, OECD countries, 1964–92
Source: OECD (1994b)

their purchases of locally made components and materials. Recent interview-based research by the Economist Intelligence Unit estimates that around 60–70 per cent of Australian manufacturers are moving in this direction (EIU 1997). Hence, Australia has seen direct offshore investment in manufacturing rise from $2bn in 1980/81 to $16bn in 1993/94 (Industry Commission 1996, p. 27). As figure 3.5 indicates, Australia has suffered the most extensive case of deindustrialisation in the OECD in recent decades. Meanwhile, over the same period, many economies in the region substantially increased their manufacturing/GDP ratios.

Kitson and Michie (1996, p. 47) outline three key reasons why deindustrialisation can affect the entire economy and 'seriously damage your wealth'. First, as noted above, there is typically a strong relationship between a strong manufacturing sector and a vibrant high-end services sector. Second, weak manufacturing trade performance, through adverse current account effects, will tend to lead to deflationary macroeconomic policies. Third, following Kaldor's ideas about sectoral linkages and 'cumulative causation' in economic development, deindustrialisation can lead to a spiral of decline which can spread out from manufacturing to other sectors. For example, if deindustrialisation exacerbates skill loss or creates a depressed environment for training,

Table 8.2 Relative productivity levels in manufacturing, 1960–95 (value added per hour, USA = 100)

	1960	1995
USA	100	100
Japan	19.2	72.8
Germany	56	81.4
France	45.9	85.1
UK	45	69.7
Canada	68.5	69.6
Belgium	45.6	104.7
Finland	45.9	100.8
Netherlands	50.8	96.5
Spain	20.4	67.6
Sweden	49.8	90.3
Australia	50.5	51.7

Source: Pilat (1996)

these problems will obstruct one of the very processes necessary for any successful shift into new sectors.

If a key indicator of the capacity for industrial upgrading and competitiveness is the capacity to increase productivity levels relative to frontrunner countries, then Australia has done very badly in this arena. As table 8.2 indicates, in the three and a half decades from 1960 to 1995, all of the listed OECD countries, *except Australia*, made substantial gains in catching up to the levels of industrial productivity found in the US, the leader country.

Also, in an increasingly competitive and high-tech world, Australia, as figure 8.3 shows, has managed to actually shed high-tech manufacturing employment and gain low-tech manufacturing employment. The leading OECD industrial economies over the same period have done precisely the opposite: they have shed low-tech employment in industry and substantially improved high-tech industrial employment.

Part of the reason for these trends is that Australian management has been unused to fierce competition or breaking into overseas markets. As the Karpin Report (Karpin 1995) found, the proportion of senior managers with degrees in Australia was around 20 per cent. In the USA and Japan, over 80 per cent of senior managers have degrees. Government programs, such as Labor's Best Practice Demonstration Program, have brought about some improvement, but this has largely been confined to 'islands of best practice' with limited diffusion of the concepts to the large majority of businesses (Rimmer et al. 1996).

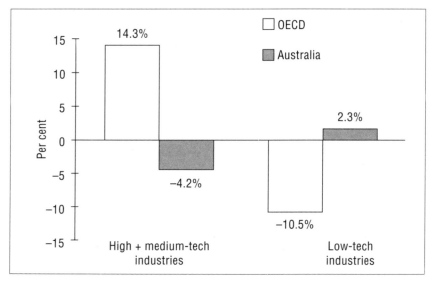

Figure 8.3 Changes in share of manufacturing employment between 1970 and 1990: Australia vs OECD 13

Source: OECD (1994b: 97)

On the investment front, there are also major problems. Despite a significant redistribution of national income towards profits in the last decade, private-sector investment has declined in each of the last two decades relative to GDP and critical investment areas such as plant and equipment have also experienced a trend decline (Bell 1997a, ch. 10). As a site for overseas investment, Australia also seems to be losing favour. Since 1988 our share of world foreign direct investment has fallen substantially as figure 8.4 indicates.

These problems, together with our history of protected industrialisation and the 'branch plant' character of much of industry, has also produced poor outcomes on the trade front. True, greater economic openness and competitive pressures have seen a rise in Australia's manufactured exports. ETM exports, for example, grew by around 16 per cent per annum during the late 1980s and into the early 1990s. These improvements, however (now tailing off), have been swamped by a far greater wave of ETM imports, as figure 8.5 shows. Sheehan (1998, p. 243) argues that a major driver of Australia's current account deterioration has been the build-up of a large ETM trade deficit, which, since the mid-1980s, has hovered around 9 per cent of GDP.

While Australian manufacturers have been losing market share domestically, the same has also occurred internationally. Australia's

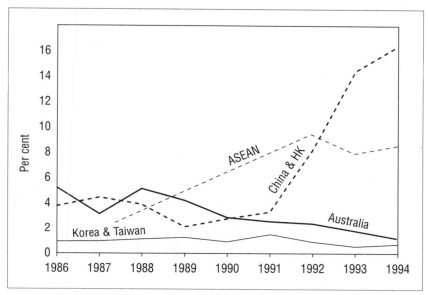

Figure 8.4 World foreign direct investment flows (% shares of total), 1986–94
Source: UNCTAD, *World Investment Report*, 1995

presence in global manufactures markets has slipped in the last two decades by almost half: from 1.4 per cent in 1970 to 0.8 per cent in 1992 (OECD 1994b). Australia is also losing market share in East Asia, in part because the strongest East Asian import sectors are manufactures, not commodities. Australia's share of East Asian imports was 4.05 per cent in 1985, but this fell to 2.89 per cent by 1993 (Hartcher 1996). It is also clear the whole economic restructuring exercise, if this is conceived as one designed to boost manufacturing and higher value-added exports, has failed. Over two decades, as figure 8.6 shows, Australia's burgeoning manufactures trade deficit has increasingly been offset by a growing non-manufactures trade surplus. This means that Australia's economic structure is regressing in this respect and is becoming *more* not less dependent on non-manufactured, largely low value-added exports in rural, mineral and tourism sectors.

The nature of the labour-market dynamics and employment created by this industrial and economic structure is also changing, largely for the worse. As argued more fully in chapters 1, 6 and 12, the most prominent shifts involve rising unemployment, increasing numbers of under-employed, the growth of part-time work, employment growth mainly in services, and rising wage inequality, job insecurity and poverty (Brosnan 1996; Burgess and Mitchell 1998; Gregory and Sheehan 1997). To take

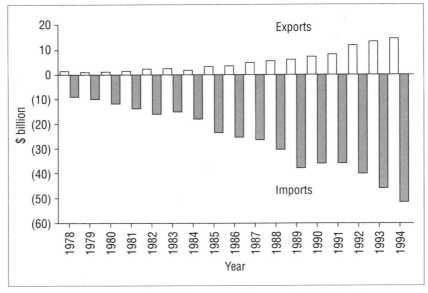

Figure 8.5 Manufactured (ETM) imports and exports ($b), 1978–94
Source: Unpublished DFAT data

just a few examples here, the manufacturing sector's share of total employment declined from 27.4 per cent in 1967 to 14.1 per cent in 1993 (Burgess and Green 1997, p. 103). Over the same period, the sector directly shed 152 000 jobs, though as Mitchell estimated in chapter 3, the net employment fall-out across the economy associated with such deindustrialisation could be as much as 300 000 jobs. Sheehan (1998, p. 241) demonstrates that since 1973, one in five full-time jobs has been lost in the economy. Put another way,

> if the 1973 ratio of full-time employment to the population of working age had been maintained through to 1996, the number of full-time jobs available in the Australian economy would have been about 2.8 million higher than was actually the case.

Moreover, as we saw in chapter 6:

- high-productivity growth has in general been achieved in those sectors that have reduced their levels of employment, e.g. mining, utilities, transport and communications;
- those sectors with the highest levels of labour productivity are those sectors that display net employment contraction: mining, manufacturing, utilities and transport and communications;

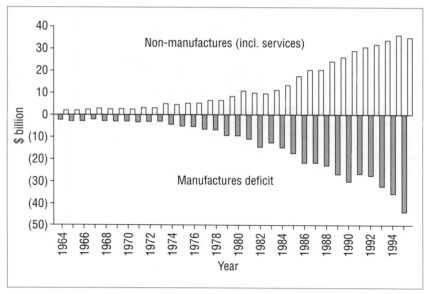

Figure 8.6 Merchandise trade: Non-manufactures trade surplus and manufactures trade deficit, 1964–94

Source: Unpublished ABS data, ABS Cat. no. 5302.0

- the *service sectors are accounting for virtually all employment growth*, but they have relatively low productivity levels and low labour productivity growth rates.

Hence, there has in effect been a transfer of employment from high-productivity sectors to low-productivity sectors, which, over time, will reduce the growth potential of the economy. Boosting productivity and associated economic restructuring to promote high-end sectors is thus essential. On the other hand, if we are interested in job generation, then it is appropriate that the service sector employment share increases. This is a key part of the answer to full employment and is discussed more fully in chapters 10 and 12.

The policies we have

Canberra boasts it has got 'the fundamentals' right (Cwth of Australia 1996). At the macroeconomic level, this reflects the progressive shift to a surplus in the federal budget, to low inflation, to lower interest rates and to growth in the 1990s better than most other OECD countries. However, as argued above, there are serious medium-term issues to consider regarding the structure of the economy. At the microeconomic level, Canberra defines the economy's chief problem as a cost-based 'competitiveness' problem. This is why competition policy has pride of place in the government's microeconomic agenda. The problem with such an agenda is that it is too limited. As argued above, Australia's major problem is not competitiveness per se, but the structure of the economy. As Roberts (1998) writes, 'our problem is primarily not one of competitiveness but what we export'.

Canberra largely overlooks the key structural issues and prefers a policy of 'structural agnosticism' which focuses mainly on economic aggregates. In part, such an approach stems from a 'comparative advantage' view of the world, which says that a country's basic economic structure is relatively fixed and rooted in 'god-given' endowments and factors of production, like abundant land or cheap labour. Hence, a comparative advantage view breeds a fatalism about economic structure and inhibits serious policy efforts to change it. The alternative view of the world is based on the notion of 'competitive advantage', which essentially says that firms and governments, guided by a vision of economic structure, can work together to effect fundamental transformation of the economy. This is exactly the sort of approach that has lifted Japan and other industrialised economies in East Asia beyond the rice paddy into the realm of high-tech manufacturing.

Because of its blinkered vision, Canberra does not have policies which are capable of actively changing the structure of the economy in a desired direction, particularly towards high-productivity production. What we have instead is a microeconomic policy focused mainly on crude cost-cutting through deregulation and competition policy, an uncertain industry policy, a trade policy centred on commodities exports, and an industrial relations system incapable of wages co-ordination and favouring 'low road' strategies of low-wage competition. Many of the reform measures directly involve job-shedding. Microeconomic reform in the public sector (as well as fiscal stringency) has seen Commonwealth employment fall by more than a third in the last decade (from 427 000 to 268 000). If we include the states as well, almost 300 000 jobs have been shed from the public sector in the last decade.

In a critique of the Productivity Commission's view of microeconomic reform, Sicklen (1996) points out cost reduction as a route to productivity and competitiveness is a strategy most applicable to low value-added commodities industries, where price is overwhelmingly the key competitive ingredient. By contrast, cost-reduction strategies, while important, should only be seen as *one* ingredient of productivity and competitiveness in high value-added or, what Arthur (1996) terms 'increasing return' industries. These are marked by high innovation and product differentiation, with competitive success depending not only on price but also on factors such as 'first mover advantages', quality, service back-up, distribution networks, client liaison and customer loyalty, brand identification and marketing strategies. Sicklen (1996, p. 4) comments that the commission's 'vision of economic reality virtually ignores increasing return industries'. This is in line with the commission's view of economic structure and specialisation based on comparative advantage theory. The implication is that the commission's (and the government's) cost-reduction strategy contains an unstated sectoral bias against high value-added increasing-return industries. Australia's increasing trade reliance on low-return industries (as figure 8.6 above shows) is the reality which follows.

A second major problem with the existing policy approach is that focusing on cost reduction as the key to productivity misses other keys to productivity growth. As Sicklen (1996) points out, there is no necessary link between cost reduction, particularly labour cost reduction, and productivity growth. Indeed, such cost reduction might even reduce productivity growth if firms substitute cheap labour for new technology. In the USA, since the early 1980s, there have been cheaper labour costs *and* lagging productivity growth. Other factors such as technological innovation, 'learning by doing', the structure of the economy, the level of public infrastructure provision, the impact of advanced human resource management strategies, the role of training, the role of clusters and linkages among firms, as well as demand conditions and the stance of macroeconomic policy, also have a major if not predominant role in spurring productivity growth (Sicklen 1996, pp. 6–10). The Productivity Commission chooses not to consider these crucial non-cost factors of productivity growth. As Phillip Holt (1996) of the Australian Business Chamber has argued:

Unless we pay a great deal more attention to the non-price aspects of com-petitiveness – which are created through human endeavour – we will be condemned to producing only slightly transformed mineral and agricultural resources, world prices for which have been on a long-term downward trend. (p. 18)

Canberra's approach to industry policy has also been problematic. The policy stance has generally favoured across-the-board, horizontal or industry-neutral approaches in areas such as generic R&D or export promotion programs. Sectoral policies have been eschewed or only tolerated temporarily as crisis measures (e.g. the 1980s steel plan). The advantages of more sectorally targeted policy approaches will be out-lined below. Despite evidence that such sectoral policies in the 1980s helped to promote critical industrial capacities in areas such as R&D and

ETM exports (Sheehan, Pappas and Cheng 1994), the Howard government revealed its views on industry policy when it drastically wound back programs and program expenditure in 1996 (Bell 1997b; Jones 1998). The government cut industry development by $3.3b over four years and even taxed imported components and machinery (raising a further $1.26b over four years). Following protest from industry, the government then conducted an inquiry into industry assistance (the Mortimer review) and in December 1997 announced new policy initiatives worth $1.26b (leaving a net deficit of about $3b compared to the earlier level of assistance). The episode is noteworthy in displaying the level of ad hockery associated with industry policy in Australia and the degree to which industry policy is vulnerable to attack.

There have also been problems because of the administrative limitations of what can only be described as a 'weak' industrial state (Jones 1994; Bell 1993). Too often policy has been poorly co-ordinated, funded and administered. Our state structures and administrative traditions have also failed to develop the kind of close and complex policy linkages with industry that typify many of the more successful industrial economies. In this sense, our policy-makers have failed to develop what might be called an effective 'microeconomic interfacing capacity' with industry. Stewart (1994) has pursued this theme and points to the fragmented nature of departments, agencies and programs, to the hostile and aggressive stance to manufacturers adopted by the Productivity Commission (and its predecessors) and to the removed and isolated nature of Canberra's bureaucratic elite (see also Jones 1994).

The lack of an effective industry policy in Australia is widely recognised in the business world. In 1997 a high-level diagnosis was dropped, bombshell-like, on Canberra by the Economist Intelligence Unit, an arm of the influential *Economist* magazine (EIU 1997). The EIU report had sampled the opinion of 55 multinational CEOs about investment in Australia and found little enthusiasm for such activity. High on the list of problems cited by the CEOs was the lack of a 'coherent industry policy'. The CEOs thought there was 'little incentive from the government to invest' and official denunciations of 'picking winners' and 'corporate welfare' did not help. In particular the majority of CEOs attacked 'the government's inability to provide a coherent, consistent and national policy for industry'. The EIU report stated:

> If there is a common response to the question of what changes in Australia would have the most impact at corporate headquarters in changing negative perceptions, it is the need for a coherent, long-term industry policy that runs across all federal ministries and across states. (quoted in the *Australian* 9 October 1996)

As Roberts (1996) comments, our policies:

> are being judged not against some academic ideal, but against the everyday policies behind so much of Asia's success in attracting investment in recent years. In Asia, multinationals find themselves dealing with governments utterly dedicated to attracting industry . . . We don't even think we have to compete. (p. 15)

In trade policy it is also clear that Canberra has expended most effort on promoting traditional commodities exports through attempts to liberalise agricultural trade. Under Labor and now under the coalition, trade policy has been aimed primarily at establishing an overarching, rule-based, free-trade regime under the auspices of the WTO and APEC. The primary thrust of this approach has been to improve access to overseas markets for Australia's commodity exporters, an approach which reflects Australia's ongoing dependence on such exports. A key problem with Australian trade policy is the feasibility of a strategy based on promoting agricultural and commodities free trade in world sectors where cartels, market power, subsidies and protectionism are very prominent. In particular, it seems that wealthy countries, for electoral and other reasons, are especially keen to protect their agricultural sectors. Scott and Williams (1995), for example, and the influential US Council on Foreign Relations (Wilson 1996), have offered a sobering prognosis on the future of APEC and cast strong doubt on the likelihood of agricultural trade liberalisation in the region, particularly in view of the recalcitrance of countries such as Malaysia and Japan (see also Beeson 1996). The future of APEC has been clouded in the wake of the Asian crisis with the most recent APEC summit in Malaysia producing little progress on trade liberalisation (Beeson and Bell 1999; Higgott 1999). Another problem with Australia's trade policy is that it does little to help *restructure* the economy or Australia's export profile. There is little formal co-ordination between trade policy and industry policy and by failing to prioritise high value-added economic restructuring, the commodity bias in Australia's trade policy helps perpetuate the fundamental structural problems of the economy (Sicklen 1995).

Australia's industrial relations policies of labour-market flexibility and atomistic bargaining also work against a 'high-road' developmental path. The shift towards decentralised bargaining, including individual contracts, the erosion of the award system and the emphasis on procedural controls over trade union activity, gives the appearance of being about deregulating wages, increasing employer prerogatives and de-unionising the workforce (Quinlan 1998). Australia already boasts a very high rate of part-time and casual employment by OECD standards, together with a growing number of workers in the unregulated employment sector (Campbell and Burgess 1997). It can be demonstrated that trade union densities are falling, that wage dispersion is increasing, that working poverty is expanding and that employment insecurity is increasing (Brosnan 1996; Campbell and Burgess 1997). Yet it is more difficult to point to dynamic efficiency gains, a permanent lift in productivity growth and an expansion in industry training. The direction of the industrial relations and labour-market policies together with the developments in the Australian workforce and industrial relations are very similar to the US model (Mishell and Schmitt 1995): low wage, low productivity, low union density and high employment insecurity.

Finally, in further distancing itself from underlying structural issues, the government has also adopted a misconceived, restrictionist fiscal policy approach to the current account deficit aimed at addressing a perceived savings shortfall. The aim is to boost national saving and thereby, so the argument goes, reduce the current account deficit. (A fuller critique of this approach can be found in Sicklen 1995; Bell 1997a, pp. 167–71; and Gelber 1998.) It can be briefly noted here, however, that some of the problems in the government's approach include: the fact that government advisers largely *assume* that it is weak savings (and associated high foreign borrowing) that is driving the current account deficit. Yet as Gregory (1991b) argues, the causality could just as easily be running the other way, with the current account and wider economic problems (such as sluggish growth and investment) driving the fall-off in savings. As a World Bank study of the East Asian economies noted: 'Studies of the income–savings relationship across a broad cross section of economies indicate that . . . growth drives savings rather than the other way round' (World Bank 1993, p. 204). Much of the foreign borrowing might also reflect lower offshore interest rates rather than weak domestic savings.

It is also the case that Australia's reduced savings level is best seen not as a cause but as a symptom of more fundamental problems. Primarily, these include the above-noted tendency to source debt offshore, but the structural problems of the economy are also important in this respect. As Sicklen (1995, p. 17) concludes, 'a single-minded attachment to increasing national saving per se, rather than rectifying the problems which have caused the current account and saving–investment deteriora- tion, may not be the most appropriate policy response'. Indeed, if any- thing, an overzealous push for saving could well undermine consump- tion, investment and growth (and thus savings), an idea long established in Keynesian economic theory (Stewart 1972, p. 178; Trethewey 1994). Critics thus point out that it is better to pursue growth and production to generate the wherewithal for savings. The implication is not to sacrifice investment and production on the altar of a too restrictive savings pattern (Black 1994). As Gelber (1998, p. 24) puts it: 'The current account deficit means . . . that we spend more than we earn'. The policy choice is either to cut spending (the savings strategy) or to produce more earnings. Only the latter route will help the unemployed.

The policies we should have

An integrated approach to policy is required to maximise employment growth and change the economic and employment structure. In the first place, as other chapters in this volume argue, macroeconomic policy can certainly be called upon to stimulate demand within the limits set by the balance of payments and create jobs directly in the public sector and through multiplier effects in the private sector as well. However, this policy stance will not be sufficient on its own to achieve sustainable jobs growth, even if it is targeted at public-sector activities with a low import propensity (though this will help minimise the problem) (European Commission 1993). An expansionary policy must also be supported by an interventionist supply-side strategy, which promotes exports and import replacement as a means of overcoming the balance of payments constraint. The main component of such a strategy will be sector-based industry and regional development policies, which, after the burst of industry plan activity in the early 1980s, virtually disappeared by the 1990s (Bell 1997b; Genoff and Green 1998). The adoption of generic cross-sector programs aimed at boosting 'competitiveness' and the export-orientation of companies may have satisfied the desire of market orthodoxy for a 'non-discriminatory' approach, but it was not the most cost-effective use of resources.

In Australia, industry policy will require greater collaboration between government, employers and unions in developing coherent strategies and visions, both for the economy as a whole and at a sectoral level. In a world of smaller, more interdependent units of production, sectors and regions are the most efficient levels for determining investment, research and development and training plans, as well as for organising customer–supplier linkages and inter-firm networking arrangements. While investment may not always lead at once to jobs growth, the long-run relationship is a strong one (see figures 3,3 and 3.4). Hence rekindling investment is an important goal. The role of government in this context should be *enabling* rather than prescriptive – it is to provide institutional support for the co-ordination of plans and assistance on the basis of transparent criteria related to the agreed goals of sector strategies and the mechanisms by which they may be translated into reality. The strategies will also provide a clear framework for enterprise bargaining and ensure that a connection is made between decision-making at the workplace and the plans and priorities developed beyond the workplace at sector level.

There will also be a role for active labour-market programs to help develop the skills base and replace passive income support for the unemployed. Such programs are now an integral part of economic and social policy in most advanced countries (see chapter 11; OECD 1995b, Calmfors 1994), and their rationale may be conceptualised in the short and longer term. In the short term, the effectiveness of programs will depend largely on their 'strategic fit' with macro policy. In a recession, public-sector job-creation programs are inherently cost-effective because they generate employment directly and increase aggregate demand through their multiplier effects, whereas wage subsidies tend to lead to job substitution and displacement (see chapter 11; Burgess 1992). However, during a recovery, wage subsidies can play a part in distributing employment growth equitably and ensuring that the long-term unemployed and other disadvantaged job-seekers have a better chance of entering the permanent workforce. This function can also be performed to some extent by work-sharing and reductions in working time.

Finally, positive industrial relations reform has a part to play not only in the job-creation task itself but also in the type of jobs created. As Australia's wage-fixing system becomes more decentralised, it is inevitable that workplace productivity gains will be pursued at the expense of wage comparability (Green 1996b). If this approach is pursued too far, however, it will actually undermine the drive to a high-productivity, high-skill economy for three reasons. First, achieving dynamic long-term efficiency gains at the workplace depends on a co-operative, motivated workforce, which will in turn be affected by perceptions of fairness. Second, an agreed industry-wide 'going rate' for the job ensures that employers compete on the basis of quality and innovation rather than wage under-cutting. Third, the skill-based classification structures that are currently being established at an industry level could be rendered unworkable by excessive pay variations within and across workplaces. Industry agreements allowing scope for local flexibility, as in Germany, would provide the best fit with a sectoral approach to industry policy, competency-based training and skill formation.

We have argued in this chapter that Australia has the wrong economic structure for the growth of high-wage, high-skill jobs. This is the product of our history – resource abundance, a relatively mediocre domestic management class and the passivity of our governing institutions in the face of global capital have shaped Australia's position in the international division of labour. The problem now is that the orthodox policy prescription of microeconomic reform, while achieving some cost reductions, is not improving the economic structure but actually making it worse, in particular through continuing adherence to notions of comparative advantage. The key to success in the world economy today lies not in access to natural endowments, which are experiencing declining terms of trade, but in building competitive advantage through high value-adding, knowledge-intensive products and processes. It is competitive advantage that will allow the Australian economy to address the medium-term balance of payments constraint on growth, and hence the expansion of employment and reduction of unemployment. Hence, any form of expansionary macroeconomic policy must be supported by interventionist supply-side policies, including industry and regional development policies, labour-market programs and a commitment to fairer and more productive workplaces.

CHAPTER 9

Dealing with the Inflation Constraint to Growth

Anis Chowdhury

> Ordinary citizens never believe economists and bankers who
> tell them unemployment is the only cure for inflation. They
> think there must be a better way, and they are right.
> *Nobel Laureate James Tobin (1987, p. 400)*

The developed industrialised countries seem to have won the battle against inflation. Australia boasts the lowest inflation in 30 years, yet the conquest of inflation required a slowdown of wage gains achieved through the Accord and monetary contraction (through high interest rates set by the Reserve Bank) leading to 'the recession we had to have' of the early 1990s. Table 9.1 presents the average unemployment rate and inflation rate over the period 1983–97 in selected OECD countries. In countries such as Germany, Italy, Netherlands, Finland and Australia where there was either some form of consensual incomes policy, such as the Accord or synchronisation of the wage-setting process, the unemployment rate is in general lower. This implies that the contractionary policies were less severe in these countries than what would have been required in the absence of labour-market co-ordination. The only exception is the USA. The recorded lower unemployment rate in the USA is often cited as a shining example of what a deregulated labour-market can achieve. However, as Nickell (1996, p. 14) points out, a further 2 per cent could be added to the official unemployment rate if the large numbers of incarcerated males in that country are counted; then, US unemployment would look very similar to many other countries. The comparative picture that emerges from table 9.1 thus vindicates Tobin's statement (1987) that unemployment is not the only cure for inflation and the war against inflation can be fought more humanely.

This chapter is critical of orthodox anti-inflationary policies. High unemployment is a costly insurance against the acceleration of inflation and damaging in the long run. Prolonged high unemployment defeats claims that inflation can be reduced quickly with a sharp recession and that the cost of such disinflation is temporary (or at least not too large).

Table 9.1 Convergence of unemployment

Country	Unemployment rate (1983–95)	Inflation rate (1983–95)	Unemployment rate (1996–97)	Inflation rate (1996–97)
Belgium	9.7	3.2	12.8	1.9
Denmark	10.0	3.6	8.3	2.2
Finland	8.5	4.4	15.4	0.9
France	10.2	3.8	12.4	1.6
Germany (W)	6.3	2.5	10.6	1.7
Ireland	15.3	4.1	10.8	1.6
Italy	7.6	6.8	12.2	2.8
Netherlands	8.6	2.0	6.0	2.1
Spain	19.5	7.0	20.0	2.8
UK	9.8	4.8	7.5	2.8
Canada	9.8	3.5	9.5	1.6
USA	6.6	3.6	5.3	2.6
Australia	*8.9*	*5.6*	*8.5*	*1.5*

Note: Inflation rate: Percentage changes of consumer price index from the previous year.
Source: OECD (1997a; 1998)

As Keynes (1931, pp. 267–8) pointed out, recessionary policies have 'unequal effects on the stronger and on the weaker groups', and cause 'economic and social waste'. The short-run economic waste is obvious – the lost output due to unemployment, the costs of which were estimated in chapter 1. The fight against inflation with recessionary policies also leaves behind long-term damage. As high unemployment persists, human capital is destroyed, especially among youths and young adults who are denied the training and experience of holding jobs. Prolonged excess capacity also adversely affects investment and hence physical capital formation, as profit is squeezed and credit financing is restricted (Bernanke 1995; Cecchetti 1995). Restrictive demand policies also mean reductions in government capital expenditure (see chapter 7). In sum, and as Watts points out in chapter 2, irreversible and durable economic costs are incurred through recessionary policies and high unemployment. The economy is stocked with less capital (both human and physical), and is less productive after the 'victory' against inflation. It is not surprising that the victory over inflation has so far failed to ignite much-expected productivity growth in any of the countries which won the fight against inflation (Chowdhury and Mallik 1998).

This chapter is based on the proposition elaborated in other chapters in this book that unemployment is essentially a macroeconomic problem and can best be reduced by policies of stronger economic growth and job creation. However, an important obstacle to such expansionary policies is the fear that so full a recovery would ignite a new inflationary fire. This chapter argues that the inflationary risk associated with expansionary policies can be minimised if such policies are complemented by incomes policy – that is, the speed limit to growth can be raised, provided growth-promoting fiscal and monetary policies are supplemented with policies to restrain wages growth.

The inflation–unemployment trade-off, the 'natural rate' and the defeatist NAIRU

As table 9.1 shows, the victory over inflation achieved with considerable unemployment for more than two decades implies that there is a trade-off between inflation and unemployment – inflation can be reduced by creating a slack in the economy. However, the cure to inflation depends on the source of the inflation. The cure-all unemployment medicine will not be equally effective in all circumstances, and it produces many adverse side-effects (see Talsim and Chowdhury 1995, ch. 12).

There are three kinds of inflation:

- excess-demand inflation,
- wage–price inflation, and
- supply-shock inflation.

The excess-demand (also known as demand-pull) inflation is caused when 'too much money chases too few goods', as when too many buyers at an auction bid up the price. Wage–price inflation occurs when workers are able to extract high wage claims over and above their productivity, and employers are able to pass this cost on to prices. A wage–price–wage spiral occurs as two social groups (workers and employers) try to outperform each other in their conflict over the economic fruit of their joint effort. Supply-shock inflation is caused by shortages of important raw materials, such as oil. Shortages of crucial raw materials increase the cost of production and hence the price level. Supply-shock inflation can also occur due to rises in various fees and statutory charges levied on producers.

In most discussions of inflation, wage–price and supply-shock are lumped together as 'cost-push' inflation, as opposed to 'demand-pull' inflation. However, there are two important differences between wage–price and supply-shock inflation. First, the wage–price–wage spiral has its own momentum – once set off, it keeps going. Supply-shock inflation, however, is based on once-and-for-all adjustments to a new supply–demand mismatch. Second, wage–price inflation does not itself impose any collective loss on society – one person's price is another's income;

when buyers pay more, sellers receive more. It only changes the relative distribution (whether such changes in distribution are socially accept-able or not can be debated). On the other hand, if raw materials are imported, their price increases are symptoms of a real national eco-nomic loss. For example, when the Organisation of Oil Exporting Countries (OPEC) raised the price of crude oil dramatically in the 1970s (first in 1973 and again in 1979), oil-importing countries had to pay higher import prices. This adverse shock in the terms of trade (import price over export price) for oil-importing countries meant a decline in the purchasing (of imports) power of their export earnings and hence a reduction in the real value of their GDP. The same argument applies even when raw materials are domestically produced, as their shortages affect production. If raw materials are primary products, incomes are transferred from the urban sector (workers) to rural sector (farmers).

The inflation–unemployment trade-off should apply strictly to excess-demand inflation. If excess demand due to 'too much money' is the cause of inflation, then the solution lies in restricting (or reducing) demand by reducing money supply and cutting government expendi-ture. On the other hand, social consensus among various sections of the community with regard to the distribution of the national pie (e.g. an incomes policy like the Accord) is required for remedying wage–price inflation. One does not need to worry too much about one-off supply-shock inflation as long as the supply–demand mismatch does not persist for too long.

The identification of types (sources) of inflation and then the appro-priate policy prescriptions, however, can be problematic if different types interact with one another. For example, an excess-demand infla-tion may lead to higher wage demands as workers try to maintain their purchasing power, and employers in a buoyant economy would generally oblige as they can pass higher wage costs on to prices. Likewise, supply-shock inflation may trigger wage–price spirals if workers (the urban sector) respond to a rise in primary producers' (the rural sector) income share by seeking higher wages and prices. Thus, after a while it becomes a chicken-and-egg problem, and at any particular point in time, the anti-inflationary policy package must include more than one instrument. However, not all instruments may have an equal role. If the predominant nature of inflation can be identified, one instrument can be assigned the primary role, while the other plays a supporting role. For example, if rising prices and wages are accompanied by *falling* unem-ployment, then the predominant source of inflation is excess demand. In that case, demand management policies assume primacy with incomes policy (social consensus) playing the supporting role. On the other hand, if rising prices and wages are accompanied by *rising* unemployment, then incomes policy takes the primary role with the support from demand management policies

Milton Friedman and his followers (known as monetarists) believe that there is only one type of inflation – the excess-demand type. According to Friedman, wage–price–wage spirals or supply-shock inflation cannot go on unless people have more money – if we spend more on one product, we must spend less on others if our money income is fixed, and then prices will fall leaving the overall price level unchanged. Employers cannot go on paying higher wages if the stock of money is constant. Friedman (1980) epitomised this principle in his famous remark, 'inflation over any substantial period is always and everywhere a monetary phenomenon arising from a more rapid growth in the quantity of money than output'. Thus, according to Friedman, there is only one anti-inflationary medicine – restrictionist measures aimed at reduction in the quantity of money and fiscal austerity.

The monetarists have been on ascendancy since the mid-1970s when the world economy was hit by the twin problems of inflation and unemployment – a situation described by the term 'stagflation'. Until about the late 1960s and early 1970s, wage–price and supply-shock inflation were almost unknown (except perhaps in theory). The inflation in the early 1970s was caused by sudden and sharp rises in prices of oil and other primary commodities (supply-shock inflation), by wage pressures (wage–price inflation), and by inflationary pressures imported from the US as it engaged in an expensive war in Vietnam. In Australia, the rate of inflation went up from 5.8 per cent in 1971/72 to 14.2 per cent in 1973/74. This meant a redistribution of income from the urban sector (workers) to the rural sector (primary producers) and to overseas oil producers. Workers sought compensation for the loss of their real income and gained large wage increases during 1974/75, resulting in wage–price–wage spirals. The Keynesian economists who were at the helm of policy-making at the time were completely unprepared for a situation where both inflation and unemployment could co-exist (the unemployment rate rose from 1.9 per cent in 1971/72 to 4.1 per cent in 1974/75).

Born out of the Depression of the 1930s, and being successful in keeping unemployment down since World War II, the Keynesians gave priority to unemployment, and applied the trade-off medicine of expansionary policies to reduce unemployment at the cost of inflation. In other words, higher wage demands were accommodated with increased money supply. This gave credence to the monetarists' claim that inflation is primarily a monetary phenomenon. When the wrong medicine was applied to a combination of wage–price and supply-shock inflation, inflation accelerated without any cure to unemployment. The matter became worse when the world economy was hit by another bout of oil price rises in 1979.

With the fall of Keynesians as the situation deteriorated, the monetarists targeted inflation and embarked on a program of tighter fiscal and monetary policies. But the problem with this kind of recessionary remedy is that it ignores the existence of wage–price and supply-shock inflation, and assumes that money is both a necessary and a sufficient condition for inflation. While economists generally agree that money is a necessary condition for inflation (that is, there has to be too much money for inflation to continue), the developments in the 1970s (commodity price and wage rises) are evidence that inflation can be ignited by factors other than excess money. Thus, when the classical remedy of restrictive monetary and fiscal policies was applied to a problem that was essentially wage–price and supply-shock inflation, the economy (both world and Australian) went into a deeper recession, with very little success with inflation.

What do you do when you do not accept the possibility of the existence of a different kind of illness and apply medicine which worsens the condition? You either deny that there is a problem and/or blame the medicine for the trouble. That is exactly what the monetarists did. They claim that the economy has a 'natural' rate of unemployment, mainly due to frictions and structural problems in the labour-market. Since this rate (no matter how high) is 'natural', nothing much can be done about it. If expansionary fiscal and monetary policies are used to reduce unemployment below this natural level, then inflation will accelerate. Furthermore, recessionary medicine required to halt (or reduce) inflation will increase the natural rate of unemployment.

The Keynesians, under siege, reluctantly accepted the diagnosis, but found a more palatable term to describe the situation as 'non-accelerating inflation rate of unemployment' (NAIRU), meaning that inflation will accelerate when the unemployment rate is below the NAIRU. There are at least two reasons why inflation accelerates if unemployment is brought down below the NAIRU. First is the enhanced market power of trade unions which can exert pressure to secure nominal wage gains. Second, the expectation of continued full employment, or at least high employment, is enough to explain both why workers ask for wage rises (the upward shift of the labour supply curve) and the employers are willing to pay wage increases (Sachs 1979; Samuelson and Solow 1960). Mainstream economists believe that the NAIRU has been chronically underestimated, so that policy has consistently erred on the inflationary side. Now with deeper and deeper recessions required to reverse the trend (reduce inflation), the NAIRU rises as the unemployed lose job skills and become marginalised. Hence, today's high unemployment is a result of underlying upward drifts of the NAIRU. If this view is accepted, complacency about unemployment can be rationalised. Thus, it is not surprising when the OECD (Elmeskov, Martin and Scarpetta 1998) describes the reduction in unemployment to 7.6 per cent a success!

Mainstream economists have travelled full circle. Once they believed that there existed a trade-off between inflation and unemployment – the reduction of unemployment required the acceptance of inflation. But then they realised that inflation had an upward bias. Once allowed, it had a tendency to accelerate to the detriment of productivity and hence employment, so it is wise to keep the inflation genie in the bottle (Bruno 1995). Thus, theorists and policy-makers accepted a 'fight inflation first' philosophy rather than making serious efforts to reduce unemployment. As a former US president stated before a cheering Wall Street audience, 'After all, unemployment affects only 8 per cent of the people while inflation affects 100%' (quoted in Tobin 1987, p. 340).

Although policy favoured fighting inflation first, the persistence of high and persistent unemployment is bound to draw the attention of the politicians and policy-makers, who put on a public display of concern or a facade of at least doing something about unemployment. Recall how the coalition in opposition declared unemployment as the main problem in the 1996 election and the Labor Party made unemployment a focus for the 1998 election. Ironically, their performance in government on the unemployment front is not very dissimilar, though Labor created more jobs. One should not be surprised as both targeted inflation first and their public concern for unemployment did not go beyond the concept of the natural rate or the NAIRU version of it. Despite discussions about the desirability of reducing unemployment to 5 per cent, the basis for orthodox policy prescriptions remains within the theoretical realm of the NAIRU. As we have seen in previous chapters, the main plank of NAIRU-based policy to deal with high unemployment is supply-side measures such as deregulation of the labour-market, supplemented with labour-market programs. While a deregulated labour-market is supposed to remove the main impediment (rigid and high real wages) to employment growth by increased wage flexibility, labour-market programs are also expected to make long-term unemployed job ready and thereby enhance competition in the labour-market.

In October 1988, the Reserve Bank and the ANU's Centre for Economic Policy Research convened a major conference on unemployment. A recurring theme was that 'labour-market programs are likely to be more effective in an environment of sustained growth' (Debelle 1998, p. 5). Yet none of the papers seriously suggested any policy required to generate growth high enough to reduce unemployment, even to a modest 5 per cent level. Two papers (Dungey and Pitchford 1998; Debelle and Vickery 1998) on the link between economic growth and unemployment are constrained by the fear of accelerating inflation. For example, according to Dungey and Pitchford (1998, p. 230), 'faster economic growth . . . is not a panacea, because higher growth will bring the potential for rising inflation'. Since bringing down inflation is very costly 'it is better not to have let it [inflation] rise in the first place' (Dungey and Pitchford 1998, p. 208). Both papers emphasise the need for slower growth of real wages for non-inflationary or steady inflation growth. Dungey and Pitchford suggest that real wages should grow about half the rate of the so-called steady inflation rate of growth (SIRG; while SIRG is an improvement over the NAIRU on empirical grounds, the concept is not much different from the NAIRU (Dungey and Pitchford 1998, p. 216)) (estimated at 4.37 per cent consistent with 2–3 per cent inflation) to reduce the unemployment rate to 5 per cent by the year 2002. Likewise, Debelle and Vickery (1998, p. 260) suggest slower growth in real wages of 2 per cent for a year to reduce unemployment permanently by 1 percentage point. However, these authors do not explain how faster economic growth or reductions in the growth of real wages can be achieved in either political or economic terms.

The role of incomes policy

So far this chapter has provided a historical and theoretical background of the fight inflation first approach of orthodox macroeconomic policy-making. These orthodox policy approaches were heavily criticised in chapters 3, 4 and 5 as both costly and ineffective. These policies are unable to generate the economic growth necessary to reduce unemployment. Reconciling high employment and price stability will remain a chronic dilemma as long as policy options are constrained by the fear of recurring inflation. This section highlights how incomes policy can remove this constraint and help reduce unemployment without aggravating inflation. Consensus-based incomes policy can generate more investment and promote the interests of the unemployed, currently the 'outsiders' in the labour-market.

'Incomes policy' is a catch-all term covering all actions initiated by the government to influence or control wages and prices to slow down the rate of inflation or, less frequently, to affect functional income distribution between labour and capital (see Dore et al. 1994). The range of incomes policy varies from 'jaw-boning' and political suasion to a wage–price freeze. In between lie wage–price guidelines and tax-based incomes policy. In Australia, we have a long tradition of some sort of incomes policy implemented by the Arbitration Commission, which is a unique feature of the Australian labour-market. The discussion here will refer to only consensual incomes policies which promote the public interest (Crouch 1985). That is, the objective of such policies is not just to promote the interests of the employed, but to achieve overall economic improvement for the benefit of the nation and the unemployed. Such an incomes policy is generally based on social contracts between the employers, employees and the government. One example of such a consensual incomes policy is Italy's Social Pact signed by the Italian government, trade unions and employers' organisations on 24 July 1993.[1] The closest to this model in Australia was the Prices and Incomes Accord that was in place in Australia during the Hawke–Keating Labor governments (1983–96). The Accord was a bipartite form of corporatism between the unions and the government in which wage moderation by the unions was used to underpin a more expansionary policy (at least initially). For their part, the unions, led by the ACTU, received various incentives involving social wage elements and greater influence in policy formation.

It is widely recognised in the literature that corporatist or centralised wage-setting systems produce both better short-run macroeconomic outcomes (in terms of inflation and unemployment) and long-term economic results (in terms of physical and human capital formation). However, as we saw in chapter 4, work in this area by Calmfors and Driffill (1988) finds that highly decentralised (laissez-faire) systems also produce good macroeconomic (inflation–unemployment) outcomes. This finding was criticised in chapter 4 and no longer has strong support in the literature. Subsequent research points not to the alleged merits of decentralised bargaining, but to the importance of workplaces being linked by forms of co-ordinated and synchronised wage bargaining. For example, in Germany (designated by Calmfors and Driffill as a 'decentralised' bargaining case) the leaders of both labour and employers' organisations meet the representatives of the central bank and the government to discuss the overall macroeconomic picture, including the monetary and fiscal policy stance for the coming year. Thus, the stakeholders are aware of the consequences of their settlements. Similarly, in both Japan and Switzerland (again designated by Calmfors and Driffill as 'decentralised' bargaining cases), the wage settlements are highly co-ordinated despite the fact that negotiations are held at the enterprise or industry level. In Switzerland, the co-ordination is achieved through an employer-organisation-dominated arbitration system which settles wage disputes in key industries. In Japan, the co-ordination takes place through informal wage cartels in the main industries, which are followed by small firms. Therefore, in contrast to Calmfors and Driffill,

Employers' strategy	Workers' strategy	
	Wage restraint	Wage militancy
High investment	Low unemployment Low inflation	Low unemployment High inflation
Low investment	High unemployment Low inflation	Potential for high inflation Moderated by high unemployment

Figure 9.1 Prisoners' dilemma

the issue is not so much whether wage settlements are centralised or decentralised. Rather it is the degree of effective co-ordination (co-operation) that produces better short- and long-term macroeconomic outcomes.

The better performance of a co-ordinated system follows from the well-known prisoners' dilemma.[2] This can be shown using a simple game-theory framework (see Henley and Tsakalotos 1995). Figure 9.1 sets up a pay-off matrix for employers and workers. In the absence of any effective co-operation, workers would choose the militant strategy, because that is likely to maximise their short-run gains in terms of higher wages for themselves (insiders). They will not accept wage restraint in an environment where there is no certainty that higher profits (due to wage restraint) would be reinvested resulting in higher productivity and higher wages later (especially not when the economy is undergoing a rapid structural change and the likelihood of separation from the current employer is extremely high). Likewise, employers would choose a low-investment, low-employment strategy in the absence of effective co-operation, because they do not want to be ransomed later on by higher wage demands once new investment takes place. Lancaster (1973, p. 1095) summarised the dilemma as follows:

The worker's dilemma: Should they forgo present consumption by handing over part of total income to the capitalists? If they do not, they will obtain no higher consumption in the future. If they do, they have no guarantee that the capitalists will actually invest sufficient of this income to bring about the desired level of increase.

The capitalist's dilemma: Should they spend now, or accumulate in order to spend later? If they spend now, they know what they have available. If they accumulate, they may fail to obtain their expected share of the increased output when they come to spend.

The result of such a dilemma if non-co-ordinated behaviour ensues is the possible co-existence of high inflation with high unemployment as a moderating influence. On the other hand, if both parties raise trust levels and co-ordinate their strategies, the outcome is much more optimal: low unemployment and low inflation. Therefore, as Kalecki (1943) pointed out, a key condition for full employment is that a capitalist society must develop social and political institutions to allow the management of distributional conflict between capital and labour. One obvious such institution is a tripartite or bipartite collective bargaining forum involving workers, employers and the government (see Dore et al. 1994 re various models of tripartism). The objective of such a bargaining mechanism is to build mutual trust so that the prisoners' dilemma does not arise. Here the role of the government is crucial. Governments may use a carrot and stick policy (such as a tax-based incomes policy) to induce workers and employers to strike a socially desirable bargain and stick to it. In short, the government must underwrite the deal and enhance the credibility of the wage–investment game.

The most common economic argument against some sort of incomes policy is that it introduces rigidity in the system and compresses the relative wage dispersion. Thus, it is alleged, incomes policy leads to resource misallocation. However, this claim has no or very little empirical validity. At the macro level, the main criticism against incomes policy is that it may work at the time of recessions, but breaks down during booms. Hence, after a period of rapid growth immediately following the breakdown, wages and prices will rise to the level that would have prevailed in the absence of any incomes policy. In Australia, the main criticism against the Accord is that it was responsible for a decline in productivity as wage moderation encouraged employment growth at a faster rate than the growth of capital stock (Chapman 1990; Lowe 1995). This is precisely the point: in the social contract resulting in a consensual incomes policy, there should be three sides of the bargain – labour, capital and the government. Workers accept lower wages now in exchange for higher wages later produced by increased investment. The job of the government is at least to underwrite the agreement, making the contract credible. The government also provides an environment through public infrastructure and a tax system conducive to investment and less painful for workers to accept wage moderation. In Australia during the Accord, capital (employers) was not a partner (Bell 1997a, ch. 8), which partly explains why wage moderation did not result in higher investment, but instead led to the acceleration of executive salaries and speculative investment.

Table 9.2 shows the growth of earnings of low-paid and high-paid workers in countries where some form of contract among social partners

Table 9.2 Real earning growth (percentage change)

	Low-paid (1st decile)		High-paid (9th decile)	
	Past 5 years	Past 10 years	Past 5 years	Past 10 years
Australia (1995)	8.4	0.8	12.6	7.7
Finland (1995)	8.8	26.9	2.0	18.5
Germany (1994)	30.8	59.6	11.7	21.5
Japan (1995)	11.4	24.3	5.9	19.9
Netherlands (1994)	3.5	8.3	2.7	9.9

Source: OECD (1997a)

exists. Earnings of high-paid employees rose at a much faster rate than did earnings of low-paid employees in Australia. In all other countries, which have stronger forms of co-ordination, the low-paid employees fared a lot better. Finland, Germany and Japan could sustain a much faster growth of earnings for both low- and high-paid employees, perhaps due to higher investment rate and higher business sector R&D. For example, fixed capital investment in Japan from 1981 to 1990 grew by an average annual rate of 7.9 per cent compared to 4.3 per cent in Australia. Business sector R&D from 1990 to 1994 in Japan was 2.08 per cent of GDP, while it was only a meagre 0.61 per cent in Australia (for Germany, the figure was 1.79 per cent).[3]

Although in Australia the government provided some relief to the workers through the tax and social welfare system as its part of the Accord bargain, it failed the business sector as public infrastructure investment fell substantially (Alesina, Gruen and Jones 1991). Why did the government cut infrastructure investment? The answer lies in the increased importance of the financial sector in the wake of global financial deregulation. Governments all over the world are under tremendous pressure from the global financial markets to balance budgets or reduce deficits. Given such pressures and Labor's unwillingness to increase taxes, plus the government's commitment under the Accord to provide higher social welfare benefits (social wage), it had no option but to cut its capital expenditure to balance the budget. It was a politically easy option in a country with a short political cycle.

The emergence of financial markets and the resultant growing dependence on equity financing may also explain the business sector's poor investment and R&D performance. Equity financing managed by the stock market makes firms more interested in short-term profit rather than long-term investment. In the words of Harrison and Bluestone (1990), the economy has become prisoner of 'impatient capital'.

This implies that the institution of capital markets also plays a crucial role in the durability of any social contract between labour and capital. As Aoki (1990) points out, ideally, for workers to accept wage restraint to deal with inflation, they must trust not only that higher profits will be reinvested, but also that the investment decisions will be wise. Otherwise employment becomes jeopardised by bankruptcy or take-overs, which is what happened in the 1980s. To the extent that workers are unlikely to have the expertise to judge the wisdom of investment, the government must play a much more active role in the capital market if it is to underwrite the reputation of the wage–investment game.

If such an ideal tripartite incomes policy model did not eventuate during the Accord, what is the chance that it would happen now? There seems a very slim possibility of resurrecting the Accord, let alone of developing a social compact involving the government, labour and business. The organised labour movement and the government now look on each other with considerable hostility; and there is not much trust between the employers and labour.

Less demanding options do exist, however. Perhaps we should look at the abovenoted German model wherein key players are made aware of the macroeconomic consequences of their wage settlements, which in turn are generally negotiated at the industry level. The best prospects for Australia lie in the development of stronger enterprise- and industry-level union organisations, with a capacity for co-ordination at higher levels. The emphasis here is on grassroots negotiating and co-ordinating capacity at the enterprise and industry level, in contrast to the top-down version of union co-ordination under the Accord. Given Australia's liberal business culture, it is unlikely that business interests will be organisationally capable or ideologically willing to engage as active players in a national incomes policy of the Accord variety. There are slightly better prospects for business involvement at the industry level. The main weight of co-ordination, however, is likely to fall on unions and government. As Quiggin and Bell argue in chapters 10 and 12 respectively, a major focus of job expansion should be on public and community services. This sectoral targeting of expansion reduces the need for a national incomes policy if employment expansion can be made conditional on wage moderation in the public sector.

As Dore et al. (1994) argue, we need to return to incomes policies. At present, the prospects for national incomes policies are not good. The prospects are somewhat better for well co-ordinated industry- and sectoral-level approaches.

Concluding remarks

As this chapter has argued, the logic behind an incomes policy makes sense. Such a policy is more preferable in economic and social terms to the harsh and costly policy of deflation. Tobin (1987, pp. 347, 365) prophetically remarked:

> The anti-inflation hawks generally ignore or denounce remedies other than the classic prescription of austere budgets and restrictive monetary policies. It is almost as if they think, like old-time physicians, the more unpleasant the medicine the better it is for the patient . . . My fear is that the purely monetary strategy of disinflation now, and inflation control thereafter, condemns our economies to chronic excess unemployment and to permanent weakness. . . . Since World War II our pragmatic amalgam of capitalism and democracy . . . spectacularly refuted the indictments and prophecies of Marx . . . It would be ironic, maybe fatal, if we were now to concede by thought and deed that our system cannot function without an industrial reserve army of unemployed.

This chapter has endeavoured to show that in principle at least we need not be condemned forever to accept a high level of unemployment as the main check on inflation. There are better ways. What is needed is a social priority and strong leadership to achieve 'full employment' and remove the social and economic waste associated with conventional anti-inflationary policies. Incomes policies are not without costs and the costs and benefits of alternative policies need to be examined. Nevile (1990, p. 348) emphasises that 'the Accord has proved a relatively low cost method of restraining inflation'. The onus lies on the anti-inflation hawks to prove that incomes policies are more costly than the conventional ones.

To hold back the economy for the fear of another inflationary spiral is self-defeating. Prolonged high unemployment becomes 'natural' and structural – a self-fulfilling prophecy. The mechanisms are obvious as unemployed workers lose, or never acquire, the skills and habits imbued by actual job experience. A depressed economy reduces both the actual and expected profit required to spur business to invest in new capacity and technology. Thus, productivity growth falters and bottlenecks develop. The economy is condemned to high unemployment rates.

The Depression of the 1930s was made worse as governments and central banks persisted with contractionary policies in the name of 'sound finance'. At the end they failed to balance budgets or protect currencies. In Europe, democracy and civilisation became hostages to Nazi Germany and fascist Italy. The parallels are disturbing as we see the rise of reactionary parties in various countries, including Australia. 'Another decade of poor economic performance can undermine the allegiance to the institutions of democratic capitalism, especially among successive cohorts of youth who fail to find jobs' (Tobin 1987, p. 387).

The Asian crisis and the present world economic environment pose both challenges and opportunities for Australia. The crisis and the resultant slowdown in both Asia and the world economy are likely to eventually impact on Australia. The government and the RBA cannot eschew expansionary macroeconomic policies when they are urging Japan to pursue traditional Keynesian policies. The fear of another inflationary surge in the current subdued (deflationary) world environment is unreal. The prospect of supply shocks of the 1970s or another Vietnam War that triggered the inflationary surge three decades ago is very remote. The community is hungry for resumption of sustained non-inflationary prosperity and growth. This is the time for leadership to capitalise on the social consensus for growth, compatible with steady inflation.

CHAPTER 10

The Public Sector
as a Job Engine

John Quiggin

In economic terms, the period since World War II can be divided into two halves, with a short period of chaos between them. The period from 1945 to 1970 was one of full employment, reductions in social and economic inequality, and a strong and growing economic role for government. The period since 1974 has been one of high unemployment, increasing inequality and declining government control over, and involvement in, the economy. In between there was an interval of confusion and dislocation, as the old postwar economic order, built around Keynesian macroeconomic policies, social democracy and the Bretton Woods system of international financial arrangements, broke down.

An appealing, but somewhat simplistic, response to historical experience is to suggest that we need only return to the economic policies of the 1950s and 1960s and full employment will be restored. An equally erroneous response to the historical experience of the postwar period is to ignore it. To have any chance of success, the design of a full-employment policy must begin with the only policy framework that has ever delivered full employment, that of Keynesian social democracy. The challenge is to strengthen that policy framework and overcome the difficulties that led to its breakdown, particularly in terms of inflation and the growing inflexibility of fiscal policy.

Langmore and Quiggin (1994) argue that the growth of public-sector employment in the postwar boom was an important contributor to the maintenance of full employment and that a full-employment strategy for today should be based on publicly funded growth in the provision of human services such as health, education, welfare and environmental services. In this chapter, the role of the public sector as a job engine is considered.

The chapter begins with a discussion of the breakdown of full employment since the early 1970s, and the increasing polarisation of the labour
force. This leads to a more general discussion of the role of human
capital and the human services sector in determining growth rates and
employment levels in an economy which has increasingly become
dominated by services employment growth. The relationship between
an expansion of the human services sector and growth in employment is
discussed in terms of a demand-switching model, in which reductions in
private consumption expenditure finance an expansion in public funding for human services. In particular, it is argued that an additional
$20 billion of public expenditure per year could form the basis of a
strategy to achieve and sustain an unemployment rate of 5 per cent.
Some options for raising the necessary revenue are presented. Obstacles
to such a strategy, including globalisation, inflationary pressures and the
need for additional tax revenue, are discussed.

Unemployment and labour-force polarisation

The twenty-five years of full employment that followed World War II was
a unique period of growth and prosperity. Debate continues on the
reasons for this 'golden age' and the factors leading to its breakdown in
the 1970s (Marglin and Schor 1990; Bell 1997a, ch. 5). Any consideration of the problem must take account of the fact that high unemployment is nothing new in the history of capitalism. Rather, the postwar
period of full employment was exceptional.

The paradox of unemployment

During the postwar boom, it was often suggested that the rate of technological improvement was so rapid as to create the possibility that
society would 'run out of jobs', in the sense that, even with reductions in
standard working hours, it would be possible to meet all social needs for
goods and services without requiring more than a small proportion of
the population to join the full-time labour force (Jones 1995). It is sometimes supposed that the mass unemployment observed today is the result
of technological change that has reduced the need for workers.

Two observations show that this idea is mistaken, at least when applied
to the economy as a whole. First, important labour-intensive services are
being cut back on the basis of claims that 'we can no longer afford
them'. Hospital waiting lists have grown longer, class sizes in schools and
universities have increased, and social welfare services have failed to
keep pace with growing needs. Second, full-time employees are working
longer and harder than they have done for decades (Quiggin 1996a).

The paradox of mass unemployment co-existing with unmet social needs was noted in the White Paper *Full Employment in Australia* (Commonwealth of Australia 1945, p. 2), in which a contrast was drawn between the free-market economy of the period before World War II and the planned economy imposed during the war:

> Despite the need for more houses, food, equipment and every other type of product, before the war not all those available for work were able to find employment or to feel a sense of security in their future. On the average during the twenty years between 1919 and 1939 more than one-tenth of the men and women desiring work were unemployed. In the worst period of the depression well over 25 per cent were left in unproductive idleness. By contrast, during the war no financial or other obstacles have been allowed to prevent the need for extra production being satisfied to the limit of our resources.

The unemployment of today displays a similar paradox, except that the most obvious unmet needs relate to services rather than goods, as will be discussed below.

In Australia, however, significant reductions in hours and intensity of work continued at least until the 1970s. Important aspects of this trend included the general shift to four weeks of annual leave, extension of long service leave, widespread adoption of maternity leave, and a reduction of standard working hours from 40 to 38 hours. The failure in the late 1970s of union campaigns for a 35-hour week signalled an end to the trend of reductions in full-time working hours.

From the mid-1980s onwards, the trend towards shorter hours was reversed. Enterprise agreements and individual contracts rarely involved reductions in total hours and frequently involved increases. Moreover, whereas flexibility had previously implied greater discretion on the part of the employee, it now implied that working hours would be varied according to the requirements of employers. In addition to these changes in formal conditions, there has been an increase in the prevalence of unpaid overtime. The increase in working hours has been accompanied by an increase in the pace of work, reflected in greater levels of stress and increasing numbers of full-time employees reporting that they would prefer a job with shorter hours and lower pay (Morehead et al. 1997; Quiggin 1996a).

As with the paradox of idle resources co-existing with unmet needs, there is nothing new about the polarisation of the labour force into a core workforce with long hours and a peripheral group subsisting on temporary and part-time jobs punctuated by frequent spells of unemployment. Except during the postwar golden age, when most workers (and nearly all adult males) had secure employment, the labour-market has always had this dual character. Polarisation increases in periods of high unemployment, when the bargaining power of labour is at its weakest.

The struggle between workers and employers over the length of the working day, and the way in which the existence of a 'reserve army' of unemployed strengthened the hand of the employers was well described by Marx more than a century ago, and has not fundamentally changed since then. A central feature of the 'microeconomic reform' policies of the past two decades, and particularly of National Competition Policy, has been an attempt to ensure that as many workers as possible are exposed to competition for their jobs. This policy is designed to ensure that as many employers as possible benefit from the increase in bargaining power they obtain when workers fear unemployment.

Technology, skills and unemployment

The idea of technologically induced jobless growth is discussed in some detail in chapters 3, 6 and 12, but here some comments are in order regarding the impact of technology on skills and human capital development. A slightly more sophisticated version of the idea that technological progress and structural change cause unemployment focuses on the differential effects of technological progress on skilled and unskilled workers. It is often argued that technological change has reduced the demand for unskilled and semi-skilled workers while increasing the demand for 'symbolic analysts' (Reich 1991) or, alternatively, that technological change encourages the substitution of physical capital for labour. In less fancy terms, technological change has reduced the need for brawn and increased the need for brains. Hence, either the wages of unskilled workers must fall or unemployment must rise (Krugman 1994b).

As with other technological accounts of the causes of unemployment, this argument is often presented in terms that suggest a totally new phenomenon associated with the development of computers, or with the disappearance of 'Fordist' methods of mass production. In fact, technology has always tended to displace low-skilled labour and to require the employment of high-skilled labour. Other things being equal, the effect of technological progress is always to reduce the wages of unskilled workers and raise the wages of skilled workers, thereby increasing the inequality of wages.

However, the effects of technological change have been offset in the past by steadily increasing levels of education or, in economic terms, investment in human capital. Increases in the average educational attainments of young people lead to an increase in the supply of skilled workers and a corresponding reduction in the number of unskilled workers. During the postwar boom, the expansion of educational opportunities led to growth in skill levels which in turn contributed to a reduction in wage inequality in most countries.

The increase in educational attainments that took place during the postwar boom came to an abrupt end in the United States during the 1970s. The proportion of young people completing school and going on to college or university remained nearly static during the 1970s and 1980s and has only recently resumed its upward trend. The consequences have been exactly as might have been predicted in an unregulated labour-market. Whereas the margin between the wages of those with and without university education declined between 1945 and 1970, it rose rapidly from the mid-1970s onwards. Because average wages were almost static, the real wages of workers with high school education or less fell steadily, and are currently no higher than they were in 1960 (Krugman 1994b).

A similar rise in income inequality has been observed in the United Kingdom and New Zealand. Both countries have reformed their labour-markets to remove minimum wages and to weaken the power of unions. In addition, average levels of education in both countries are lower than in most OECD countries which suggests that, in an unregulated labour-market equilibrium, the margins for skill should be large. These two cases are somewhat different from that of the United States, since educational attainments are rising from a low base in the United Kingdom and New Zealand, rather than being static at a relatively high level. Hence the rise in inequality in these countries may be seen as the result of the removal of policies and institutions that tended to equalise wages and, particularly, to keep minimum wages high.

In most other OECD countries, wage inequality has not increased to the extent observed in the United States, United Kingdom and New Zealand (see chapter 4). In some cases, wage inequality has actually declined. However, many of these countries have experienced persistently high unemployment. It may be argued that, if minimum wages had been reduced, there would have been less unemployment and more wage inequality. Against this it should be noted that educational attainments have continued to rise in most of these countries. In addition, although unemployment rates for unskilled workers are considerably higher than for skilled workers, the rise in unemployment rates since the 1970s has affected all workers. The unemployment rate for university graduates is now around 4 to 5 per cent, while the rate for those with high school education or less is above 10 per cent.

The human services sector

Changes in the pattern of output and employment are a natural response to technological progress. During the first half of this century, manufacturing displaced agriculture as the primary source of employment. Service industries also grew in importance, but mainly in areas

such as transport, wholesaling and retailing, which were associated with
the distribution of goods produced in the manufacturing sector. It was
therefore possible to conceive of the economy in terms of primary industries (agriculture and mining) supplying raw materials to be turned into
finished goods by secondary industries (manufacturing) which were
assisted in the tasks of distribution, finance and so on by tertiary industries (services).

Although this way of thinking about the economy is still common-
place, it is really only appropriate for an economy based primarily on
unskilled labour. In a developed economy, where the supply of skilled
labour is at least as important as that of raw materials, the industries
that should be regarded as primary are those concerned directly with
people, and particularly those which ensure that the population is
healthy, well educated, secure and so on. With some important excep-
tions like food, the majority of these industries produce services rather
than goods.

These industries will be referred to collectively as the human services
sector. In statistical terms, the human services sector corresponds
broadly speaking to the Australian Bureau of Statistics categories of community services, recreation and personal services, and public services
and defence.

In chapter 6 of this volume, Burgess and Green give a detailed description of the shift towards employment in the human services sector. They
show that, between 1967 and 1993, employment in the traditional
primary and secondary sectors (agriculture, mining, manufacturing and
construction) fell substantially from 46 per cent of the employed workforce in Australia to 29 per cent. Over the same period, employment in
the human services sector rose from 16 per cent to 27 per cent of the
employed workforce. Of the traditional tertiary activities, employment
in retail and wholesale trade remained constant at about 20 per cent of
the workforce. Employment in finance and banking grew substantially
between 1967 and 1993, but has contracted since 1993 as a result of
mergers and rationalisation in the retail banking industry.

Human capital and economic growth

Human capital has long played an important role in the economic
analysis of growth. In 'old growth theory', exemplified empirically by the
'growth accounting' work of Denison (1962, 1984), growth in human
capital is regarded as one among a number of forms of factor accumulation, all of which work in a similar way. Growth accounting involves
studying the performance of individual countries over time and attempting to apportion observed economic growth to factors such as growth in

the labour force, investment in physical capital and increases in education levels (human capital).

Growth accounting analyses such as those of Denison showed that investments in human capital produced higher economic returns than investments in physical capital. These findings were reinforced by the disappointing results experienced by developing countries which attempted to promote growth by building up heavy industries reliant on large investments in physical capital. The results of growth accounting analysis were reflected in the 'new growth theory' (Romer 1990), where human capital and knowledge play a central role in generating self-sustaining growth.

Emphasis on human capital is supported by a growing empirical literature on cross-section regressions of growth performance. Many factors have been suggested as conducive to economic growth but the literature displays few consistent results, with the important exception of human capital. Systematic studies of factors conducive to economic growth found that the great majority of proposed correlations (for example, between growth and inflation, or between growth and public spending) are not robust to changes in the specification of estimating equations (Levine and Renelt 1992; Levine and Zervos 1993). One of the few stable causal relationships that has been identified in these systematic studies is that the higher the proportion of school-age people attending school at the beginning of any given period, the higher the growth rate over the subsequent period.

A number of studies, notably including Barro (1991) and Mankiw, Romer and Weil (1992), conclude that human capital growth is a centrally important contributor to economic growth. Mankiw, Romer and Weil (1992) used the fraction of the working-age population attending secondary school as a measure of human capital investment at any point in time. Whereas a model using only physical investment variables performed poorly in explaining relative economic growth, the same models performed well when human capital was included. Although analysis of the role of human capital normally focuses on education, a wide range of human services contribute to the development of human capital. Lack of education is one factor which prevents people from achieving their full potential, but so are ill-health and family breakdown. Expenditure on health services and social services should therefore be classed, at least in part, as investment in human capital.

The expansion of education spending under the Whitlam Labor government from 1973 to 1975 was one of the biggest changes in Australian public policy in the postwar period. It was a response to a widespread public recognition that improvements in education were essential to the future of young people in a society that offered fewer and fewer jobs for the unskilled. As argued above, this concern is supported by economic theory and empirical evidence.

The most striking single change that may be attributed to the expansion of education spending in the 1970s was a dramatic increase in the proportion of students completing high school from 34 per cent in 1980 to 77 per cent in 1992. Growth in enrolments in higher education has been similarly dramatic. However, this progress is now being reversed, at least partially because public spending on education has been insufficient to keep pace with growing needs. In important areas such as higher education, funding has been cut substantially. Not surprisingly, the effects are reflected in declining rates of high school completion and university enrolment.

The human services sector and employment

Economists interested in the economics of human services such as education have focused mainly on the long-term effects of investment in human capital. By raising the average skill level in the workforce, services that contribute to human capital development make it possible to meet the increasing demand for skilled labour and therefore, as argued above, reduce the pressure for expansion in wage differentials that would otherwise result from technological change.

In the short run, however, it is the direct employment benefits arising from expansion of the human services sector that are of most interest. Human services are large employers of labour and are less affected than other sectors of the economy by the labour-saving bias of technological change.

Significant parts of the human services sector have experienced relatively limited technological progress. For example, the technology of cutting hair has changed very little in the past 50 years, even if fashions in hairstyles have changed radically. Similarly, despite repeated attempts to automate teaching, based first on television, then on computers and more recently on the internet, the basic technology of classroom teaching is much the same today as it was in the days of Plato's Academy. As Burgess and Green argue in depth in chapter 6, the human services sector is characterised by relatively high employment growth and low productivity growth, at least on conventional measures of output.

In other cases, technological change has taken place, but its primary effect has been to raise the quality and variety of the services that labour can provide, rather than to permit the substitution of capital for labour. Health care is a good example. Improvements in surgical, diagnostic and other procedures have led to better outcomes for patients and have extended the range of ailments that can be treated. The effect has been to increase the demand for the services of doctors, nurses, medical technicians and so on. Demand for the services of ancillary workers, such as nurses' aides and clerical staff, has risen accordingly, though the potential for labour-saving technological change is greater in some of these cases.

The growth of the services sector was first analysed in these terms by Baumol (1967), who argued that if labour productivity grew more slowly in the services sector than in other sectors such as manufacturing, and maintenance of output in the services sector at least as a constant proportion of total output was desirable, resources should be progressively transferred towards the services sector. Arguments of this kind have gradually displaced the older view of services as ancillary costs associated with the production and delivery of physical goods. However, the older view remains widespread, particularly in relation to publicly provided services.

Baumol's analysis of productivity trends may be reinforced by the observation that the demand for services such as education, health, police, urban amenities, environmental protection and the arts tends to rise with income, and to increase as a proportion of total demand as income rises. At low levels of income a large share of expenditure must be devoted to necessary goods such as food, shelter and basic clothing, and services may be regarded as luxuries. In communities with the income levels of developed countries like Australia, the satisfaction of these basic needs requires only a small proportion of total income. It is therefore possible to move up Maslow's (1968) hierarchy of needs, and to address the needs for health, security, self-esteem and the esteem of others. In addressing these needs, which largely concern relationships between people, services are necessities, while physical goods are luxuries, largely associated with the desire for the esteem of others.

Burgess and Green present a more detailed discussion of the implications of structural change for growth in GDP, productivity and employment. The crucial observation, for the purposes of this chapter, is that the greater the proportion of economic activity allocated to the human services sector, the greater is the share of demand for labour in aggregate demand, and hence the higher is the level of employment for any given level of GDP. In other words, growth in the human services sector is a jobs-intensive growth path.

Growth in the demand for services of all kinds and the limited effects of labour-saving technological change in the human services sector imply that growth in employment in the human services sector is a natural economic response to technological progress and structural change in the economy. Hence, if the economy were on an equilibrium growth path, declining employment in the mining, manufacturing and agriculture sectors would be offset by expanding employment in the human services sector.

The structural shift away from employment associated with the production and processing of goods and towards the human services sector commenced during the later part of the postwar boom. As noted above, during the period 1967–93, employment in mining, agriculture and manufacturing fell from 46 per cent of the workforce to 29 per cent. Although this decline was associated with an increase in the rate of unemployment from 1 or 2 per cent in the 1960s to around 5 per cent in the late 1970s, it was largely offset by an increase in the proportion of the workforce employed in human services from 16 to 27 per cent. Other sectors of the economy remained broadly stable. This expansion of employment in the human services sector was particularly pro-nounced in the publicly funded areas of education, health and community services and government administration. This growth largely ceased after 1980, however, with the proportion of the workforce employed in these sectors remaining static at 20 per cent.[1] Continuation of the previous trend would have implied that between 25 and 30 per cent of the labour force should be employed in publicly funded human services. If such a trend had continued, total employment would be between 5 and 10 per cent higher than it is at present. Allowing for increased labour-force participation rates, this increase in employment would be consistent with an unemployment rate of 5 per cent or less.

The stagnation of employment in the human services sector is in part a reflection of the 'fiscal crisis of the state' (O'Connor 1973) which has arisen because of the conflict between growing demands for expansion of publicly provided services and transfer payments and increasingly vigorous resistance to increases in taxation, particularly among high-income earners. The fiscal crisis of the state has been exacerbated by the ideological dominance of free-market, small-government ideology during the 1980s and 1990s. On the other hand, the need for expansion of the human services sector has grown increasingly evident, and attempts to cut public expenditure have encountered strong opposition. The result, in Australia at least, has been a stalemate. After rising from 20 per cent in the 1960s to 30 per cent by 1983, the ratio of general government current expenditure[2] to GDP has remained virtually static for the past 15 years.

International experience

The contrasting experiences of Sweden and Norway illustrate the importance of public-sector employment. Sweden retained nearly full employment during the 1970s and 1980s, focusing primarily on expansion of public employment in the human services sector, along with extensive use of active labour-market programs. This approach, combined with generous universal social welfare programs, relied on high levels of public expenditure as a share of GDP (more than 50 per cent by the late 1980s).

In 1990, however, the interaction of a number of political and economic forces produced a severe crisis. First, Sweden's planned entry to the European Community required harmonisation of the tax system with that of the other members of the Community and generated external pressure for lower taxes. The demand for harmonisation exacerbated the general pressure for lower taxes on business arising from real and threatened capital flight (Meidner 1993).

Second, an influential group of Swedish economists, notably including Lindbeck (1997), had become vocally hostile to the welfare state. Like Australian advocates of free-market reform, they argued, on the basis of dubious statistics on economic growth, that as a result of the disincentives created by the tax–welfare system, Swedish economic performance was worse than that of other OECD countries. Also, as in Australia, the Swedish economics profession contributed to a consensus that a move towards 'economic rationalism' was needed. Finally, Sweden was hit by an asset boom and bust caused, not by the welfare state, but by financial deregulation, the first instalment of economic rationalism.

Following the onset of recession in 1990, the Social Democrats, who had held office for most of the postwar period, were defeated. The incoming government adopted a policy of free-market reform based on cuts in taxation (particularly company tax, which was cut from 52 per cent to 40 per cent) and in public expenditure. Not surprisingly, unemployment rose rapidly, reaching 8 per cent, with a further 4 per cent of the population being engaged in labour-market programs.

Norway experienced a similar boom and bust resulting from financial deregulation. However, partly because of the availability of revenue from North Sea oil, there was less pressure for cuts in public expenditure. The critical difference between Sweden and Norway was that, in Norway, public-sector employment continued to expand, both absolutely and relative to the private sector. Although Norway's unemployment rate rose above 8 per cent during the 1990 recession, it had fallen back to 4.4 per cent by 1997.

Benefits of expanding the human services sector

The current state of the human services sector in Australia is a clear example of the paradox referred to in the White Paper on *Full Employment* (Commonwealth of Australia 1945). While resources lie idle, there is clear and growing evidence of unmet needs. Inadequate investment in human capital is hampering our future growth prospects while inadequate provision of publicly funded services is reducing current living standards. The long-term costs of inadequate education have already been discussed.

Health care is another vital area of need where inadequate public expenditure is leading to severe problems, such as long waiting lists for admission to public hospitals. The central cause of the difficulty is the acceptance by successive governments of the idea that health care is a cost burden on the economy that should not be increased, or more precisely that the share of total GDP allocated to health should not rise. This view gains superficial support from the example of the United States, where high levels of expenditure on health co-exist with life expectancy levels below those of many other developed countries. However, the poor performance of the United States reflects grossly unequal access to health resources.

Although provision of health and education services remains inadequate, Australians are healthier and better educated than they were 30 years ago. However, living standards have deteriorated in important respects, including increased economic insecurity, higher rates of family breakdown, and increased vulnerability to crime. These problems are closely related. As indicated in chapter 2, there is considerable evidence that unemployment and economic insecurity contribute to crime, family breakdown and other social problems.

Even as the severity of the problems becomes increasingly apparent, resources to deal with them are cut because of budgetary stringency. Stricter enforcement of the law has been the most politically popular response to the symptoms of social breakdown, but even here, police numbers have barely kept pace with population growth. Other emergency services have fared even worse. The privatisation of the Victorian ambulance dispatch service and cuts in funding for fire services in New South Wales have resulted in increasing delays in responses to emergency calls (Rix 1997).

The situation in the welfare services sector is even worse, since this sector is seen as an easy target for budget cuts. Services to youth, to families and to the mentally ill have all been cut at a time of growing need. With the budgetary stringency which prevails at present, welfare workers are faced with the unattractive choice between hasty decisions to remove children from their families or to leave them in potentially dangerous situations. The resources needed to undertake proper assessment and to help families to deal with their problems are not available. Yet the costs of failing to address social problems are both large and long-lasting. The effects of child abuse are lifelong and are frequently passed on to the next generation. In a society where human capital is the crucial variable, the provision of inadequate services to families is simply bad economics.

With so many unfulfilled and urgent social needs, discussion of increased funding for arts, culture and the environment may seem something of a luxury. This is an indication of the extent to which a policy debate dominated by economic fundamentalism has narrowed our horizons. The social democratic vision of a civilised society has always centred on basic needs such as health, education and housing, but it has extended beyond meeting those needs to the development of a society where the full fruits of human cultural achievement are available, not to a tiny elite, but to every member of society.

The preservation of the environment is another area of public activity often seen as a luxury. Yet it is increasingly apparent that an economic policy that does not take account of the need for environmental preservation is inherently unsound. Countries that have neglected the environment in a push for rapid economic growth have paid a high price. The havoc caused in much of Eastern Europe by industrial pollution and in Southeast Asia by forest fires are graphic illustrations of this point. Leaving aside the direct benefits provided by a healthier environment and our moral obligation to preserve our natural heritage, the importance of environmental preservation to the growth of the tourism and recreation industries (the most rapidly growing component of the private sector) is increasingly being recognised.

The macroeconomic effects of public-sector expansion

In setting a target for unemployment it is useful to begin with an estimate of the likely average rate of unemployment in the absence of policy change. Although unemployment has been at or above 8 per cent throughout the 1990s, it seems likely that a rate of around 7 per cent or even a bit lower could be achieved without substantial changes in policies, simply by maintaining moderate output growth and avoiding the use of excessively restrictive fiscal and monetary policies (see chapter 6).

Although rates of unemployment were maintained below 2 per cent for most of the postwar golden age, it seems unlikely that such low rates can be restored in the near future. Adverse changes in the structure of labour-markets, such as the increase in casual and contract employment and the demoralisation produced by decades of high unemployment, will take time to overcome. It seems reasonable for the moment to treat rates of unemployment from 4 to 5 per cent as a 'full employment' target.

As pointed out in chapter 6, an increase in employment does not translate directly into a reduction in measured unemployment. As jobs become available, people who want work but who have not been actively searching and immediately available for employment (the official definition of unemployment) re-enter the labour force, and take jobs. This growth in participation has no effect on measured unemployment, though it reduces the number of 'hidden unemployed' who are not counted in official statistics.

Although definitions and estimates of the number of hidden unemployed vary, it seems likely that about half the people who want work, but are unable to find it, are not counted in official statistics (see chapter 2). This estimate is consistent with the observation that when employment rises at a rate faster than that required to absorb natural growth in the labour force, about half of the increase in employment is offset by an increase in labour-force participation, while half is reflected in a reduction in unemployment. Thus, creation of 100 000 jobs would reduce unemployment by around 50 000, or about 0.5 percentage points. A reduction in the unemployment rate from 8 per cent to between 4 and 5 per cent would require the creation of between 600 000 and 800 000 additional jobs.

Labour-market programs

Part of this task could be addressed through active labour-market programs, an approach tried briefly under the Keating Labor government through the *Working Nation* program. This program of wage subsidies and short-term direct job creation was introduced in 1994, but was cut back in the 1995 budget, then scrapped by the Howard Liberal–National government in 1996.

Evaluation of *Working Nation* is difficult in view of the fact that the programs were only in operation for two years. Official evaluations have varied from glowing (Crean 1995) to circumspect (Department of Employment, Education, Training and Youth Affairs 1996a) to damning (unpublished research cited by the Howard Liberal–National government) according to the political demands of the occasion. The critical issue relates to the cost of creating jobs through programs of this kind. Piggott and Chapman (1995) give an *ex ante* evaluation suggesting that the net budgetary cost per job created would be low, a view broadly supported by the *ex post* studies of Junankar and Kapuscinski (1997) and Stromback, Dockery and Ying (1997) (see also chapter 11). A net budgetary cost of around $10 000 per job will be assumed in subsequent analysis.

In the analysis presented below, it is assumed that active labour-market programs are expanded to provide 300 000 program places per year, at an annual budgetary cost of $3 billion. This would be sufficient to meet the original *Working Nation* objective of 'reciprocal obligation' in which the obligation of unemployed workers to seek work actively is matched by the acceptance by society of an obligation to provide appropriate work opportunities for all long-term unemployed workers.

Demand-switching and the human services sector

The claim that expansion of the human services sector would reduce unemployment is a straightforward application of the idea of demand-switching. If aggregate demand is held constant, but the composition of demand is changed to include more labour-intensive goods and services, employment will rise. Similarly, if demand is switched from import-intensive consumption to domestically produced goods and services, demand for imports will decline for any given level of the exchange rate. This is important because, as argued in chapter 8, growth in the current account deficit might otherwise constrain expansion in employment.

One way of assessing the impact of changes in expenditure patterns on the demand for labour, capital and imported inputs is through the use of a computable general equilibrium model of the economy such as ORANI (Dixon et al. 1982). Models of this kind combine a description of the economy derived from an input–output matrix such as that prepared by the Australian Bureau of Statistics (ABS) (1994a) with assumptions about elasticities of demand and supply, and about the quantities and prices which are allowed to vary to bring the economy into equilibrium. For any given set of assumptions, it is possible to predict the impact of an external shock or a change in economic policy.

A simple and robust alternative is to use the input–output matrix directly. The input–output matrix shows the inputs of labour, capital, domestically produced goods and imports used to generate the final output of each good or service in the economy. The matrix can be used to trace the second round and subsequent effects of an initial change in demand, leading to estimates of effects on employment, import demand and so on.

As an illustration of the approach, the ABS input–output matrix shows that an increase of $1 billion in demand for publicly provided human services is associated with additional imports of $40 million. An increase of $1 billion in private final consumption expenditure is associated with additional imports of $140 million. This means that if additional public expenditure of $1 billion is financed by higher taxes, leading to a reduction of $1 billion in private final consumption expenditure, the net effect on import demand is a reduction of $100 million.

A similar analysis may be applied to employment effects. The human services sector is more labour intensive than the economy as a whole. Between 75 and 80 per cent of final expenditure in the human services sector is allocated to wages and salaries, compared to only 40 per cent of private final consumption expenditure. Given an increase of $1 billion of expenditure in the human services sector, about $750 million is allocated to employment, generating about 25 000 additional jobs at average wages of $30 000 per year. (Average wages are somewhat higher in the public than in the private sector. However, this difference is primarily due to the higher proportion of full-time jobs in the public sector.) By contrast, each $1 billion of private final consumption expenditure is associated with about 13 000 jobs. Hence, an increase of $1 billion in human services expenditure, and a corresponding reduction in general consumption expenditure, would be associated with a net gain of 12 000 jobs.

To maintain equilibrium, a policy program must be consistent with internal and external balance. As noted above, an expansion of the human services sector, financed by higher taxation, would reduce demand for imports and therefore create pressure for an appreciation of the currency. This pressure could be partially offset by reductions in domestic interest rates, resulting in some expansion of domestic demand and a neutral impact on inflation. For the purposes of analysis we assume that public expenditure on human services is increased by $20 billion per year or 4 per cent of GDP, and that the net effect of higher taxation and lower interest rates is to reduce private final consumption expenditure by $12.5 billion per year or 2.5 per cent of GDP. Thus, demand-switching is associated with a net expansion of output equal to 1.5 per cent of GDP.

Assuming that $3 billion of public expenditure is allocated to active labour-market programs creating 300 000 places, the remaining $17 billion generates approximately 450 000 additional jobs. This is offset by a loss of approximately 150 000 jobs associated with a contraction of private-sector demand, yielding a net gain of 600 000 jobs and program places. As argued above, such an employment gain would reduce unemployment by about 3 percentage points. With an initial rate of unemployment between 7 and 8 per cent, this would be sufficient to achieve a target rate of between 4 and 5 per cent.

The role of infrastructure investment

Large-scale infrastructure projects have long been a favoured response to unemployment and are commonly used to illustrate the Keynesian approach to counter-cyclical policy. The basic idea is that workers displaced from their regular employment in a recession are employed to build public works such as roads. Public works spending is maintained at high levels during recessions and wound back during booms.

However, the case for large-scale infrastructure spending as an employment policy is no longer a strong one because the characteristics of infrastructure projects have changed. Whereas in the first half of this century, infrastructure projects such as road construction employed large numbers of unskilled and semi-skilled workers, today such projects are highly capital intensive, employing only a small number of workers, many with specialised skills. In addition, the planning time for infrastructure projects has increased, making them less useful as counter-cyclical instruments. As the experience of the *One Nation* program showed, projects which are funded as a response to a recession may not commence until well after the economy has recovered. The program was announced in 1992 as a response to the recession that commenced in 1990, but many of the infrastructure projects funded under the program did not begin until 1993 or 1994, by which time the economy was growing strongly.

Although infrastructure projects can no longer be regarded as an appropriate instrument of macroeconomic policy, as John Nevile mentioned in chapter 7, there is a strong microeconomic case for an expansion of public investment in physical infrastructure. Public investment in infrastructure has declined markedly over the past 30 years from 9 per cent of GDP to 5 per cent. This decline is of particular concern in view of evidence suggesting that infrastructure projects have high external benefits associated with increases in the productivity of the private business sector (Aschauer 1988; Kenyon 1998).

Admittedly, there has been some substitution of private investment for public investment. In many cases, however, reliance on private investment has been an expensive and inefficient way of undertaking projects which could have been done more efficiently in the public sector, except for ideological objections to public debt. So-called BOOT (build, own, operate and transfer) schemes have been particularly costly (Quiggin 1996c; EPAC 1995a, b; H of R 1997). Infrastructure investment should be financed by the issue of debt and supported, as far as possible, by user charges designed to achieve a rate of return to capital at least equal to the rate of interest on public debt.

Tax and revenue implications

Since a policy of expanding the human services sector represents a long-term response to unemployment, rather than a short-term macro-economic stabilisation policy, it is necessary that any increase in public expenditure should be matched by an increase in taxation. In estimating the increase in taxation required to finance an extra $20 billion of human services, it is necessary to take account of the fact that employment growth automatically reduces public expenditure on unemployment benefits. A more expansionary macroeconomic policy would also lead to a higher level of output and therefore a higher level of tax revenue. Finally, because the effective tax rate on wage income is generally higher than the tax rate on capital and other income, growth in employment is associated with an increase in tax revenue even if aggregate output remains unchanged.

Assuming that GDP is increased by 2 per cent and employment by 5 per cent, the government could expect to save around $1 billion in outlays on unemployment and other benefits, and to receive around $4 billion in additional tax revenue. Thus, the net revenue requirement would be about $15 billion, or about 3 per cent of GDP. This would still leave Australia's ratio of government revenue to GDP below the OECD average.

Assuming revenue gains and expenditure savings of $5 billion, the net cost of an increase in government outlays, financed by additional taxation, would thus be about three-quarters of the gross cost. This proportion is considerably higher than that estimated by Boltho and Glyn (1995), who suggest that the net cost will be about one-third of the gross cost. However, Boltho and Glyn's estimate does not take account of the effects of contraction in private-sector demand arising from increased taxation. This estimate would be appropriate if interest rates were reduced so as to ensure that private-sector demand remained unchanged. The feasibility of such a reduction depends on the severity of balance of payments constraints and the capacity of labour-market institutions to maintain stable real wages. These issues are discussed below.

Options for raising additional revenue have been explored in detail by Quiggin (1998) and the Australian Council of Social Service (ACOSS 1998). Several revenue options were canvassed in chapter 6. Although the primary focus of the tax packages released by the major political parties in the lead-up to the 1998 federal elections was on cuts in taxes, they also provided some useful information on options for increasing revenue. The following list of revenue options draws on these sources:

- *Restrictions on tax avoidance through trusts and company structures, along with a general campaign to improve tax compliance.* The minimal measures announced by the government are estimated to yield revenue of $500 million per year. ACOSS (1998) proposes somewhat stronger measures estimated to raise $1.5 billion per year. However, as argued in Quiggin (1998), there is very little justification for the existence of most trusts or for the proliferation of loss-making private companies.

A radical attack on these tax-avoidance mechanisms could raise at least $4 billion per year.

- *Cuts in tax expenditures, including withdrawal of superannuation and savings concessions and elimination of fringe benefits tax concessions.* Depending on the approach taken to superannuation, reductions in tax expenditures would raise between $3 and $5 billion per year.
- *Extension of the indirect tax base to encompass a range of services, while preserving the existing exemptions for food, health and education.* Quiggin (1998) shows that a goods and services tax, levied at a rate of 12 per cent, could finance the abolition of wholesale sales tax and payroll tax while still yielding net revenue of $4 billion per year.
- *A jobs levy, calculated on the same basis as the existing Medicare levy.* A jobs levy at a rate of 2 per cent would raise additional revenue of $5 billion per year.
- *Reintroduction of some form of inheritance tax.* This could raise between $1 billion and $2 billion per year.
- *Increasing charges for urban road use to a level which accurately reflected the social costs of road use.* This could raise between $7 billion and $10 billion per year.
- *Limits on the exemption of residential property from capital gains tax and state land taxes.* Such limits could raise $1.5 billion per year.

Beyond the measures above, Quiggin (1998) proposes a comprehensive program of tax reform that would raise additional revenue of $20 billion and shows that the net impact of such a program on the distribution of income would be progressive.

A complete set of expenditure proposals is outside the scope of this book. However, expenditure increases of at least $5 billion per year would be required simply to restore services cut by state and Commonwealth governments during the 1990s. An extra $5 billion per year would be required to eliminate waiting lists in public hospitals and to bring Australia up to the OECD average in terms of health expenditure as a share of GDP. An active labour-market policy on a scale consistent with a goal of 5 per cent unemployment would cost at least $3 billion per year. Providing all young people with the right to an adequately funded place at university or TAFE would cost around $4 billion per year. In summary, additional public spending of $20 billion per year would barely suffice to cover the most urgent needs for services.

Obstacles to expansion

In this section, several obstacles to a full-employment policy based on publicly funded employment in the human services sector will be considered. First, there is the 'fiscal crisis of the state', reflected in resistance to the higher levels of taxation needed to finance a sustainable expansion in the human services sector. Second, it is necessary to consider the danger that a tighter labour-market will lead to inflation and the argument that inflation will necessarily rise if unemployment falls below its 'natural rate' (see chapter 9). Third, there are the constraints imposed by the growth of international financial markets, commonly referred to as 'globalisation'.

The fiscal crisis of the state

The most important obstacle to full employment arises from resistance to higher taxation, and the associated 'fiscal crisis of the state'. As noted above, the ratios of tax revenue to GDP and of general government current expenditure to GDP have remained virtually static for the past 15 years. However, in part because the social welfare system is tightly targeted and means-tested, these ratios are lower in Australia than in most other OECD countries (by some measures, lower than in all except Turkey). This means that Australia has greater scope than other countries to raise additional tax revenue and increase public expenditure on human services. A comparison with six other OECD countries is presented in table 10.1.

Even with increases on the scale proposed in this chapter, Australia would still be a low-tax country. There is evidence to suggest that Australians are willing to accept higher taxes in return for improved services (Withers, Throsby and Johnston 1994; Baldry and Vinson 1998), but it is obviously necessary to mobilise that support. Both the Hawke–Keating Labor government and the Howard coalition government have been committed to the ideology of cutting taxes. Neither major party has presented the case for increased public expenditure.

Labour-market pressure and the NAIRU

The most common objection to a policy of employment creation is that inflation will accelerate if unemployment falls too low. As we have seen in previous chapters, this claim is often presented in terms of the concept of the non-accelerating inflation rate of unemployment (NAIRU). This rate, commonly thought to be around 7 per cent, is supposed to be the lowest that can be achieved without setting off a steady increase in the rate of inflation. However, estimates of the NAIRU have been so volatile that many economists reject the concept as useless (Eisner 1995; Stiglitz 1997; Galbraith 1997).

Whatever analytical framework is used, it is clear that an employment policy will fail if it sets off an inflationary spiral. Two difficulties arise for

Table 10.1 Tax revenue as percentage of GDP in seven OECD countries, 1994

	Australia	USA	Japan	UK	Germany	France	N'lands
Personal income tax	13.6	9.9	7	9	10	5	11
Payroll and social security tax	1.6	9	11	7.5	15	20	18
Company income tax	3.6	1.5	4	1.8	1	1	3
Goods, services and property tax	10.7	9.3	8	17.6	12	16	15
Total	*29.5*	*29.7*	*30*	*35.9*	*38*	*42*	*47*

Source: Pender (1997)

an employment policy based on expansion of the human services sector. The first is that the provision of additional human services will, in general, require a reduction in post-tax incomes. If wage earners and others seek to raise prices and wages to restore their post-tax incomes, inflation will inevitably result. Hence, as Boltho and Glyn (1995) observe, it is important that the policy be implemented with wide popular support, particularly from trade unions. The idea that improvements in the social wage, provided through human services, can substitute for increases in private income must be widely accepted. The proposal for a jobs levy is one way of making explicit the link between higher taxes and improved services.

The second difficulty for a full-employment policy arises from the fact that, however a reduction in unemployment is achieved, the effect is to reduce the downward pressure on wages created by the existence of a large pool of unemployed workers. It is useful to consider the impact on the public and private sectors separately. Since most of the proposed expansion would be in the public sector, it is here that wage pressure would be most likely to arise. However, public employers can bargain with unions over wages and employment levels simultaneously. More precisely, expansion of funding for any given area can be made conditional on the acceptance of real wage bargains consistent with stable inflation (assuming an inflation rate of 2 per cent and underlying productivity growth of 2 per cent, the rate of growth of nominal wages should be around 4 per cent per year).

Governments have less direct influence in the private sector. However, under the proposed policy, aggregate output and employment in the private sector will contract or remain stable, so that pressure from

employed workers for wage increases will be limited, even if unemployment is falling. The need for wage restraint should be reinforced
through a return to a more centralised system of wage-setting, with
awards retaining a substantial role in the determination of wages and
conditions.

Globalisation

Many objections to the feasibility of a full-employment program, from
both the right and the left, are tied in some way to the concept of
globalisation. This term refers to the expansion in world trade and
particularly in capital flows that has taken place since World War II and
is associated with a claim that this increase in international economic
integration has removed the power of national governments to undertake independent economic policies. On the right, the claim is cast in
terms of the need to be internationally competitive, and therefore to
reduce what are seen as cost burdens on the productive private sector.
On the left, attention is focused on the capacity of international financial capital to frustrate national governments and to impose the policies
they desire.

The growth of international financial markets and the collapse of
regulations controlling those markets have been a negative phenomenon. It has substantially worsened the performance of domestic capital
markets and has constrained the ability of governments to pursue
policies aimed at macroeconomic stability.

Advocates of full employment must recognise this, without being
paralysed into inaction. The displeasure of the money markets may
generate a devaluation and a temporary increase in interest rates but it
cannot ultimately undermine a government that adopts sustainable
fiscal and monetary policies (Argy 1998, ch. 9). Australia has suffered
more over the past decade as a result of overvalued exchange rates, and
the resulting losses to exporters, than as a result of devaluation. Policies
such as privatisation and competitive tendering may fit the world view
associated with terms like globalisation, but they are not in any mean-
ingful sense demanded by globalisation. An Australian government that
pursues policies in the national interest and avoids persistent budget
deficits cannot be derailed by the displeasure of financial markets.

In the present context, the crucial observation is that expansion of the
public sector, financed by higher taxation, will tend to reduce imports,
the current account deficit and, therefore, overseas borrowing. These
policies will make Australia less dependent on foreign capital and less
vulnerable to crises arising from breakdowns in international financial
markets.

Concluding comments

The economic policies pursued in Australia and other industrialised countries for the past two decades have failed to meet their most important objective – the provision of socially useful work for all. Only by restoring full employment as the pre-eminent goal of government policy can this failure be remedied. There is no shortage of socially useful work to be done. The crucial problem is to match idle resources and unmet needs.

This chapter has argued that, in tandem with the more general expansionary policies outlined in chapter 7 by John Nevile, expansion of the jobs-intensive human services sector offers a reasonable prospect of full employment at socially acceptable wage levels. As argued above, a program based on additional expenditure of $20 billion per year could generate sufficient employment growth to reduce the rate of unemployment to 5 per cent. The main obstacle to such a policy is political resistance to increases in taxation. As a community we face a clear choice. We can maintain our present status as a very low-tax country, and accept continuing high unemployment, or we can choose to pay a little more tax in return for better services, more jobs and a more civilised society.

CHAPTER 11

What Role for Labour-Market Programs?

Elizabeth Webster

In the broadest terms, labour-market programs are public expenditures designed to affect the demand for or supply of labour in one or several labour-markets. They are distinguished from other government expenditure primarily by their selective targeting at uncompetitive labour-market segments. Since the 1970s these programs have taken the form of a grant or subsidy to the worker, the firm or the job-broker, and during the 1990s it has become prevalent to compel many job-seekers to accept individualised employment counselling. Labour-market programs, which can be traced to the sixteenth century, are time-honoured policy responses not only to rising unemployment but also to labour and skill shortages. Their tenacity as a policy tool may be explained by their perceived ability to offer different solutions to different classes of economic theorist and policy-maker. The rationale for them has shifted with the evolution of economic theory and they are not the exclusive preserve of one school of thought. Little pattern is apparent between those who reject or embrace them.

Four main types of active labour-market programs reappear with regular frequency over time and space. Early schemes were most commonly job-creation programs which provided complete funding for all wage and material costs for projects which employed the target group. Wage-subsidy schemes provide temporary subsidies towards the wage costs incurred by employers (private and public) who hire designated job-seekers. It has become increasingly common in both Australia and overseas, to require wage-subsidy and job-creation schemes to provide the participant with some level of informal on-the-job training as well. Training-subsidy schemes pay for part or all of the costs of placing a person in a formal training program and, finally, placement services offer either intensive job counselling to job-seekers or a matching service with potential employers.[1]

It has become customary in contemporary literature to distinguish these 'active' programs from basic income support or 'passive' labour-market programs. A high ratio of active to passive expenditure is generally regarded as good (see OECD 1993, 1996; Martin 1998). However, since passive income support (e.g. the dole) is precedent to active support, a comparatively high proportion or a high level of active support indicates either low unemployment benefits or high overall spending on labour-market programs. Hence, a government cannot easily switch funding from passive support to active support without incurring additional program costs.

This chapter focuses on active labour-market programs. It discusses the transformation of labour-market programs over time, outlines their theoretical rationale and summarises recent evidence regarding the ability of programs to achieve their aims. Finally, the role these programs should play in contemporary unemployment policy is discussed. It is argued that contemporary labour-market programs are essentially supply-side policies, which have, on balance, little effect on aggregate demand. Accordingly, when the macroeconomy is demand constrained, their capacity to raise aggregate employment is negligible. However, as the economy moves closer to full employment, these programs have the potential to help reduce unemployment by assisting the matching process between labour and employers and by increasing competition in specific labour-markets. There are some a priori grounds for believing that labour-market programs may equalise the equality of access to employment by specifically targeting the long-term unemployed; however, formal evidence for this assertion is largely absent.

Labour-market programs: Description and trends
Early history

As a remedy for idleness, labour-market programs have a longer tradition than formal economic theory. Their appearance coincided with the transition from agrarian feudalism to industrial capitalism and the emergence of unemployment as defined today. Workhouses which offered the poor food and board in exchange for work have existed in Amsterdam, for example, since 1596. Similar organisations have been mentioned in the writings of seventeenth-century English and French authors (Garraty 1978). Among these were schemes to provide vocational training for pauper children, to force labour at 'moderate' wages, to coerce work for one's board and lodgings and to compel service at sea. At times, these measures were reinforced by law and penal sanctions, and at others, they were run by charitable institutions for the moral benefit of paupers, vagrants and the destitute. Some institutions, such as the French Hôpital Général, aimed to become self-supporting through the work of their inmates, but it has been claimed by historians that these were rarely successful. In part, this was attributed to the inefficiency and lack of motivation of the participants and, in part, because the workhouses produced a glut of goods that could not be sold (Garraty 1978, ch. 3). It was commonly believed that poverty, idleness and vice were due to personal defects.

During the Depression, labour-market programs became larger, more systematic and more clearly the responsibility of governments. The US, German, Italian and Swedish governments undertook public works programs on a large scale, but the British, French and Belgian governments used them more sparingly. In Australia, labour-intensive capital works were instigated during the major recessions of the 1840s, 1890s as well as the 1930s (Bureau of Labour Market Research 1984, p. 20). These programs, however, ended with the ultimate job creator: World War II.

In the three decades following the war, labour-market programs did a complete turn-around from their established tradition of 'doing something' *with* the unemployed to doing something *about* labour shortages. Under the apt nomenclature of 'manpower programs', they were ordinarily aimed at the male labour force and few efforts were made to address regulations and overt and covert forms of discrimination which kept the female labour force artificially low. Attempts to overcome basic labour shortages were made by assisted immigration programs and guest worker schemes. Skilled labour shortages were met by education, training and mobility grants and subsidies.

Australian labour-market programs since 1974

Although the dominant concern during the 1940s, 1950s and 1960s was labour-market shortages, small job-creation programs were funded in rural areas during the 1960s and early 1970s as forms of drought relief (Bureau of Labour Market Research 1984, p. 20). The quantum rise in unemployment during 1973/74 caused a major attitudinal shift and a subsequent reallocation of expenditure towards programs to assist the unemployed (see figure 11.1).[2] Since then, expenditure has followed the conventional pattern of rising in response to growing unemployment levels and easing as recessions ended. These expenditures exclude basic employment placement or job-broking under the Commonwealth Employment Service (CES) which operated from 1946 to 1998. Despite the shift towards programs to reduce labour surpluses, programs to encourage the formation of trade skills still attract significant funding in absolute terms.

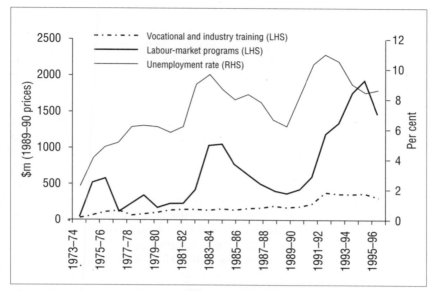

Figure 11.1 Commonwealth government labour-market expenditure, Australia, 1973/74 to 1995/96
Sources: Stretton and Chapman (1990); Webster (1997, appendix)

Between 1991/92 and 1992/93, the government more than doubled the labour-market assistance to job-seekers. Under the auspices of *Working Nation* (formally introduced in 1994), it re-emphasised intensive counselling services and targeting towards the very long-term unemployed (those unemployed for over 18 months) and those deemed at risk of becoming so. In addition to guaranteeing a job through improved access to wage- and training-subsidy programs, it imposed higher penalties upon people who did not participate.

Most of the cyclical variation in total program expenditure is due to changes to job-creation programs. Major schemes have included the Regional Employment Development Scheme (1974 to 1976), the Wage Pause Program (1982 to 1983), the Community Employment Program (1983 to 1987/88) and most recently JobSkills (1991 to 1996), Landcare and Environment Action Program (1992/93 to 1996) and New Work Opportunities (1995 to 1996). Funding for wage-subsidy schemes, while less volatile, has nonetheless tended to vary pro-cyclically as well. The main programs have included the youth wage- and training-subsidy scheme, SYETP (from 1976 to 1985), the Adult Wage Subsidy Scheme (1981 to 1985) and Jobstart (1985 to 1996). Job-placement services (excluding the CES) include additional job-search assistance and intensive employment counselling, and are a relatively new form of labour-market program. These have included Job Clubs (1988 to 1996), Skill Share (1989 to 1996), and case management (1994 to 1998). Funding for training programs has been more even over time. The most recent significant example is Jobtrain, which operated from 1988/89 to 1996.

A notable feature since the late 1980s has been the blending of program characteristics. Placement programs have included training and work experience situations, job-creation schemes have required the provision of training and case management schemes have acted as an agent to ensure individuals have a combination of assistance. Since 1989, a 'principle of reciprocal obligation' requiring unemployment recipients to accept referral to jobs or training positions has operated.

While there has been a clear and consistent pattern of increasing spending as unemployment rises over the last quarter of a century, there has also been a pattern of continually chopping and changing program names, conditions and payment schedules. While some modification can be justified as fine-tuning, these reoccurring changes have probably imparted a degree of confusion and uncertainty and considerable information costs upon job-seekers, government service providers, policy analysts and employers. Furthermore, funding volatility generally makes it difficult to establish efficient programs. Administrators are often required to devise and spend money very quickly with little assurance of a continuity of funding.

Programs since 1998: The Jobs Network

Following its election in March 1996, the incoming coalition government announced a complete reorganisation of the employment services programs and a significant reduction in spending on employment services for the coming three-year period. The CES was abolished in May 1998, the Department of Social Security was restructured, provision of employment services was almost completely outsourced and funding for those services was cut by about half. In addition, changes in the structure and level of funding have implied a shift away from the lengthy job-creation and wage-subsidy programs towards placement services.

Centrelink, a one-stop, government-owned shop, was established to form the centre of employment services and link it to the social security system. The role of provider of employment services was transferred from the CES and the case management network to a new Jobs Network. The Network comprises over 300 government, private and community organisations that have successfully tendered to provide one or more defined services. The rights to provide services for basic job-matching and job-search training were awarded on a competitive price basis. These prices range from under $100 to a few hundred dollars per successfully placed client. The right to provide more intensive assistance is funded along a payment schedule fixed by the government (see Webster 1998a).

The Commonwealth, under the Jobs Network scheme, funds several categories of employment services, from the provision of basic recruitment services (Flex 1), intensive job-search training (Flex 2), through to case management for the most disadvantaged (Flex 3). There are no formally defined labour-market programs and the providers of these services have a relatively free hand in designing and funding any subsidies for wages, training costs or counselling. However, not only do funding levels for Flex 3 scarcely cover the cost of assistance on par with the previous Jobstart or job-creation programs, but in addition, the payment schedules give service providers little incentive to do more than basic job-matching (see Webster forthcoming). This is significant since some of the most recent Australian research indicates that wage-subsidy and job-creation programs produce the greatest employment impact per dollar spent (Stromback, Dockery and Ying 1998a, 1999). In addition, the new Jobs Network offers basic recruitment services for seasonal labour-markets such as those involving fruit-picking, assistance for job-seekers who want to become self-employed and a 'one-stop shop' service for employers, apprentices and trainees. Of all the services offered, however, job-matching, job-search training and intensive assistance are the most important.

While the replacement of the CES and case management network with the Jobs Network has been hailed as a bold innovation, these changes should be seen in the context of reviews and reforms carried out under both the Hawke–Keating Labor government and two successive Victorian governments (see e.g. DEETYA 1996a). These relate to the increased emphasis on case management, outsourcing and the introduction of competitive market incentives in the employment services area. What is new and bold, however, is the dramatic and fast pace of change and the significantly reduced level of program funding. Unlike earlier reforms, the birth of the Jobs Network was once-off and no phase-out period was allowed for the old system.

International context

Australia spends less than the average OECD member country on active labour-market programs although it had been growing more strongly in the decade to 1996 (table 11.1). By 1996, spending was very high relative to East Asian members, high relative to other Anglo-Saxon countries but low compared with the European Union countries. However, spending

Table 11.1 Active labour-market programs, percentage of GDP

	1985	1996	Annual percentage change 1985 to 1996
Australia	0.4	0.7	5.2
Canada	0.6	0.5	−1.6
New Zealand	0.9	0.7	−2.3
United Kingdom	0.7	0.4	−5.0
United States	0.3	0.2	−3.6
EU	0.9	1.2	2.6
OECD	0.7	0.9	2.3

Source: Martin (1998, Table 1)

on active labour-market programs in Australia since 1996 has been cut by about a half.

It is difficult to assess whether the relative position of Australia is to be commended or condemned for the value of spending on labour-market programs depends on the economic context of a country and, in particular, on complementary macroeconomic policies.

Labour-market programs: Theoretical rationale and evaluations
Rationale

Since the emergence over the last quarter of a century of high and sustained levels of unemployment across the industrialised western world, labour-market programs have been regarded either as a possible solution to unemployment or as the means of ameliorating the adverse effects unemployment has on equality of access to a job. Economists and policy-makers who advocate these programs believe they achieve their ultimate objective by making it more profitable for employers, in both the short and longer term, to hire the unemployed without aggravating inflation, the external trade account or the assets markets.

Programs may increase expected profitability via three main routes. First, they may reduce the job-search process by improving access to relevant employers. This will not only increase the chances that the participant will get a job offer but should also assist them to find a job for which they are more suited. Second, labour-market programs may raise the intrinsic profitability of hiring the person by improving the participant's formal and informal work-related skills and increasing their motivation and confidence.[3] Whether these improvements are exploited depends on whether the participant can readily move into open employment, for the benefits are likely to depreciate quickly. Third, by providing the employer with more knowledge about the person, labour-market programs reduce the uncertainty associated with hiring them.

The four different labour-market program types mentioned above have been developed in response to differing job-seekers' requirements and different stages of the economic cycle. Job-creation programs, while expensive, are most suitable for the very disadvantaged job-seekers. This program gives policy-makers a large degree of control over work content, the selection of people into jobs and provides recruitment certainty even during times of economic downturn. Wage-subsidy programs are generally more suitable for the more able and skilled job-seekers who on average have experienced shorter durations of unemployment. However, experience shows that take-up rates can be low during periods of low economic growth. Training programs are mainly suitable for job-seekers who have specific identified skill needs and are capable of acquiring information through a formal classroom setting. However, like training in general, the benefits from training can be low if it is not articulated with employment, especially since skills initiated under formal training programs require consolidation through immediate practical repetition. Finally, intensive placement services have been devised for two disparate groups. Job-search training represents short courses for the 'job ready'. These programs are comparatively cheap but their success will depend critically on the stage of the macroeconomy. Case management services are targeted at the most disadvantaged job-seeker and are usually integrated with one or more of the other types of programs. As such, the whole case management package can be expensive per participant.

Microeconomic evaluations

To assess the success of a program, it is not enough to maintain that program participants, on average, are more employable because of the program. It needs to be cogently argued that the jobs gained by participants have not been wholly at the expense of other job-seekers and people already in employment. If there is significant substitution between program participants and other labour-market participants, then the ultimate goal of increasing aggregate employment is compromised. Further, unless we know something about the characteristics of the displaced workers, we cannot make very firm statements about the equity effects.

Microeconomic evaluations of labour-market programs seek to measure the difference in labour-market experience of participants with an equivalent set of non-participants (control group) at some defined post-program set of dates. While they can give an estimate of the proportion of program participants who would have obtained open employment without the program, they cannot give any information about the extent of employment substitution and thus whether aggregate employment or equality of employment access has been extended. Nevertheless, as a partial equilibrium analysis, they provide data for a more embracing macroeconomic analysis. They are also useful for defining the maximum level of benefits we can expect from a program.

There has been considerable progress in the quality of microeconomic evaluations and the associated data set in Australia since the late 1970s. Many evaluations during the 1970s and early 1980s suffered from a lack of a control group population, and programs were often so large that most of the target group had participated in the program in some way.[4] Even when control groups were used, these early evaluations were not able to cater for a bias, which occurs when more able, motivated or knowledgeable people are systematically selected into or excluded from a program.

Longitudinal (panel) evaluations, which have been designed to control for the (possibly very large) bias in evaluations from this type of program selection, have been conducted overseas since the late 1970s. However, while there are two suitable Australian data sets (ABS Survey of Employment and Unemployment Patterns (SEUP) and the DEWRSB longitudinal survey), there have not been any evaluations which have controlled for selection biases to date (1998). Stromback, Dockery and Ying have, however, conducted alternative microeconomic evaluations from the ABS SEUP. These have been used to calculate the significance of factors associated with both a move from unemployment to employment (hazard functions) and labour-force status.

The other main source of microeconomic evaluation is the regular post-program evaluations based upon Commonwealth government monitoring surveys. Only the most recent evaluations compare participants' post-program employment status with a selected control group. Results from both types of evaluation are summarised in table 11.2

Both sets of evaluations find that wage subsidies have the largest impact upon an individual's outcome; however, the ranking of job-creation, training and job-placement programs differs. Stromback et al. consistently find that job creation has the second-highest effect, while the government evaluations place them on equal par with the other two programs. However, none of the evaluations have been able to control for the probability that people who were selected into programs had unobservable characteristics, relating to motivation and commonsense, which significantly differentiate them from a control group selected on the basis of observable characteristics. As such, even these evaluation

Table 11.2 Summary of evaluation results of labour-market programs

Program type	Summary of SEUP results	Summary of government post-program monitoring (with a control group)
1. Wage subsidies	Stromback, Dockery and Ying (1998a, 1998b) and Stromback and Dockery (1998) find a significant increase in the post-program employment rate. Stromback, Dockery and Ying (1998b, p. 18) estimate the employment rate of participants to be 20 percentage points higher than comparable non-participants up to a year after the program has ended.	DEETYA (1997) and DEET (1993a, 1989) found employment rates about 30 percentage points higher at between 3 and 6 months compared with control group.
2. Job creation	Stromback, Dockery and Ying (1998a, 1998b) and Stromback and Dockery (1998) find a significant positive increase in post-program employment rate. Stromback, Dockery and Ying (1998b, p. 18) estimate this to be 25 percentage points higher than a comparable group up to a year after the program has ended.	DEETYA (1997, 1996b) found a post-program effect of between 9 and 11 percentage points.
3. Training	Stromback, Dockery and Ying (1998a, 1998b) did not find training courses had any effect on post-program employment status. However, Stromback and Dockery (1998) estimated the effects as significant but about half as large as the wage-subsidy effect.	DEETYA (1997) and DEET (1993b) estimate that post-program employment rate for up to 12 months is 7 to 10 percentage points higher than the control group.
4. Intensive job placement	Stromback, Dockery and Ying (1998a, 1998b) estimate the effect is insignificant or very small. Stromback and Dockery (1998) find the effect is significant but about half as large as the wage-subsidy effect.	DEETYA (1997) and DEET (1994) found that post-program employment rate for up to 12 months is 10 to 12 percentage points higher than for a control group.

results may be substantially revised when evaluations that cater for selection biases are undertaken.

Macroeconomic evaluations

The microeconomic evaluations cited above suggest that, at best, the chance an individual who has undergone a labour-market program has of finding a job improved by 10 to 30 percentage points during the post-program year. However, as previously mentioned, some of this gain to the individual is likely to come at the expense of another job-seeker or person in employment.

One archaic view, which enjoyed currency during the 1970s, was that labour-market program expenditure was a net addition to aggregate demand and thus participants' jobs were a net addition to employment. However, for a given fiscal and monetary stance, the cost of labour-market programs is forgone spending in other government portfolios and is thus unlikely to lead to any addition to aggregate demand. On the other hand, an addition to aggregate employment could possibly arise from the higher domestic labour intensity of program expenditure. While there are many possible expenditure counterfactuals, some possibly more employment intensive than labour-market programs, labour-market programs do not intrinsically contribute to aggregate demand or employment.

Contemporary pro-employment or pro-efficiency arguments for labour-market programs reside in more subtle arguments about the nature of the macro labour-market. A common argument is that while unemployment is caused by a deficiency of aggregate demand, an expansion of demand on its own may not be the remedy, due to labour-market bottlenecks or concentrations of market power which produce inflation rather than higher employment.[5] High public debt levels, current account problems and overheating in asset markets are also reasons limiting government-induced expansion of aggregate demand. Nevertheless, because of its labour-market focus, most of the literature addresses the complication of wage inflation.

The microeconomic mechanism by which a demand stimulus translates into higher wages rather than higher production and employment is the subject of several hypotheses, of which the insider–outsider and efficiency wage hypotheses are pre-eminent. With respect to the former, Lindbeck and Snower (1986) have argued that incumbent employees – insiders – have considerably greater bargaining power over the unemployed – outsiders – because the firm has invested considerable resources into equipping them with a knowledge and understanding of its internal and external operations. The tighter the labour-market, and accordingly the less the threat of dismissal, the greater the incentive for and ability of labour to successfully bargain for higher wages. The presence of active labour unions further adds to workers' power. Variations of this theory also hold that the power of insiders is directly reinforced by the poor quality of informal work skills held by outsiders. The longer 'outsiders' are out of work, the more they become out of touch with the world of work and subsequently the less intense are wage pressures they may bring to bear upon insiders' wage negotiations.

As we saw in chapter 4, a distinct but related efficiency wage theory argues that employers initiate wage rises to keep valued employees keen, enthusiastic and hard working, and reduce their propensity to quit.[6] These types of employers will not drop nominal wages and will always seek to keep wages above 'market clearing' and in line with their competitors.

The literature, especially in Europe, suggests that the more removed outsiders are from the world of work and the more depleted and obsolete their skills, the less threat they pose to persons in work. Growing firms would rather poach existing workers from rivals, by offering better wages, than hire someone who has been out of work for over a year. Thus, it is argued that it is the portion of the labour force in short-term unemployment, not the total unemployment rate, which acts to keep the labour-market competitive and wage pressures low. However, when unemployment is rising, people are more likely to move out of short-term unemployment into long-term unemployed rather than a job. Thus rising or sustained unemployment over time does not progressively increase the portion of short-term unemployment and thus act as a brake upon wage demands.

Under these theories, labour-market programs can play a role in reducing the anticipated heating of the labour-market during expansions if they can reverse the skill atrophy of the long-term unemployed and maintain them as an effective, work-ready labour force. If this transformation is successful, it will allow an expansion of aggregate demand without contributory wage pressures. However, there is little point having measures to contain inflation if their benefits are not exploited by instigating discretionary mechanisms to stimulate economic growth (Quiggin 1993a; Mitchell 1994b; Heylen, Goubert and Omey 1996). Under this model of the economy, labour-market programs are *complementary* to expansionary policies of economic growth, and expenditure on labour-market programs should increase during cyclical upturns or when the government is taking active steps to raise aggregate demand. This does not appear to have been the case in Australia where labour-market program expenditure has been counter-cyclical (see figure 11.1).[7] Overseas literature suggests that active labour-market programs of this sort are used anti-cyclically as much as pro-cyclically.

The evaluation literature can test for the effects of lower unemployment stemming from labour-market programs in one of two ways. Either it directly tests for a relationship between labour-market programs and aggregate unemployment (usually by a pooled time series cross-section data analysis), or it may infer from theory and partial evidence. It is difficult to get direct evidence on the macroeconomic effects of labour-market programs using time series data. The small size of the programs relative to GDP inevitably means that their effects can be swamped by other influences. Unfortunately, there are few international rules of thumb to glean from the aggregate data and the econometric evidence is mixed (Calmfors 1993). Low unemployment in Sweden has frequently been attributed to the Swedish interventionist labour-market policies; however, at the same time, low Japanese unemployment has always been associated with very low expenditure on labour-market programs (OECD 1994a).[8] Moreover, because the government's policy stance is often endogenous, that is governments increase labour-market program expenditures in response to the (worsening) state of the labour market, care must be taken to disentangle cause and effect in statistical work.[9] One approach therefore has been to enter the labour-market program variable as a lagged variable.

There are a limited number of studies that seek to directly test for a causal relationship between labour-market programs and unemployment. An international study by Bellmann and Jackman (1996) used pooled cross-sectional time series data from 17 OECD countries during the period 1975 to 1993. They estimated the equation:

Rate of unemployment = f(labour market program expenditure per unemployed person, the replacement ratio, duration of unemployment benefits, degree of centralisation of wage bargaining, institutional sclerosis, union density and usage of temporary employment)

They did not find that the labour-market program had any influence on the rate of unemployment (although it did affect the incidence of long-term unemployment) or the rate of growth of employment.

The alternative evaluation approach has involved testing whether labour-market programs improve the unemployment/vacancy trade-off (the Beveridge curve) and whether they reduce wage inflation.

With respect to the former, labour-market programs may shift the Beveridge curve inward if they increase the speed at which vacancies are filled. Over the period 1979 to 1998, the average vacant job in Australia took between 5 and 15 days to fill according to the tightness of the labour-market (figure 11.2).[10] Reducing the fill time from 15 to 5 days could potentially reduce 1998 unemployment levels by 7 per cent if all

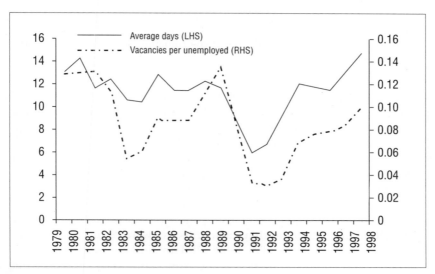

Figure 11.2 Estimated average number of days to fill a vacancy and ratio of vacancies per unemployed person, Australia, 1979–98

Note: Annual estimates for 1998 exclude November and December data. Average day estimates cannot be calculated for 1993, 1995 and 1997 and these are accordingly interpolated.

affected vacancies were taken by unemployed job-seekers and not those outside the labour force. A casual glance at figure 11.2 however supports the view that neither the two peak periods of labour-market program expenditure (1983 to 1985 and 1994 to 1996) nor the growth of job-placement services since the early 1990s has had a large and systematic effect on the average number of days taken to fill a vacancy.

Two econometric studies by Jackman, Pissarides and Savouri (1990) and Webster (1998b) have examined the relationship between labour-market programs and the unemployment/vacancy relationship. Using data from 14 OECD countries over the period 1971 to 1988, Jackman et al. found some evidence to support the theory that labour-market programs shift the Beveridge curve inward. However, the Australian results found by Webster are either insignificant or small. The most optimistic econometric results indicate that a 10 per cent increase in training subsidies per unemployed person would reduce the unemployment rate by 0.1 percentage points. The equivalent effect for placement services was 0.01 percentage points.

Layard, Nickell and Jackman (1991) appear to belong to a minority of economists who have tried to find a direct relationship between labour-market programs and inflation. Using data from 20 countries from 1983 to 1988, they estimated:

Change in inflation = f(duration of unemployment benefits, replacement ratio, expenditure on labour market programs, unions coverage, co-ordination between unions, degree of co-ordination between employers, the rate of unemployment)[11]

They obtained significant results for all variables. Forslund and Kreuger (1994) re-estimated this equation with 1993 data and found the labour-market program variable lost its significance and changed sign (see Calmfors and Skedinger 1995, p. 93). Two further studies from Sweden have found contradictory conclusions over whether or not labour-market programs have added to or subtracted from wage inflation (OECD 1993; Calmfors and Lang 1995). A study by Calmfors argued that labour-market programs might raise inflation because they diminished the consequences of losing one's job; however, another study by Forslund in 1992 found that wage pressures were reduced by labour-market programs. Carling et al. (1996) did not find any evidence that an increased availability of labour-market programs in Sweden makes the unemployed less inclined to search for open employment.

Finally, an Australian study by Webster and Summers (1998) using pooled time series industry data found evidence that, collectively, wage-subsidy, job-creation and training programs had a significant effect in reducing wage inflation over the 1989/90 to 1996/97 period. The average number of labour-market program participants varied over this period from 0.09 per cent of the labour force in agriculture, forestry and fishery to about 1 per cent in personal services. The econometric results indicate that if this coverage was doubled, nominal wages would have been 1 per cent lower *ceteris paribus*. No significant results were obtained for the effect of labour-market programs on the rate of growth of nominal wages.

Our interim conclusion on the effect of labour-market programs on wage inflation is that their effects are small or ambiguous. In the case of Australia, they may affect the level of nominal wages but not their rate of growth. However, these evaluations may reveal low-level macroeconomic effects because data were drawn from periods of high excess supply of labour. Better placement services, top-up training and subsidised work experiences may make the difference between delaying the filling of a vacancy (or poaching workers from a rival) and hiring an unemployed person only in the context of a tight labour-market.

In sum, Australian microeconomic evaluations indicate that the most effective program, wage-subsidy schemes, enhances the employment prospects of between 20 and 30 per cent of participants. However, macroeconomic evaluations suggest that most of this gain has been at the expense of other job-seekers and people already in employment. A higher level of program participants by industry does appear to reduce nominal wages by a small level but whether this translates into more employment depends on how this affects government policies and the profitability of employing new labour.

What should be done?

Both inductive and deductive reasoning suggest that as a device for alleviating unemployment, labour-market programs should *complement* demand expansion policies as the economy approaches full employment and not substitute for it. The major obstacle facing many unemployed people is a lack of vacancies not a lack of work experience, skills or contacts with firms. We know from microeconomic evaluations that many non-participants in labour-market programs with similar characteristics to participants find and retain employment. Program participation in many cases merely pushes a person further up the labour queue. Job-seekers generally benefit more from ongoing employment rather than a temporary job.

If we are only interested in labour-market programs as a means of increasing competition in specific labour-markets and thus reducing wage inflation, then one must also ask whether other, more effective ways of achieving this exist. Some studies have found evidence that wage-setting institutions (i.e whether we have a centralised Accord system or not) and the level and severity of employment protection regulations are more important factors in containing inflation than the total or short-term unemployment rate. Reducing the very high marginal effective tax rates on households receiving unemployment benefits, increasing the flexibility of the wage-setting process, altering wage structures to reflect the costs and benefits of training more closely, minimising the skill loss caused by firms which downsize and shed skilled staff, and increasing the transferability of skills between several related occupations may contribute as much or more to reducing wage inflation as labour-market programs. If we find that bilateral monopoly power is a major contributory factor in fuelling inflation, then a broader incomes policy arrangement may be more appropriate.

With respect to the effects that labour-market programs have on equality of opportunity, the prospects are more sanguine. While full employment is also the best policy countering inequality of access to employment, labour-market programs offer a second-best alternative over which central governments have more immediate control. However, given the paucity of macroeconomic work in this area, it cannot be given a full vote of confidence. There is no surety that the same type of person would or would not have gained a job, or training and job combination, in the absence of the program. Programs could have merely selected the more 'job-ready' members of the target group at the direct expense of other members of the (disadvantaged) target group.

The type of programs which should be promoted in pursuit of the objectives above depends on both the estimated cost per participant who obtained open employment, estimates of the effect on wage inflation and speed of vacancy filling, and the suitability of each program type for different classes of job-seeker. Most microeconomic estimates regard wage subsidies as the most cost-effective type of labour-market program. However, even if they were very effective against wage inflation and hard-to-fill vacancies, wage subsidies are not considered suitable for many of the most disadvantaged types of job-seeker nor are they easy to use in times of low job growth. While very long-term unemployed job-seekers exist in the community, direct job-creation programs may be required to act as a bridge between idleness and open employment.

In sum, from an efficiency perspective, labour-market programs could be used to complement economic growth and should not be regarded as a method which can directly stimulate growth on their own. At best, labour-market programs should be regarded as one of several measures governments may adopt to permit high economic growth. The decision to fund complementary anti-inflationary policies should however be undertaken in the context of other education, training, industrial relations and social security changes which may have similar effects. From an equity perspective, labour-market programs are probably a faster way of assisting the most marginalised members of the labour force than the alternative trickle-down method.

Conclusion

While enhancing the skill level and career flexibility of the labour force may provide complementary conditions for sustainable full employment, it is not clear that labour-market programs designated for those out of work are the best or most efficient way to achieve this. Arguably, jobs growth and sustained work experience are the most effective way of acquiring higher level work skills. Good early formal education may provide the theoretical basis and instil good learning habits for subsequent informal on-the-job skill development. Formal training may accelerate the skill acquisition process if logically articulated with practical experience. However, these measures cannot substitute for learning on the job.

To state that a permanent expansion of jobs is the best solution clearly begs the question of how to achieve this. While this is not the subject of this chapter, it is worth noting that as a device for attaining full employment, labour-market programs should at best accompany policies to stimulate economic growth. The most optimistic Australian estimates of labour-market programs' macroeconomic effects suggest positive but only small effects and, accordingly, consideration should be given to alternative policies which have a greater impact.

Finally, labour-market programs may have a positive role in equalising access to employment opportunities; however, until some estimates are made of these effects, programs are advocated more on intuition than on sound evidence.

CHAPTER 12

Unemployment, Inequality and the Politics of Redistribution

Stephen Bell

Since the mid-1970s, GDP growth rates across the advanced economies, including Australia, have averaged about half the rate achieved during the postwar golden age (see table 12.2). Nevertheless, and due to the magic of compound growth, it is still the case that the advanced capitalist economies have never been wealthier. In Australia, for example, average real per capita incomes have roughly doubled since the mid-1960s. Despite this, we still have an unemployment crisis and economic insecurity has become a leitmotif of the age: inequality is rising and those with jobs worry about losing them. Krugman (1994a, pp. 19–20) sums up the situation thus: 'the economic problems of the West present a paradox of growing misery in the face of growing wealth'.

As previous chapters have argued, one of the explanations for this is insufficient economic growth. Partly due to the stance of macro-economic policy, GDP growth has averaged less than 3 per cent per annum over the last 25 years and this has not been enough to prevent rising unemployment, or associated increases in inequality. In short, jobs growth has not kept up with rising demand. Another part of the explanation, which is the focus of this chapter, is the changing nature of the developmental process itself and related structural change in the economy.

In key respects a new economy is emerging, one which *distributes* jobs and incomes less effectively than in the past. Even in low-tech Australia, at the top end of the labour-market the impact of new technology and production systems is placing an employment premium on skill, knowledge and flexibility, leaving many less skilled and less talented workers behind. Structural economic change is also transforming the postwar growth, employment and wage relationships into a far less accommodating form. In particular, the shift to an increasingly services-dominated

252

economy, and in Australia, a predominantly 'low end' services economy, is producing a less equal pattern of wage outcomes and growing distributional tensions. In this more difficult employment regime, neoliberal economic orthodoxy has settled on the view that the major market route to reduced unemployment is through wage reductions at the lower end of the labour-market. It is clear, however, as previous chapters have argued, that such an approach offers only limited employment growth and does not solve but simply reshuffles the underlying distributional problem. In effect, those at the lower end are being asked to fund jobs growth through wage reductions with rising inequality as a key outcome. The implication is that societies confronted by the new economy, if they wish to retain some semblance of civility, must now confront distributional issues head on. Current difficulties in mounting such a response stem from major changes to the broader economic governance regime. So far, neoliberalism in its various societal and policy manifestations has stymied an effective response. Possible ways beyond this impasse are discussed.

The new economy

The type of economy that has evolved since the 1970s is in key respects very different to the postwar economy. In the postwar era, a major driver of employment growth was the expansion of manufacturing which entailed mass production and mass consumption of standardised consumer goods and by low to medium technology and low to medium skill-based forms of work. By contrast, one of the most important changes in the evolving economy since the 1970s has been the shift from manufacturing to a services-dominated employment growth pattern. In part this change reflects shifts away from earlier mass consumption patterns towards services or more specialised forms of consumption. Changing production systems, the impact of technology and changing labour-markets have increasingly meant that the ability to obtain reasonably secure, well-paid jobs increasingly depends on achieving high educational and skill levels. In combination, these developments, considered more fully below, have substantially eroded the earlier distributional capacities of the market economy.

Technology and skills

The relationship between technology, employment and unemployment is a complex one (Padalino and Vivarelli 1997). Many have claimed that labour-displacing technology is a major factor driving unemployment. Others claim that advanced technology creates many new jobs. The key idea in the former scenario is that as technology increasingly replaces labour, we get 'jobless growth'. Yet from an aggregate, long-term perspective in the advanced economies, it is widely agreed that technology enhances aggregate employment growth, thus avoiding the 'jobless growth' pattern. As the OECD (1994a, p. 33) explains: 'Historically, the income-generating effects of new technologies have proved more powerful than the labour-displacing effects: technological progress has been accompanied not only by higher output and productivity, but also by higher overall employment'. In some respects, however, the veracity of this conclusion can be questioned. As indicated in table 12.1, in the period between 1960 and 1994, jobless growth has been a feature of the UK economy. The employment intensity of growth has been quite weak in Europe, and not particularly strong in Japan. Indeed, only in North America (US, Canada), where there has been a relatively robust link between GDP growth and employment growth, do we find strong contrary evidence to the 'jobless growth' thesis. As table 12.1 also shows, jobless growth in the manufacturing sector has occurred in four of the G-7 economies, while relatively weak employment responses characterise a further two of these economies. As indicated below, 'jobless growth' has also been a feature of Australian manufacturing in recent decades.

Contrary to the OECD orthodoxy above, jobless growth does seem to be a relevant issue, at least in some countries and in some sectors (particularly manufacturing). This poses the following question: is this a developing, post-'golden age' trend, perhaps driven by advancing labour-displacing technology? This may well be true for manufacturing, but it seems less the case for whole economies. First, if the labour-displacing technology argument was true in aggregate we should expect to find an acceleration in labour productivity growth as part of a process by which new technology reduces labour input. In fact, the opposite has been the case in recent decades. Across the advanced economies, particularly in the 1970s and 1980s, labour productivity growth slowed very substantially (Eatwell 1995; Singh 1995). Second, on the question of whether jobless growth is a new development, table 12.2 indicates that it is not. If we compare the job intensity of growth over two periods – 1960–73 and 1980–94 – which correspond to the golden age and post-golden age eras, we find that the later period is generally more jobs rich. In the G-7 countries between 1960 and 1973, there was on average a 0.17 jobs growth response to every 1 per cent increase in GDP. Yet for the period 1980–94, this response had increased to 0.26. In Australia, there is a similar pattern of increasing jobs intensity per quantum of GDP growth. Indeed, as table 12.2 shows, the jobs intensity of growth in Australia has been much higher than the G-7 average in both periods and has been close to the level achieved by the US. The main

Table 12.1 Aggregate and manufacturing GDP and employment growth averages, G-7 countries, 1960–94

	Whole economy		Manufacturing	
	Real GDP rate	Employment growth	Product growth	Employment growth
USA	2.99	1.87	3.87	0.61
Japan	6.22	1.09	6.37	1.48
Canada	3.92	2.24	3.72	0.75
Germany	2.95	0.27	2.60	−0.32
France	3.40	0.34	2.78	−0.28
Italy	3.52	0.20	3.46	−0.73
UK	2.32	−0.18	1.42	−2.20

Source: Padalino and Vivarelli (1997, p. 201)

explanation for this broad comparative shift towards greater jobs intensity, as argued more fully below, has been the growing shift towards (jobs-rich) services employment. The weak labour productivity performance across the OECD economies in the 1970s and 1980s has also helped employment growth in this respect. Hence, at the aggregate level, these trends seem to have more than offset jobless growth in manufacturing.

The arguments above suggest that the impacts of technology-driven jobless growth are far from uniform, both across sectors and across countries. A more uniform effect, however, is the impact of technology and changing production systems on the *composition* of employment. The OECD (1994a, p. 33) argues that 'technology both destroys jobs and creates jobs. Generally, it destroys lower wage, lower productivity jobs, while it creates jobs that are more productive, high-skill and better paid'. This change in the composition of employment is important. At the top end of the market, the impact of technology, but also the changing nature of production systems, rapidly changing patterns of demand, short product cycles and the associated increasing 'flexibilisation' of production (as well as the rise of certification and professionalism), have all raised the bar to obtaining gainful forms of employment. Increasingly, obtaining a well-paid job requires higher and higher levels of education, skill, commitment and experience. Flexibilisation, heightened competitive pressures, the growing stress on bottom-line returns, the downsizing of corporate hierarchies, and outsourcing through contractual networks have also altered employment relationships, placing less emphasis on earlier forms of secure, long-term employment. One implication of this is the growth of what Hancock (1999, p. 24) refers to as the 'floating' component of the labour force, which, because of heightened job

Table 12.2 GDP growth and employment growth, G-7 and Australia

Growth	US	Japan	Canada	Germany	France	Italy	UK	G-7	Australia
GDP (real)									
1960–73	4.0	9.7	5.5	4.4	5.4	5.3	3.2	5.4	5.1
1980–94	2.3	4.0	2.3	2.0	1.9	2.0	1.9	2.3	2.7
Employment									
1960–73	2.0 (0.5)	1.3 (0.13)	2.9 (0.53)	0.3 (0.07)	0.7 (0.13)	−0.2 (−0.04)	−0.5 (−0.16)	0.93 (0.17)	2.5 (0.49)
1980–94	1.5 (0.65)	1.1 (0.27)	1.3 (0.56)	0.5 (0.25)	0.05 (0.03)	0.2 (0.1)	−0.5 (−0.26)	0.59 (0.26)	1.6 (0.59)

Note: The numbers in brackets are the ratios of employment to GDP growth

Sources: Padalino and Vivarelli (1997); Foster (1996)

turnover, increased 'churning' and shifting contractual work relationships, inevitably drives up frictional unemployment. In Hancock's view, there is an important relationship in these terms between unemployment and the growing *insecurity* of employment. Another implication is that many workers, either because of their own limitations or because of inadequate education, training and experience, now find it difficult to enter the world of gainful, well-paid employment. A key dimension of the new economy is that it is leaving large numbers of the low skilled and less talented behind (Nickell and Bell 1997). An important result, in the US, for example, is what Krugman (1994a, p. 20) refers to as a 'startling polarisation in the earnings distribution' as the less skilled become unemployed, 'economically inactive', or scramble for low-paying jobs in what is increasingly becoming a core/periphery labour-market (Cox 1987, ch. 9).[1]

Education, retraining and skills upgrading programs are seen by many as the obvious answer to this problem. While useful, particularly in the longer term as part of a national economic upgrading process, in the short to medium term the training route can only be a partial answer to unemployment because it focuses only on the supply of labour and not on the supply of jobs. At present, in Australia, the unemployment/job vacancy ratio is about 10:1. In a recent study of the relationship between skills upgrading and unemployment, Chapman (1999) wrote that the 'major conclusion is that the answer to Australian job creation, at least in the short to medium term, does not lie in increasing the skills of the unemployed'. Serious consideration also needs to be given to the little debated possibility that the level of commitment, intellect and knowledge required to *successfully* participate in the labour-market may be increasingly beyond the capacity of many. As the American writer Larry Letich (1995) has argued: 'It is possible that over the last 100 years, and especially the last 40, we may have created a society that demands more brain power than most people are able to give'. If so, even an advanced 'training augmented' labour-market will fail the key distributional tasks of providing jobs and adequate incomes for many of those at the bottom. *In this situation, the only solution is to explicitly supply jobs with reasonable wages that match feasible capabilities and talents.* This is an explicitly distributional issue which in the new economy the market is not solving.

Structural change and the new service economy

The postwar golden age economy was one in which rapid expansion of the manufacturing sector served as an important engine of jobs growth featuring a 'virtuous circle' of rising demand, productivity and employment, together with falling prices (Iversen and Wren 1998; Appelbaum and Schettkat 1995a). This was driven by several factors. First, demand for manufactured goods and consumer durables was income elastic – as incomes grew so did demand. Second, above-average productivity increases in manufacturing allowed the relative prices of goods to fall. Third, demand for manufactures and consumer durables was price elastic – lower relative prices saw large increases in demand. Fourth, there was a tendency for productivity growth not to be fully absorbed by wage increases which meant that growing demand and falling relative prices could support growing employment. Fifth, rising real incomes were used to purchase more consumer durables. Hence, the system could support growing incomes and employment linked to growing demand and productivity growth – the virtuous circle.

Since the late 1960s, however, this equation has changed. Manufacturing expansion has increasingly featured decreasing income and price elasticity due to market saturation and changes in consumption patterns away from volume towards quality. As Appelbaum and Schettkat (1995a, p. 244) argue:

> At the heart of the change in the relationship between productivity growth and employment growth is the change in the price elasticity of demand for consumer durables from elastic to inelastic as most households in the industrialised economies have achieved ownership of these goods. While advances in productivity in these industries still lead to reductions in relative prices, these price reductions no longer lead to an expansion of the market for the products sufficient to increase (or, in some cases, even to maintain) employment in the relevant industries.

Hence, in this new situation, increases in productivity no longer generate sufficient demand to compensate for the labour-saving effects of productivity growth. For those that remain in manufacturing employment, wages improve but employment declines. In the 1980s, for example, Appelbaum and Schettkat (1995a) find a significant negative relationship between manufacturing productivity growth and employment in most OECD countries – a reversal of the postwar pattern.

This pattern has certainly been evident in Australia. Between the late 1960s and early 1990s, the manufacturing sector featured 'jobless growth' as the sector expanded output but underwent a 12 per cent fall in the total numbers of workers employed. As Burgess and Green indicate in chapter 6, in Australia the impacts of such jobless growth, combined with the impacts of a comparatively large dose of 'deindustrialisation', have seen employment in manufacturing fall from around 27 per cent of total employment in the late 1960s to only around 13 per cent by the early 1990s. Net employment losses have also been a feature

Table 12.3 Industry output, employment and productivity growth over the period 1984/85–1992/93

	Industry output growth	Labour productivity growth rate	Employment growth
Agriculture	12.3	12.3	0.0
Mining	40.8	47.3	−6.5
Manufacturing	12.3	16.4	−4.1
Utilities	28.5	58.0	−2.9
Transport and communications	48.7	51.6	−2.9
Construction	−0.4	−16.0	16.2
Wholesale and retail	15.3	−7.4	22.7
Finance and property	37.3	−0.3	37.6
Community services	41.3	14.4	26.9
Recreation and personal services	21.3	−21.0	42.3

Source: Burgess and Green, ch. 6

of other high-productivity sectors in areas such as mining, utilities and transport and communications. Table 12.3 illustrates these trends for the period from the early 1980s to the early 1990s.

As table 12.3 indicates, this transition has also been accompanied by the rise of services as virtually the sole form of employment growth. Overwhelmingly, employment growth (mostly part-time) has occurred in only four service sectors: wholesale and retail trade, finance and property, community services, and recreation and personal services. These growth patterns are also reflected in the shifting sectoral composition of employment, as figure 12.1 illustrates.

The main reason why this pattern of employment growth poses major distributional problems is that the services sector typically features low levels of productivity and low labour productivity growth. This is particularly true of Australia where most of the services sector development is concentrated at the low end of the market in areas such as personal services, accommodation, etc. In part because of Australia's rapid deindustrialisation and the associated failure to develop sufficient high-end services employment, the employment growth structure, as indicated in table 12.3, has shifted from high-productivity to low-productivity sectors. This not only reduces the medium- to long-term growth potential of the economy, it also means that any significant expansion of services employment (to help compensate for losses in other areas) is

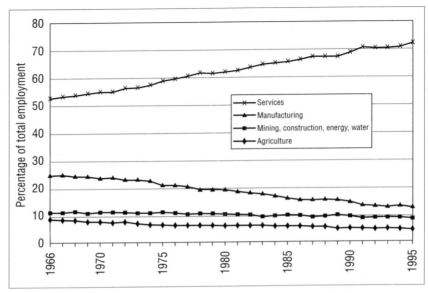

Figure 12.1 Sectoral composition of employment, Australia, 1966–95
Source: ABS *The Labour Force*, Cat. no. 6203

likely to be associated with low or even negative wages growth. This is especially so in the market services 'Mcjobs' sector featuring part-time and casual work. As Iversen and Wren (1998, p. 512) put it, 'high growth in market-provided services . . . therefore presupposes a more *inegali-tarian* wage structure'. This is illustrated for Australia not only by various measures of growing market-based wage inequality (Harding 1997), but also by figure 12.2 which indicates that the areas of strongest employment growth in the economy generally pay below-average weekly earnings.

New governance

John Nevile points out in chapter 7 that Keynesian policy played a useful role in stimulating the postwar economy in cases of cyclical downturns and in helping to support expansionary sentiments on the part of business and consumers. Beyond this, however, the basic strength of the postwar virtuous circle outlined above tended to override institutional differences across the advanced economies. According to Appelbaum and Schettkat (1995a, p. 243) such institutional differences were masked or 'swept away by the market forces unleashed by a full employment economy'. Hence, as Rowthorn (1992) argues, policy and institutional

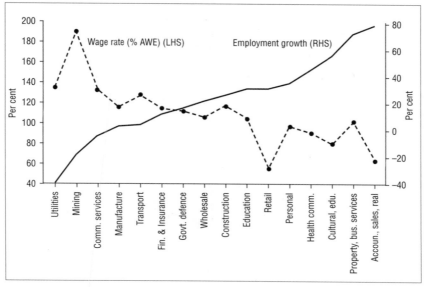

Figure 12.2 Employment growth and wages by industry, 1985–95
Source: ABS Cat. nos. 6248.0 and 6203.0

responses to the labour-market have mattered more since the 1970s as the strength of the postwar market-based full-employment order declined.

In this context there have been several paradigmatic policy responses to the new economy, probably best illustrated by the divergent cases of the US and Sweden. The deregulated neoliberal route traditionally followed in the US (and emulated more recently in countries such as New Zealand, the UK and increasingly Australia) saw an expansion of employment in low-productivity market services; a process facilitated by 'flexible' labour-markets and high-wage differentials. In Sweden, by contrast, a highly organised social democratic labour movement maintained low-wage differentials and inhibited the expansion of low-wage market services. Instead, the government's preferred strategy was public-sector and public services expansion financed by taxes, a strategy that was defeated and reversed by business and neoliberal forces by the late 1980s (Meidner 1993).

In the case of Australia, particularly under the period of Labor rule between 1983 and 1996, various combinations of the above approaches and outcomes were witnessed. For example, unlike the US, Australia's Accord-based incomes policy played a role in constraining wage dispersion, at least for a period. On the other hand, the shift to low-

Table 12.4 Wage and salary earners ('000s) – public sector, Commonwealth and states, 1988–98

State	Aug. 1988	Aug. 1989	Aug. 1990	Aug. 1991	Aug. 1992	Aug. 1993	Aug. 1994	Aug. 1995	Aug. 1996	Aug. 1997	Aug. 1998	1988–98 change	% change
NSW	375.8	367.6	361.5	367.7	351.4	360.6	345.1	363.6	358.5	356.8	348.7	–27.1	–7.21
Vic.	318	317.2	317.1	292.6	291.8	265.4	248.4	233.8	226.4	230.9	207.2	–110.8	–34.84
Qld.	174.9	179.2	185.9	191.8	192	195.9	190.4	198.5	208.1	211.7	207.2	32.3	18.47
SA	109.2	109.2	113.2	109.6	108	106.5	99.6	93.5	93.7	90.3	88	–21.2	–19.41
WA	122	124.1	127.8	121.7	122.2	127	116.8	118.6	113.3	110.4	108.8	–13.2	–10.82
Tas.	40.3	40.6	38.8	38.5	36.8	35.7	32.8	34.1	34	32.1	29.6	–10.7	–26.55
NT	15.1	16.2	16.6	15.8	15	15.4	15.5	16.1	16	16.1	16.1	1	6.62
ACT	0.5	19	19.7	20.8	18.8	20.3	19.7	19.7	18.8	17.7	17.9	17.4	348.00
C'wealth	427.3	397.4	400.7	448.8	388.5	370.3	350.9	339.2	302.5	282.6	268.2	–159.1	–37.23
Totals	*1583.1*	*1570.5*	*1581.3*	*1607.3*	*1524.5*	*1497.1*	*1419.2*	*1417.1*	*1371.3*	*1348.6*	*1291.7*	*–291.4*	*–18.41*

Note: August 1988 ACT data precede self-government.
Source: ABS Cat. no. 6248.0

productivity services employment in the market sector (most of it non-unionised) pushed in the opposite direction. So too did Labor's incremental shifts (under the Accord) towards an enterprise bargaining framework from the early 1990s. The net effect of these trends was widening market wage inequality. In contrast to Sweden, Australia saw a major reduction in public-sector employment, as table 12.4 indicates. Overall, about 300 000 jobs were shed between 1988 and 1998 at federal and state level.

The main way in which Labor's social democratic impulse was reflected was in a kind of 'residual welfarism' involving large increases in transfer payments, and, more positively from 1994 to 1996, an expansion of labour-market programs. The transfer programs went most of the way in offsetting the effects on family incomes of rising market inequality (Harding 1997). Yet in the context of Labor's fiscal restrictionism, such programs were financially unsustainable and depended increasingly on stop-gap measures such as running down public infrastructure expenditures, reduced payments to the states, selling off public assets and pursuing stricter welfare targeting and user-pays schemes (Dwyer and Larkin 1996). With Australian taxation rates the second lowest in the OECD (Bell 1997a, p. 273), Labor was attempting to run a European welfare system off US-style tax rates (Latham 1998, p. 33). The final factor in the equation has been broadly deflationary macroeconomic policy aimed squarely at fighting inflation (Bell 1997a, ch. 7; Argy 1998, 41–4).[2] Even during the early 1990s, in the midst of the worst recession since the 1930s, the authorities decided to pursue an anti-inflationary stance and delay reductions in interest rates. As the current governor of the Reserve Bank, Ian Macfarlane, admitted in 1992, there was a willingness to take some 'risks' with unemployment in the name of fighting inflation (*Australian*, 22 May 1992).

In the wake of Labor's defeat in the 1996 federal election, the incoming conservative coalition government axed many of Labor's labour-market programs and tightened welfare payments. The general trend in policy has been in the direction of orthodox labour-market deregulation strategies.

The trilemma

In the new economy there are two broad paths to promoting the growth of employment, which, as argued above, will mainly be in the services sector. The first approach, as mentioned above and in previous chapters, is the US-inspired neoliberal route where falling wage levels are thought to reduce prices and hence increase demand and employment in low-end market services. The key links in this equation concern those between wages, prices, demand and employment but there are doubts about the strength of these links, and, as we have seen in previous chapters, the neoliberal employment strategy is open to serious criticism as an employment growth strategy. The neoliberal route will increase market wage inequality. Arguably, in Australia, there is not much scope for actively contemplating trade-offs between unemployment and inequality for we already have far too much of both. True, Australia might not be one of the worst offenders in a comparative sense when it comes to inequality (Whiteford 1998), but it is also true that market inequality has worsened in Australia over the last decade or more and this trend should not be further exacerbated.

The second solution path is the one advocated in this book: namely, the combination of a more expansionary macroeconomic policy, in part derived through fiscal stimulation, combined with a strategy of direct public-sector job creation at reasonable wages. The obvious problem with this approach is that it costs money and compromises government efforts at budgetary stringency.

The two solution paths and their problems constitute what Iversen and Wren (1998), following Swensen (1989), term the 'trilemma of the service economy'. Nowhere it seems have governments managed to combine employment growth, wage equality and budgetary restraint. 'While it is possible to achieve two of these goals simultaneously, it has so far proved impossible to achieve all three' (1998, p. 508). As argued above, the growth of private services employment typically is associated with rising inequality. The growth of public services employment sacrifices budgetary restraint and what in recent decades has become a neoliberal and business fixation on lower taxes.

The utility of the trilemma framework is that it clearly reveals the stark moral and policy choices that are at stake as we enter the new millennium. Unlike the postwar situation, we are returning to an order where the market economy is breeding inequality and is increasingly divisive. This situation can only be overcome through explicitly confronting distributional issues, something that even in the postwar order was only done in a relatively indirect way, mainly through the trickle-down effects of strong economic growth.

Social democracy and the politics of redistribution

Strongly supported by a job-rich, expansive economy, Keynesian social democracy worked well in the postwar period. As argued above, a manufacturing-centred growth dynamic operating in the market economy was a key ingredient of postwar full employment. This was buttressed by a supportive Keynesian policy of demand management that dampened recessions and encouraged a growth psychology (Matthews 1968). Yet we have seen that the central market element of this full-employment dynamic was in transition by the 1970s towards a very different market structure dominated by services employment growth. This new economy places a premium on skill at the top end of the employment scale and at the bottom end pays low wages. In Australia's case, most of the new employment in the last decade has been in low-productivity, low-pay market services. In tandem with various skills mismatches, the damage to victims of long-term unemployment and a deflationary, 'fight inflation first' macroeconomic policy, the net effect has been rising unemployment and inequality.

This book has proposed two complementary solutions to the twin problems of unemployment and inequality. Both involve reinvigoration of the public sector as an ameliorative force which counterbalances market tendencies. As argued in chapter 7, one arm of policy should be directed towards a more expansionary macroeconomic policy based on fiscal stimulation and an accommodating monetary policy. As argued in chapters 8 and 9, an expansionary policy approach needs to be supported by medium-term policies aimed at economic restructuring and wage restraint. These policies are needed in order to make an expansionary program *sustainable*. Australia's problems with unemployment and inequality reflect the failure to distribute jobs and incomes effectively. However, as argued in chapter 8, Australia's 'low road' developmental path also raises the even more fundamental medium-term issue of wealth creation and the wherewithal for economic expansion. If this issue is not tackled and Australia's medium to longer term living standards are threatened, then the fate of effective redistributive strategies will become even more problematical.

Beyond aggregate Keynesian expansionism, a second complementary strategy proposed in this book is direct job creation, primarily in the jobs-rich public and community services sector. Part of the rationale for such an approach could come down to timing. It is possible that in the short to medium term, aggregate expansionism could aggravate current account problems. Dealing with the current account constraint on growth through structural change policies is a medium- to long-term project. Hence, jobs growth now rather than later implies that more resources be applied to direct job creation. As John Quiggin points out in chapter 10, a targeted approach to job creation in the community services sector is also less likely to aggravate the current account position because it is a less import-intensive pattern of growth than more broadly based expansion.

We also need to acknowledge, as noted above, that the skills and capacities needed to operate effectively at the middle to top end of the

labour-market in an increasingly knowledge-based economy may be
beyond the reach of many. Also, the spatial and regional nature of
labour-market dynamics means that unemployment and disadvantage
tend to be highly concentrated in regions and neighbourhoods. All this
suggests the need for more specialised and targeted demand policies to
help tackle these structural problems. On this point, Argy (1998, p. 151)
suggests that 'many of our unemployed are regrettably unable or
unwilling to be trained or retrained, and others are immobile and live
in areas which offer few work opportunities'. To deal with this, Argy
stresses the importance of governments 'altering the characteristics
of jobs (the pattern of demand for labour) to match those of the
unemployed' (1998, p. 151). As pointed out above, there are four
services sectors that are mainly driving employment growth. A central
aspect of employment policy, as John Quiggin argues in chapter 10,
should be to recognise the fundamental importance of these sectoral
issues and promote jobs-intensive development in areas with large
community spin-offs such as education, skills enhancement health care,
community services and environmental protection. As Argy points out,
the jobs on offer should, where needed, match the existing capacities of
many of those currently out of work.

The issue of how we pay for an expansionary jobs program has been
discussed in chapters 7 and 10. As noted there, deficit-based financing
should be minimised, in part because of the possibility of retaliation
from financial markets. Hence, any expansionary program should be
financed mainly through the tax system although there may be some
scope for the deficit financing of longer term infrastructure projects that
contribute to the economy's net worth. The tax options here were
discussed in most detail by John Quiggin in chapter 10. Another option
has been presented by Richard Blandy (1998), who suggests a 3.5 per
cent 'full employment levy' on the wages and salaries of the currently
employed. He estimates that if this were done the resulting gain in
public- and private-sector jobs would see unemployment fall to around
3 per cent within a few years. With respect to private-sector job creation,
Blandy proposes that employees could be given the option of contributing their levy to a company-based 'extra employees fund'.

In weighing the pros and cons of an expansionary approach, it is useful to recall the estimates by Watts in chapter 2 that the total economic
costs of unemployment could be as much as $40b per annum. Add to
this the magnitude of the personal suffering involved and it is clear that
reducing unemployment along the lines suggested here makes good
economic and social sense. A comparison of the neoliberal employment
strategy and the public-sector expansion model advocated here is
presented in table 12.5.

Table 12.5 Alternative employment strategies

Effects	Labour-market deregulation	Tax-financed public spending
Extra jobs	Private-sector services	Government services and supplying industries
Predictability of jobs	Low; depends on the effect of deregulation on relative wages or on the effect of relative prices on demand	High; jobs directly created by higher spending
Aggregate consumption	Rises; greater consumption mainly of private-sector services	Unchanged or small rise; spending power redistributed by higher taxes
Post-tax real wages	Rise for consumers of private-sector services; fall for producers of these services	Fall because of higher taxation (but net cost of public spending less than gross cost)
Balance of of payments	Little impact; import content of private-sector services low; reductions in low pay may raise competitiveness	Little impact; import content of government services and infrastructures is low
Long-term competitiveness	Focuses jobs growth in low-productivity market services	Improvements in infrastructure and human capital

Source: Adapted from Boltho and Glyn (1995, p. 469)

At present, the costs of unemployment fall most heavily on the weak and vulnerable. An expansionary jobs model of the kind proposed in this book will inevitably place extra costs on employed middle and upper class taxpayers. Whether business taxation should rise in a context of competitiveness pressures and 'globalisation' is a moot point. In any case, reducing unemployment down to acceptable levels, as well as spin-offs regarding more equality and the expansion of community services and public infrastructure, is quite achievable if enough people are willing to pay. Importantly, as Peter Kenyon (1998) points out, this kind of choice has never been clearly or explicitly presented to the public. As Glyn (1995, p. 39) explains, the tax-based program proposed here 'redistributes consuming power from taxpayers to those finding work'. The task is explicitly redistributional. This was less so during the postwar golden age where the rising tide of growth tended to lift all. This is no longer so. Unlike the postwar era, as Glyn (1995, p. 39) argues, 'there is no longer a free lunch in the literal sense of nobody having to pay in reduced consumption for full employment'. Latham (1998, p. 73) is quite right to conclude that the 'distributional tasks of social democracy have been placed under immense pressure'.

In weighing the pros and cons of the approach advocated in this book, it is useful to recall the estimates by Martin Watts in chapter 2 that the total economic costs of unemployment could be as much as $40b per annum. It is clear that the deadweight costs of unemployment are enormous. Nor should we ignore the cost burdens imposed on economies by rising levels of inequality. In stark contrast to earlier orthodox views about an equality/ efficiency trade-off, revisionist research conclusively demonstrates that high levels of inequality damage long-run growth prospects (Benabou 1996; Alesina and Rodrick 1994). Empirical research has also cast doubt on other orthodox propositions. For example, a range of studies have found that public-sector investment, particularly infrastructure invest- ment, plays a strong role not in 'crowding out' but in stimulating and supporting private-sector investment (Aschauer 1989a, b; Munnell 1992; Otto and Voss 1994; Erenburg 1994). Furthermore, in a wide-ranging quantitative study, Perotti (1996, p. 170) concluded that 'not only taxation but redistributive expenditures are positively associated with growth'. Quite apart from the moral and social issues, then, reducing unemploy- ment and inequality along the lines suggested in this book ultimately makes good economic sense.

Before concluding it is worth saying something about two further issues: first, alternative distributional mechanisms. Beyond the aggregate and sectoral expansionism outlined above, there are three other distri- butional options: guaranteed minimum incomes, wage subsidies and work-sharing. In my view, there are problems with each of the three options. The problem with guaranteed minimum income schemes is that they perpetuate the postwar residual welfarist model of income maintenance and run a strong risk of creating a dependent and margin- alised subgroup of 'recipients' vulnerable to the politics of downward envy (Pixley 1993; Latham 1998, p. 203). Wage subsidies aimed at reducing the costs private employers face in hiring labour have been much debated but most analysts agree that they confront serious 'sub- stitution' effects whereby subsidised employees tend to replace existing full-cost labour. The effectiveness of job subsidies is strongly related to the economic cycle and they tend to be of limited usefulness in periods of sluggish growth. Work-sharing might play a useful though limited role. The advantage is that it potentially provides a way of reducing excessively high work levels for some categories of workers. Its problems are that it involves substantial transaction costs and does not provide any net expansion of employment levels or services provision. Employers also tend to respond to shorter hours by increasing paid or unpaid over- time for the already employed or by lifting productivity by intensifying work effort. Moreover, a major site of excessive working hours is in the high-skilled professional arena. The main problems with work-sharing in this arena involve the potential shortages of such high-skilled workers and the fact that most of the unemployed are concentrated in low-skilled areas of work.

Second, the links between investment and employment growth need to be considered. It is clear that the link is a strong one. Figures 3.3 and 3.4 are suggestive in this respect and depict a strong long-term correlation between investment and unemployment levels in Australia and across the OECD economies. Boreham, Dow and Leet (1999, pp. 136–9) present pooled data from a sample of 16 OECD countries which suggest a strong link between public- and private-sector investment levels and employment growth, while Rowthorn (1995) reaches similar conclusions in relation to links between private-sector investment and employment growth. As previous chapters, particularly chapters 7 and 10, have suggested, public-sector infrastructure investment is worth pursuing for employment reasons and for the positive effects on private-sector investment noted above. Increased public- and particularly private-sector investment is also essential for the medium to longer term project of restructuring and rebuilding the economy, as chapter 8 argued. The position adopted here, however, is that the investment route is best seen as a medium to longer term complement to the main public-sector expansion/community services model advocated in this book. In the short term, investment in public infrastructure projects will certainly generate jobs, but this sector is not as jobs intensive as the community and human services sector. Therefore, in the short to medium term, say over the period of the next five years, stimulation of the community services sector is the quickest, surest and most cost-effective way of substantially reducing unemployment levels.

Conclusion

As Krugman (1994a, pp. 19–20) points out, 'something has gone wrong with the promise of economic growth'. In Australia's case we have a richer economy than 20 years ago and yet far too many Australians have been marginalised through unemployment, job insecurity and low pay. Left to itself the market drive of the new economy is failing to produce enough jobs or the right kinds of jobs. As is often the case with labour-markets, public intervention is required to effect a redistribution of resources. These should be aimed primarily at job creation and greater equality, and also, as Elizabeth Webster argues in chapter 11, at the promotion of education, training and other labour-market programs aimed at the supply side of the labour-market.

So far, the unemployment debate in Australia has been confused and the public has not been party to a serious discussion regarding the costs and benefits of the main options for dealing with the problem. If we are to move in the direction of the model just outlined, the debate will need to become more enlightened. It will also need to move up to a new normative level where it is recognised that dealing with unemployment (and inequality) is essentially a redistributive issue. We need, as Hirsch (1977) puts it, a 'moral re-entry', one capable of configuring a rough consensus on income distribution.

How do we do this? Public education and wide discussion of the issues at stake are obviously essential. But how can such a process be driven? Organisations such as ACOSS, for example, as well as the churches and unions could play an important role. But the cause must also be taken up by a major party. Among these, the ALP and the Democrats would be the ones most sympathetic to the arguments outlined herein. However, in the last two federal elections, tax, not unemployment, has been the dominant issue. The ALP ran a conservative fiscal policy in the 1998 federal election, and senior ALP leaders seem to be of the view that public cynicism and distrust of government are major problems confronting the 'positive government' and redistributive strategies outlined here. In this context, bold political leadership, which must start by clearly outlining the options to the public and then building a winning political coalition, is the only way forward. Politicians, community leaders and the electorate must stop falling for the right's agenda that ever lower taxes and the running down of public-sector services and infrastructure are compatible with a civilised society. We should be emboldened by the fact that Australia is one of the lowest taxed countries in the OECD and that polling evidence suggests that Australians are willing to pay higher taxes for improved services and that community attitudes towards proposals such as a jobs levy have been positive (Withers, Throsby and Johnston 1994; Hamilton 1998). As Blandy (1998, p. 6) argues,

> there are effective, immediate, democratic solutions to the present unemployment situation which require essentially that those now-employed get a little less so that those now unemployed get a great deal more . . . When the chips are down, cultures impose expectations on people. In the case of Australians, we are required not to abandon each other.

In the end if nothing is done, unemployment and growing inequality will split society. As Krugman (1994a, p. 30) points out, 'even an economist can see that such a split demoralises those at the bottom and coarsens those on the top'. He adds that 'the ultimate effect of growing social and economic disparities on our social and political health may be hard to predict, but it is unlikely to be pleasant'.

Notes

1 The Unemployment Crisis and Economic Policy

1   This inflation accelerationist view, central to the NAIRU framework, has been challenged. As Stiglitz (1997, p. 9) argues: 'Contrary to the accelerationist view, not only does the economy not stand on a precipice – with a slight dose of inflation leading to ever-increasing levels of inflation – but the magnitude by which inflation rises does not increase when the unemployment rate is held down for a prolonged period of time . . . [This] suggests that even risk averse policy makers might want to engage in moderate experiments with unemployment' (see also Galbraith 1997).

2   Australian Council of Trade Unions (ACTU) (1998) 'Cutting Low Wages Will Not Boost Jobs', Media Release, 26 October.

3   Brain (1999), for one, is far from sanguine about the CAD.

2 The Dimensions and Costs of Unemployment in Australia

1   A full definition of the state of employment can be found in ABS, *Persons Not in the Labour Force* (Cat. no. 6220.0), p. 35.

2   Since 1 May 1998 labour-market assistance to job-seekers has been provided through competing employment placement enterprises, that is, private and community employment agencies and the corporatised Employment National that replaced the publicly funded CES.

3   The ABS (1997b) argues that the concept of employment must be aligned with other economic concepts such as economic activity, as defined by the national accounts. All economic activity, of whatever duration, is considered to be contributing to the national product. The definition used by ABS is the one established by the ILO and adopted by other countries. Any other definition will necessarily incorporate an arbitrary definition of hours worked.

4   Goodridge, Harding and Lloyd (1995) note that, since the 1960s, the average rate of economic growth in each succeeding business cycle has been lower than in the previous cycle. This would be an important factor in explaining the trend in the unemployment rate.

5   Ross (1985) is critical of measures of unemployment and under-employment based on headcounts, because they ignore the extent of the under-

employment for each individual. He devises a 'monthly labour under-utilisation rate' to address this problem.

6 Watts and Rich (1992) note that the pattern of occupational gender segregation in the service and blue-collar occupations appears to be resistant to change, which would further contribute to the problem of insufficient male employment opportunities. Also it is becoming more difficult to obtain unemployment benefits and disability pensions, which threatens the access to long-term income support of the male unemployed.

7 This debate raises an important conceptual issue in labour economics which is the extent to which labour productivity resides in the worker, as in human capital theory, or in the job.

8 Under diminishing returns, pure competition and profit maximisation, workers are paid their marginal products, but a more appropriate character-isation of production and pricing is markup pricing founded on constant per unit labour costs. In this case productivity per worker exceeds the wage.

9 Full-time equivalent employment is usually denoted as full-time plus 0.50 multiplied by part-time employment.

10 Likewise, in a model of labour hoarding, the demand for skilled labour will exhibit lower variance over the business cycle than the demand for unskilled (Oi 1962). Thus, to the extent that relative wage rates are positively correlated with shifts in labour demand, wage differentials should be counter-cyclical.

11 The increased incidence of long hours worked has been accompanied by an increase in unpaid hours of work. Wooden et al. (1994) put forward four explanations for this phenomenon, of which two are linked to the level of unemployment. The high levels of unemployment and under-employment contribute to greater job insecurity, along with the greater competition for jobs because of rising labour-force participation and the concentration of the growth of job opportunities in part-time and casual employment. Also high unemployment and the growth of non-standard employment have contributed to the slow rate of real wage growth, which have increased the preparedness of employees to increase hours of work without an increase in earnings, to increase their promotion opportunities.

3 The Causes of Unemployment

1 The 'Keynes and the classics' debate on the relationship between rigid wages and unemployment is well documented and is not considered here (Blaug 1978 is a good source of references).

2 There are many versions of implicit contract theory, some of which are supportive of the price-auction approach. For example, Azariadis (1975) attempts to introduce asymmetric risk-aversion in the labour-market contract and presents a model of rigid wages with uncertain employment status. There is no empirical support for this type of model.

3 Thurow (1983, pp. 192–3) says: 'Whatever one believes about unions, they can at most only be blamed for wage rigidity in the 20 percent of the labour force they control . . . [in the USA] . . . A rigid union wage does not lead to a rigid nonunion wage'.

Orthodox theorists argue that non-union employers have to pay union wages to stop them entering their labour-markets. However, this still doesn't explain why unemployment has not decreased as the power of trade unions has declined in the OECD block.

4   The real unit cost measure is identical to the wage share in national income. It is the ratio of the real wage to labour productivity. It was developed by the Australian Treasury in the mid-1970s as a method of measuring the so-called 'real wage overhang', reflecting the bias towards neoclassical employment theory held by that organisation. Unfortunately, it was a flawed measure for this purpose, because changes in it could also support Keynesian interpretations, given that deficient demand reduces productivity growth and so real unit labour costs rise.

5   For Australia, it has been estimated that the labour-force participation rate increases by approximately 0.4 per cent every time the unemployment rate falls by 1 per cent. In other words, for every ten jobs created, six people leave the unemployment queue (as measured) and four people enter employment from outside the labour force. Pro-cyclical productivity patterns are also observed, due to the adjustment costs of employment changes. Employment growth is thus less if both output and productivity increase together, and these two cyclical adjustments will modify the rules of thumb based on stable assumptions of the variables in the identities.

6   To estimate the employment elasticities, generalised autoregressive-distributed lag models were run (with lags up to 2) to eliminate residual auto-correlation. The dependent variable and the output variable were expressed in logged first differences. Structural break intercept dummy variables were tested at 1974(1), 1978(1), 1983(1) and 1989(1) and all were insignificant. The resulting equations were solved for their long-run properties.

7   Elasticities were examined by splitting the sample up into sub-periods in addition to testing the full sample for structural breaks at strategically chosen points.

8   Okun's (1973) results are summarised as follows:
    1) The most cyclically sensitive industries had large employment gaps, were dominated by prime age males, offered high-paying jobs, offered other remuneration characteristics (fringes) which encouraged long-term attachments between employers and employees, and displayed above-average output per person hour;
    2) In demographic terms, when the employment gap is closed in aggregate, prime age males exit low-paying industries and take jobs in other higher paying sectors and their jobs are taken mainly by young people;
    3) In the advantaged industries, adult males gain large numbers of jobs but less than would occur if the demographic composition of industry employment remained unchanged following the gap closure. As a consequence, other demographic groups enter these 'good' jobs, and
    4) the demographic composition of industry employment is cyclically sensitive. The shift effects are in total estimated (in 1970) to be of the same magnitude as the scale effects (the proportional increases in employment across demographic groups assuming constant shares). This indicates that a large number of labour-market changes (the shifts) are generally of the ladder-climbing type within demographic groups from low-pay to higher pay industries.

4 Are Wage Cuts the Answer? Theory and Evidence

1   In formal terms, they hire workers until the real wage rate equals the marginal product of labour.

2   Walras, in *Elements of Pure Economics* (1874), suggested that an auctioneer would costlessly iterate on prices until an equilibrium price set was obtained,

no trade would take place except at equilibrium prices. This meant that the equilibrium price was independent of the dynamic path of price adjustment.

3 In a curious twist of history, one of these authors (Rapping), whose name is so closely tied to this neoclassical model, decided to change his paradigms and became a Marxist scholar. Lucas has remained a true blue neoclassical economist and went on to win the Nobel Prize in Economics for his contribution to the 'rational expectations revolution'.

4 Ask any of your unemployed friends of their experience of getting loans or overdrafts from their bank!

5 Also see Kalecki (1943) for an elaboration of this argument.

6 Henry Ford who doubled workers' wages in 1914 said: 'Of course the higher wage drew a more productive worker. But that wasn't the real reason. The fact was, it was no good mass producing a cheap automobile if there weren't masses of workers and farmers who could afford to buy it' (quoted in Schmid 1995, p. 433).

7 More formally, the efficiency wage is that wage where the elasticity of effort with respect to wages is unity.

8 For example, wages for full-time males in the bottom fifth of the labour-market fell by over 23% between 1973 and 1993 (Thurow 1996, p. 23). This, combined with extraordinary increases at the top end of the remuneration scale, has effectively produced in the US what Jessop (1988) refers to as a 'two nations' project. According to one study, the 'growth in the incomes of the richest one per cent of Americans has been so large that just the increase between 1980 and 1990 in the after-tax income of this group equals the total income of the poorest twenty per cent of the population' (Goldsmith and Blakely 1992, p. 20). Thurow (1996 p. 21) also points out that in the 1980s, 64% of all income gains went to the top 1 per cent of income earners (see also Palley 1998).

5 The Impact of Labour-Market and Economic Reforms in the UK, NZ, Australia and the US

1 We cannot list all the New Zealand reforms here. A good description of the reforms and their date of introduction can be found in Evans et al. (1996), and Silverstone, Bollard and Lattimore (1996).

2 The OECD database used in this analysis provides population estimates for those aged 15–64 years (Australia, UK, US) and for those aged 15 years and over (New Zealand).

3 The crisis came to a peak in June 1984 when the Reserve Bank of New Zealand announced the day after the election that it was ceasing to convert NZ dollars into foreign currency.

4 The poor growth rate performance of NZ was not a new phenomenon. It has been estimated that in 1939 NZ GNP per capita was 92 per cent of that of the US. Half a century later it was about half of the US level (Maddison 1989).

5 Economists have also emphasised many other objectives of reform such as moving the government deficit into a surplus, reducing the rate of inflation, reducing the size of the government sector and encouraging user-pay charging practices for government services and state-owned enterprises. Most of these objectives should not be thought of as final objectives but as means to increase GDP per capita. It is surprising therefore to see so much emphasis placed on these intermediate objectives and no discussion of the

GDP per capita growth rate in the major survey of New Zealand reforms by Evans, Grimes, Wilkinson and Teece (1996).
6 For an introduction to some of the literature see Basu, Fernald and Kimball (1998).

6 Is Growth the Answer?

1 Since there are difficulties in maintaining industry concordance together with obtaining reliable industry employment data over a long period, table 6.5 goes back as far as 1967. Note that it does not include all sectors as a result of these problems.

7 Can Keynesian Policies Stimulate Growth in Output and Employment?

1 These effects are taken up in the broader subject of public finance.
2 In heavily regulated economies, monetary policy may use quantitative regulations and restrictions on interest rates which relate to particular classes of borrowers, but this is no longer the case in Australia or most OECD countries.
3 For most OECD countries exchange rates remained fixed for decades.
4 A significant recession is defined as occurring in a year in which output (GDP measured in constant prices) declines or rises by less than a quarter of its trend rate of growth.
5 Rates of growth of government expenditure quoted in this chapter exclude expenditure on inventories.
6 Changes in unemployment lag behind changes in output.
7 In most circumstances the bigger the first round effect the bigger the total effect. Nevile (1975, ch. 4) sets out the theory why this is not always the case.
8 As more and more of the workforce were younger, with no memories of the 1930s depression, the Kaleckian argument, that full employment removes the power to discipline workers, leading to declining efficiency and inflation, was no doubt becoming more important, but the Vietnam War spending was the inflationary trigger.
9 These unemployment rates are standardised by the OECD. Both countries had structural deficits in this period, but that in the US averaged 2.9 per cent of GDP, that in Germany less than 1 per cent of a slower growing GDP.
10 The argument also applies to an increase in private consumption expenditure brought about by a cut in tax rates, but it is usually expressed in terms of increased public expenditure crowding out an equal amount of private expenditure. It is a simplification to ascribe to all holding this view a belief in 100 per cent crowding out, but they do hold that it approaches 100 per cent (Mayer 1978).
11 Nevile (1983) contains a longer and more technical survey of earlier empirical evidence which comes to the same conclusion.
12 Inflation is measured by the implicit deflator for gross national expenditure. These figures start in a recession year and end in a boom year, but the recession which followed did not owe its length to the factors that enabled the simultaneous fall in inflation and unemployment. As was shown earlier the major reason for the severity of the recession was a policy gamble which tried to entrench a much lower level of inflation without undue cost in higher unemployment and only succeeded in the first of these two aims. The speculative excesses of the late 1980s also probably contributed to the severity of the recession.

13 Real wages need not fall if productivity gains are big enough to offset higher import prices.

14 Hence, the calls for major countries to co-ordinate domestic macro-economic policy and to work together to assist those of their number that have low levels of economic activity.

15 This reduces the force of the French experience in the early 1980s as an example of the reduction in national policy-making power. In any case, the major problem in this case was basically domestic: a high level of inflation led to expectations of a devaluation; the current account deficit was only 2.2 per cent of GDP.

8   Speed Limits to Growth and the Quality of Jobs: Economic Structure and the Current Account

1 Parts of this chapter are drawn from Bell (1997b), Burgess and Green (1997) and Green and Burgess (1997).

2 As of December in the 1998/99 financial year, net foreign debt equalled almost $237 billion.

9   Dealing with the Inflation Constraint to Growth

1 See *International Labour Review*, 132(4): 431–5, 1993 for a detailed description of Italy's Social Pact.

2 The problem arises from the 'isolation paradox'. Let the preference ordering of individuals in a society be such that 1) given the set of actions of the others (no matter what they are), an individual is better off doing A rather than B and 2) given the choice between doing A and everyone doing B, each individual prefers the latter to the former. In the absence of collusion, each individual will prefer to do A rather than B, for no matter what the others do each is himself better off doing A. Yet the outcome A will be regarded as strictly worse off by each than the alternative B, and hence the outcome is inferior. See Sen (1961).

3 OECD, *Economic Survey* (various issues).

10   The Public Sector as a Job Engine

1 Data for the period since 1990 are not directly comparable with data for the period between 1966 and 1980 because of a change in the classification of industries used by the Australian Bureau of Statistics. This does not affect the validity of the conclusion that the proportion of the workforce employed in the human services sector grew rapidly before 1980 and has remained static since then.

2 General government public expenditure includes interest and transfer payments and expenditure on the provision of services, but excludes investment in physical capital.

11   What Role for Labour-Market Programs?

1 In addition, Australia has smaller programs to assist unemployed people start their own businesses and for youth in general to access formal training. This chapter focuses however on the four main types of program listed here.

2 For a discussion of labour-market programs since 1974, see Jarvie and McKay (1993) and Freeland (1998).

3 Psychological studies in Australia and overseas have found support for the hypothesis that the experience of unemployment increases the person's feelings of helplessness and loss of control over their lives. These attributes in turn affect the person's ability to recognise problems, retrieve, evaluate and interpret information and their decision-making capacities. See Goldsmith, Veum and Darity (1996). A large UK study has found that men's unemployment experience has only a temporary effect on earnings if the man subsequently regains stable employment (Gregory and Jukes 1997).

4 E.g. the Australian Special Youth Employment and Training Program during the 1980s.

5 This theory has evolved out of the family of hypotheses which attempt to explain the historical correlation between wage or price inflation and the rate of unemployment. Beginning with the early Phillips Curve, the ideas metamorphosed into a natural rate of unemployment (NRU) and subsequently a collation of non-accelerating inflationary rate of unemployment (NAIRU) theories. Part of the difficulty of summarising these arguments lies with the inconsistency in the terminology between authors and it will suffice to say here that most economists of this ilk accept that raising aggregate demand will spill over into both prices and employment. As other chapters have argued, unemployment is a crucial factor which acts to control inflation. The level of unemployment at which average prices are constant (all else being equal) is the equilibrium rate of unemployment (alias NRU or NAIRU). The attainment of lower unemployment with constant inflation depends therefore on reducing the NRU or NAIRU.

6 Although the term 'efficiency wage' emerged during the early 1980s, the underlying concepts were 'known' by labour-market economists well before then.

7 One could of course argue that in Australia, the aim of labour-market programs has been purely to promote equality of access to a given set of jobs. In this case, it would be logical to vary program expenditure counter-cyclically.

8 In fact, Calmfors (1993) has argued that Swedish unemployment is more affected by their macroeconomic stance than the level of their labour-market program expenditures.

9 OECD (1993) tried unsuccessfully to model whether labour-market programs affected the relationship between aggregate employment growth and GDP growth (via improving labour-market matching).

10 Average days are estimated by dividing the average annual level of vacancies times 365 by the average number of workers who had held their current job for under a year as at February. Accordingly, the estimate overstates the number of days per job to the extent that people hold multiple jobs or change jobs more than once in a year (ABS AUSSTATS, cat. 6354.0, 6209.0).

11 The first 6 variables were meant to be the structural determinants of the NAIRU.

12 Unemployment, Inequality and the Politics of Redistribution

1 One elaboration of this idea is Will Hutton's notion of a 30/40/30 society. The top 30 per cent are those in secure high-paying jobs that under market

and neoliberal shifts in the last two decades have become much better off. The middle 40 per cent have employment but are increasingly insecure regarding incomes and employment tenure. The bottom 30 per cent are effectively excluded, being unemployed, retired or in some other way 'economically inactive'. See Hutton (1996), and (1995) 'High risk society not paying off', *Guardian Weekly*, 12 November.

2   As indicated in chapter 1, the failure to deal effectively with the 'Kaleckian' problem of wage-driven inflation stands as a key failure of the postwar full-employment order. The shift in many countries to a broadly deflationary approach to controlling inflation reflects powerful neoliberal preferences but is also indicative of the problems social democratic regimes have had in establishing or maintaining an effective incomes policy, the only real alternative to a deflationary approach (see Glyn 1995).

References

ABS (1991) *Labour Force Projections, 1992–2005* (Cat. no. 6260.0).

ABS (1994a) *Australian National Accounts, Input–Output Tables 1989–90* (Cat. no. 5209.0).

ABS (1994b) *The Labour Force*, August (Cat. no. 6203.0).

ABS (1995) *Australian Economic Indicators* (Cat. no. 1350.0).

ABS (1997a) *Persons Not in the Labour Force*, September (Cat. no. 6220.0).

ABS (1997b) *The Labour Force*, May (Cat. no. 6203.0).

ABS (1997c) *Government Financial Statistics, Australia* (Cat. no. 5512.0).

Akerlof, G. (1982) 'Labor Market Contracts as Partial Gift-Exchange', *Quarterly Journal of Economics*, vol. 97, pp. 543–69.

Akerlof, G., Dickens, W. and Perry, G. (1996) 'The Macroeconomics of Low Inflation', *Brookings Papers on Economic Activity*, no. 1, pp. 1–76.

Akerlof, G.A. and Yellen, J.L. (1986) *Efficiency Wage Models of the Labour Market*, Cambridge University Press, Cambridge.

Albo, G. (1994) 'Competitive Austerity and the Impasse of Capitalist Employment Policy', *The Socialist Register*, Merlin, London.

Alesina, A., Gruen, D. and Jones, M. (1991) 'Fiscal Adjustment, the Real Exchange Rate and Australia's External Imbalance', *Australian Economic Review*, vol. 24, pp. 38–51.

Alesina, A. and Rodrick, D. (1994) 'Distributive Politics and Economic Growth', *Quarterly Journal of Economics*, vol. 109, pp. 465–90.

Amable, Bruno, Henry, J., Lordon, F., and Topol, R. (1993) 'Unit-Root in the Wage-price Spiral Is Not Hysteresis in Unemployment', *Journal of Economic Studies*, vol. 20, pp. 123–35.

Anderson, T. (1995) 'Corporate Foreign Debt and the Current Account', *Journal of Australian Political Economy*, no. 36, pp. 48–67.

Aoki, M. (1990) 'Toward an Economic Model of the Japanese Firm', *Journal of Economic Literature*, vol. 28, pp. 1–27.

Appelbaum, E. and Schettkat, R. (1995a) 'Economic Development in the Industrialised Countries and the Prospects for Full Employment', in Arestis, P. and Marshall, M. (eds), *The Political Economy of Full Employment*, Edward Elgar, London.

Appelbaum, E. and Schettkat, R. (1995b) 'Employment and Productivity in Industrialised Economies', *International Labour Review*, vol. 134, pp. 605–23.

Argy, F. (1998) *Australia at the Crossroads: Radical Free Market or Progressive Liberalism?*, Allen & Unwin, Sydney.

Armstrong, P., Glyn, A. and Harrison, J. (1991) *Capitalism Since 1945*, Blackwell, Oxford.

Arthur, W.B. (1996) 'Increasing Returns and the New World of Business', *Harvard Business Review*, July–August, pp. 101–9.

Aschauer, D. (1988) 'Is Public Expenditure Productive?', *Journal of Monetary Economics*, vol. 23, pp. 177–200.

Aschauer, D.A. (1989a) 'Is Public Expenditure Productive?' *Journal of Monetary Economics*, vol. 23, pp. 177–200.

Aschauer, D.A. (1989b) 'Does Public Capital Crowd Out Private Capital?' *Journal of Monetary Economics*, vol. 24, pp. 171–88.

Australian Council of Social Service (ACOSS) (1997) *Jobspack*, ACOSS Policy Paper, ACOSS, Sydney.

Australian Council of Social Service (ACOSS) (1998) *Agenda for Tax Reform: Background to the ACOSS Proposals*, ACOSS, Sydney.

Australian Manufacturing Workers Union (AMWU) (1998) *Meeting the Challenge by Going for Growth*.

Australian Metal Workers Union (AMWU) (1997) *Rebuilding Australia: Industry Development for More Jobs*, Sydney.

Azariadis, C. (1975) 'Implicit Contracts and Underemployment Equilibria', *Journal of Political Economy*, vol. 83, pp. 1183–1202.

Bacon, R. and Eltis, W. (1976) *Britain's Economic Problem: Too Few Producers*, Macmillan, London.

Baldry, E. and Vinson, T. (1998) 'The Current Obsession with Reducing Taxes', *Just Policy*, no. 13, pp. 3–9.

Banerjee, A., Dolado, J.J., Hendry, D.F. and Smith, G.W. (1986) 'Exploring Equilibrium Relationships in Econometrics Through Static Models: Some Monte Carlo Evidence', *Oxford Bulletin of Economics and Statistics*, vol. 48, pp. 253–77.

Barro, R.J. (1974) 'Are Government Bonds Net Worth', *Journal of Political Economy*, vol. 82, pp. 1095–1117.

Barro, R.J. (1991) 'Economic Growth in a Cross-section of Countries', *Quarterly Journal of Economics* , vol. 56, pp. 407–43.

Barro, R.J. and Grossman, H.I. (1971) 'A General Disequilibrium Model of Income and Employment', *American Economic Review*, vol. 61, pp. 82–93.

Basu, S., Fernald, J. and Kimball, M. (1998) 'Are Technology Improvements Contractionary?', *International Finance Discussion Papers*, Board of Governors of the Federal Reserve System.

Bates, W. and Snape, R. (1998) Discussants: 'Microeconomic Reform: The New Zealand Experience', in *Micro Economic Reform and Productivity Growth*, Workshop Proceedings, Productivity Commission and Australian National University, Canberra, pp. 182–91.

Baumol, W. (1967) 'Macroeconomics of Unbalanced Growth: The Anatomy of the Urban Crisis', *American Economic Review*, vol. 57, pp. 415–26.

Beeson, M. (1996) 'APEC: Nice Theory, Shame About the Practice', *Australian Quarterly*, vol. 68, pp. 35–48.

Beeson, M. and Bell, S. (1999) 'Australia in the Shadow of the Asian Crisis', in Robison, R. et al., (eds), *Politics and Markets in the Wake of the Asian Crisis*, Routledge, London.

Bell, S. (1993) *Australian Manufacturing and the State: The Politics of Industry Policy in the Post-War Era*, Cambridge University Press, Cambridge.

Bell, S. (1996) 'Inequality, Trade and Investment: The Failure of Supply-Side Market Liberalism', *Journal of Australian Political Economy*, no. 37, pp. 29–48.

Bell, S. (1997a) *Ungoverning the Economy: The Political Economy of Australian Economic Policy*, Oxford University Press, Melbourne.

Bell, S. (1997b) 'Scorched Industry Policy', *Journal of Economic and Social Issues*, vol. 2, pp. 5–19.

Bell, S. (1999) 'The Scourge of Inflation?: Unemployment and Orthodox Monetary Policy', *Australian Economic Review*, vol. 32, pp. 74–82.

Bellmann, L. and Jackman, R. (1996) 'The Impact of Labour Market Policies on Wages, Employment and Labour Market Mismatch', in Schmid, G., O'Reilly, J. and Schömann, K. (eds), *International Handbook of Labour Market Policy and Evaluation*, Edward Elgar, Cheltenham, Brookfield.

Benabou, R. (1996) *Inequality and Growth: NBER Macroeconomics Annual*, MIT Press, Cambridge, Mass.

Berheim, D. (1987) 'Budget Deficits and the Balance of Trade', in Summers, L.H. (ed.), *Tax Policy and the Economy*, Cambridge, Mass., National Bureau of Economic Research.

Bernanke, B. (1995) 'A Conference Panel Discussion: What Do We Know About How Monetary Policy Affects the Economy?', *Federal Reserve Bank of St. Louis Review*, vol. 77, pp. 127–30.

Bewley, T.F. (1998) 'Why Not Cut Pay?', *European Economic Review*, vol. 42, pp. 459–90.

Biddle, D. and Burgess, J. (1998) 'Youth Unemployment and Contemporary Labour Market Policy in Australia', paper to AIRAANZ Conference, Dunedin, NZ, February.

Black, M. (1980) 'Pecuniary Implications of On-the-job Search and Quit Activity', *Review of Economics and Statistics*, vol. 62, pp. 222–9.

Black, T. (1994) 'The FitzGerald Report on National Saving: Economic Utopia or Economic Stagnation', *Economic Papers*, vol. 13, pp. 10–16.

Blanchard, O.J. and Summers, L.H. (1988) 'Hysteresis and the European Unemployment Problem', in Cross, R. (ed.), *Unemployment, Hysteresis and the Natural Rate Hypothesis*, Basil Blackwell, Oxford.

Blandy, R. (1998) *A Scheme for Full Employment*, Austral Asia Economics, Adelaide.

Blaug, M. (1978) *Economic Theory in Retrospect*, 3rd edn, Cambridge University Press, Cambridge.

Boltho, A. (1989) 'Did Policy Activism Work?', *European Economic Review*, vol. 33, pp. 1709–26.

Boltho, A. and Glyn, A. (1995) 'Can Macroeconomic Policies Raise Employment?', *International Labour Review*, vol. 134, pp. 451–70.

Boreham, P., Dow, G. and Leet, M. (1999) *Room to Manoeuvre: Political Aspects of Full Employment*, Melbourne University Press, Melbourne.

Borland, G. (1997) 'Unemployment in Australia: Prospects and Policies', *Australian Economic Review*, vol. 30, pp. 391–404.

Borland, J. and Kennedy, S. (1998) 'Dimensions, Structure and History of Australian Unemployment', in Debelle, G. and Borland, J. (eds), *Unemployment and the Australian Labour Market*, Reserve Bank of Australia, Sydney.

Bradbury, B., Ross, R. and Doyle, J. (1990) 'Unemployment Benefit Replacement Ratios', paper to Department of Social Security Policy Research Centre.

Brain, P. (1999) *Beyond Meltdown: The Global Battle for Sustained Growth*, Scribe, Melbourne.

Brosnan, P. (1996) 'Labour Markets and Social Deprivation', *Labour and Industry*, vol. 7, pp. 3–34.

Brosnan, P. and Campbell, I. (1995) 'Labour Market Deregulation in Australia: Towards New Forms of Workforce Division', Paper to Conference of the International Working Party on Labour Market Segmentation, Siena, Italy.

Bruno, M. (1995) 'Does Inflation Really Lower Growth?', *Finance and Development*, vol. 32, pp. 35–8.

Burdett, K. (1978) 'A Theory of Employee Job Search and Quit Rates', *American Economic Review*, no. 68, pp. 212–20.

Bureau of Labour Market Research (1984) *Public Sector Job Creation: Interim Report on the Wage Pause program*, Interim report series no. 1, Canberra, BLMR.

Burgess, J. (1992) 'A Case for Public Sector Job Creation Schemes', *Economic and Labour Relations Review*, vol. 3, pp. 115–30.

Burgess, J. (1998) 'Working Time Patterns and Working Time Deregulation in Australia', *Economic Papers*, vol. 17, pp. 35–47.

Burgess, J. and Campbell, I. (1998) 'The Nature and Dimensions of Precarious Employment in Australia', *Labour and Industry*. vol. 8, pp. 5–22.

Burgess, J. and Green, R. (1997) 'Economic Growth and Employment Reduction in Australia: The Changing Equation', *Journal of Economic and Social Policy*, vol. 2, pp. 96–110.

Burgess, J. and Mitchell, W. (1998) 'Unemployment, Human Rights and a Full Employment Policy for Australia', *Australian Journal of Human Rights*, vol. 4, pp. 76–94.

Burgess, J., Mitchell, W., O'Brien, D. and Watts, M. (1998) 'Workfare in Australia: A Critical Assessment', paper to conference of the International Working Party on Labour Market Segmentation, Arco, Italy.

Burgess, J., Strachan, G. and Watts, M.J. (1998) 'Labour Market Deregulation and Gender Equity in the Australian Workforce: Complementary or Incompatible?', paper to the Path to Full Employment and Equity Conference, University of Newcastle, December.

Calmfors, L. (1993) 'Lessons From the Macroeconomic Experience of Sweden', *European Journal of Political Economy*, vol. 9, pp. 25–72.

Calmfors, L. (1994) 'Active Labour Market Policy and Unemployment: A Framework for the Analysis of Crucial Design Features', *OECD Labour Market and Social Policy Occasional Paper* No. 15, Paris.

Calmfors, L. and Driffill, J. (1988) 'Bargaining Structure, Corporatism and Macroeconomic Performance', *Economic Policy*, vol. 6, pp. 14–61.

Calmfors, L. and Lang, H. (1995) 'Macroeconomic Effects of Active Labour Market Programmes in a Union Wage-setting Model', *Economic Journal*, vol. 105, pp. 601–19.

Calmfors, L. and Skedinger, P. (1995) 'Does Active Labour Market Policy Increase Employment? Theoretical Considerations and Some Empirical Evidence from Sweden', *Oxford Review of Economic Policy*, vol. 11, pp. 91–109.

Campbell, I. and Burgess, J. (1997) 'National Patterns of Temporary Employment: The Distinctive Case of Casual Employment in Australia', *Working Paper* no. 53, National Key Centre in Industrial Relations, Monash University, Melbourne.

Card, D. and Krueger, A. (1995) *Myth and Measurement: The New Economics of the Minimum Wage*, Princeton University Press, Princeton, NJ.

Carling, K., Edin, P.A., Harkman, A. and Holmlund, B. (1996) 'Unemployment Duration, Unemployment Benefits and Labour Market Programs in Sweden', *Journal of Public Economics*, vol. 59, pp. 313–34.

Carter, C. (1992) 'A Vision Targeted on Asia', *Australian*, 13–14 June.

Cecchetti, S. (1995) 'Distinguishing Theories of the Monetary Transmission Mechanism', *Federal Reserve Bank of St. Louis Review*, vol. 77, pp. 83–97.

Chapman, B. (1990) 'The Australian Labour Market in the 1980s', in Grenville, S. (ed.), *The Australian Macro-Economy in the 1980s*, Reserve Bank of Australia, Sydney.

Chapman, B.J. (1999) 'Could Increasing the Skills of the Jobless be the Solution to Australian Unemployment?', in Richardson, S. (ed.), *Regulating the Labour Market: Regulation, Efficiency and Equity in Australia*, Cambridge University Press, Cambridge.

Chapman, B.J., Dowrick, S.J. and Junankar, P.N. (1991) 'Perspectives on Australian Unemployment: The Impact of Wage-setting Institutions', in *Australian Economic Policy: Conference Proceedings*, Gruen, F.H. (ed.), Centre for Economic Policy Research, Australian National University, Canberra.

Chapman, B.J. and Gruen, F. (1990) 'An Analysis of the Australian Consensual Incomes Policy: The Prices and Income Accord', *Centre for Economic Policy Research Discussion Paper*, no. 221, ANU, Canberra.

Chenery, H. and Syrquin, S. (1975) *Patterns of Development, 1950–1970*, Oxford University Press, Oxford.

Chowdhury, A. (1994) 'Centralised Vs. Decentralised Wage Setting Systems and Capital Accumulation: Evidence from OECD Countries, 1960–90', *The Economic Labour Relations Review*, vol. 5, pp. 84–101.

Chowdhury, A. and Mallik, G. (1998) 'A Land Locked into Low Inflation: How far is the Promised Land', *Economic Analysis and Policy*, September, pp. 233–43.

Clark, D. (1997) *Student Economic Briefs*, Australian Financial Review Books, Sydney.

Clark, K. and Summers, L. (1982) 'The Dynamics of Youth Unemployment', in Freeman, R. and Wise, D. (eds), *The Youth Labour Market*, University of Chicago Press, Chicago.

Coe, D.T. and Gagliardi, F. (1985) 'Nominal Wage Determination in Ten OECD Economies', *OECD Economics and Statistics Department Working Paper, no. 19*, OECD, Paris.

Coelli, M., Fahrer, J. and Lindsay, H. (1994) 'Wage Dispersion and Labour Market Institutions: A Cross Country Study', *Research Discussion Paper*, no. 9404, Reserve Bank of Australia, Sydney.

Cohen, S. and Zysman, J. (1983) 'Why Manufacturing Matters: The Myth of the Post-Industrial Economy', *California Management Review*, vol. 29, pp. 2–26.

Commonwealth of Australia (1945) *Full Employment in Australia*, Commonwealth Government Printer, Canberra.

Commonwealth of Australia (1993) *Restoring Full Employment: A Discussion Paper* (Green Paper), AGPS, Canberra.

Commonwealth of Australia (1996) *Budget Statements 1996/1997*, Statement no. 2, AGPS, Canberra.

Conway, P. and Hunt, B. (1998) *Productivity Growth in New Zealand: Economic Reform and the Convergence Hypothesis*, Reserve Bank of New Zealand, June.

Corden, W.M. (1992) 'A Perspective', in Blundell-Wignall, Adrian (ed.), *Inflation, Disinflation and Monetary Policy*, Sydney, Reserve Bank of Australia, Sydney.

Cornwall, J. (1983) *The Conditions for Economic Recovery*, Martin Robertson, Oxford.

Cornwall, J. (ed.) (1984) *After Stagflation*, Basil Blackwell, Oxford.

Cox, R.W. (1987) *Production, Power and World Order: Social Forces in the Making of History*, Columbia University Press, New York.

Crean, S. (1995) *Working Nation: The First Year 1994–95*, Department of Employment, Education and Training, Canberra.

Cross, R. (1986) 'Phelps, Hysteresis and the Natural Rate of Unemployment', *Quarterly Journal of Business and Economics*, vol. 25, pp. 56–64.

Cross, R. (1993) 'On the Foundations of Hysteresis in Economic Systems', *Economics and Philosophy*, vol. 9, pp. 53–74.

Crouch, C. (1985) 'Conditions for Trade Union Wage Restraint', in Lindberg, L. and Maier, C. (eds), *The Politics of Inflation and Economic Stagnation*, Washington DC: Brookings Institution.

Daly, A., Duc, N.H., Eldridge, D., Gabbitas, O. and McCalman, P. (1998) *Youth Wages and Unemployment*, Productivity Commision Staff Research Paper, AusInfo, Canberra.

Daniels, P.W. (1993) *Services Industries in the World Economy*, Blackwell, Cambridge, Mass.

Davidson, P. (1998) 'Post Keynesian Employment Analysis and the Macroeconomics of OECD Unemployment', *The Economic Journal*, vol. 108, pp. 817–31.

Dawkins, P. (1996) 'The Distribution of Work in Australia', *Economic Record*, vol. 72, pp. 272–86.

Dawkins, P. and Freebairn, J. (1997) 'Towards Full Employment', *Australian Economic Review*, vol. 30, pp. 405–417.

Debelle, G. (1998) 'Introduction', in Debelle, G. and Borland, J. (eds), *Unemployment and the Australian Labour Market*, Reserve Bank of Australia, Sydney.

Debelle, G. and Borland, J. (eds) (1998) *Unemployment and the Australian Labour Market*, Reserve Bank of Australia, Sydney.

Debelle, G. and Swann, T. (1998) 'Stylised Facts of the Australian Labour Market', *Discussion Paper*, 9804, Reserve Bank of Australia, Sydney.

Debelle, G. and Vickery, J. (1998) 'The Macroeconomics of Unemployment', in Debelle, G. and Borland, J. (eds), *Unemployment and the Australian Labour Market*, Reserve Bank of Australia, Sydney.

Denison, E. (1962) *The Sources of Growth in the US*, Committee for Economic Development, New York.

Denison, E. (1984) 'Productivity Analysis Through Growth Accounting', in Brief, A.P. (ed.), *Productivity Research in the Behavioural and Social Sciences*, Praeger, New York.

Department of Employment, Education and Training (DEET) (1989) *Jobstart Evaluation*, Program Review and Income Support Branch, Canberra.

Department of Employment, Education and Training (DEET) (1993a) *Evaluation of Jobstart*, Evaluation and Monitoring Branch, EMB Report 7/93, Canberra.

Department of Employment, Education and Training (DEET) (1993b) *Evaluation of Skill Share*, Evaluation and Monitoring Branch, EMB Report 5/93, Canberra.

Department of Employment, Education and Training (DEET) (1994) *Net Impact Study of Job Clubs*, Evaluation and Monitoring Branch, EMB Report 5/94, Canberra.

Department of Employment, Education and Training (DEET) (1995) *Australia's Workforce 2005: Jobs in the Future*, AGPS, Canberra.

Department of Employment, Education, Training and Youth Affairs (DEETYA) (1996a) *Working Nation: Evaluation of the Employment, Education and Training Elements*, Evaluation and Monitoring Branch, EMB Report 2/96, Canberra.

Department of Employment, Education, Training and Youth Affairs (DEETYA) (1996b) *Evaluation of JobSkills Program*, Evaluation and Monitoring Branch, EMB Report 7/96, Canberra.

Department of Employment, Education, Training and Youth Affairs (DEETYA) (1997) *The Net Impact of Labour Market Programmes*, Evaluation and Monitoring Branch, EMB Report 2/97, Canberra.

Department of Employment, Education, Training and Youth Affairs (DEETYA) (1998) *Small Area Labour Markets, Australia: Analysis and Evaluation*, AGPS, Canberra.

Department of Foreign Affairs and Trade (DFAT) (1994) *The APEC Region: Trade and Investment*, AGPS, Canberra.

Dickey, D.A., Bell, W.R. and Miller, R.B. (1986) 'Unit roots series models: Tests and implications', *American Statistician*, vol. 40, pp. 12–26.

Dickey, D.A. and Fuller, W.A. (1979) 'Distribution of the Estimators for Auto-regressive Time Series with a Unit Root', *Journal of the American Statistical Association*, vol. 74, pp. 427–31.

Dickey, D.A. and Fuller, W.A. (1981) 'Likelihood Ratio Statistics for Autoregressive Time Series with a Unit Root', *Econometrica*, vol. 49, pp. 1057–72.

Dickey, D.A. and Fuller, W.A. (1984) 'Testing for Unit Roots 2', *Econometrica*, vol. 52, pp. 1241–69.

Dickey, D.A., Hasza, D.P. and Fuller, W.A. (1984) 'Testing for Unit Roots in Seasonal Time Series', *Journal of Business and Statistics*, vol. 5, pp. 455–61.

Dixon, D. (1992) *Unemployment: The Economic and Social Costs*, Brotherhood of St Laurence, Melbourne.

Dixon, P.B., Parmenter, B.R., Sutton, J. and Vincent, D.P. (1982) *ORANI: A Multi-sectoral Model of the Australian Economy*, North-Holland, Amsterdam.

Doeringer, P. and Piore, M. (1971) *Internal Labor Markets and Manpower Analysis*, Heath, Mass.

Dore, R., Boyer, R. and Mars, Z. (1994) *The Return to Incomes Policy*, Pinter, London.

Dornbusch, R. and Fischer, S. (1987) *Macroeconomics*, 4th edn, McGraw Hill, New York.

Dowrick, S. (1993) 'A Review of New Theories of Economic Growth and Their Implications for Policy', *Economic Analysis and Policy*, vol. 23, pp. 105–22.

Dowrick, S. (1994a) 'Fiscal Policy and Investment: The Supply Side Economics', *Discussion Paper* no. 311, Centre for Economic Policy Research, ANU, Canberra.

Dowrick, S. (1994b) 'Impact of Investment on Growth: Externalities and Increasing Returns', in *Investment for Growth*, Economic Planning Advisory Council, Background Paper no. 39.

Drake, P. and Niewenhuysen, J. (1988) *Economic Growth for Australia: An Agenda for Action*, Oxford University Press, Melbourne.

Drucker, P. (1986) 'The Changed World Economy', *Foreign Affairs*, vol. 64, pp. 768–91.

Dungey, M. and Pitchford, J. (1998) 'Prospects for Output and Employment Growth with Steady Inflation', in Debelle, G. and Borland, J. (eds), *Unemployment and the Australian Labour Market*, Reserve Bank of Australia, Sydney.

Dwyer, T. and Larkin, T. (1996) 'Living Standards in Decline?', *Business Council Bulletin*, no. 127, pp. 6–17.

Easton, B. (1998) 'Microeconomic Reform: The New Zealand Experience', in *Micro Economic Reform and Productivity Growth*, Workshop Proceedings, Productivity Commission and Australian National University, AusInfo, Canberra.

Eatwell, J. (1995) 'The International Origins of Unemployment', in Michie, J. and Grieve-Smith, J. (eds), *Managing the Global Economy*, Oxford University Press, Oxford.

Economic Planning Advisory Council (EPAC) (1992) *Current Account Adjustment: Options for the 1990's*, Council Paper no. 50, AGPS, Canberra.

Economic Planning Advisory Commission (EPAC) (1992) *Unemployment in Australia*, AGPS, Canberra.

Economic Planning Advisory Commission (EPAC) (1995a) *Interim Report of the Private Infrastructure Task Force*, AGPS, Canberra.

Economic Planning Advisory Commission (EPAC) (1995b) *Final Report of the Private Infrastructure Task Force*, AGPS, Canberra.

Economic Planning Advisory Commission (EPAC) (1996) *Future Labour Market Issues for Australia*, AGPS, Canberra.

Economist Intelligence Unit (EIU) (1997) *Make or Break*, Metal Trades Industry Association, Sydney.

Edey, M. and Britten-Jones, M. (1990) 'Saving and Investment', in Grenville, S. (ed.), *The Australian Macro-Economy in the 1980s*, Sydney, Reserve Bank of Australia.

Eisner, R. (1995) 'Our NAIRU Limit: The Governing Myth of Economic Policy', *The American Prospect*, no. 21, pp. 58–63.

Elmeskov, J., Martin, J. and Scarpetta, S. (1998) 'Key Lessons for Labour Market Reforms: Evidence from OECD Countries' Experiences', paper presented to the Economic Council of Sweden Conference on The Political Economy of Labour Market Reform, Stockholm, 25 May.

Engle, R.F. and Granger, C.W.J. (1987) 'Cointegration and Error Correction: Representation, Estimation, and Testing', *Econometrica*, vol. 55, pp. 251–76.

Engle, Robert F. and Yoo, S. (1989) 'A Survey of Cointegration', mimeo, University of California, San Diego.

Erenburg, S.J. (1994) 'Public Capital: The Missing Link Between Investment and Economic Growth', *Public Policy Brief*, No. 14/1994, Jerome Levy Economics Institute, New York.

European Commission (1993) *Growth, Competitiveness and Employment*, EC, Brussels.

Evans, L., Grimes, A., Wilkinson, B. and Teece, D. (1996) 'Economic Reform in New Zealand 1984–95: The Pursuit of Efficiency', *Journal of Economic Literature*, vol. XXXIV, pp. 856–902.

Evatt Foundation (1995) *Unions 2001: A Blueprint for Trade Union Activism*, Evatt Foundation, Sydney.

Fazzari, S.M. (1994–5) 'Why Doubt the Effectiveness of Keynesian Fiscal Policy', *Journal of Post-Keynesian Economics*, vol. 17, pp. 231–48.

Flatau, P. and Simpson, M. (1996) 'Part-time Youth Employment and Training', *Labour Economics and Productivity*, vol. 8, pp. 131–62.

Forslund, A. and Kreuger, A. (1994) 'An Evaluation of the Swedish Active Labour Market Policy: New and Received Wisdom', *National Bureau of Economic Research Working Paper*, no. 4802, July.

Foster, R. (1996) *Australian Economic Statistics*, Reserve Bank of Australia, Sydney.

Foster, R. and Stewart, S. (1991) *Australian Economic Statistics*, Reserve Bank of Australia, Sydney.

Franz, W. (1990) 'Hysteresis in Economic Relationships: An Overview', *Empirical Economics*, vol. 15, pp. 109–84.

Fraser, B. (1996) 'Reserve Bank Independence', *Reserve Bank Bulletin*, September, pp. 14–20.

Freeland, J. (1997) 'The Anatomy of Vulnerability: The State of the Unemployed in Australia', in *Turning Point*, Evatt Foundation, Sydney.

Freeland, J. (1998) 'Employment and Training Policy and Programs: Past Lessons and Future Prospects', *Evatt Papers*, vol. 6, no. 2.

Freeman, R.B. (1988) 'Labour Market Institutions and Economic Performance', *Economic Policy*, vol. 3, pp. 64–80.

Freeman, R.B. (1998) 'War of the Models: Which Labour Market Institutions for the 21st Century?', *Labour Economics*, vol. 5, pp. 1–24.

Freeman, R.B. and Wise, D. (eds) (1992) *The Youth Labour Market*, University of Chicago Press, Chicago.

Friedman, M. (1969) *The Optimum Quantity of Money*, Macmillan, London.

Friedman, M. (1977) 'Inflation and Unemployment', *Journal of Political Economy*, vol. 85, pp. 451–72.

Friedman, M. (1980) 'Memorandum', Treasury and Civil Service Committee, House of Commons, UK, Session 1979–80, *Memoranda on Monetary Policy*, HMSO, London.

Fuller, W.A. (1976) *Introduction to Statistical Time Series*, John Wiley and Sons, New York.

Galbraith, J. (1996) 'Inequality and Unemployment: An Analysis across Time and Countries', mimeo, University of Texas, Austin.

Galbraith, J. (1997) 'Time to Ditch the NAIRU', *Journal of Economic Perspectives*, vol. 11, pp. 93–108.

Garraty, J.A. (1978) *Unemployment in History*, Harper Colophon Books, New York.

Garrett, G. (1996) 'Capital Mobility, Trade, and the Domestic Politics of Economic Policy', in Keohane, R. and Milner, H. (eds), *Internationalisation and Domestic Politics*, Cambridge University Press, Cambridge.

Gelber, F. (1998) 'Tackling the Current Account Deficit', in Genoff, R. and Green, R. (eds), *Manufacturing Prosperity: Ideas for Industry, Technology and Employment*, Federation Press, Sydney.

Genoff, R. and Green, R. (eds) (1998) *Manufacturing Prosperity: Ideas for Industry, Technology and Employment*, Federation Press, Sydney.

Gilbert, M. (1981) 'A Sociological Model of Inflation', *Sociology*, vol. 15, pp. 185–209.

Glyn, A. (1995) 'Social Democracy and Full Employment', *New Left Review*, no. 211, pp. 31–55.

Glyn, A., Hughes, A., Lipietz, A. and Singh, A. (1990) 'The Rise and Fall of the Golden Age', in Marglin, S. and Schor, J. (eds), *The Golden Age of Capitalism*, Clarendon, Oxford.

Goldsmith, A.H., Veum, J.R. and Darity, W. (1996) 'The Psychological Impact of Unemployment and Joblessness', *Journal of Social-Economics*, vol. 25, pp. 333–58.

Goldsmith, W.W. and Blakely, E.J. (1992) *Separate Societies: Poverty and Inequality in US Cities*, Temple University Press, Philadelphia.

Goodridge, S., Harding, D. and Lloyd, P. (1995) 'The Long Term Growth in Unemployment', Discussion paper, Series 2/95, Institute of Applied Economic and Social Research.

Grattan, M. and Gruen, F. (1993) *Managing Government: Labor's Achievements and Failures*, Macmillan, Melbourne.

Green, R. (1995) 'How Manufacturing Can Help Young People to Get High Wage Jobs', *ESC Working Paper no. 20* (University of Newcastle), October.

Green, R. (1996a) 'Productivity: Current Trends and Prospects', in *Industrial Relations under the Microscope*, ACIRRT Working Paper no. 40 (University of Sydney), April.

Green, R. (1996b) 'The Death of Comparative Wage Justice', *Economic & Labour Relations Review*, vol. 7, pp. 224–53.

Green, R. and Burgess, J. (1997) 'A Policy Program for Growth, Jobs and the Current Account', *Journal of Australian Political Economy*, vol. 40, pp. 1–26.

Green, R., Mitchell, W. and Watts, M. (1992) *Economic Policy in Crisis: A Proposal for Jobs and Growth*, Evatt Foundation, Sydney.

Green, R., Mitchell, W. and Watts, M. (1997) 'The Accord, Trade Unions and the Australian Labour Market', in Kriesler, P. (ed.), *The Australian Economy*, Sydney, Allen & Unwin.

Gregg, P. and Manning, A. (1997) 'Labour Market Regulation and Unemployment', in Snower, D.J. and de la Dehesa, G. (eds), *Unemployment Policy: Government Options for the Labour Market*, Cambridge University Press, Cambridge.

Gregory, M. and Jukes, R. (1997) 'The Effects of Unemployment on Subsequent Earnings: A Study of British Men 1984–94', mimeo, University of Oxford.

Gregory, R.G. (1986) 'Wages Policy and Unemployment in Australia', *Economica*, Supplement, vol. 53, pp. S53–S75.

Gregory, R.G. (1991a) 'Jobs and Gender: A Lego Approach to the Australian Labour Market', in Clements, K.W., Gregory, R.G. and Takayama, T. (eds), *International Economics Postgraduate Research Conference*, volume supplement to the *Economic Record*, pp. 20–40.

Gregory, R.G. (1991b) 'The Current Account and Economic Policy in the 1980s', in Hamilton, C. (ed.), *The Economic Dynamics of Australian Industry*, Allen & Unwin, Sydney.

Gregory, R.G. (1993) 'Aspects of Australian and United States Living Standards: The Disappointing Decades 1970–1990', *Economic Record*, vol. 69, pp. 61–76.

Gregory, R.G. (1994) 'Unemployment: What to Do?', *Sydney Papers*, Spring, Sydney Institute.

Gregory, R.G. (1996) 'Wage Deregulation, Low Paid Workers and Full Employment', in Sheehan, P. et al. (eds), *Dialogues on Australia's Future*, Victoria University Press, Melbourne.

Gregory, R.G. (1998) 'Solutions to Australian Unemployment: Three Perspectives', in Debelle, G. and Borland, J. (eds), *Unemployment and the Australian Labour Market*, Reserve Bank of Australia, Sydney.

Gregory, R. and Hunter, B. (1995) 'The Macro Economy and the Growth of Ghettos and Urban Poverty in Australia', Australian National University Centre for Economic Policy Research, DP325.

Gregory, R.G., Klug, E. and Martin, Y.M. (1999) 'Labour Market Deregulation, Relative Wages and the Social Security System', in Richardson, S. (ed.), *Regulating the Labour Market: Regulation, Efficiency and Equity in Australia*, Cambridge University Press, Cambridge.

Gregory, R.G. and Sheehan, P. (1997) 'Poverty and the Collapse of Full Employment', in Fincher, J. and Nieuwenhuysen, J. (eds), *Australian Poverty: Then and Now*, Melbourne University Press, Melbourne.

Gregory, R.G. and Sheehan, P. (1998) 'Unemployment Trends in Australia and the US: The Natural Rate, Wage Flexibility and Path Dependence', in Sheehan, P. and Tegart, G. (eds), *Working for the Future*, Victoria University Press, Melbourne.

Hall, R. (1970) 'Why is the Unemployment Rate so High at Full Employment?', *Brookings Papers on Economic Activity*, vol. 3, pp. 369–402.

Hamilton, C. (1998) 'In Search of the Fourth Way', *Australian Economic Review*, vol. 31, pp. 409–21.

Hancock, K. (1998) 'The Needs of the Low Paid', in *Wealth, Work and Wellbeing*, Academy of Social Sciences in Australia, Occasional Paper, no. 1, pp. 1–26.

Hancock, K. (1999) 'Economics, Industrial Relations and the Challenge of Unemployment', keynote address to the Association of Industrial Relations Academics of Australia and New Zealand, Adelaide, 4 February.

Harding, A. (1995) 'The Impact of Health, Education and Housing Outlays Upon Income Distribution in Australia in the 1990s', *Australian Economic Review*, vol. 28, pp. 71–86.

Harding, A. (1997) *The Suffering Middle: Trends in Income Inequality in Australia 1982–93*, NATSEM Discussion Paper, no. 21, June.

Harrison, B. and Bluestone, B. (1990) 'Wage Polarisation in the US and the "Flexibility" Debate', *Cambridge Journal of Economics*, vol. 14, pp. 351–73.

Hartcher, P. (1996) 'Lost: $12bn in Exports to Asia', *Australian Financial Review*, 16 September.

Heilbroner, R.L. (1979) 'Inflationary Capitalism', *New Yorker*, 8 October.

Henley, A. and Tsakalotos, E. (1991) 'Corporatism, Profit Squeeze and Investment', *Cambridge Journal of Economics*, vol. 15, pp. 425–50.

Henley A. and Tsakalotos, E. (1995) 'Unemployment Experience and the Institutional Condition of Full Employment', in Arestis, P. and Marshall, M. (eds), *The Political Economy of Full Employment*, Edward Elgar, London.

Herr, H. (1991) 'External Constraints on Fiscal Policy: An International Comparison', in Matzner, E. and Streeck, W. (eds), *Beyond Keynesianism: The Socio-Economics of Production and Full Employment*, Edward Elgar, Aldershot and Vermont.

Heylen, F., Goubert, L. and Omey, E. (1996) 'Unemployment in Europe: a Problem of Relative or Aggregate Demand for Labour?', *International Labour Review*, vol. 135, pp. 17–58.

Higgins, C. (1990) 'The Australian Economy Entering the 1990s', *Economic Papers*, vol. 9, pp. 1–18.

Higgott, R. (1999) 'The International Relations of the Asian Economic Crisis: A Study in the Politics of Resentment', in Beeson, M. and Robison, R. (eds), *From Miracle to Meltdown: The End of Asian Capitalism?*, Routledge, London.

Hirsch, F. (1977) *Social Limits to Growth*, RKP, London.

Holt, P.M. (1996) *Influencing Australia's Future*, Australian Business Chamber, Sydney.

House of Representatives Standing Committee on Communications, Transport and Microeconomic Reform (H of R) (1997) *Planning not Patching: An Inquiry Into Federal Road Funding*, The Parliament of the Commonwealth of Australia, AGPS, Canberra.

Humphrey, T. (1982) 'Changing Views on the Phillips Curve', in Humphrey, T. (ed.), *Essays on Inflation*, Federal Reserve Bank of Richmond, Richmond.

Hutton, W. (1996) *The State We're In*, Vintage Books, London.

Hylleberg, S., Engle, R., Granger, C. and Yoo, B. (1990) 'Seasonal Integration and Cointegration', *Journal of Econometrics*, vol. 44, pp. 215–38.

Indecs (1992) *State of Play* 7, Allen & Unwin, Sydney.

Indecs (1995) *State of Play* 8, Allen & Unwin, Sydney.

Industry Commission (1996) *Implications for Australia of Firms Locating Offshore*, AGPS, Canberra.

International Labour Organisation (ILO) (1995), *World Employment 1995*, ILO, Geneva.

Iversen, T. and Wren, A. (1998) 'Equality, Employment and Budgetary Restraint: The Trilemma of the Service Economy', *World Politics*, vol. 50, pp. 507–46.

Jackman R., Pissarides, C. and Savouri, S. (1990) 'Labour Market Policies and Unemployment in the OECD', *Economic Policy*, vol. 11, pp. 450–92.

Jackson, F. and Pettit, P. (1992) 'In Defence of Explanatory Ecumenism', *Economics and Philosophy*, vol. 8, pp. 1–21.

Jaikumar, R. (1986) 'Post-Industrial Manufacturing', *Harvard Business Review*, November–December, pp. 69–76.

Jarvie, W. and McKay, R. (1993) 'Perspectives on DEET Labour Market Programs', *ANU Discussion Paper*, no. 296, Centre for Economic Policy Research, ANU, Canberra.

Jessop, B. (1988) *Thatcherism: A Tale of Two Nations*, Polity Press, Cambridge.

Johansen, S. (1988) 'Statistical Analysis of Cointegration Vectors', *Journal of Economic Dynamics and Control*, vol. 12, pp. 231–54.

Jones, B. (1995 [1982]) *Sleepers, Wake! Technology and the Future of Work*, 4th edn, Oxford University Press, Melbourne.

Jones, E. (1994) 'The Politics of Industry Policy in the Cook Era', *Australian Geographer*, vol. 25, pp. 153–60.

Jones, E. (1998) 'The Howard Government's Industry Policy', paper delivered at the Back to the Future Conference, University of Newcastle.

Junankar, P.N. (1997) 'Lessons from Britain's Thatcherite Experiment', *Economic Papers*, vol. 16, pp. 65–70.

Junankar, P.N. and Kapuscinski, C.A. (1991) 'The Incidence of Long Term Unemployment in Australia', *Australian Bulletin of Labour*, vol. 17, pp. 325–52.

Junankar, P.N. and Kapuscinski, C.A. (1992) *The Costs of Unemployment in Australia*, Economic Planning Advisory Council Background Paper no. 24, AGPS, Canberra.

Junankar, P.N. and Kapuscinski, C.A. (1998) 'Was Working Nation Working? *Journal of Industrial Relations*, vol. 40, pp. 25–41.

Junankar, P.N., Waite, M. and Belchamber, G. (1998) 'The Youth Labour Market: Anecdotes, Fables and Evidence', paper presented to the Joint Workshop on Do youth wages matter?, at the Centre for Economic Policy Research, ANU and Productivity Commission, 23 November 1998.

Kalecki, M. (1943) 'Political Aspects of Full Employment', *Political Quarterly*, vol. 14, pp. 322–31.

Karpin, D. (1995) *Enterprising Nation: Renewing Australia's Managers to Meet the Challenge of the Asian-Pacific Century*, AGPS, Canberra.

Katz, L. and Krueger, A. (1992) 'The Effects of the Minimum Wage in the Fast Food Industry', *Industrial and Labour Relations Review*, vol. 46, pp. 6–21.

Kearney, C., Chowdhury, K. and Fallick, L. (1996) 'Public Infrastructure and Private Investment in Australia', in Johnson, M., Kriesler, P. and Owen, A. (eds), *Issues in the Australian Economy*, Sydney, Allen & Unwin

Kenyon, P. (1998) 'Infrastructure Spending and Unemployment: Government Responsibility for Growth and Jobs', *Australian Economic Review*, vol. 30, pp. 421–32.

Keohane, R.O. and Milner, H.V. (eds) (1996) *Internationalisation and Domestic Politics*, Cambridge University Press, Cambridge.

Keynes, J.M. (1931) 'The Economic Consequences of Mr. Churchill', *Essays in Persuasion*, Macmillan, London.

Keynes, J.M. (1964 [1936]) *The General Theory of Employment, Interest and Money*, Harcourt Brace Jovanovich, New York.

Keynes, J.M. (1973) *The Collected Writings of John Maynard Keynes*, XIII, Macmillan, London.

King, J.E., Rimmer, R.J. and Rimmer, S.M. (1992) 'The Law of the Shrinking Middle: Inequality of Earnings in Australia 1975–89', *Scottish Journal of Political Economy*, vol. 39, pp. 391–412.

Kitson, M. and Michie, J. (1996) 'Manufacturing Capacity, Investment and Employment', in Michie, J. and Grieve-Smith, J. (eds), *Creating Industrial Capacity: Towards Full Employment*, Oxford University Press, Oxford.

Kniest, P., Lee, J. and Burgess, J. (1997) *Introduction to Macroeconomics*, Macmillan, Melbourne.

Krugman, P. (1994a) 'Europe Jobless, America Penniless', *Foreign Affairs*, no. 95, pp. 19–34.

Krugman, P. (1994b) *Peddling Prosperity: Economic Sense and Nonsense in the Age of Diminished Expectations*, W.W. Norton, New York.

Lancaster, K. (1973) 'The Dynamic Inefficiency of Capitalism', *Journal of Political Economy*, vol. 81, pp. 1092–1109.

Langmore, J. and Quiggin, J. (1994) *Work for All: Full Employment in the Nineties*, Melbourne University Press, Melbourne.

Latham, M. (1998) *Civilising Global Capital: New Thinking for Australian Labour*, Allen & Unwin, Sydney.

Layard, R., Nickell, S. and Jackman, R. (1991) *Unemployment, Macroeconomic Performance and the Labour Market*, Oxford University Press, Oxford.

Leeson, R. (1993) 'Policy Induced Recessions: What Have we Learnt?' *Economic Papers*, June, pp. 85–96.

Letich, L. (1995) 'Is Life Outsmarting Us?' *Washington Post*, 2 April.

Levine, R. and Renelt, D. (1992) 'A Sensitivity Analysis of Cross-country Growth Regression', *American Economic Review*, vol. 82, pp. 942–63.

Levine, R. and Zervos, S.J. (1993) 'What We Have Learned About Policy and Growth from Cross–country Regressions?', *American Economic Review*, vol. 83, pp. 426–30.

Lindbeck, A. (1993) *Unemployment and Macroeconomics*, MIT Press, London.

Lindbeck, A. (1997) 'The Swedish Experiment', *Journal of Economic Literature*, vol. 35, pp. 1273–1319.

Lindbeck, A. and Snower, D. (1986) 'Wage Setting, Unemployment and Insider Outsider Relations', *American Economic Review*, Supplement, vol. 76, pp. 235–39.

Lombard, M. (1998) 'Unemployment in Australia: The Effects of Macro-economic Policies', *Journal of Australian Political Economy*, no. 41, pp. 65–76.

Lowe, P. (1995) 'Labour Productivity Growth and Relative Wages: 1978–1994', in Andersen, P., Dwyer, J. and Gruen, D. (eds), *Productivity and Growth*, Reserve Bank of Australia, Sydney, pp. 93–134.

Lucas, R.E. Jr and Rapping, L.A. (1969) 'Real Wages, Employment, and Inflation', *Journal of Political Economy*, vol. 77, pp. 721–54.

McDonald, I.M. (1999) 'Can Unemployment Be Reduced Without Violating the Inflation Target', *Australian Economic Review*, vol. 32, pp. 89–95.

Macfarlane, I. (1997a) 'Monetary Policy, Growth and Unemployment', *Reserve Bank of Australia Bulletin*, June, pp. 1–9.

Macfarlane, I. (1997b) 'Job Security v. Job Creation', *Australian Financial Review*, May 16.

Macfarlane, I. (1997c) 'The Economics of Nostalgia', *Reserve Bank of Australia Bulletin*, March, pp. 1–7.

Macfarlane, I. and Stevens, G. (1989) 'Overview: Monetary Policy and the Economy', in Macfarlane, I. and Stevens, G. (eds), *Studies in Money and Credit*, Sydney, Reserve Bank of Australia, Sydney.

McGuire, P. (1994) 'Changes in Earnings Dispersion in Australia, 1975–92', *Labour Economics and Productivity*, vol. 6, pp. 27–53.

Machin, S. and Manning, A. (1994) 'Minimum Wages, Wage Dispersion and Employment: Evidence from UK Wages Councils', *Industrial and Labour Relations Review*, vol. 47, pp. 319–29.

Maddison, A. (1989) *The World Economy in the 20th Century*, OECD, Paris.

Maddison, A. (1991) *Dynamic Forces in Capitalist Development: A Long-run Comparative View*, Oxford University Press, Oxford.

Malinvaud, E. (1982) 'Wages and Unemployment', *Economic Journal*, vol. 92, pp. 1–12.

Mankiw, N.G., Romer, D. and Weil, D.N. (1992) 'A Contribution to the Empirics of Economic Growth', *Quarterly Journal of Economics*, vol. 107, pp. 407–37.

Marceau, J., Sicklen, D. and Manley, K. (1997) *The High Road or the Low Road?: Alternatives for Australia's Future*, Australian Business Chamber, Sydney.

Marglin, S.A. and Schor, J.B. (1990) *The Golden Age of Capitalism: Reinterpreting the Post-War Experience*, Clarendon Press, Oxford.

Martin, J.P. (1998) 'What Works Among Active Labour Market Policies: Evidence from OECD Countries' Experiences', in Debelle, G. and Borland, J. (eds), *Unemployment and the Australian Labour Market*, Reserve Bank of Australia, Sydney.

Maslow, A. (1968) *Toward a Psychology of Being*, Van Nostrand, Princeton, NJ.

Matthews, R. (1968) 'Why Has Britain had Full Employment Since the War?', *Economic Journal*, vol. 78, pp. 555–69.

Mattila, P. J. (1969) 'Quit Behaviour in Labor Markets', *American Statistical Association Proceedings*, Economics Statistics Section.

Mayer, T. (1978) *The Structure of Monetarism*, New York, Norton.

Meidner, R. (1993) 'Why Did the Swedish Model Fail?', *Socialist Register 1993*, Merlin Press, London.

Mishell, L. and Schmitt, J. (1995) *Beware the US Model: Jobs and Wages in a Deregulated Economy*, Economic Policy Institute, Washington DC.

Mitchell, D.J.B. (1984) 'The Australian Labour Market', in Caves, R.E. and Krause, L.B. (eds), *The Australian Economy: A View from the North*, Allen & Unwin, Sydney.

Mitchell, W.F. (1987a) 'The NAIRU, Structural Imbalance and the Macro-equilibrium Unemployment Rate', *Australian Economic Papers*, vol. 26, pp. 101–18.

Mitchell, W.F. (1987b) 'What is the Full Employment Unemployment Rate', *Australian Bulletin of Labour*, vol. 11, pp. 321–36.

Mitchell, W.F. (1993) 'Testing for Unit Roots and Persistence in OECD Unemployment Rates', *Applied Economics*, vol. 25, pp. 1489–1501.

Mitchell, W.F. (1994) 'Restoring Full Employment: A Problem of Policy Balance', *Australian Economic Review*, vol. 27, pp. 24–30.

Mitchell, W.F. (1994a) 'Productivity Bonuses in the Recovery', mimeo, Department of Economics, University of Newcastle.

Mitchell, W.F. (1994b) 'Restoring Full Employment: Great Idea, But Where is the Policy?' mimeo, Department of Economics, University of Newcastle.

Mitchell, W.F. (1996) 'Unemployment and Inflation: A Demand Story', Paper to European Unemployment Conference, European University, Florence, Italy, November.

Mitchell, W.F., Mitchell, C.E., Watts, M.J. and Butterworth, A. (1995) *Women's Prospects in the Economic Recovery*, AGPS, Canberra.

Mitchell, W.F. and Watts, M.J. (1997) 'The Path to Full Employment', *Australian Economic Review*, vol. 30, pp. 436–44.

Mitchell, W.F. and Wu, P.X. (1995) 'Evidence of Unit Roots in Quarterly OECD Unemployment Rates', *Department of Economics Research Monograph*.

Moore, A. (1998) 'The Globalisation of the National Economy: The Impact on Public Policy', PhD thesis, Australian National University, Canberra.

Moore, B. and Rhodes, J. (1976) 'The Relative Decline of the UK Manufacturing Sector', *Economic Policy Review*, no. 2, pp. 36–41.

Moore, D. (1997) 'The Effects of the Social Welfare System on Unemployment', *Australian Bulletin of Labour*, vol. 23, pp. 275–94.

Morehead, A., Steele, M., Alexander, M., Stephen, K. and Duffin, L. (1997) *Changes at Work: The 1995 Australian Workplace Industrial Relations Survey*, Addison Wesley Longman Australia, Melbourne.

Morris, M., Bernhardt, A.D., and Handcock, M.S. (1994) 'Economic Inequality: New Methods for New Trends', *American Sociological Review*, vol. 59, pp. 205–19.

Mortensen, D.T. (1970) 'Job Search, the Duration of Unemployment, and the Phillips Curve', *American Economic Review*, vol. 60, pp. 847–62.

Munnell, A. (1992) 'Policy Watch: Infrastructure Investment and Economic Growth', *Journal of Economic Perspectives*, vol. 6, pp. 189–98.

National Board of Education, Employment and Training (NBEET) (1992) *Disadvantaged Job Seekers*, Report no. 18, AGPS, Canberra.

National Commission of Audit (1996) *Report to the Commonwealth Government*, AGPS, Canberra.

Nelson, Charles R. and Plosser, Charles I. (1982) 'Trends and Random Walks in Macroeconomic Time Series', *Journal of Monetary Economics*, vol. 10, pp. 139–62.

Nevile, J.W. (1975) *Fiscal Policy in Australia: Theory and Practice*, 2nd edn, Cheshire, Melbourne.

Nevile, J.W. (1983) 'The Role of Fiscal Policy in the Eighties', *Economic Record*, vol. 59, 1–15.

Nevile, J. (1990) 'Discussion of J. Carmichael, Inflation: Performance and Policy', in Grenville, S. (ed.), *The Australian Macro-Economy in the 1980s*, Reserve Bank of Australia, Sydney.

Nevile, J.W. (1996) 'Deregulation and the Welfare of the Less Well Off', *International Journal of Social Economics*, vol. 23, pp. 310–25.

Nevile, J.W. (1997) 'Fiscal Policy in Australia', in Kriesler, P. (ed.), *The Australian Economy*, 2nd edn, Allen & Unwin, Sydney.

Nguyen, D. and Sirwardana, A. (1988) 'The Relationship Between Output Growth and Unemployment: A Re-examination of Okun's Law in Australia', *Australian Economic Review*, 1st quarter, vol. 21, pp. 16–27.

Nickell, S. (1996) *Unemployment and wages in Europe and North America*, Institute of Economics & Statistics, University of Oxford.

Nickell, S. (1997) 'Unemployment and Labor Market Rigidities: Europe versus North America', *Journal of Economic Perspectives*, vol. 11, pp. 55–74.

Nickell, S. and Bell, B. (1997) 'The Collapse in Demand for the Unskilled and Unemployment Across the OECD', *Oxford Review of Economic Policy*, vol. 11, pp. 40–62.

Norris, K. (1996) *The Economics of Australian Labour Markets*, 4th edn, Longman, Melbourne.

Norris, K. and Wooden, M. (1996) 'The Changing Australian Labour Market: An Overview', in Norris, K. and Wooden, M. (eds), *The Changing Australian Labour Market*. EPAC Commission Paper no. 11, AGPS, Canberra.

O'Connor, J. (1973) *The Fiscal Crisis of the State*, St Martin's Press, New York.

OECD (1993) 'Active Labour Market Policies: Assessing Macroeconomic and Microeconomic Effects', *Economic Outlook*, pp. 39–80.

OECD (1994a) *The Jobs Study – Facts, Analysis, Strategies*, OECD, Paris.

OECD (1994b) *Industry Policy in OECD Countries*, OECD, Paris.

OECD (1995a) *Economic Outlook*, no. 58, Paris.

OECD (1995b) *Employment Outlook*, OECD, Paris.

OECD (1996) *Employment Outlook*, OECD, Paris.

OECD (1997) *Economic Survey, Australia*, OECD, Paris.

OECD (1997a) *Employment Outlook*, OECD, Paris.

OECD (1997b) *Economic Outlook*, OECD, Paris.

OECD (1998) *Economic Outlook*, OECD, Paris.

OECD (1998a) *Employment Outlook*, OECD, Paris.

Oi, W. (1962) 'Labor as a Quasi-Fixed Factor', *Journal of Political Economy*, vol. 70, pp. 538–55.

Okun, A.M. (1970) *The Political Economy of Prosperity*, Norton, New York.

Okun, A.M. (1973) 'Upward Mobility in a High-Pressure Economy', *Brookings Papers on Economic Activity*, 1, pp. 207–52.

Okun, A. M. (1981) *Prices and Quantities: A Macroeconomic Analysis*, Basil Blackwell, Oxford.

Okun, A.M. (1983) *Economics for Policymaking*, MIT Press, Cambridge.

Osberg, Lars (1984) 'The Pyrrhic Victory – Unemployment, Inflation and Macroeconomic Policy', in Cornwall, J. (ed.), *After Stagflation*, Basil Blackwell, Oxford.

Otto, G. and Voss, G.M. (1993) 'Public Capital and Private Sector Productivity', *Economic Record*, vol. 70, pp. 121–32.

Otto, G. and Voss, G.M. (1994) 'Public Capital and Private Sector Productivity', *Economic Record*, vol. 70, pp. 121–32.

Padalino, S. and Vivarelli, M. (1997) 'The Employment Intensity of Economic Growth in the G-7 Countries', *International Labour Review*, vol. 136, pp. 191–213.

Palley, T.I. (1998) 'Restoring Prosperity: Why the US Model is Not the Answer for the United States or Europe', *Journal of Post-Keynesian Economics*, vol. 20, pp. 337–53.

Pappas Carter Evans Koop-Telesis (1990) *The Global Challenge*, Australian Manufacturing Council, Melbourne.

Pender, H. (1997) *The Joy of Tax: Australian Tax Design – Directions for Long Term Reform*, Australian Tax Research Foundation, Sydney.

Perotti, R. (1996) 'Growth, Income Distribution and Democracy: What the Data Say', *Journal of Economic Growth*, vol. 1, pp. 149–87.

Perry, G.L. (1970) 'Changing Labour Markets and Inflation', *Brookings Papers on Economic Activity*, no. 3, pp. 411–448.

Perry, George L. (1971) 'Labor Force Structure, Potential Output, and Productivity', *Brookings Papers on Economic Activity*, vol. 3, pp. 541–2.

Phelps, E.S. (1970) *Microeconomic Foundations of Employment & Inflation Theory*, N.W. Norton, New York.

Phillips, P.C.B. (1987) 'Time Series Regression with Unit Roots', *Econometrica*, vol. 55, pp. 277–302.

Phillips, P.C.B. and Perron, P. (1988) 'Testing for a Unit Root in Time Series Regression', *Biometrika*, vol. 75, pp. 332–46.

Phipps, A. and Sheehan, J. (1995) 'Macroeconomic Policy and Employment Growth in Australia', *Australian Economic Review*, vol. 28, pp. 86–102.

Piggott, J. and Chapman, B. (1995) 'Costing the Job Compact', *Economic Record*, vol. 71, pp. 313–28.

Pilat, D. (1996) *Labour Productivity Levels in OECD Countries: Estimates for Manufacturing and Selected Services Sectors*, OECD, Paris.

Piore, Michael J. (ed.) (1979) *Unemployment and Inflation: Institutionalist and Structuralist Views*, M.E. Sharpe, Inc., White Plains.

Pitchford, J. (1989) 'A Sceptical View of Australia's Current Account and Debt Problem', *Australian Economic Review*, 2nd Quarter, pp. 5–13.

Pitchford, J.D. (1990) *Australia's Foreign Debt: Myths and Realities*, Allen & Unwin, Sydney.

Pitchford, J. (1992) 'Current Account Deficits, External Liabilities and Economic Policy', *Discussion Paper* no. 262, Centre for Economic Policy Research, Australian National University, Canberra.

Pitchford, J. (1995) *The Current Account and Foreign Debt*, Routledge, London and New York.

Pixley, J. (1993) *Citizenship and Employment: Investigating Post-Industrial Options*, Cambridge University Press, Cambridge.

Porter, I. (1996) 'Manufacturing Sector Facing Gloomy Outlook', *Australian Financial Review*, 16 September.

Pressman, S. (1995) 'Deficits, Full Employment and the Use of Fiscal Policy', *Review of Political Economy*, vol. 7, pp. 212–26.

Productivity Commission (1996) *Stocktake of Progress in Microeconomic Reform*, AGPS, Canberra.

Productivity Commission (1998) *Micro Economic Reform and Productivity Growth*, Workshop Proceedings, Productivity Commission and Australian National University, AusInfo, Canberra.

Quiggin, J. (1993a) 'A Policy Program for Full Employment', *Australian Economic Review*, vol. 26, pp. 41–7.

Quiggin, J. (1993b) 'Growing Our Way to Full Employment', *Labour and Industry*, vol. 5, pp. 91–104.

Quiggin, J. (1996a) *Great Expectations, Microeconomic Reform and Australia*, Allen & Unwin, Sydney.

Quiggin, J. (1996b) 'The Intensification of Work and the Polarisation of Labor', paper presented at Academy of the Social Sciences in Australia Workshop, Canberra, February 5.

Quiggin, J. (1996c) 'Private Sector Involvement in Infrastructure Projects', *Australian Economic Review*, vol. 29, pp. 51–64.

Quiggin, J. (1997) 'The Market for Labour and the Market for Tomatoes', *Journal of Economic and Social Policy*, vol. 1, pp. 84–95.

Quiggin, J. (1998) *Taxing Times: A Guide to Australia's Tax Debate*, University of New South Wales Press, Sydney.

Quinlan, M. (1998) 'Recent Industrial Relations Policy Developments in Australia: A Critical Review', paper presented at the Back to the Future Conference, University of Newcastle.

Reder, M.W. (1955) 'The Theory of Occupational Wage Differentials', *American Economic Review*, vol. 45, p. 833.

Reich, R. (1991) *The Work of Nations*, Simon & Schuster, New York.

Reserve Bank of Australia (RBA) (1993) *Towards Full Employment*, Occasional Paper, no. 12, Reserve Bank of Australia, Sydney.

Reynolds, L.C. (1951) *The Structure of Labor Markets*, Westport, Greenwood Press.

Rimmer, M. et al. (1996) *Reinventing Competitiveness: Achieving Best Practice in Australia*, Pitman, Melbourne.

Rix, S. (1997) 'Seriously Prejudiced: the State of Emergency Services', in Sheil, C. (ed.), *Turning Point: The State of Australia and New Zealand*, Evatt Foundation and Allen & Unwin, Sydney.

Roberts, P. (1996) 'Forget Those Pats on the Back, We're on the Nose', *Australian Financial Review*, 9 October.

Roberts, P. (1998) 'Fundamental Weakness in Canberra's Values', *Australian Financial Review*, 13 February.

Robinson, M. (1996) 'The Case Against Balanced Budgets', *Australian Journal of Public Administration*, vol. 55, pp. 48–63.

Rodrik, D. (1995) 'Getting Interventions Right: How South Korea and Taiwan Grew Rich', *Economic Policy*, vol. 20, pp. 53–108.

Romer, P. (1989) 'Human Capital and Growth: Theory and Evidence', *NBER Working Paper* no. 3173, National Bureau of Economic Research, Cambridge, Massachusetts.

Romer, P. (1990) 'Are Non-Convexities Important for Understanding Growth', *American Economic Review*, vol. 80 (2), pp. 97–103.

Ross, R.T. (1985) 'Improved Labour Market Information: Beyond Unemployment Statistics', *Australian Bulletin of Labour*, vol. 11, pp. 236–45.

Rowthorn, R.E. (1977) 'Conflict, Inflation and Money', *Cambridge Journal of Economics*, vol. 1, pp. 215–39.

Rowthorn, R.E. (1992) 'Centralisation, Employment and Wage Dispersion', *Economic Journal*, vol. 102, pp. 506–23.

Rowthorn, R.E. (1995) 'Capital Formation and Unemployment', *Oxford Review of Economic Policy*, vol. 11, pp. 26–39.

Rowthorn, R.E. and Wells, J.R. (1987) *De-Industrialisation and Foreign Trade*, Cambridge University Press, Cambridge.

Sachs, J. (1979) 'Wages, Profits and Macroeconomic Adjustments: A Comparative Study', *Brookings Papers on Economic Activity*, vol. 2, pp. 269–332.

Sachs, J. and Roubini, N. (1988), 'Sources of Macroeconomic Imbalances in the World Economy: A Simulation Approach', in Suzuki, Y. and Okabi, M. (eds), *Toward a World of Economic Stability*, University of Tokyo Press, Tokyo.

Said, S.E. and Dickey, D.A. (1984) 'Testing for Unit Roots in Autoregressive-Moving Average Models of Unknown Order', *Biometrika*, vol. 71, pp. 599–608.

Salter, W.E.G. (1960) *Productivity and Technical Change*, Cambridge University Press, Cambridge.

Samuelson, P. and Solow, R. (1960) 'Problem of Achieving and Maintaining a Stable Price Level: Analytical Aspects of Anti-inflation Policy', *American Economic Review*, vol. 50, pp. 177–94.

Sargent, T.J. (1973) 'Rational Expectations, the Real Rate of Interest, and the Natural Rate of Unemployment', *Brookings Papers on Economic Activity*, no. 2, pp. 429–72.

Schmid, G. (1995) 'A New Approach to Labour Market Policy: A Contribution to the Current Policy Debate on Efficient Employment Policies', *Economic and Industrial Democracy*, vol. 16, pp. 429–56.

Schott, K. (1984) *Power, Policy and Order: The Persistence of Economic Problems in Capitalist States*, Yale University Press, New Haven, Conn.

Scott, R. and Williams, J.B. (1995) 'APEC and the Political Economy of "Recalcitrance"', *Current Affairs Bulletin,* vol. 72, pp. 15–21.

Sen, A.K. (1961) 'Isolation, Assurance and the Social Rate of Discount', *Quarterly Journal of Economics*, vol. 81, pp. 112–24.

Sen, A.K. (1997) 'Inequality, Unemployment and Contemporary Europe', *International Labour Review*, vol. 136, pp. 155–71.

Shapiro, C. and Stiglitz, J.E. (1984) 'Equilibrium Unemployment as a Worker Discipline Device', *American Economic Review*, vol. 74, pp. 433–44.

Sheehan, P. (1996) 'Economics and the National Interest', in Sheehan, P. et al. (eds), *Dialogues on Australia's Future*, Victoria University Press, Melbourne.

Sheehan, P. (1998) 'Rebirth of Australian Industry Revisited', in Genoff, R. and Green, R. (eds), *Manufacturing Prosperity*, Federation Press, Sydney.

Sheehan, P. and Gregory, R.G. (1998) 'Poverty and the Collapse of Full Employment', in Fincher, R. and Nieuwenhuysen, J. (eds), *Poverty Then and Now*, Victoria University Press, Melbourne.

Sheehan, P., Pappas, N. and Cheng, E. (1994) *The Rebirth of Australian Industry*, Centre for Strategic Economic Studies, Victoria University Press, Melbourne.

Shone, R. (1989) *Open Economy Macroeconomics*, Harvester Wheatsheaf, London.

Sicklen, D. (1995) 'GATT and Australia's Trade Policy', *Industry Policy Briefing Note*, no. 18, Australian Economic Analysis, May.

Sicklen, D. (1996) *The Productivity Commission's Stocktake of Progress in Micro-economic Reform: Some Critical Comments*, Australian Economic Analysis, Sydney.

Sicklen, D. (1998) 'Free Trade Mythology and the Importance of Manufacturing', in Genoff, R. and Green, R. (eds), *Manufacturing Prosperity: Ideas for Industry, Technology and Employment*, Federation Press, Sydney.

Siegel, R.L. (1994) *Employment and Human Rights: The International Dimension*, University of Pennsylvania, Philadelphia.

Silverstone, B., Bollard, A. and Lattimore, R. (eds) (1996) *A Study of Economic Reform: The Case of New Zealand*, North-Holland.

Simler, N.J. and Tella, A. (1968) 'Labour Reserves and the Phillips Curve', *Review of Economics and Statistics*, vol. 50, pp. 32–49.

Singh, A. (1977) 'UK Industry and the World Economy: A Case of De-industrialisation?', *Cambridge Journal of Economics*, vol. 1, pp. 113–36.

Singh, A. (1989) 'Third World Competition and De-industrialisation in Advanced Countries', *Cambridge Journal of Economics*, vol. 13, pp. 103–20.

Singh, A. (1994) 'Employment and Unemployment: North and South, Notes for a Global Development Agenda for the 1990s', mimeo, Cambridge University, Cambridge.

Singh, A. (1995) 'Institutional Requirements for Full Employment in Advanced Economies', *International Labour Review*, vol. 134, pp. 471–95.

Sloan, J. (1997) 'Lower Wages the Key to Jobs', *Australian*, 8 August.

Sloan, J. and Wooden, M. (1998) 'Industrial Relations Reform and Labour Market Outcomes: A Comparison of Australia, New Zealand and the United Kingdom', in *Unemployment and the Australian Labour Market*, Reserve Bank of Australia, Sydney.

Smith, M. and Mahony, G. (1993) 'Macroeconomic Stabilisation Policy', in Mahony, G. (ed.), *The Economy Under Labour*, Allen & Unwin, Sydney.

Solow, R. (1990) *The Labour Market as a Social Institution*, Blackwell, Oxford.

Soskice, D. (1990) 'Wage Determination: The Changing Role of Institutions in Advanced Industrialised Countries', *Oxford Review of Economic Policy*, vol. 6, pp. 36–61.

Standing, G. (1990) 'Labour Flexibility and Insecurity: Towards an Alternative Strategy', in Brunella, R. and Dell Ariga, C. (eds), *Labour Relations and Economic Performance*, Macmillan, London.

Standing, G. (1997) 'Globalisation, Labour Flexibility and Insecurity: The Era of Market Regulation', *European Journal of Industrial Relations*, vol. 3, pp. 7–37.

Stein, B. (1983) 'Economic Purple Hearts', *New York Times*, 12 January.

Stevens, G. and Robertson, R. (1993) 'The Australian Labour Market 1967–1992: A Brief International Perspective', *Research Discussion Paper*, no. 292, Centre for Economic Policy, Australian National University, Canberra.

Stewart, M. (1972) *Keynes and After*, Penguin Books, Harmondsworth.

Stewart, M. (1994) 'Should we Concern Ourselves With Foreign Debt?', *Economic Papers*, vol. 13, pp. 114–21.

Stiglitz, J.E. (1997) 'Reflections on the Natural Rate Hypothesis', *Journal of Economic Perspectives*, vol. 11, pp. 3–10.

Stilwell, F. (1991) 'Wages Policy and the Accord', *Journal of Australian Political Economy*, no. 28, pp. 27–52.

Stretton, A. and Chapman, B. (1990) 'An Analysis of Australian Labour Market Programs', *Discussion Paper*, no. 247, Centre for Economic Policy Research, Australian National University, Canberra.

Stricker, P. and Sheehan, P. (1981) *Hidden Unemployment, The Australian Experience*, Melbourne, Institute of Applied Economic and Social Research.

Stromback, T. and Dockery, M. (1998) 'Labour Market Programs, Unemployment and Employment Hazards: An Application of the Survey of Employment and Unemployment Patterns', paper presented to the 27th Conference of Economists, University of Sydney, NSW, 28 September–1 October, 1998.

Stromback, T., Dockery, M. and Ying, W. (1997) 'Labour Market Programs and Labour Market Outcomes', *Working Paper*, Curtin University and Centre for Labour Market Research, Perth.

Stromback, T., Dockery, M. and Ying, W. (1998a) 'Transitions in the Labour Market: Evidence from the Survey of Employment and Unemployment Patterns', *Australian Bulletin of Labor*, vol. 25, no. 2, pp. 159–78.

Stromback, T., Dockery, M. and Ying, W. (1999) 'Labour Market Programs and Labour Market Outcomes', *Melbourne Institute Working Paper Series*.

Summers, L. (1988) 'Should Keynesian Economics Dispense with the Phillips Curve?', in Cross, Rod (ed.), *Unemployment, Hysteresis and the Natural Rate Hypothesis*, Basil Blackwell, Oxford.

Summers, L. and Carroll, C. (1987) 'Why is U.S. National Saving so Low?', *Brookings Papers on Economic Activity*, no. 1, pp. 607–35.

Swensen, P. (1989) *Fair Shares: Unions, Pay and Politics in Sweden and Germany*, Cornell University Press, Ithaca, NY.

Taslim, M. and Chowdhury, A. (1995) *Macroeconomic Analysis*, Prentice-Hall, Sydney.

Thurow, L.C. (1975) *Generating Inequality*, Basic Books, New York.

Thurow, L.C. (1983) *Dangerous Currents: the State of Economics*, Random House, New York.

Thurow, L.C. (1996) *The Future of Capitalism*, Allen & Unwin, Sydney.

Tobin, J. (1967) *Full Employment & Growth*, Edward Elgar, Vermont.

Tobin, J. (1972) 'Inflation and Unemployment', *The American Economic Review*, vol. 62, pp. 1–18.

Tobin, J. (1987) *Policies for Prosperity: Essays in an Keynesian Mode*, Wheatsheaf Books, Sussex.

Tobin, J. (1996) *Full Employment and Growth*, Edward Elgar, London.

Trethewey, M. (1994) 'Does Low Saving Restrain Investment?: A Note Relevant to the FitzGerald Report From a "Keynesian" Perspective', *Economic Papers*, vol. 13, pp. 10–16.

UNCTAD, *Word Investment Report*, 1995.

Vroman, W. (1978) 'Cyclical Earnings Changes of Low-wage Workers', *Research in Labour Economics*, vol. 2, pp. 191–235.

Wachter, M.L. (1970) 'Cyclical Variation in the Inter-industry Wage Structure', *American Economic Review*, vol. 60, pp. 75–84.

Wallich, H.C. (1956) 'Conservative Economic Policy', *Yale Review*, vol. 46, pp. 68–81.

Walras, L. (1874) *Elements of Pure Economics*, Allen & Unwin, London.

Watts, M.J. (1997) 'The Accord and Wage Polarisation in Australia: Some Evidence and Tentative Explanations', in Wilson, K. (ed.), *Australia in Accord: An Assessment of Australia's Incomes Policy During the Hawke–Keating Years*, Victoria University Press, Melbourne.

Watts, M.J. and Mitchell, W.F. (1990) 'Australian Wage Inflation: Real Wage Resistance, Hysteresis and Incomes Policy: 1968(3)–1988(3)', *The Manchester School*, vol. LVIII, pp. 142–64.

Watts, M.J. and Rich, J. (1991) 'Equal Employment Opportunity in Australia?: The Role of Part-Time Employment in Occupational Sex Segregation', *Australian Bulletin of Labour*, June, pp. 160–79.

Watts, M.J. and Rich, J. (1992) 'Labour Market Segmentation and the Persistence of Occupational Sex-Segregation in Australia', *Australian Economic Papers*, vol. 31, pp. 58–76.

Webster, E.M. (1997) 'Labour Market Programs: A Review of the Literature', *Working Paper* 23/97, Melbourne Institute, University of Melbourne.

Webster, E.M. (1998a) 'What is Job Network?' *Mercer-Melbourne Institute Quarterly Bulletin of Economic Trends*, 4/98.

Webster, E.M. (1998b) 'Labour Market Programs and the Australian Beveridge Curve: 1978 to 1997', mimeo, Melbourne Institute, University of Melbourne.

Webster, E.M. (forthcoming) 'Job Network: What can if offer?' *Just Policy*.

Webster, E.M. and Summers, P. (1998) 'The Effect of Labour Market Programs on Wage Inflation', mimeo, Melbourne Institute of Applied Economic and Social Research, University of Melbourne.

Whiteford, P. (1998) 'Is Australia Particularly Unequal? Traditional and New Views', in Cass, B. and Smyth, P. (eds), *Contesting the Australian Way*, Cambridge University Press, Cambridge.

Wilson, P. (1996) 'APEC no Quick Fix for Trade, Clinton Warned', *Australian*, 13–14 April.

Withers, G. (1984) 'Crime, Punishment and Deterrence in Australia: An Empirical Investigation', *Economic Record*, vol. 60, pp. 176–85.

Withers, G., Pitman, D. and Whittingham, B. (1986) 'Wage Adjustments and Labour Market Systems: A Cross-country Analysis', *Economic Record*, vol. 62, pp. 415–26.

Withers, G., Throsby, D., and Johnston, K. (1994) *Public Expenditure in Australia*, Economic Planning Advisory Council (EPAC), Commission Paper no. 3, AGPS, Canberra.

Wooden, M. (1994) 'The Labour Market Experience of Immigrants', in Wooden, M., Holton, R., Hugo, G. and Sloan, J. (eds), *Australian Immigration: A Survey of the Issues*, 2nd edn, AGPS, Canberra.

Wooden, M. (1996) 'The Youth Labour Market: Characteristics and Trends', *Australian Bulletin of Labour*, vol. 22, pp. 137–60.

Wooden, M. (1997) 'The Path to Full Employment? They're Dreamin!', *Australian Economic Review*, vol. 30, pp. 445–47.

Wooden, M., Sloan, J., Kennedy, S., Dawkins, P. and Simpson, M. (1994) 'Work Sharing and Unemployment', National Institute of Labour Studies, *Working Paper*, no. 129, Flinders University, Adelaide.

World Bank (1993) *The East Asian Economic Miracle; Economic Growth and Public Policy*, Oxford University Press, Oxford and New York.

Wu, P.X. (1992) 'Testing Fractionally Integrated Time Series', *Working Paper Series*, 9, Graduate School of Business and Government Management, Victoria University of Wellington.

Wu, P.X. (1993) 'Trend Stationarity vs Difference Stationarity: New Tests and Some Empirical Evidence', *Working Paper Series*, 10, Graduate School of Business and Government Management, Victoria University of Wellington.

Index